CINEMA ILLUMINATING REALITY

CINEMA
ILLUMINATING REALITY

Media Philosophy through Buddhism

VICTOR FAN

UNIVERSITY OF MINNESOTA PRESS

Minneapolis
London

The University of Minnesota Press gratefully acknowledges the financial assistance provided for the publication of this book by the Chiang Ching-kuo Foundation for International Scholarly Exchange.

A portion of chapter 1 was previously published in a different form in "Cinematic Imaging and Imagining through the Lens of Buddhism," *Paragraph* 43, no. 3 (November 2020): 364–80, https://www.euppublishing.com/. Another portion of chapter 1 was previously published in "Illuminating Reality: Cinematic Identification Revisited in the Eyes of Buddhist Philosophies," in *The Structures of the Film Experience by Jean-Pierre Meunier: Historical Assessments and Phenomenological Expansions,* ed. Julian Hanich and Daniel Fairfax, trans. Daniel Fairfax, 245–58 (Amsterdam: Amsterdam University Press, 2019); published with permission. A portion of chapter 4 was previously published in "Szukają *tungzi dingjing:* Kultura filmowa i kino LGBTQI+ od roku 1997" [Locating *tungzi* cinema: Hong Kong LGBTQI+ films since 1997], in *Made in Hong Kong: Kino czasu przemian* [Made in Hong Kong: Cinema of a changing time], 157–80 (Warsaw: Wydawnictwo w Podwórku, 2019).

Published by the University of Minnesota Press
111 Third Avenue South, Suite 290
Minneapolis, MN 55401-2520
http://www.upress.umn.edu

ISBN 978-1-5179-0991-8 (hc)
ISBN 978-1-5179-0992-5 (pb)

A Cataloging-in-Publication record for this book is available from the Library of Congress.

Printed in the United States of America on acid-free paper

The University of Minnesota is an equal-opportunity educator and employer.

UMP BmB 2022

To Bhāṇaka Ch'ang-hwai,
Thomas Elsaesser, and
Christine Lamarre

CONTENTS

DEPENDENT ORIGINATIONS

On July 14, 2015, I underwent a major surgery in London. During my hospitalization and recovery, I was accompanied by copies of the *Vajracchedikā Prajñāpāramitā Sūtra* [*Diamond Sūtra*] and the *Shorter Sukhāvatīvyūha Sūtra*. These texts were brought to me by my father, Samuel Fan, a devout *upāsaka* and avid researcher of Buddhism. We both had the honor of becoming students of Bhāṇaka Ch'ang-hwai and his two loving disciples Ting-yin and Ting-yan.

In my life's journey, I have encountered a number of *bhikkhunīs/ bhikṣuṇīs* and *bhikkhus/bhikṣus*, who have been instrumental in my research. They include Foon-chai of the Buddhist Youth Association, my friend Rongdao from McGill University, and the *sanghas* of Dharma Drum Mountain, the London Fo Guang Shan Temple, and Plum Village. I am also indebted to lay communities, including the Dharmasthiti Group, the Buddhist Educational Foundation, and the Vajrayana Buddhism Association. My former student Sanjay Dalugoda also offered me invaluable insights into the Theravādin and Yogācāra debates in South Asia.

I shall always miss—until we meet again—the generous mentorship, care, and support from Thomas Elsaesser. Every conversation with Thomas—in Amsterdam, Rotterdam, New York, and New Haven—was a portal to multiple potentialities. Even at times of fear, anxiety, and despair, Thomas gave me hope by supporting me with inspiration, reassurance, and rigor.

This monograph would not have been completed without the unconditional support, friendship, and guidance of Thomas and Christine

Lamarre and Earl Jackson Jr. I am also grateful for the encouragement and advice of Dudley Andrew, Francesco Casetti, D. N. Rodowick and Dominique Bluher, Haun Saussy and Olga Solovieva, David Martin-Jones (DMJ), William Brown, and Marc Steinberg. I must also thank Aaron Gerow and Yamamoto Naoki for their attentive and incisive feedbacks during my research.

This project was first presented, in its inchoate form, in the Film Theory in Media History conference in Shanghai, June 2016, co-organized by Bao Weihong. After my presentation, Jin Danyuan, Zhong Dafeng, and Chen Xihe kindly offered me a two-hour pep talk on their research experiences. I also exchanged ideas with Thomas Pringle, Vinzenz Hediger, Malte Haganer, and Johannes von Moltke on methods of comparative studies. This gathering led to three further occasions. First, Weihong co-organized a follow-up conference in Berkeley in October 2017 to celebrate the achievements of Paul Fonoroff, at which Zhang Zhen offered me heartfelt advice. A month later, Vinzenz and Weihong invited me to a conference in Frankfurt, which celebrated the work of Jean-Pierre Meunier. There, I received feedback from Vivian Sobchack, and my presentation was also included in the conference proceedings, edited by Julian Hanich and Daniel Fairfax. Then, in June 2019, many of us reconvened at Columbia University, where I had the opportunity to discuss my ideas with Jane Gaines.

In July 2016, I was invited by Peng Hsiao-yen to attend a conference at Academia Sinica, on Hou Hsiao-hsien's new release, *The Assassin*. I was showered with constructive comments from Hsiao-yen, Timmy Chen, Nichole Huang, and Hsiu-Chuang Deppman. Thanks to Hsiao-yen, I had my first publication on Buddhism and cinema in her edited volume on that film. She kindly invited me back to Academia Sinica in 2018 to give a talk, during which she generously shared with me her research experience. I will never forget the pleasure of spending three days with Lo Wai-luk, Peter Reist, Tan See Kam, Wayne Wong, and Gary Bettinson in Lancaster to converse on *Chinese* aesthetics over wine. Wei-luk's advice was instrumental in shaping the fifth chapter of this book.

My research in Hong Kong and Taiwan would not have been possible without the Visiting Scholarship offered by the Centre for China Studies, Chinese University of Hong Kong in 2016 and 2017, when I received help from Jan Kiely and from one of my best friends, Kristof Van Den Troost. I felt highly honored to receive a University Fellowship from the Hong

Kong Baptist University (HKBU) in 2018, where I worked with an amazing group of scholars and writers at its Department of Humanities and Creative Writings. I especially want to thank K. C. Lo and John Erni, who made me feel at home at the department. I was also deeply inspired by my colleagues Chow Yiu Fai, Louis Ho, Amy Lee, Mette Hjort, Patrick Holland, Man Kit Wah, Kenny Ng, James Shea, Daisy Tam, Tong Yui, Dorothy Tse, and Jessica Yeung. I was also grateful for their supporting staff, which included Chester Chan, Bonnie Fung, Jacky Ho, and Fiona Lu.

During my stay in Hong Kong, besides giving two very productive talks at HKBU, I was also invited by Nichole and Gina Marchetti to offer a research seminar at the Department of Comparative Literature, University of Hong Kong. Gina's passionate comments on the Kyoto school scholars gave me further inspiration for my fifth chapter. During this period, I also penned two articles on this topic, under the sagacious editorship of Kyle Stevens and Sarah Cooper. In 2019, I was honored with an invitation from David Sofra and Dario Linares to give a keynote address at the Film-Philosophy Conference in Brighton, which was kindly introduced by DMJ. I was later invited by Lucy Bolton to give a shorter version of the talk at the Screen Study Group Training Day. On both occasions, I received enthusiastic and thoughtful feedback from numerous scholars. I also want to thank Pema Tseden for his long-term support and Catherine Wheatley for introducing *Transit* to me. I am grateful for Jean Ma's invitation to and Apichatpong Weerasethakul's own explanation of *Sleepcinemahotel* at the International Film Festival Rotterdam (IFFR) 2018. I also thank May Adadol Ingawaij for kindly introducing me to Apichatpong.

During the difficult 2020–21 academic year, I felt extremely honored when a number of great friends and cohorts invited me to give talks and participate in seminars based on this monograph. These incredible scholars included Jane Gaines at Columbia University (including the inaugural Thomas Elsaesser Memorial Lecture); Alex Zahlten and Yoda Tomiko at Harvard University; Rick Warner at the University of North Carolina; and Michael Goddard at the University of Westminster. I also want to thank Deborah Levitt, Laura Marks, Shane Denson, Markos Hadjioannou, Kiki Yu, Ruby Cheung, Tim Bergfelder, and Ivan Girina and his students for their inspiration.

Besides my father, I want to thank my mother, Jackie Mak, and my partner, John Christiansen, for their unconditional love and care. I also feel very grateful to be surrounded by loving companions during this writing process, including Scotty, Peter Restrick, Archie Wolfman, Francesco Quario, Sagara Masaaki, Alfie Woodhead, Scott Williams, and Ross Hansbury. Every word of this book has been mulled over and challenged productively by Archie. I am also grateful to George Crosthwait, Xu Tianhao, Liu Siqi, Fan Weiting, Lilly Zhuang, Sophia Doyle, and Markus Beeken for their friendship and intellectual inspiration.

Amitābha,
Jhāna-sukha (Victor Fan),
London, September 2020

NOTE ON LANGUAGES

Buddhism has always been a multilingual field. The earliest oral traditions and written records of Sakyamuni/Śākyamuni Buddha's (circa 563 or 480 B.C.E.–circa 483 or 400 B.C.E.) teachings were in Pāli, which is still the language of Theravāda Buddhism. Between the second and first centuries B.C.E., Sanskrit texts began to emerge. In this book, all Buddhist terms that originated from these texts are given in the format of Pāli/Sanskrit unless a term is identical in both languages.

Most Buddhist texts were translated into Middle Chinese between the Six Dynasties (220 or 222–589 C.E.) and the Dhang/Tang dynasty (618–90 and 705–907 C.E.). Chinese terms and names from this period are given in the main text of this book in the Middle Chinese/Putonghua (pinyin) format. The Glossary toward the back of this book provides a list of all the Buddhist terms, names, and titles in multiple languages that I use in the text.

Middle Chinese pronunciations have been historically reconstructed by linguists according to the rhyme dictionary Tsethiàn/Qieyun [601]. The editors of the Tsethiàn sought to construct a standardized language by reconciling the difference between the Mandarins spoken in the north and in the south. Northern Mandarin corresponds largely to the Kan-on (Han pronunciations) in modern Japanese, whereas Southern Mandarin is closer to the Go-on (Wu pronunciations).

Most dictionaries today use the International Phonetic Alphabet (IPA) to notate the Tsethiàn pronunciations, with modifications and simplifications. This book uses primarily a system developed in the 1990s and 2000s by Zhengzhang Shangfang (1933–2018), with some minor modifications:

VOWELS AND DIPHTHONGS

1. Sounds from the [a/e] family are notated in this order: [ɑ] (long throaty *a*), [ɐ] (long *a*), [ʌ] (medium-long *a*), [a] (regular *a*), [æ] (a near-open *e* sound, as in *air*), [ɛ] (a medium *e* sound, as in *es*), [ə] (a medium *a* sound, as in *un*), [e] (a medium *i* sound, as in *ee*).

2. The regular [i], [o], and [u] are pronounced as in the Latin *i, ou,* and *u.* The IPA letter [ɨ] is a short *i.* Put immediately after a consonant and before another vowel or diphthong, it is read as a very brief and subtle *i.* Meanwhile, [ɨng] sounds closer to the English pronunciation of *ing.* When the letter [ɨ] is not followed by a consonant, it is considered interchangeable with the letter [i]. The letter [ʉ] is a long *u.* Finally, the letter [y] is pronounced like a German *ü.*

3. Diphthongs are pronounced as is, though four common ones can be confusing. They are [iə], which is pronounced like the English *leer;* [iɛ], which is pronounced like *bite* in English; [iɪ], which is pronounced closer to the English *ai,* as in *exercise;* and [iʌ], which is almost identical to *ü.*

CONSONANTS

1. The IPA uses the letter [ʔ] (half Q) to indicate a silent glottal stop. This silent letter merely shortens the vowel that follows. The letter [h] is throatier than the English letter *h.*

2. The [d], [t], [s], [ś] (close to the English *sh*), [z], and [ž] (a post-alveolar *z*) family in the IPA system is extremely subtle.

   The letters [d] and [t] can be added in front of the letters [s], [z], and their variations to create compounds.
   When the letter [h] is added to the end of a consonant or a compound, it indicates a subtle aspiration, whereas the compound [hh] is added to indicate a strong aspiration.
   A ['] added after a consonant or compound refers to the palato-alveolar ejective fricative version of its original.

The only exceptions are [dh'] and [th'], which are the
retroflex versions of [dh] and [th].

3. The letter [ñ] replaces the IPA letter [ɲ], and the [ng] replaces
the IPA letter [ŋ]. Meanwhile, the IPA letter [j] indicates the
English *y* sound.

4. The IPA letters [p, k, t] are pronounced more like *bh, gh,* and *dh*
in English.

INTONATIONS

1. This book uses the pinyin intonation symbols. In a diphthong, if
a symbol cannot be added to an IPA letter directly, it is added
either to the IPA or Latin letter next to it, or immediately after
the diphthong.

2. It is widely acknowledged that the *Tsethiэ̀n*'s recording of
intonations is incomplete and some entries are contestable.
Most words are recorded as *b'iæng/ping* (level tone). Modern
linguists speculate that in practice, Middle Chinese speakers,
when confronted with a sequence of level tones, would inflect
alternate words in the sequence, thus producing an effect
similar to the difference between *jiɛngb'iæng/yangping* (light
level) and *ʔ'iimb'iæng/yinping* (dark level).

3. The *dzhiɛ̀ng/shang* (rising tone) and the *khiʌ̀/qu* (departing
tone) are indicated in the same way as modern Mandarin.
Meanwhile, the *ñiip/ru* (entering tone) is indicated by a silent
consonant ending, which "interrupts" the final vowel or
diphthong. This practice is identical to the way Cantonese
words with entering tones are spelled today.

In this book, Old Chinese terms are given in pinyin only. This is because modern reconstructions of Old Chinese are still considered less
reliable than their Middle Chinese counterparts. I use the English or
European names of historical and regional figures from China and
Japan, based on the preferred forms in their publications or other historical documents. Between 1906 and 1949, place names throughout
Mainland China were transliterated with the Postal Map Romanization
(PMR) system, a historical practice that will be observed throughout
this book.

INTRODUCTION

CINEMA

A Technicity-Consciousness

WHAT IS CINEMA AS A TECHNICITY-CONSCIOUSNESS?

More than two decades after the publication of Gilles Deleuze's
(1925–95) two volumes on the cinema, scholars in film and media studies
began to examine these books' indebtedness to the thoughts of Gilbert
Simondon (1924–89).[1] Such a line of investigation has been motivated
by an urge to reevaluate the pertinence of Deleuze's works in an age
when the definition of the cinema has been put into crisis by a proliferation of new technico-technological modes of image-generation,
manipulation, dissemination, and reception, including social media,
mobile electronic devices, and corporate- or state-controlled biometric
data collection and surveillance systems. These new technics have been
actively rewriting the relationships between human and machine, and
self and other. They do so by obfuscating the boundary between human
consciousness and a range of technically generated perceptual-conceptual
formations—including memories.

More perturbingly, these new modes of *anthropotechnical* existences,
in their processes of becoming, affect—and are affected by—impulses,
desires, and powers.[2] These modes of existence operate as perpetual
cycles, in which affective impulses actualize desires as consumable and
livable forms and virtualize these forms as desires. Our desire for desire
and our ignorance of such desire have been harnessed by corporate and
state powers as preemptive measures to consolidate biopolitical management, with seemingly no room for resistance.[3]

1

As cinema and media scholars, we have an ethical responsibility to scrutinize ways in which such impulses, desires, and powers can be repurposed to offer an insight into how such anthropotechnical existences operate as *the way it is*. In this book, I make an intervention into such an investigation by introducing Buddhist philosophy into our scholarly conversation in order to address an aporia that has been left open by Deleuze and Simondon: the intricate relationship between technicity (substrate) and consciousness (form). As I shall demonstrate in the rest of this introduction, Buddhist philosophy is particularly useful in addressing this unanswered conundrum because its *point de départ* is precisely a wholesale deconstruction of the substrate-form/technicity-consciousness divide that has haunted Euro-American thinking of media and mediation. It does so by adhering unfailingly to one single axiom: dependent originations.

APORIA

An aporia is best understood as a seemingly irresolvable conundrum that gives rise to a philosophical debate. It can be considered the *ground* of the debate. Nonetheless, as Thomas Lamarre suggests, this ground usually *disappears* in the discursive process, as it is often concealed underneath—and manifested under the disguise of—a more concrete problematic on the *formal* level. As a result, scholars and thinkers are often attracted to resolving the problematic itself, without addressing the philosophical impasse that gives rise to them in the first place.[4]

In order to understand what this aporia is and why it is important for us to wrestle with it through Buddhism, we need to first locate this problematic: the ontological crisis triggered by the emergence of digital technology in the cinema circa the late 1980s. In this book, I follow Simondon to use the term *technicity* to refer to the configurative codes, operational principles, and technical impetus that in-form the formational process of technical *existence*. In a Cartesian sense, technicity can be considered the *essence* of technics, whereas technology refers to a specific technical *instantiation,* an ecology of technical layouts or assemblages that enables technical objects and beings to be actualized or transindividuated.[5]

The perceived ontological crisis I have just mentioned is often attributed to the fact that digital technology can no longer guarantee a direct relationship between the cinematographic image and the *reality* it claims to have captured, preserved, and reactivated. In other words, the digital image challenges André Bazin's (1918–58) understanding of the photographic image as an imprint or trace of reality.[6] This is because the light particles (protons) that constitute the image we see, once having been refracted and transmitted by the camera lens, no longer leave an imprint on a piece of celluloid film. Rather, they are transduced into electrons, which are then sampled and quantized as numbers that can be stored in a memory chip and eventually recalled, recomposed, and reedited as an image. The resulting image, as Philip Rosen argues, often *reconstructs* its relationship with reality as though it were still an imprint.[7] However, as William Brown and Shane Denson argue respectively, it also disconceals perspectives that are too macroscopic or too microscopic, too fast or too slow, for human perception, thus *subsuming* the human experience under a larger technico-technological one.[8]

One of the earliest ways to circumvent this crisis is Lev Manovich's relocation of cinema's ontological ground from reality to animation. For him, cinema was historically configured as a technology of animating still photographs, until live-action cinema energized an intellectual debate on its relationship with reality after the First World War (1914–18). Therefore, digital cinema merely returns to cinema's historical root, which uses live-action footage as one among many kinds of materials it animates.[9] Yet, as Thomas Elsaesser (1943–2019) points out, although Manovich argues that digital technology has triggered an ontological shift (or *return*), he (Manovich) maintains that the fundamental stylistic principles and industrial mode of operation in Hollywood have remained "business as usual."[10] This argument is therefore challenged by scholars including Vivian Sobchack, Laura Mulvey, Mary Ann Doane, and Laura Marks.[11] They argue respectively that digital technology has fundamentally put into question—or allowed us to rethink—the subject-object relationship and reciprocity in celluloid cinema by privileging the technical and the nonhuman perspective. Moreover, for Lamarre and Deborah Levitt, animation (or, in the Japanese context, anime) is not simply a technique. Rather, it is a technological milieu that intersects with the cinematic eco-assemblage. Like the cinema, the animation/anime assemblage has reconfigured—and been reconfigured by—digital technology both conjunctively (the production of production) and disjunctively (the production of consumption). It means that there is something more fundamental that drives—and is driven by—the operation of both ecologies.[12]

As Stanley Cavell (1926–2018) argues, celluloid cinema can be considered ontologically grounded in a temporal difference between a past that is absent (the profilmic) and a present that is the presence of such absence (the spectatorial). For Markos Hadjioannou, digital technology renders this temporal difference unreliable.[13] As I argued in *Cinema Approaching Reality* [2015], the unreliability of any direct relationship between the cinematographic image and reality requires us to rethink and relive time nonlinearly.[14] Meanwhile, as Brown and Denson argue respectively, contemporary digital cinema's fascination with compositing time by vertically layering diegetic temporalities (for example, presenting multiple planes of temporal existence in a single shot or sequence) grafts us onto machinic or other nonhuman modes of temporal existence.[15] As Sobchack and D. N. Rodowick argue respectively, the *subsuming* of the human to the non-/post-human in digital (post-)cinema also implies the potentiality of its being instrumentalized by state and corporate powers as an apparatus: one that capitalizes on our willful participation and enjoyment by surrendering our own *humanity*. A case can be made that the emergence and configuration of digital technology has been part of an ecological reconfiguration of the relationship between human and nonhuman.[16]

In other words, digital technology has transformed human consciousness and it mirrors, facilitates, and exacerbates the extension and proliferation of corporate and state surveillances by controlling and propelling individual affects.[17] However, as Bernard Stiegler (1952–2020) and Peter Sloterdijk argue respectively, this line of investigation assumes that technicity and humanity are fundamentally opposed to each other in a power asymmetry.[18] Such a presupposition overlooks the fact that humanity has been historically defined by technics, and that consciousness is an anthropotechnical operation.[19] In Simondon's terms, a technological transduction inevitably initiates a new mode of anthropotechnical existence.[20] Therefore, we must pay attention not only to how a new mode comes to be in-formed, but also to the technicity of the formational process that produces that new mode.

However, as Ted Nannicelli and Malcolm Turvey argue, this debate often conflates the substrate of the digital medium with form. In other

words, when we speak of an ontological shift, are we referring to a shift in the medium itself or to the form it takes?[21] In response, Denson points out that (1) a technical substrate is inseparable from form, as form is the manifestation of its substrate, and (2) on the ontological level, a substrate (or, some say, an essence) is not a transcendental plane that lies beyond sensuous forms; rather, it is immanent in—and can only be apprehended and understood through—form.[22]

Hui Yuk argues that the digital crisis is only a problematic manifested on the formal level. Such a problematic is rooted in a deeper philosophical and logical aporia: European philosophy's attachment to the divide between substrate and form. As a philosopher trained exclusively in European thinking, Hui demonstrates how European philosophers since Immanuel Kant (1724–1804) have devoted their works to deconstruct their reliance on this axiom in their ontological investigation, to the extent that our technico-technological ecology is *still* configured as a paradox. For Hui, the digital object, concretized as technological platforms such as the computer, smart phone, smart TV, and other devices that are currently being embodied as lived experiences, continues to operate on a binary logic that differentiates substrate from form, subject from object, and self from other. Meanwhile, the digital, which consists of the mathematical and technical configurative principles and processes that produce the digital object, is relational. The digital is often considered by engineers as the substrate of the digital object (form). What they overlook is that the digital and the digital object are both modes of operation and of configuration that are instantiations of a digital *existence*. For Hui, digital existence is not a substrate in the Aristotelian sense. Rather, it is the pure relationality between the digital and the digital object as they are engaged in a mutually dependent process of becoming.[23]

In other words, in order to determine whether there is an ontological shift, locate where this shift is initiated, and scrutinize what kind of shift it is, we need to rethink *this* aporia: the substrate-form divide that has in-formed and haunted all ontological investigations. Such an aporia lurks beneath the surface of the way Deleuze appropriates Simondon's thoughts in his conceptualization of the cinema.

In the fourth chapter of *Cinéma 1. L'image mouvement* [*Cinema 1: The Movement Image*, 1983], Deleuze defines the cinema as a consciousness. For him, consciousness does not belong to an individuated being (for instance, a spectator) or a technical body (for instance, a camera). Rather, consciousness is a mobile and changing process (movement) that in-forms an *agencement* (layout) of interrelated modes of existence: subject and object, observer and observed, and various beings and objects that constitute a milieu of existence. Such a milieu of existence therefore includes the sentient and perceiving body (of the spectator), the embodied mind (which is inseparable from the body), the technical body (that is, the mechanical or digital apparatus), and what the body perceives as a projected image on screen. The boundaries between these configurative components (that is, the various bodies and the projected image) are constantly changing. For example, as I shall demonstrate in chapter 1, although perception requires a contact between data that we consider as external (for instance, light particles) and our internal data (for instance, molecules that constitute our body), the image that seems to be projected out there is informed in our optico-neurological system. Hence, the boundary between our interiority and exteriority is always in flux. In this sense, the consciousness is best understood neither as the "mind" nor the human body together with its embodied mind. Instead, it refers to the entirety of the *anthropotechnical* milieu. One can say that such a milieu, as a whole, can be regarded as an anthropotechnical body (or technicity-consciousness) that can sense, perceive, act, affect and be affected by creative impulses, understand, and think.[24]

Furthermore, borrowing Simondon's critical framework, Deleuze sees the cinematographic milieu as an ecology of energies or potentialities, whose perpetual operation enables the technical body and the organic one (the human body) to be transduced into a transient, mobile, and changing metastable phase.[25] The resulting *form*, precisely, is the anthropotechnical body or technicity-consciousness: a mode of existence that drives—and is driven by—*conatus* (*puissance*, or power) or an impetus to subsist, which is immanent in the mode itself and emanative to the whole.[26]

The aporia at hand is subtle. In order to avoid anthropocentrism, Simondon never regards a milieu as a consciousness.[27] Rather, he focuses on how an ecology of potentialities, in its process of becoming, unleashes and reconfigures affective and creative energies that enable technical, biological, psychic, and social individuations (or, in relational terms, *transindividuations*).[28] He therefore illustrates how potentialities are actualized as forms from the perspective of technicity. Working on the cinema as an embodied experience, Deleuze is obliged to explain how this process is perceived and conceptualized as a consciousness (that is, from the perspective of *humanity*). One can argue that Simondon and Deleuze offer a parallax view on the same formational process. Yet, what remains unanswered is how a technical operation relates to an operation of the consciousness. This intricate interconnectedness between technicity and consciousness, I argue, is precisely where affective impulses and powers operate. Such an intersection is what constitutes the *cinema* as an ecology of mediation. However, if we put Simondon and Deleuze side by side, the relationship between technicity and consciousness is *still* configured as one between substrate and form.

As a philosophy, Buddhism circumvents this substrate-form conundrum by adhering to one single axiom: dependent originations. For Buddhist scholars, all forms are initiated and extinguished, from one moment to another, from a layout of interdependent relationships. Hence, forms are by definition empty of existential values. The substrate-form divide is therefore a logical violation of this axiom.[29] As I shall demonstrate in the rest of this book, the substrate-form divide does *return* to the Buddhist discourse on the formal level, though it means that what cinema and media scholars have identified so far—an ontological crisis brought about by the emergence of digital technology—is a problematic in form, not an aporia. The *aporia* lies in how mediation, as a process of becoming, has been perceived and conceptualized as a *technicity-consciousness* in the first place. The terms *technicity* and *consciousness* are hyphenated when linked here to indicate that, as a formational process (or process of interbecoming), it is neither a substrate nor a form, neither not a substrate nor not a form. Rather, technicity-consciousness needs to be reconceptualized and rescrutinized as a *relationality*.

This book is largely about cinema and media today and, as a discursive process, it is initiated by the scholarly debate on the digital. However, my discussion is not going to focus on how specific technical modes (such as digital versus celluloid or theatrical versus home) operate and perform differently. The following pages are written in response to a challenge proposed by Thomas Elsaesser in a graduate seminar he conducted at Yale University in 2006. For him, technico-technological modulations persuade us that something fundamental about the cinema has changed, or perhaps that cinema itself has already disappeared *into* the multiplicity of its technical proliferations. He argues that by deliberately bypassing the question of technico-technological modality, we can better focus on how *cinema* has been understood and defined.[30] This does not mean that I am going to ignore the digital altogether in my discussion. Rather, I posit the digital neither as a cause nor an effect of an ontological shift, but rather as one of the many technical reconfigurations that affect—and are affected by—a larger ontogenetic layout. Moreover, in our process of examination, we must be mindful that knowledge constantly affects—and is affected by—almost unnoticeable shifts of observational positions in the process of ontological investigation. As Tanabe Hajime (1885–1962) and Thomé H. Fang (1899–97) argue respectively, a Buddhist investigation does not depart from—or arrive at—an ontology. For Tanabe and Fang, if what philosophers call an ontological ground is ultimately constituted by dependent originations, such a *ground* is not an essence. Instead, it is a pure relationality that is empty of any existential value. If so, ontology itself is also empty of existential value. It is merely a perceptual-conceptual proliferation. Fang calls such a philosophical investigation meontology (meta-ontology), whereas Tanabe calls this metanoetics (an investigation into the emptiness of ontology).[31]

   This book is, first and foremost, an investigation into film and media philosophy. Such an investigation begins with a meontological study of the cinema by comparing established notions of cinema ontology with Buddhist logic and epistemology. It then *walks through* the trajectory of Deleuze's two volumes on the cinema and tests the edges and limitations of their critical framework. In so doing, this book locates the interconnectivity between technicity and consciousness and rethinks how certain modes of cinema and media can redirect formational impulses to initiate changes in our physical, psychic, and sociopolitical relationalities. In this sense, our journey can be divided into five interrelated phases: meontology, epistemology, ethics, aesthetics, and politics. In my discussion, I also pay attention to the historical and cross-cultural contexts of the debates and discuss how their historicities affect and inflect our understandings of specific concepts. The question of historicity especially comes to the fore in my discussion of aesthetics, since what we consider to be "Buddhist aesthetics" is a complex discourse that bears traces of philosophical syncretism, linguistic and cultural (mis)translations, and colonial interventions.

While some film and media examples I analyze in this book (especially the historical ones) are chosen to corroborate the philosophical framework at hand, I use this opportunity to study how contemporary independent filmmakers in the Tibeto-Sinophone communities and beyond (Thailand and Germany) have adopted both Buddhist and non-Buddhist relational modes of thinking in their works. These films are mostly chosen out of my experience of interacting with their makers directly or through my work as a film festival consultant. Hence, they are best regarded not as a comprehensive sample space, but as a few windows that open onto some current trends and concerns in global independent filmmaking. I am especially interested in analyzing how these films negotiate conflicting affects associated with prescriptive political powers by actively questioning our sense of tangible reality, and exploring how they address crises of political deindividuation, desubjectivization, and deautonomization. In short, this book seeks not only to propose a philosophical framework to *work through* cinema and media, but also to use Buddhism as a tool to *converse with* contemporary independent filmmakers regarding what sorts of media intervention we can make in order to rebuild a world that appears to be beyond reparation.

BUDDHISM AS METHOD

As a philosophy, what we call Buddhism today is a culturally diverse and discursively polyphonous ecology built on a singular axiom: dependent originations. *Sutta* (SA)-298 of the *Saṃyuktāgama* [*Connected discourses*], which is probably the earliest collection of the oral traditions circulated within the *saṅgha/sangha* (monastic community), defines dependent originations as such: "The existence of a consequent depends on the existence of a cause-condition; the origination of the consequent depends on the origination of that cause-condition."[32] As Fyodor Stcherbatsky (1866–1942) argues, by adhering to this axiom rigorously, Sakyamuni/Śākyamuni Buddha (circa 563 or 480 B.C.E.–circa 483 or 400 B.C.E.) himself and generations of Buddhist scholars have produced scrupulous discourses on the interconnectedness between technicity and consciousness, and how impulses, desires, and powers can be repurposed as a key to unlock our agency to make changes.[33]

In my investigation, I choose the debates on Buddhism occurring between Śākyamuni Buddha's lifetime and their decline in India beginning around the sixth century C.E. as my main discursive space. I also refer to Chinese and Japanese scholarships on these debates since the third century. I compare their discussions of technicity and consciousness, movement, temporality, ethics, and aesthetics with those proposed by Euro-American scholars that are pertinent to film and media philosophy.

Most of these texts were originally written in Pāli and Sanskrit. While some survive in their original languages, others are available today only in Chinese and Tibetan. It is important to remember that translation *is* production, as translators often employ words that carry conceptual frameworks specific to the host language. Thus, by "throwing together" two words that mean different things in their respective languages, translators often produce a new semiotic difference: a discursive space that instantiates a contention between these two culturo-linguistic frameworks.[34]

Translation does not always corrupt the original text. Rather, the original and translated texts often form a palimpsest, whose differences initiate a productive semiotic layout.[35] For example, two fundamental terms in Buddhism—*bhava/bhāva* (becoming or existence) and *suñña/śūnya* (empty)—have been historically translated as *hiŭ/you* and *khung/kong*. While *hiŭ* does mean existence, the term *khung* presents a set of problematics. In Pāli and Sanskrit, *suñña/śūnya* is understood transitively as being empty *of* existential value. When I say that my existence is *suñña/śūnya,* I refer to the fact that my body and psyche are not initiated out of a permanent self. Rather, they are dependently originated with other forms (such as beings and objects) out of a layout of causes and conditions. Hence, from one *kṣaṇa* (moment or smallest unit of time) to another, *my* becoming is empty of any existential value.

Meanwhile, *khung,* a term borrowed from Daoism (Taoism), is understood intransitively. It refers to the idea that my body and psyche are in-formed out of an impetus emanating *from* emptiness. Such a (mis)translation, nonetheless, has produced a rich literature in both Chinese and Japanese scholarships on the meaning of *tathatā/tathātā* (thusness, or *the way it is*), based on the discursive difference between *suñña/śūnya* and *khung* (a topic I will return to later in this book).[36] Understanding Buddhism as discourses therefore requires us not only to recover how conceptual frameworks were configured within the historical debates among Indian scholars and practitioners, but also to reevaluate those culturo-linguistic contestations found in subsequent Sino-Japanese and Euro-American discussions. Productive (mis)translations are sometimes deliberately deployed in comparative studies. For example, two terms that run through this book are *technicity* and *consciousness*. I take these terms from Gilbert Simondon and Gilles Deleuze in order to ground my discussion in film and media studies. Nonetheless, there is no direct term in Pāli or Sanskrit that corresponds to "technicity." In the Mahāyāna discourses, however, two concepts are discussed: *sammuti/saṁvṛti* (conventional reality) and *paramārtha* (ultimate reality). Conventional reality refers to a reality constituted by perceptual-conceptual forms (consciousness), which operates on dependent originations. Meanwhile, the ultimate reality refers to *the way it is*.

For Duŏzhiùn/Dushun (557–640), the founder of H'ua'ngiɐm/ Huayan Buddhism, dependent originations are best understood as *lǐ/li* (principles), while the image-consciousness (conventional reality) is to be regarded as *dʑì/shi* (matters).[37] William Edward Soothill (1861–1935) and Lewis Hodous (1872–1949) translated *lǐ* as noumena and *dʑì* as phenomena.[38] Their translations have grafted H'ua'ngiɐm thinking onto the epistemic space of Immanuel Kant, which can be regarded as an act of cultural imperialism.[39] Yet these translations enabled Stcherbatsky to conduct a productive reading between the logic and epistemology of Dinna/Dignāga (circa 480–540) and Dharmakīrti's (circa sixth or seventh century) with those of Kant and other European thinkers.[40] He did so by analyzing precisely the productive differences between these terms.

Lǐ refers to the operational principles of the conventional reality. As a concept, it bears little pertinence to media studies until we (mis)translate it productively as "technicity": meaning the *operating principles and processes of the image as consciousness*. Meanwhile, the *pure relationality* between technicity and consciousness is the ultimate reality. In Buddhism, such pure relationality refers to *the way it is:* that technicity and consciousness are neither the same nor different, neither not the same nor not different. This is not to say that we replace *lǐ* unquestionably with technicity. Rather, in this book, when I use the word "technicity," I negotiate the discursive potentiality that lies within the difference between it and *lǐ*, and I use their distinct, yet mutually related, epistemes to produce a renewed understanding of both concepts.

We must remember that productive (mis)translations, when being performed carelessly, can be acts of political violence. As Shih Shu-mei argues, theory in the humanities is often built on universalizing the exceptional.[41] For example, Simondon's abandonment of the notion of consciousness and his employment of a mechanical language to analyze the relationship between the human and machine in relational, configurational, and functional terms betrays a technocentric worldview that was specific to 1950s Europe (a historical and regional exception).[42] As Aijaz Ahmad argues, politically, European exceptions have always been universalized through colonial and postcolonial discourses. These frameworks have been, in turn, used to theorize Asia as an exception—what Gayatri Chakravorty Spivak calls an epistemic violence.[43]

My work too has been criticized by some scholars and cohorts for performing such violence. For example, in *Cinema Approaching Reality*, I argue that introducing Asian theories and criticisms into cinema and media studies is not simply a matter of throwing two sets of critical languages together. Efforts to build a dialogue between Chinese and Euro-American theories in the 1980s, for example, were conducted with the presumption that these epistemes are fundamentally different. However, by claiming a priori that these discourses are radically distinct, scholars ruled out the possibility that a *topos* can be built on a shared aporia in these discussions. Moreover, critical thinking in semi-colonial Shanghai and colonial Hong Kong was produced out of two sociopolitically, linguistically, and culturally extraterritorial public spheres, where contesting notions and values of the cinema were appropriated, rewritten, and reconfigured from both Euro-American and Asian sources. In other words, these theoretical discourses are in themselves comparative.[44]

However, for Aaron Gerow, in Japan, *riron* (theory) was often considered from the late nineteenth century to the 1960s as a concept imported from Europe and North America. By grouping intellectual debates on the cinema and media retroactively as theory, we force these Asian critical writings to perform those functions that historically were fulfilled by Euro-American theories.[45] For Sheldon Lu, excavating Asian writings on film and media should remain a task specific to the historicity of Asia. This is to avoid grafting concepts that are particular to Asia's lived experience onto the Euro-American discourse.[46] As Chen Kuan-hsing and Spivak argue respectively, decolonizing Euro-American theories may also open a space for *orthodox* Han-Chinese, Japanese, and Indian methods to recolonize them. Moreover, in the process of decolonization, scholars often conveniently forget that knowledge production in capitalist Asia since the second half of the twentieth century—what we identify as *indigenous* or *local* knowledge—was often produced through the lens of the United States as an unnamed and unmarked geopolitical center.[47]

We therefore come to an impasse. *Either* we insist that Asian theories and philosophies can only be understood within their discrete historical contexts and we acknowledge that cross-cultural dialogues are impossible without performing epistemic violence. *Or*, we build a conversation by using (mis)translations as an access into the discourse.[48] One way or another, Asian theory is doomed—Asia simply does not have nor does it need theory.

In this thorny debate, I appreciate immensely Marc Steinberg and Alexander Zahlten's proposal to replace "theory" with *theorization*—that is, to see critical discourses not as historically and geopolitically constituted formations, but instead as a media and a mediating ecology that is in a process of interbecoming.[49] In Buddhist philosophy, there is a valuable concept called *sati/smṛti.* A *sati/smṛti* means an "awareness" when it is produced out of ignorance (as in "I am not aware of an awareness"). When the consciousness *is* aware of its awareness, *sati/smṛti* is called mindfulness. Being mindful does not mean paying attention to or being careful of, but *engaging in.*[50] Engaging in the historical contexts of the theories and philosophies we discuss, I argue, is different from incarcerating them within their historical cages and rendering them incommunicable with scholars who work from other culturo-historical contexts. Understanding a concept within its historical context is important. It means that we engage in its meanings and implications that were once produced out of a specific discursive space. Yet, such a concept should not be treated simply as a historical legacy. Rather, we can repurpose it mindfully. We can resuscitate it and keep it alive by establishing another comparative process between its historical semiotic assemblage and our contemporary one. Such a concept can therefore be transferred, displaced, and reconfigured not by unquestioningly grafting it from one episteme onto another, but by engaging in their very *epistemic difference.*[51]

In the rest of this introduction, I first preview the key historical debates and concepts of Buddhism, which will be crucial to our subsequent discussion of its application in film and media philosophy. These

14	INTRODUCTION

discourses and ideas will be reintroduced and elaborated more substantially in the main chapters. I then introduce the specific topics and case studies I discuss in each chapter of this book.

THERAVĀDA BUDDHISM

The multifarious colloquies that constitute Buddhism can be traced back to two parallel philosophical movements in India during the Vedic period (1500–500 B.C.E.): the Upanishads and the Śramaṇa. The earliest texts that constitute the Upanishads were composed around the seventh to sixth centuries B.C.E. Early Buddhism is formulated as a rejoinder to the two key concepts discussed in the Upanishads, the ātman (self) and Brahman (ultimate being). For early Buddhists, if all beings and objects are in-formed by dependent originations, rather than unchanging self-natures or an absolute being (substrate), they are anicca/anitya (impermanent) and anattā/anātman (nonself). For the same reason, we can say that they are empty of self-natures.[52] Meanwhile, the practices of satipaṭṭhāna (establishing mindfulness) and asceticism by early Buddhists were part of the Śramaṇa tradition, which were observed by other concurrent schools, including Jainism and Cārvāka (materialism).[53]

According to the Samantapāsādikā, the Pāli translation of the Sinhala commentaries on the vinaya (monastic regulations) by Buddhaghosa (fifth century C.E.), the suttas (discourses) and the vinaya of Śākyamuni Buddha were recited approximately thirty years after his death by his disciples Ānanda (fifth to fourth centuries B.C.E.) and Upāli (also fifth to fourth centuries B.C.E). This recitation is commonly known as the First Buddhist Council. Nearly seventy years later, a group of monks known as the Mahāsāṃghikas (Commoners) demanded a reform of the vinaya in the Second Buddhist Council at Vaiśālī. After their proposal was rejected by the Sthaviras (Elders), the Mahāsāṃghikas broke away from the sangha, an event known as the First Schism.[54] During the time between these two councils, the Abhidhamma/Abhidharma (meta-discourses) were compiled. These texts are records of scholarly debates on the suttas. These three genres—the suttas, the vinaya, and the Abhidhamma—are collectively known as the Tipiṭaka/Tripiṭaka (Pāli Canon), and the collections of suttas are called the āgamas.[55]

Subsequent schisms gave rise to Theravāda (Doctrines of the Elders) Buddhism, which observed the Pāli Canon as the only legitimate texts. Based on the axiom of dependent originations, the four Theravādin

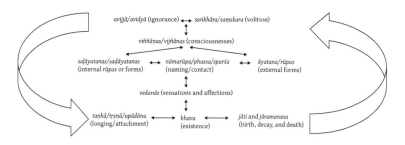

FIGURE 1. The twelve *nidānas*

principles are: impermanence, *dukkha/duḥkha* (suffering), emptiness, and nonself. Suffering is caused by an *avijjā/avidyā* (un-enlightenment, or ignorance) of impermanence and emptiness of forms, which produces an *upādāna* (attachment) to forms as existent states of things or beings that endure in time.[56] The axiom of dependent originations is also developed into an epistemology on the formational process of the consciousness called the twelve *nidānas* (see Figure 1). For the Theravādins, ignorance is dependently originated with *saṅkhāra/ samskara* (volition) and *viññāṇa/vijñāna* (consciousness).[57] Consciousness refers to the overall formational process and the forms (both internal and external) being constituted (a definition similar to Gilles Deleuze's), whereas volition refers to an impetus that generates—and is generated by—the process itself. Consciousness has six domains: the consciousnesses of the eyes, ears, nose, tongue, body, and thought organs. Each domain performs two functions: differentiating forms from one another and manifesting such differences as an image.[58]

These six domains operate interdependently. With them, the abilities to *nāmarūpa* (name and give form) are dependently originated. *Nāmarūpa* refers to the differentiation between the *salāyatanas/ ṣaḍāyatanas* (internal *rūpas* or forms: eyes, ears, nose, tongue, body, and thought organs) and the *āyatana* (external forms: sight, sound, odor, taste, touch, and thought). As the internal and external forms make *phassa/sparśa* (contact), *vedanās* (sensations and affections) and *taṇhā/ tṛṣṇā* (longing or desire) are dependently originated. With desire, an attachment to forms as that which exists is generated. Existence endures in time. Thus, an existing being or object goes through *jāti* (birth) and *jarāmaraṇa* (old age and death).[59] If consciousness refers to the overall formational process of an image (again, including the body—together with the embodied mind—and its associated milieu), the operation of the twelve *nidānas* is the technicity on which the image is in-formed.

During this period, a methodological split emerged between the Sthaviras and the Sarvāstivāda (School of all that exists). The Sarvāstivādas developed a rigorous epistemology by studying the way consciousness is driven by *kamma/karma*, a concept inherited from other Vedic schools of philosophy.[60] In the Vedic tradition, karma is an enduring *impetus* that is immanent in the formational process, that is to say, in the consciousness itself. This impetus is immanent in Brahman and emanative to all beings and modes of existence, and it remains perpetually operative and cannot be conceived otherwise. Such an impetus codifies the way consciousness is manifested as a series of representations (*vijñaptis*). At the same time, these representations reconfigure the way the impetus (karma) codifies the consciousness. In other words, it codifies both the technicity and the technical configuration of the consciousness.

However, the concept of karma creates two points of contention in the Buddhist debates. First, if karma is a perpetual impetus that is immanent in the formational process, an insight into the pure relationality between technicity and consciousness will enable the consciousness to be mindful of how karma operates, but it will not interrupt its operation. In this light, *nibbāna/nirvāṇa* (enlightenment) is not to be understood as a release from forms or an extinction of them. If so, what is absolute mindfulness? Second, by suggesting that karma endures in time, the Sarvāstivādas imply that karma is a force that initiates dependent originations and impermanent forms. Yet, as a technicity, it stands *outside* of dependent originations and is in-itself permanent. This is a violation of the most fundamental axiom in Buddhism: dependent originations.

THE MIDDLE WAY

These aporias were first raised by a Theravādin text called the *Kathāvatthu,* or *Points of Controversy,* often dated back to the reign of the Indian emperor Ashoka (268–232 B.C.E.). According to the book, the Theravādins had already established that all forms are dependently originated. An insight into dependent originations as technicity enables the consciousness to become mindful of its own emptiness. When such mindfulness becomes the only point of reference at each moment of becoming, consciousness *is* mindfulness. According to the *āgamas*, an *arahant/arhat* (enlightened one) arrives at this absolute mindfulness when: *Khīṇā jāti, vusitaṃ brahmacariyaṃ, kataṃ karaṇīyaṃ, nāparaṃ itthattāyā'ti pajānātī"ti* (My life is exhausted, my monastic living has come to perfection, what needs to be done has been done, there is no coming back to another state of being).[61]

This seems to suggest that when one arrives at absolute mindfulness, the relationality between technicity and consciousness is dissolved. The precarity of this suggestion lies in the phrase *nāparaṃ itthattāyā'ti pajānātī"ti* (there is no coming back to another state of being). If karma operates perpetually and cannot be conceived otherwise, being mindful of the technicity of consciousness cannot possibly *dissolve* their relationality and operation.

I shall use the cinema as an example to illustrate this conundrum. The cinematographic image-consciousness is dependently originated out of many conditions: technical components such as the camera and projector (or monitor), our sensory-perceptual organs and abilities to perceive and conceptualize, and an avalanche of formational impulses that configures this perceptual-conceptual process and the corresponding forms. Dependent originations, for my purpose here, are to be considered the technicity of this formational process.

However, if, in this process, the consciousness becomes mindful of such technicity, forms will continue to be initiated as a series of contiguous initiations-extinctions (which is to say, the film will go on). The difference is that mindfulness now replaces consciousness in the operation. In such an operation, mindfulness (formerly "consciousness") remains mindful of its relationality with technicity, as their relationality is disconcealed as *the way it is*. When mindfulness is mindful of the way in which each formational impulse initiates desires, afflictions, and power relations (as, for example, with self and others), it no longer either affects them or is affected by them. Rather, it lets desires, afflictions, and powers *be*, and it engages in each moment of their initiation with equanimity.

While *Kathāvatthu* dismisses this notion as heresy, Mahāyāna scholars developed a debate around it.[62] For Richard Gombrich, Donald Lopez, and David McMahan, as a *religious* practice, the Mahāyāna movement emerged around the first and second centuries B.C.E. During this period, a large number of Sanskrit *sūtras* emerged. Unlike the Pāli *suttas*, which are concise discourses that can be transmitted orally, *sūtras* are considerably longer, carefully composed, and well-structured sermons intended for literary transmission.[63] As religious texts, their authenticity has been dismissed by the Theravādins. As philosophical texts, however, they are records of prolific debates on the conundrums left unaddressed by the Pāli Canon.

A fundamental concept in Mahāyāna Buddhism is best summarized in the *Prajñāpāramitāhṛdaya* [*Heart Sutra*]:

> *iha śāriputra rūpaṃ śūnyatā śūnyataiva rūpaṃ, rūpān na pṛithak śūnyatā śunyatāyā na pṛithag rūpaṃ, yad rūpaṃ sā śūnyatā yā śūnyatā tad rūpaṃ; evam eva vedanā-saṃjñā-saṃskāra-vijñānaṃ.*
>
> Here, O Śāriputra, form is emptiness and the very emptiness is form; emptiness does not differ from form, form does not differ from emptiness; whatever is form, that is emptiness, whatever is emptiness, that is form, the same is true of feelings, perceptions, impulses, and consciousness.[64]

Let us return to the cinema for a moment. The image-consciousness (form) is dependently originated out of a layout of conditions and is therefore empty. Here, emptiness does not refer to a state of things or being, but rather to the technicity of the formational process (consciousness). In this sense, the technicity (substrate) is not different from the formational process (form). Thus, the form-itself (self-nature) of the image-consciousness is its technicity, and the technicity-itself is the formational process. This is not to say that technicity is entirely the same as consciousness. Dwelling in consciousness (form), as it were, I often ignore its technicity; dwelling in technicity, I can lose sight of forms as embodied experiences. Therefore, in the opening of the *Vajracchedikā Prajñāpāramitā Sūtra* [*Diamond Sutra*], Śākyamuni Buddha's disciple Shubūti asks, "when virtuous men and virtuous women initiate the mind of *anuttarasamyaksambodhi* [absolute mindfulness], how should their minds [mindfulness] dwell?"[65]

The answer to this question, according to the *Diamond Sutra*, is "should thus dwell" (meaning: should dwell as *the way it is*). In the *Connected Discourses*, this is referred to as "not landing on either side."[66] This is to say that *neither technicity (substrate) nor consciousness (form) is the way it is.* Rather, both are manifestations of *the way it is.* Nonetheless, this reasoning seems to suggest that thusness is a transcendental plane—a notion rejected by Śākyamuni Buddha.

In the first century, Nāgārjuna (150–250 C.E.) composed the *Mūlamadhyamakakārikā* [*Fundamental Verses of the Middle Way*], a *śāstra* (treatise) that works through logically what is meant by "not landing on either side." It does so by examining a wide range of forms, including existence, temporality, spatiality, movement, karma, and emptiness. In each of his twenty-seven chapters, Nāgārjuna employs an exhaustive method called *hetuvidyā* (illuminating causes or logic). Here is a simplified example:

1. The Theravādins have established that if forms are dependently originated, from one *kṣaṇa* to another, we cannot claim that a form is initiated out of its self-nature. It is therefore nonself and impermanent.
2. However, in saying so, the Theravādins imply that a form is initiated, sustained, and extinguished at a *kṣaṇa*. If so, a *kṣaṇa* must be divisible into smaller units of time, which is absurd.
3. We must then accept that a form is initiated, sustained, and extinguished over three *kṣaṇas*. To say so means that a form endures over time (three *kṣaṇas*) and that it changes qualitatively. It also means that, despite these qualitative changes, these forms are considered *one* because they share an underlying self-nature. This notion is against the axiom of dependent originations.
4. If we argue that initiation, endurance, and extinction are three contiguous forms, there arises another conundrum. At the *kṣaṇa* of initiation, the form in question has yet to be in-formed. At the *kṣaṇa* of extinction, the form is no longer in-formed. This means that this form exists only at the *kṣaṇa* of its endurance, independent of any other forms. However, according to the axiom of dependent originations, a form cannot be in-formed unless it is dependently initiated and extinguished.
5. Therefore, form, the formational process, and the technicity of formation are perceptual-conceptual proliferations, which are empty of any existential values.
6. Existence and emptiness can both be refuted by following the same reasoning.

Nāgārjuna calls the way it is the *mādhyamaka* (middle way): not literally somewhere in the middle, but the emptiness of emptiness. For him:

(1) emptiness (substrate) has no self-nature; (2) as an indication of non-form, emptiness is perceived and conceptualized as the negation of form; (3) hence, in order to attain—or to return to—*the way it is,* the negation of form, the negation of the difference between form and emptiness, and the notions and actions of negation must be negated.[67] In the *Mahāprajñāpāramitāśāstra* [*Treatise on the Great Prajñāpāramitā*], Nāgārjuna clarifies that the middle way is neither a transcendental plane nor a nihilistic state of nonexistence. This is because a negation of negation refers neither to a return to a positive assertation nor to a transcendental plane, but instead to a *pure relationality* between form and emptiness. In other words, *the way it is* (thusness) is neither a form nor emptiness, neither not a form nor not emptiness.[68]

Based on the principle of the middle way, Nāgārjuna argues that karma is not an enduring operating impetus (see Figure 2). Rather, in the perceptual-conceptual reality, the initiation and extinction of a transient form is affected by a layout of conditions at a *kṣaṇa.* This form, in turn, affects and reconfigures this layout of conditions. This reconfigured layout, at the immediately contiguous *kṣaṇa,* will affect—and be affected by—the initiation and extinction of a new form. As the consciousness perceives and conceptualizes a series of modulations from one contiguous form to another and begins to discern repetitions, retributions, reversals, transferences, and delays between forms, it produces an impression that a series of karmic *impulses* has codified these modulations. Or that these modulations are perceived and conceptualized as qualitative changes of a singular enduring form mediated by a

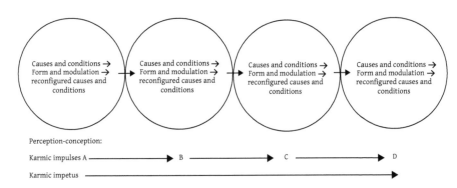

FIGURE 2. Nāgārjuna's understanding of karma

karmic impetus. In other words, karma is a perceptual-conceptual proliferation.[69]

YOGĀCĀRA BUDDHISM AND THE TATHĀGATAGARBHA

In the *Fundamental Verses of the Middle Way,* Nāgārjuna uses logical reasoning to work through the technicity of absolute mindfulness and karma. In so doing, he does not explain how such a technicity is instantiated as consciousnesses. In short, we ask: how are these operations actualized as embodied experiences?

From the fourth to seventh centuries, a school of scholars worked through the Abhidharma and arrived at a line of investigation called Chittamatra/Cittamātra (Consciousness or Manifestation Only) theory—also known as Yogachara/Yogācāra Buddhism. Yogācāra practitioners believe that their philosophical system was first proposed by Metteyya/Maitreya, a bodhisattva (enlightened sentient being) who now resides in the inner court of a universe called Tusita/Tuṣita. Historically, the scholar Asaṅga and his half brother Vasubandhu (circa fourth–fifth centuries) are considered the founders, who, according to Yin Shun (1906–2005), took their concepts from the Sarvāstivāda. Their ideas were then further debated by their disciples Buddhasimha (circa fifth and sixth centuries) and Dignāga. Their works were then revised by a new generation of scholars, including Sthiramati (475–555) and Dharmapāla (530–61), whose ideas were later debated by Tibetan and Chinese scholars. The popularity of Yogācāra Buddhism, however, began to decline in India around the time of Dharmakīrti, as a result of a revival of Mādhyamaka Buddhism.[70]

Yogācāra scholars produced an epistemology based on the theory of *bījas* (seeds or potentialities) and on the *ālaya*-consciousness (eighth consciousness). This epistemology has been known for its logical complexity and meticulousness, and many first-time readers and practitioners find it intimidating. As I mentioned earlier, the following paragraphs are best treated as a preview. In the main chapters, I will elaborate each concept closely, with more concrete examples.

The Theravādins had already established that the six consciousnesses are separate, though interdependently related, domains, which are unified by volition. Yogācāra scholars argue that as a force that initiates an *attachment* to the six consciousnesses as a unified whole, volition operates as a consciousness known as *manas* (seventh consciousness;

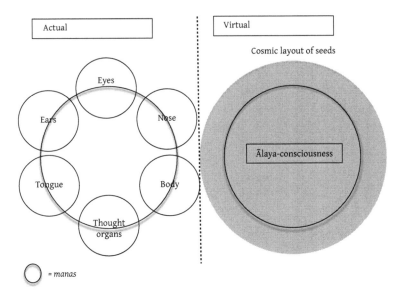

FIGURE 3. The eight consciousnesses

see Figure 3). Some scholars, for convenience, simply call it the ego, even
though *manas* does not correspond directly to the ego (see chapter 4).
Manas is therefore best understood not as a domain independent of the
six consciousnesses, but rather, as Thich Nhat Hanh (1926–2022) argues,
a magnetic force that is immanent in the six consciousnesses.[71]

The six consciousnesses are forms, which operate on the axiom of
dependent originations. Forms are manifestations or actualizations of
the potentiality to perceive and conceptualize and also the potentiality
to generate signs. As forms are instantiations of causes and conditions
that were *planted and laid dormant* in the past, and have been reactivated
in the present, such causes and conditions can also be considered potentialities. These potentialities, like seeds, were planted and laid dormant as a cosmic layout, while *manas* attaches itself to a specific subset
called the *ālaya*-consciousness (storehouse or eighth consciousness).
These seeds are mobile and perpetually circulating, and their circulation drives—and is driven by—karma.

In this sense, the six consciousnesses are the manifestations or actualizations of the seeds. When a sub-layout (known as an "avalanche")

of seeds is actualized as forms (six consciousnesses), the configuration of their relationalities (as causes and conditions) is also revised. When the forms are extinguished, they are virtualized, planted, and laid dormant again as seeds in the *ālaya*-consciousness. In this sense, the reconfigurations of the seeds and their inter-relationalities are stimulated or activated by the operation of the six consciousnesses. For example, a benevolent thought, speech, or act, once extinguished, will be planted in the *ālaya*-consciousness as seeds that will facilitate the proliferation of potentialities to exercise benevolence.[72]

Perceptually and conceptually, karma is experienced as an impetus that drives—and is driven by—the overall operation of the eight consciousnesses (the six consciousnesses, *manas,* and the *ālaya*-consciousness). It codifies the seeds, their relationalities, and their actualizations. Technically, Yogācāras follow Nāgārjuna's argument that they are impulses. However, where these impulses are located and how exactly they operate are subject to debate. Asaṅga, for example, argues that these impulses are perceived and conceptualized as formal modulations from one *kṣaṇa* to another. Hence, the idea of an impulse is a perceptual-conceptual proliferation when the consciousness observes a series of actual configurational changes. Vasubandhu, by contrast, argues that the mobile relationalities between the seeds (and their manifestations) are the impulses themselves.[73]

We can compare a cosmic layout of seeds to a roomful of dust particles. *Manas* can be imagined as a mobile light that sheds on a sublayout of dust (*ālaya*-consciousness) within this cosmic layout. This light makes visible (actualizes) these dust particles as existent forms, based on the principle of dependent originations. As the actualized forms perish, they are virtualized as seeds again, and they circulate around the *ālaya*-consciousness. However, by comparing the *ālaya*-consciousness and the cosmic layout to a room, we are presuming that it is a predefined space. We should reimagine this *room* not as a preexisting container but as a *layout* of paths traveled by the dust particles. The *ālaya*-consciousness is then best understood not as a terrain, but as a layout of mobile relationalities between the dust particles. These relationalities are empty of existential values *until* the potentialities are actualized as forms. In this sense, while the potentialities and their manifestations (forms) are constantly changing and moving, the relationalities are neither moving nor not moving.[74] It is in this sense that the *ālaya*-consciousness (technicity) does not *exist* unless there are moving dust particles and their manifestations, and the six consciousnesses will not be manifested unless the *ālaya*-consciousness (technicity) is in operation. Later scholars called the pure relationalities—as a layout—the Tathāgatagarbha (the womb from which Buddhahood is conceived), a concept that was then further developed and debated by Chinese and Japanese scholars alike.[75]

MEONTOLOGY

As I stated earlier, this book can be divided into five interrelated transductive phases: meontology, epistemology, ethics, aesthetics, and politics.

In the first chapter of this book, "Meontology," I argue that the cinematographic technicity-consciousness along with any ontological investigation into it are *papañcas* (perceptual-conceptual proliferations), defined by Bodhi as the "propensity of the worldling's imagination to erupt into an effusion of mental commentary that obscures the bare data of cognition."[76] Therefore, such an investigation must be conducted with a mindfulness of the subtle changes of observational positions in our process of scrutiny, a process in which imaging *is* imagining. Tanabe Hajime and Thomé H. Fang call this meta-ontological method "metanoetics" and "meontology," respectively.[77]

In this chapter, I first put the Buddhist debates on dependent originations in dialogue with the sciences and European philosophy, so as to remap the formational process of the cinema as a technicity-consciousness. I then follow the Theravādin argument that the dependent originations underlining the contact between forms (both internal and external) on the one hand, and sensations and affections on the other, drive—and are driven by—karmic impulses. Such impulses turn what appears to be an objective layout of dependent originations (a perceptual-conceptual configuration) into an objectivized-subjective consciousness (another perceptual-conceptual configuration).[78]

By adjudicating on the debates between the Mādhyamikas and their Yogācāra counterparts, I define karma as impulses that configure the initiation-extinction of forms ranging from one *kṣaṇa* to another, which affect—and are affected by—the configuration itself. With this concept of karma, I revisit Bazinian ontology: a belief that the photographic—and, *by extension*, the cinematographic—image is an imprint of reality.[79] If we read Bazin carefully, however, his ontology is not hinged on the relationship between photography (a technico-technological transduction) and reality, but instead on the death drive as an initiating impetus (ontological ground) that sets in motion the formational process. By differentiating the *technico-technological* (or *ontogenetic*) from the *ontological* in Bazin, a conversation can be established between his notion of ontology with that of Buddhism. They both see imaging as imagining—a karma-driven, perceptual-conceptual proliferation that is meontologically empty. By the end of chapter 1, I will have analyzed Bi Gan's *Diqiu zuihou de yewan* [*Long Day's Journey into Night*, 2018] in relation to the emergence of the Chinese independent mind-game film, in order to illustrate how perceptual-conceptual configurations proliferate as an image-consciousness. I also will have discussed how the negotiation between imaging and imagining enables the consciousness to be mindful of its political technicities.

EPISTEMOLOGY

Chapter 2, "The Karma-Image," and chapter 3, "The Insight-Image," are phase-by-phase reworkings of the two key concepts proposed by Gilles Deleuze: the movement-image and the time-image. In Deleuze's formulation of the movement-image, *puissance* is immanent in each mode of being and emanative to all. In the formational process, it is instantiated as impulses, which serve as intermediaries among perceptions, affections, and actions.[80] According to the Yogācāras, impulses are actualized, *here and now*, from the seeds stored in the ālaya-consciousness. These impulses are perceived and conceptualized as an avalanche of initiating forces that impels the formation of a series of awarenesses. In this sense, karmic impulses are always at work in the formational process of the movement-image. Therefore, the movement-image is better understood as a karma-image.

By analyzing the cinematographic technicity-consciousness as a karma-image, we can become mindful of how karmic impulses affect—and are affected by—the formational process from one kṣaṇa to another. We can also see how affects are dependently originated with an attachment not only to the image-consciousness as that which exists, but also to desires and afflictions. In this process, cinematic identification is best reunderstood as a series of affective transductions and transindividuations, which constantly reconfigures the subject-object relationships in the image. In chapter 2, "The Karma-Image," I use a classical Hollywood example, *The Searchers* [directed by John Ford (1894–1973), 1956] to shed light on every phase of this formational process, including how this process negotiates conflicting values on both gender and race. Meanwhile, an insight-image is an image-consciousness that is mindful of its own technicity. In the first five chapters of *Cinéma 2*. *L'image-temps* [*Cinema 2: The Time-Image*, 1985], Deleuze uses and reconfigures concepts of time and temporalities propounded by Henri Bergson (1859–1941) to illustrate various modes of the time-image. For Deleuze, the time-image is in-formed when the cinematic technicity-consciousness travels across different planes of temporal existences—as in recollections, dreams, and the crystal image (crystallization of the pure difference between the past, present, and future). As *pure optical and sound situations* whose sensory-motor connections are in question, these travels leave indiscernible the boundaries between memories and fantasies (potentialities) and lived realities (actualities), and the observer and the observed.[81]

In chapter 3, "The Insight-Image," I rework Deleuze's notion of the time-image through the Theravādin, Mādhyamika, and Yogācāra understandings of time and reanalyze one of his film examples, *Le jour se lève* [*Daybreak*, Marcel Carné (1906–96), 1939]. I argue that what fascinates Deleuze is not time. Rather, as the time-image draws the consciousness's attention to its sensory-motor (dis)connections, it becomes mindful of its own technicity: the karmic impulses that initiate sense-formations, thought-formations, and time-formations.[82] For Deleuze, in pure optical and sound situations, the present is no longer an interval between which the consciousness relates itself to the past and anticipates the future (Chronos). Rather, the consciousness fully engages in the present as the *here and now* (Cronos, or *kairos*).[83]

Toward the end of chapter 3, I demonstrate that such a mindfulness can be attained either through the Dzhiɛn/Chan (Zen) Buddhist notions of *dziǎmnguò/jianwu* (gradual awakening) or through *tuǎnnguò/dunwu* (sudden awakening).[84] Gradual awakening corresponds to what we now call "slow cinema," which I illustrate with an analysis of Apichatpong Weerasethakul's *Sleepcinemahotel* [2018]. Sudden awakening is achieved in the cinema through formal and temporal manipulations, which I illustrate with an analysis of another example of Deleuze's, *L'Année dernière à Marienbad* [*Last Year in Marienbad*, Alain Resnais (1922–2014), 1961]. Finally, I conduct a close reading of Pema Tseden's *Tharlo* [2015] to examine how mindfulness is mobilized as a technology that gives the consciousness an agency over its own becoming, and how such a technology addresses a Tibetan person's position of political deindividuation, desubjectivization, and deautonomization.

ETHICS AND AESTHETICS

When a consciousness assumes an agency over its technicity, it is called a *paññā/prajñā* (insight into pure relationalities). The rest of the book, chapters 4 and 5 and the conclusion, is devoted to defining how relational thinking enables us to reconceptualize the cinema as a process of transindividuation and also to rethink its ethical, aesthetic, and political implications.

According to Mahāyāna philosophy, relational thinking enables the consciousness to attain—and return to—the four *brahmavihārās* (heightened states of mind): *mettā/maitrī* (benevolence), *karuṇā* (compassion), *muditā* (empathy), and *upekkha/upekṣā* (equanimity).[85] These four *brahmavihārās* form the foundation of Mahāyāna ethics. However, the ways in which relationalities are reconfigured and Buddhist understandings of relationalities can be compared to their Euro-American counterparts are eminently contestable.

In chapter 4, "Cinema Ecology," I turn to some provocative discourses of relational thinking in film and media studies, including phenomenology, the debate on the relationship between human and technics, and theories of affect.[86] I then propose to use the four *brahmavihārās* to rethink cinema ecologically, with the aid of Imamichi Tomonobu's (1922–2010) reconfiguration of Martin Heidegger's (1889–1976) notion of *hypokeimenon* as the Tathāgatagarbha, Brian Massumi's understanding of ontopower (an im-mediate—as in temporal immediacy and without mediation—agency over an affective impulse), and Zen Buddhism's understanding of sudden awakening.[87]

In that chapter I argue that relational thinking reveals what we do in the cinema (identification), what the cinema does (negotiating powers), how the power asymmetry between the human and machine is configured, and, most important, how we can instigate changes. By the end of the chapter, I push this idea further by analyzing contemporary *tongzhi* (comrade) or queer cinema in Mainland China as both a media ecology and a form of political activism, giving special attention to three films: *Xing xing xiang xi xi* [*Star Appeal,* Cui Zi'en, 2013], *Huoxing zonghezheng* [*Martian Syndrome,* Kokoka, 2013], and *Canfei kehuan* [*Deformity Sci-Fi,* Kokoka, 2013].

In chapter 5, titled "In-Aesthetics," I argue that the concept of aesthetics stands at odds with Buddhist philosophy itself.[88] Instead, in the process of becoming mindful of its own technicity, the cinematographic consciousness *abduces* an in-aesthetics: the emptiness on which aesthetic judgment is based. The term "abduces," together with the noun "abduction," were coined by Charles Sanders Peirce (1839–1934), which refer to a process of drawing a meta-analytical conclusion from which the differentiation between logicality and illogicality arises.[89]

In that chapter, I first explain how certain aesthetic choices came to be defined as Buddhist through the lens of colonial discourses, and discuss how these choices can be more properly contextualized within the larger East Asian Buddhist philosophical debates. Through a historical approach, I explicate on how "Buddhist aesthetics" came to be defined in the twentieth century through the works of Shaku Soyen (1860–1919) and Suzuki Teitarō Daisetz (1870–1966). Such aesthetics then became part of the debate of the Kyoto school over the definition of the Pure Land—a mode of existence that is a manifestation of absolute mindfulness.[90]

Meanwhile, from the 1870s to the 1940s, Yang Wenhui (1837–1911) and his disciple Ouyang Jian (1871–1943) debated the influence of Taoism on Chinese Buddhism, initiating the Buddhist Renaissance.[91] While philosophers have since then tried to reexamine the delineation between Indian and Chinese scholarships on the Tathāgatagarbha, aesthetes such as Wang Guowei (1877–1927), Chu Kuang-ch'ien (Zhu Guangqian, 1897–1986), Zong Baihua (1897–1986), and Lam Nin-tung (1944–90) developed a syncretic approach to aesthetics, adjudicating on Buddhist, Taoist, Confucian, as well as European frameworks to arrive at a theory of art—and eventually, cinema—as an image-consciousness.[92] By the end of this final chapter, however, I maintain that none of these notions can be called Buddhist aesthetics. Rather, with their aid, we can understand better what is meant by the term "in-aesthetics." I illustrate how one can conduct an in-aesthetic analysis by discussing the reception history and film forms of the works of Ozu Yasujirō (1903–63).

POLITICS

In the "Conclusion: Cinema and Nonviolence," I mobilize the key concepts presented in this book to rethink the relationship between cinema and nonviolence. In the formational process of a consciousness, the subject comes to believe that it stands outside all relationalities. Such a position is effectively made sacred: untouchable and severed from any relationality.[93] It *enjoys* the sights, sounds, sensations, and thoughts of violence, under the impression that it plays no part in affecting violence or being affected by it. The truth is: subjectivization-objectivization is, by default, an act of violence on the overall technicity of consciousness. It merely defers and delays the technological, physical, psychical, and even sociopolitical harm to the subject.

In this conclusion, I examine how the cinematic consciousness and its various technico-technological instantiations have been historically configured in ways that preempt potentialities of creative and radical changes from being actualized. When the entire sociopolitical milieu is in-formed cinematographically in accordance with such preemptive technicity, there seems to be no room for reparation. Through a comparative study between the Theravādin and Mahāyāna understandings of nonviolence, some of which have been appropriated by both historical and contemporary political powers to justify violence, I reinstate and elaborate how nonviolence can be exercised as an active engagement in radical changes.[94] By the end of the conclusion, I will have conducted an analysis of Christian Petzold's film *Transit* [2018] as a user manual that illustrates how microperceptual changes can be made to gradually—but surely—repair *our* technicity-consciousness.

CHAPTER 1

MEONTOLOGY

Defining cinema as a technicity-consciousness requires an ontological—and meontological—investigation. Historically, such an investigation has been associated with André Bazin ever since the publication of his essays "Ontologie de l'image photographique" ["Ontology of the Photographic Image"] in the journal *Problèmes de la peinture* [Problems of painting, 1945] and "Le mythe du cinéma total" ["The Myth of Total Cinema"] in *Critique* [1946].[1] This is not to say that Bazinian ontology is the only model ever proposed in our discipline.[2] Nonetheless, what scholars today perceive as cinema's ontological crisis has been triggered by a belief that the emergence of digital technology has fundamentally challenged two interrelated presuppositions of Bazinian ontology: (1) that the photographic image is the technico-technological basis of the cinema and (2) that the photographic image is an imprint of reality.[3] A renewed ontologico-meontological investigation into the cinema therefore requires us to rethink where the edges and limitations of Bazinian ontology lie and to locate the core aporia that we can address with the aid of Buddhist philosophy.

As Dudley Andrew points out, Bazin's two articles were composed toward the end of the Nazi Occupation (1940–44), based on two blueprints. From *L'imaginaire* [*Imaginary*, 1940], Bazin borrows Jean-Paul Sartre's (1905–80) notion of the photographic image as being an imperfect analogon that offers the beholder a trace of the photographed being. Such a trace recalls either the beholder's memory of this being or a prototype they have encountered in the past, thus invoking in them a

31

mental image. This imagination then enables the beholder to bypass the materiality of the photographic print and apprehend an animated image-consciousness of that being.[4]

Bazin's second blueprint is *Esquisse d'une psychologie du cinéma* ["Sketch for a Psychology of the Moving Pictures," 1940], in which André Malraux (1901–74) regards the cinema as a myth in its psychoanalytical sense—a fetish that both conceals and indicates the site of the death drive. For him, technical innovations, formal strategies, and cultural practices of the cinema are ontologically grounded and teleologically driven toward the death drive, until the cinema reaches an asymptote in relation to its totality-cum-annihilation.[5]

An ontology of the cinematographic image seeks to expound on how the cinema comes into being and how it is posited in the order of things. However, it does so only within a given epistemological framework. For Michel Foucault (1926–84), ontology posits itself in a larger *dispositif,* which in-forms—and is in-formed by—a network of sociopolitical discourses, laws, moral values, governmental decisions, and scholarly statements. This network manipulates the relations of forces and occupies the strategic intersection between "power relations and relations of knowledge."[6] In this sense, an ontological investigation is a political and ethical act.

In the introduction to this book, I discussed the political and ethical implications of the Euro-American understanding of knowledge production. As Shih Shu-mei argues, in the humanities, theory is often arrived at by universalizing the exceptional.[7] As Aijaz Ahmad argues, under colonialism and postcolonialism, European exceptions have always been universalized as the truth. The lived experiences and methods developed in Asia and elsewhere, which do not always conform to such *truth,* are configured in the Euro-American imagination as exceptions. Gayatri Chakravorty Spivak calls this an epistemic violence.[8]

In the "Madhupiṇḍika Sutta," ontology is regarded as a *papañca,* defined by Kañukurunde Ñaṇananda as a perceptual-conceptual proliferation. Bodhi defines *papañca* as the "propensity of the worldling's imagination to erupt into an effusion of mental commentary that obscures the bare data of cognition."[9] Ñaṇananda argues that the starting point of an ontological investigation is an observer's bare cognition, what he calls the "impersonal phase." Through a close reading of §16 of the "Sutta," he points out that an "impersonal note," indicated by the text's use of the third-person objective pronoun, "is sustained only up to the point of *vedanā* [sensation or affection]." After that, the "formula now takes a personal ending suggestive of deliberate activity" (the subjective phase). The employment of the first-person subjective pronoun in this second half of the "Sutta" suggests that cognition after the emergence of sensations and affections "is no longer a mere contingent process, nor is it an activity deliberately directed, *but an inexorable subjection to an objective order of things* [ontology]. At this final stage of sense-perception (objective subjective phase), he who has hitherto been the subject now becomes the hapless object."[10] In other words, a *papañca* universalizes the subjective and turns it into an *ontology*. Such an ontology is in turn employed as a perceptual-conceptual framework to constitute an objectivized subjectivity.

From a Buddhist perspective, ontology is not purposeless. Rather, ontological investigations need to be conducted with a mindfulness of those minute transformations of observational positions in our process of examination. In this perceptual-conceptual process, imaging is imagining. Thus, as Tanabe Hajime and Thomé H. Fang argue, ontology entails a meta-ontological study, which they call "metanoetics" and "meontology" respectively.[11]

In this chapter, I first put the Buddhist discourses on dependent originations in conversation with the sciences and European philosophy to schematize the formational process of the cinema as a technicity-consciousness. As Ñāṇananda argues, the initiation of sensations and affections in this process marks the conversion from technicity to consciousness.[12] If so, the interconnectedness between technicity and consciousness is in-formed by an abject impulse: karma. Based on the debates between the Mādhyamikas and their Yogācāra counterparts, I define "karma" as impulses that configure the initiation-extinction of forms from one *kṣaṇa* (smallest unit of time) to another, which function like codes that affect—and are affected by—the configuration itself. Such impulses convert an objective layout of dependent originations (technicity) into an objectivized subjective consciousness.

Toward the end of this chapter, I use the theory of karma to address an aporia in Bazinian ontology. What problematizes such ontology is not its failure to anticipate digital technology, which has put the direct (or, some say, indexical) relationship between the image and reality in crisis.[13] If we read Bazin carefully, his ontology is not hinged on the relationship between photography (a technico-technological transduction) and reality, but on the death drive as an initiating impetus (ontological ground) that sets in motion the formational process. The trouble, I argue, is our tendency to conflate the *technico-technological* (or *ontogenetic*) with the *ontological* in Bazin. By recognizing their difference, a conversation can be established between his notion of ontology with Buddhism's via the concept of karma. At the end of this chapter, I analyze Bi Gan's *Diqiu zuihou de yewan* [*Long Day's Journey into Night*, 2018] in relation to the Chinese independent mind-game film to illustrate how perceptual-conceptual configurations proliferate as an image-consciousness.

DEPENDENT ORIGINATIONS

SA-298 of the *Saṃyuktāgama* [Connected discourses], which Sujato regards as the earliest collection of the oral traditions circulated before the Great Schism in the Third Buddhist Council (circa 250 B.C.E.), defines dependent originations as such: "The existence of a consequent depends on the existence of a cause-condition; the origination of the consequent depends on the origination of that cause-condition."[14] The subjects and objects of this statement are neither the consequent nor the cause-condition. Rather, they refer to a perception and conception of a state of being (existence) and to a process of becoming (origination). Hence, a more accurate way to understand this statement is: "The perception and conception of a state of being depend on the perception and conception of another state of being; the perception and conception of a process of becoming depend on the perception and conception of another process of becoming." In other words, ontology is a perceptual-conceptual proliferation.

In Sanskrit, the term *hetu-pratyaya* (cause-condition) refers to the interdependency between a direct cause and a layout of conditions. It means that the existence and origination of a direct cause must depend on the existences and originations of other conditions.[15] For example, the existence and origination of light particles are fundamental to the existence and origination of a cinematographic image. Yet, the existence and origination of the image both depend on the existence and origination of a layout of technical, physio-psychic, historical, and sociopolitical conditions. Each of these conditions is dependent on another layout of conditions, ad infinitum. Thus, it is impossible to perceive and conceptualize the existence of an unmoved mover unless we violate the axiom of dependent originations.[16]

Let us conduct a phase-by-phase technico-technological analysis of the core components of the anthropotechnical assemblage on which the existence and origination of a cinematographic image both depend. For my analysis, I choose an arbitrary starting point: our *objective reality*. From a technical perspective, this can be defined as an electromagnetic field in-formed by a layout of photons and other waves and particles, whose momentum is polarized into a sinusoidal plane that is represented perceptually and conceptually as a spatiotemporal cone.[17] The existence and origination of this analytical starting point, which seem to be posited in objective reality, depend on the existence and origination of perception as well as conception. In Buddhism, the dependent originations between the ability to perceive-conceptualize and perception-conceptualization is called *ālambana-pratyaya* (foundational condition).[18] In other words, this *objective reality* is a subjective proliferation objectivized in accordance with an ontological order.

As a momentum, this electromagnetic field is transmitted through the camera lens into the camera body by means of refraction. The size of the lens determines the width of the electromagnetic field it can transmit, the dynamic range of its intensity (brightness), and the frequency range of its spectrum (colors). These are made adjustable by the camera's iris, which forms an aperture that can be opened or closed by a photographer. These factors determine the acuity of the image. A smaller aperture that transmits more-intense light beams through the lens will enable the sensors to register a sharper image with a clearer rendition of its spectrum.[19]

As an optical process, refraction transmits collimated beams of photons and converges them at a focal point, which will be ready to be registered by the sensors. This part of the process is common in both celluloid and digital single-lens reflex (DSLR) cameras. In a celluloid camera, these collimated beams of photons will be registered directly on the silver particles of a piece of 35 mm film, which forms an analogon of the electromagnetic field *out there*.

Meanwhile, a DSLR camera uses a charge-couple device (CCD), which is a cascade of synchronized electric circuits called flip flops. Each flip flop is a latch that registers either a transmission of an electrical charge or the absence of it. On registering the data, the circuit shifts by one position in a bit array.[20] When the photons hit the CCD, they are first categorized by a Bayer filter into a square grid of primary additive filter layers—red, green, and blue (RGB)—arranged alternately into BGGR, RGBG, GRGB, or RGGB.[21] Each capacitor of the CCD will produce an electrical charge proportional to the intensity of the electromagnetic field of a square analogically. The last capacitor that forms the bit array will output its electrical charge into an amplifier, which will then convert it to a voltage. Repeatedly, this process generates a sequence of voltages, which will then be sampled from a series of continuous analogue signals to a series of intervals. Each interval will be represented by a sequence of digits. These digital sequences will then be stored in a memory card.[22]

The DSLR camera can reverse this process and convert the digitized samples back to an RGB grid via a liquid-crystal display (LCD), while the 35 mm film in a celluloid film camera can be processed and printed as a photograph—or, in the cinema, as a projectable print. When the photons from the LCD or the physical print hit the human corneas, they pass through the lenses of the eyes, which refract the light beams and transmit them to the back of the retinas. The two types of photoreceptive cells in the retinas—rods and cones—transduce these photons into neuronal signals. Rods are sensitive to low light intensity, to the extent that they can respond to a single photon, but they produce vision of lower acuity in only one photosensitive pigment. Cones are less sensitive to light intensity, but they are more sensitive to changes. They can also produce high visual acuity with all three photosensitive pigments. Once a cell is activated, its membrane rises and falls rapidly to produce hyperpolarization, that is, an effect that turns the electrical charges in the axon—the body of the cell—into a series of predominantly negative ones. This activates the subsequent cell in the chain to do the same, thus producing a sequence of binary electric impulses. These signals are then transmitted by the optical nerve from the retinas to the lateral geniculate nucleus (LGN).[23]

The LGN receives electrical signals not only from the retinas, but also from other regions of the optico-neurological system. It combines the signals from both retinas in order to produce a single field of vision in relationship to the body. It also computes the focal point of the field and the spatial differences, velocities, and directions of movements between differentiated optical elements and the perceiving body.[24] Signals from the LGN are transmitted to the primary visual cortex (V1) on each hemisphere of the brain, which processes optical data and identifies patterns. These processed signals are then transmitted to V2, the brain's secondary visual cortex, where a cognitive map of the visual field is configured. These signals are then sent to V3 and V4. V3 identifies and configures patterns of motion, while V4 configures both attention (one's gaze) and the spatial relations between the optical elements. The information from V1, V2, and V3 is also sent to V5 and V6. The V5 cortex processes and outputs signals that define the velocity and direction of movements, while V6 defines self-motion.[25] In this sense, vision is best understood not as a static image *out there*. Rather, it is a layout of mobile forms that instantiates the relationship between the perceiving body-as-form and the field of vision posited at a distance, as well as the mobile forms between the different optical elements in this field.

In this anthropotechnical layout, the existence and origination of each condition depend on the existence and origination of a contiguous one. In Buddhism, this relationship is called *anantara-pratyaya* (seed condition) and *samanatara-pratyaya* (matching condition). These two conditions are often, in combination, called a condition of contiguity.[26] These conditions explain the formational process of bare cognition, but not how this visual field and the human body are recognized as an image-consciousness. For Buddhist scholars, this process of turning bare cognition into recognition is initiated by *saṅkhāra/saṃskara* (volition; see Figure 1 in the introduction to this book). Volition is originated dependently with the *viññāṇa/vijñāna* (consciousness) and an operation called *nāmarūpa* (naming and in-forming). *Nāma* refers to the cognitive process of identifying and differentiating one form from another. The existence and origination of this process depend on the existence and origination of *saḷāyatanas/ṣaḍāyatanas* (sensory-perceptual organs, that is, internal forms). *Rūpa* refers to the process of positing those forms in the sensory-perceptual field as *āyatana* (external forms).[27]

For Buddhist philosophers, consciousness at this stage is not a unified operation. Rather, each sensory-perceptual process is a discrete consciousness. Thus, there are consciousnesses of the eyes, ears, nose, tongue, body, and mind (thought; see Figure 3 in the introduction). Neurosciences have by now located where in the neurological path these acts of naming and in-forming take place (the LGN and V1–V6). However, they have not yet been able to explain where these abilities (technicity) come from and how a bare cognition is recognized as an objectivized subjective reality (consciousness).

Both Ñaṇananda and Yin Shun identify the generation of *vedanās* (sensations and affections) as the turning point between bare cognition and recognition. The existence and origination of sensations and affections depend on the existence and origination of the perceptual-conceptual difference between internal and external forms. Such a difference provides the condition for the *phassa/sparśa* (contact) between internal forms and their external counterparts. This is what Ñaṇananda calls the subjective phase. Affections can be pleasurable, unpleasurable, or indifferent, which produce a *taṇhā/tṛṣṇā* (longing) for the perpetuity of these feelings. Such longing produces an *upādāna* (attachment) to the *bhava/bhāva* (existence) of all forms. Thus, forms, which were subjectivized in the phase of *vedanās,* are now projected as the objectivized subjective.[28]

The existence of a form is conditioned on the existence of a layout of other forms that serve as its *adhipati-pratyaya* (dominant condition). This means that the existence of a form only lasts as long as the dominant conditions exist. Moreover, Buddhist scholars argue that forms are originated and extinguished from one *kṣaṇa* to another. A form that seems to persist in time is a sequence of contiguously reproduced forms that we misrecognize as only one form. Thus, forms are by default *anicca/anitya* (impermanent), and they go through cycles of *jāti* (birth or origination) and *jarāmaraṇa* (decay, and death or extinction).[29]

The cinematographic image, however, is never recognized as a layout of existent beings and objects. Let us say that we are in a darkened movie theater watching a fiction film, where our sensory-perceptual organs are drawn predominantly to the visual field on the screen in front of us and also to the audio field around us. In such an environment, the LGN and V1–V6 will configure an attentive gaze by limiting the muscular movements of our eyes and body, thus enabling the optical elements on the screen and the forms they represent to be the dominant conditions on which our sensations, affections, longing, attachment, and sense of existence depend. However, even in this situation, a triple recognition is in operation, which involves: (1) the recognition of the optical image as a physical form that exists *outside of* the perceptual

body (objectifying the subjective); (2) the reliance of the forms on the
screen as the dominant conditions on which (the existence and origination of) the internal forms depend, which generates what Gilbert Simondon calls a transindividuation between the sensory-perceptual body
and the technical body (especially the camera); and (3) the recognition
of the audiovisual field as an existent objective reality, which produces
a transindividuation between the spectator's body and the film's protagonist's. The second and third recognitions are what Christian Metz
(1931–93) calls primary and secondary identifications.[30]

In this formational process, the technical difference between
celluloid and digital is a matter of storage (celluloid film versus the memory card) as well as the modes of transduction (chemical versus electromagnetic). Hence, the materiality of the electromagnetic field (which we
call the film image) has nothing to do with the way the eventual image-
consciousness is in-formed. The qualitative difference lies not *in* the
materiality of the image (as if one were to say "I love the 35 mm graini-
ness!"). Rather, it is a perceptual-conceptual proliferation initiated by
both sensations and affections (as if one were to remark "I *feel* a qualitative difference, and hence, these two technological modes appear to
instantiate two different *ontological* relationships"). In Simondon's terms,
there *is* a difference between celluloid and digital, but such a difference
is an ontogenetic-affective one, not an ontological one. I shall elaborate
this point later.

I also want to bring our attention to the relationship between
the starting point and the endpoint of this formational process. The
endpoint of this process is the existence and origination of an image-
consciousness: a perceptual-conceptual proliferation. Meanwhile, the
starting point of my analysis, the *objective reality,* is also a perceptual-
conceptual proliferation: an image-consciousness. The difference is that
in the beginning, the existences and originations of smell, taste, and
touch depend on the direct contact between the external and internal
forms. By the end, these three sensations and affections are, as Vivian
Sobchack argues, supplemented synesthetically by the operation of the
consciousnesses.[31] In other words, the entire process of becoming is a
perceptual-conceptual proliferation, which is *anatta/anātman* (nonself)
and *suñña/śūnya* (empty of existential value). Our unawareness of this
is called *avijjā/avidyā* (ignorance). This cyclical process is often called
the twelve *nidānas* (interdependent relationships).[32]

INTRODUCTION TO KARMA: MODULATIONS
AS MEDIATION

The Theravādin notion of the twelve *nidānas* seems to suggest that ignorance either operates as, or emanates, an impetus, which propels the operation of the six consciousnesses—in our case, the cinematographic image-consciousness. If so, such an impetus can be regarded as a force of mediation. In Buddhist philosophy, however, the suggestion that there is an enduring force that mediates the formational process contradicts the axiom of dependent originations. Understanding cinema as a technicity-consciousness and knowing how the formational process operates therefore require us to scrutinize what this impetus is and how it works.

Both Gilbert Simondon and Gilles Deleuze are suspicious of the idea of mediation. For Simondon, in any given process of mediation, anthropotechnical forms, which seem to perform their functions as media, are merely instantiations of this process.[33] In other words, mediation is formless. It is best understood as a potentiality that does not exist until it is actualized as qualitative changes in forms. If so, we may say that there is no mediation, but there are only qualitative changes whose relationalities are perceived and conceptualized as mediation. Moreover, as Michel Foucault argues, mediation involves a code (*dispositif*), which defines how an act of mediation is configured, which is likewise formless.[34]

For Deleuze, the concept of mediation stems from a semiotic approach to media, which "reduces the image to an analogical sign belonging to the enunciation on the one hand and codifies these signs in order to discover the (non-analogical [digital]) linguistic structure underlying these enunciations." For him, such an approach of mediation regards the image as two molds: a sensible form (resemblance) supported by an intelligible structure (substrate). This intelligible structure codifies the sensible form, which maintains a consistent relationship with the object to which it refers (resemblance). For Deleuze, such an understanding overlooks that each qualitative change is a *mode* (of existence) transindividuated anthropotechnically from one phase (moment) to another. Therefore, what we conceive of as mediation is in fact a series of modulations. When we observe a consistency in the relationship between the sign and the object to which it refers over a period of time, we get the impression that there is an underlying structure of codes.[35]

What Deleuze identifies is a conundrum debated by Buddhist scholars from the third century B.C.E. to the sixth century C.E. This conundrum was first uncovered in a debate on the relationship between a seed
condition and a matching condition. According to the axiom of dependent originations as understood by the Theravādins, the origination,
existence, and extinction of a condition takes place at one kṣaṇa. When
we say that the origination and existence of a matching condition depend on the origination and existence of a seed condition, we give the
impression that when the seed condition is extinguished, a code remains, which actively rewrites—and is rewritten by—the matching condition as a reproduction of or retribution to the seed. If the originations
and existences of the seed and the matching conditions are immediately
contiguous, we will have the impression of temporal continuity. Yet, if
the originations and existences of these two conditions appear to be
spatiotemporally discrete, we will get the impression that the consequence of the seed is deferred, delayed, and displaced, a phenomenon
known as kamma/karma.[36]

According to the Sarvāstivādas, karma is an impetus that remains
dormant and formless after the extinction of a seed condition, until it is
reactivated by other conditions and actualized as a matching condition.
Moreover, karma itself is avyākata/avyākṛta (unmarked: neither benevolent nor malevolent). Hence, whether the matching condition is benevolent or malevolent depends on the dominant conditions at the time of
its actualization.[37] Nonetheless, the idea that an enduring impetus can
be reactivated and actualized as codes insinuates that there is something
akin to sabhāva (self-nature), of which each form is an instantiation. This
idea goes against the principles of impermanence, emptiness, and nonself. Yet, such a theory helps explain why the cyclical relationship between technicity and consciousness remains perpetually operative.

In the "Karmaphalaparīkṣa" [On karma] chapter of the Verses on the
Middle Way, Nāgārjuna proposes an analogy to reconcile the notion of
karma with the axiom of dependent originations (previewed in the introduction to this book). For him, a seed does not produce a piece of fruit
directly. Rather, it produces stages of growth until a plant is generated
and bears fruit. If we simply observe the seed condition (seed) and the
matching condition (fruit), we will probably arrive at the same conclusion as the Sarvāstivādas'.

For Nāgārjuna, what happens is that the origination and existence of a seed condition enables the origination and existence of an immediately contiguous matching condition, that is, a new stage of growth (see Figure 2 in the introduction). Perceptually and conceptually, each new form is a new mode of existence that configures—and is configured by—the dominant conditions at the instant of its origination. Nāgārjuna's model is closer to Deleuze's idea that the cinematographic image-consciousness is not in-formed by an enduring mediating force, but instead by a series of modulations ranging from one mode of transindividuation to another. For Nāgārjuna, if a contiguous matching condition gives rise to a form that is identical or similar to the preceding one, it is not because a code exists that governs its formation. Rather, it simply means that the originations and existences of these two forms depend on nearly identical or similar conditions. Hence, for Nāgārjuna, even though what we misrecognize as karmic relationships between causes and consequences are undeniable phenomena, karma, like any other forms, is empty of existential value.[38]

If so, karma is a mentally fabricated technical operation that we deduce from the way consciousness is *experienced.* The Yogācāras, however, contend that this goes against Śākyamuni Buddha's claim, in the *Connected Discourses,* that karma is an actual (not imagined) technical operation. In SA-102, Śākyamuni Buddha even claims that what the Brahmins regard as Brahman (ultimate being) is karma.[39] The Yogācāras therefore seek to maintain Nāgārjuna's position that karma is part of dependent originations, on the one hand, and acknowledge karma as an actual power that drives—and is driven by—the operation of the technicity-consciousness, on the other. In order to do so, they work through Nāgārjuna's idea via three theoretical domains: the theory of seeds, the *ālaya*-consciousness as an actual existence, and the concept of potentiality. The resulting epistemology (previewed in the introduction) is known for its logical and conceptual complexity, and some of the finer points are still being debated by scholars today.

For the Yogācāras, forms that are constituted by dependent originations are called nominal or virtual existences, whereas the layout of these dependent originations is called an actual existence. For convenience, we can think about this distinction in semiological terms: (1) *paroles* (speeches), as instantiations of differences, exist nominally; (2) a *langue* (language system), as a system of differences or a set of relations that are fundamentally empty, exists in actuality.[40] Virtuality and actuality are interdependent, synchronic, and relative to each other. Therefore, Yogācāra scholars treat them as shifting signifiers until they arrive at a point where their structural difference is rendered purposeless.

Perceptually and conceptually, the origination and existence of forms can be traced back to the operation of the six consciousnesses, which depends on the *ālambana-pratyaya* (foundational condition)—that is, naming and constituting internal and external forms. According to Dignāga, what we call a *viññāṇa/vijñāna* (consciousness) is also a *vijñapti* (manifestation or representation). The governing potentiality that enables—and is enabled by—the origination and existence of seeing (such as sensing, perceiving, and recognizing) is called *darśana bhāga* (potentiality to perceive and conceptualize). The origination and existence of this potential is dependent on the origination and existence of the *nimitta bhāga* (potentiality to generate signs). In the operation of the six consciousnesses, the originations and existences of the acts of seeing and the signs being seen are confirmed by the *svasaṃvedana/svasaṃvitti* (potentiality to take the act of seeing and the signs being seen as self-evident).[41] Dharmapāla argues that *svasaṃvedana* can be further subcategorized into the potentiality to perceive and conceptualize a consciousness as self-evident, and also the potentiality to generate a self-evident consciousness.[42]

According to Yogācāra scholarship, a consciousness can therefore be defined as an interdependent relationship between a potential condition and a being-conditioned condition. Hwendzàng/Xuanzang (602–64), who traveled from Dhiᵊngʔan/Chang'an (nowadays Xi'an) to Nālandā to study with Sthiramati and Dharmapāla, calls this relationship one between the *siɪm/xin* (mind) and *siᵊnˇg/xiang* (perception or *sañña/ saṃjñā*). For him, the objective representation of *siᵊnˇg* is called *k'iᵊ̌ng/ jing* (milieu or image). In the *Dzhiᵊng jiuɪshɪk lùan/Cheng weishi lun* [*Vijñapatimātratāsiddhi* or *Discourse on the Perfection of Consciousness-Only*], Hwendzàng argues that the originations of all dharmas (phenomena) depend on the dependent originations between the mind and its perception.[43]

The discrete dependent originations and existences of the six consciousnesses are perceptually and conceptually unified by *manas* (volition; see Figure 3 in the introduction). The relationship between the potentiality to perceive and conceptualize volition and the potentiality to represent it as the self is called the *manas*-consciousness (volition-consciousness). Yogācāra scholars call this the seventh consciousness. For the Yogācāras, all the dependent originations we have encountered thus far are synchronic. In other words, in a single *kṣaṇa*, a system of differences is instantiated as: (1) the actualization of potentialities and the virtualization of actualities; (2) the unification of the discrete operation of the six consciousnesses by volition and the proliferation of volition into the six consciousnesses; (3) the dependent originations and existences between the potentiality to see and the potentiality to generate signs, and between the potentiality to perceive and conceptualize self-evidentiality and the potentiality to generate self-evident consciousnesses; (4) the dependent originations and existences between the mind (the *internal* portions of the consciousnesses) and perceptions, and between the perceptions and their objective representations; and finally (5) the mutual dependency between origination and extinction, existence and nonexistence.

While origination and existence are dependent on the actualization of potentialities, extinction and nonexistence are dependent on the virtualization of actualities. In Sarvāstivāda terms, forms *in turn* function as seed conditions (or potentialities), which are formless and unmarked. These seeds are *planted* or deposited into a layout called the *ālaya*-consciousness (storehouse or eighth consciousness), where they circulate perpetually. Hence, their actualizations—the six consciousnesses—also circulate perpetually. In this light, potentialities and conditions are mutually dependent, so as their layouts—that is, the *ālaya*-consciousness and the six consciousnesses themselves—are also mutually dependent.

The mutual dependency between the *ālaya*-consciousness and the six consciousnesses enables potentialities and conditions to proliferate interdependently ad infinitum. For Yogācāra scholars, as actualizations and representations of the *ālaya*-consciousness, the six consciousnesses and the volition consciousness that summon them as a unity exist in name only. In other words, the only *thing* that actually exists is the *ālaya*-consciousness itself, a layout of potentialities that are formless, unmarked, and dormant. Meanwhile, the *ālaya*-consciousness is a sub-layout of a cosmic layout of potentialities to which *manas* attaches. In other words, *manas* is responsible for setting aside this specific domain, amid a cosmic layout of causalities, as *my own*.

As a start, the ālaya-consciousness is often imagined as a predefined domain or terrain. However, it is better understood as a layout constituted by the paths traveled by the seeds in the process of circulation. In other words, the ālaya-consciousness is a layout of pure relationalities. The layout itself (the Deleuzian whole) is neither moving nor not moving, and the moving relationalities that constitute it are empty until their instantiations—the potentialities that are in circulation—are actualized as forms. As the Saṃdhinirmocana Sūtra [Sutra of the Explanation of the Profound Secrets] argues, the ālaya-consciousness can be understood as the ultimate sabhāva (self-nature) of the six consciousnesses and manifestations, which is characterized by its nihsvabhāvatā (self-nature-less-ness).[44] For Duŏzhiùm from the H'ua'ngiɐm school of Buddhism, the ālaya-consciousness is termed lǐ (technicity; see the introduction), whereas the six consciousnesses are called džǐ (matters).

Fyodor Stcherbatsky argues that the ālaya-consciousness is timeless. Hence, to imagine that the infinite proliferation of potentialities and conditions takes place in one kṣaṇa is merely an analogy. For him, this timeless layout is conceptualized by Henri Bergson as the durée, an overall duration from which individuated originations and existences are activated.[45] Once it is represented as forms, they are perceived and conceptualized as a process of becoming consisting of an ever-operating saṃsāra (cycle).[46] In each kṣaṇa, a cycle will produce a sati/smṛti (awareness). The origination and existence of one awareness is followed by another cycle of origination and existence in immediate contiguity: a sequence of modulations that will be perceived and conceptualized as a temporally continuous process of mediation (consciousness as a flux). This sequence of awarenesses can be subcategorized into:

1. A sh'iùmiě siim/shuai'er xin (sudden awareness): a kṣaṇa of bare cognition, which is normally imperceptible
2. A series of ziimgiu siim/xunqiu xin (seeking awarenesses): driven by a longing for knowing what the sudden awareness was
3. A series of kwetdèng siim/jueding xin (determining awarenesses): a process of mental differentiations and formations
4. A series of ñiěmdzièng siim/ranjing xin (polluting or purifying awarenesses): a process of generating sensations and affections
5. A series of tɣ̌ngliu siim/dengliu xin (ontological awarenesses): a process of affirming the existence of those forms one perceives and conceptualizes, as well as the ways they come into being in the overall order of things[47]

In this light, Yogācāra thinkers borrow from Nāgārjuna's argument that karma operates from one *kṣaṇa* to another as a series of impulses that initiates a sequence of awarenesses. As these awarenesses are perceived and conceptualized as a continuous mobile form, karma appears to be an enduring impetus that propels its qualitative changes. Yet, karma is not a mental fabrication. Like forms, these impulses are actualized from the modulating relationalities between seeds that are deposited in the *ālaya*-consciousness. We can say that the relationalities themselves, *in movement,* are the karmic impulses. As the constitutive configurations of the *ālaya*-consciousness, these relationalities exist in actuality. This notion therefore conforms to the Buddha's claim in SA-102: what the Brahmins regard as Brahman is karma. In chapter 2, I will discuss further debates on karma in relation to the formational process of the movement-image and karma-image.

BAZINIAN ONTOLOGY REVISITED

As I pointed out earlier, the formational process of the image-consciousness is not directly affected by its technico-technological instantiation (an ontogenetic change). Rather, any reconfiguration of the consciousness has to be initiated on the level of its technicity, precisely by karma. If so, it will be worthwhile for us to examine why we have been under the impression that Bazinian ontology has failed because of the emergence of digital technology.

In the introduction to this book, I have already summarized the key discourses in this ontological debate. Here, I focus on two specific perspectives within this debate. First, as William Brown and Lev Manovich argue respectively, digital technology has rendered unreliable the relationship between the cinematographic image and reality. Manovich thus defines digital cinema as "*a particular case of animation that uses live-action footage as one of its many elements.*"[48] More recently, Shane Denson and Markos Hadjioannou even argue that such a relationship no longer matters in digital post-cinema, as it is subsumed under non-/ post-human perspectives and existential concerns.[49] That is to say, digital cinema belongs to a different order of technics and technologies.

Second, D. N. Rodowick, Vivian Sobchack, and Brown himself suggest that such a technological change is symptomatic of a more fundamental crisis of how human beings as well as societies have come to define themselves under postcolonial neoliberalism. The most troublesome aspect is the way in which corporate and state powers galvanize digital technology to initiate, manage, and control our desires for consumption and fears of political threats. In such a system, every biopolitical life voluntarily participates in the consolidation of corporate and state powers by surrendering their own data, political subjectivity, individuality, rights, and liberty through consumption, and further by devoting every moment of their living—including time for leisure—to production and preemption of violence. As a result, these lives are dehumanized as biometric data and mere consumers.[50] Therefore, technological shifts, including digital production, reproduction, and dissemination of the moving image, are symptomatic of the ontological crisis of humanity.

Both sides of the argument, nonetheless, focus on cinema as a technology. In Gilbert Simondon's terms, technological and anthropological modulations are inseparable. In this light, the emergence of digital technology and the crisis of humanity are transindividuated out of a layout of causes, conditions, and energies as a *new* mode of anthropotechnical existence. What these scholars have identified thus far is therefore an ontogenetic transduction, not an ontological shift. It means that the impulses that propel the layout to dephase from the previous anthropotechnical existence (what Sobchack calls a cinematic existence) to the current one (a digital or post-cinematic existence) have always been in the layout itself. In other words, they are part and parcel of the relationalities that constitute the layout. While the relationalities affect—and are affected by—anthropotechnical transductions, the layout itself remains unchanged. Such an understanding of technicity therefore mirrors the Yogācāra understanding of the consciousness. In short, we need to distinguish the *technical* from the *ontological* in Bazin.

Bazin wrote "Ontology of the Photographic Image" primarily for a readership of art historians. The first issue he tackles is whether the cinema is a form of mimetic art. For him:

> The originality of photography in relation to painting resides . . . in its essential objectivity. Also, the group of lenses that constitutes the photographic eye, which substitutes the human eye, is called precisely the *objectif.* For the first time, no other object comes between the initial object and its representation. For the first time, an image of the exterior world is formed automatically without any creative intervention of man, according to a rigorous determinism.[51]

Bazin's argument that the photographic image is formed without
the creative intervention of a human being is often criticized as naïve
and technically inaccurate. After all, the photographer is responsible
for choosing the type of lens, the amount of light admitted through it,
the speed of the filmstock, its composition, and eventually, in the labo-
ratory, its color saturation or its grayscale, contrast, and brightness. But
what Bazin means by "creative intervention" is mimesis: an imitation
of forms. In one register, this may seem obvious to us. For example, a
painter employs brushstrokes to portray a landscape, and a sculptor
chisels a piece of marble to produce a human or animal form. In a deeper
register, the term "creative intervention" refers not to the techniques
the artist utilizes, but to the volition that motivates the artist to use
these techniques.

In classical philosophy, an act motivated by desire—thought and
will—is considered by Plato as a *praxis* (practice), as opposed to a creation (or pro-duction). Therefore, Plato dismisses art as *technē*: a mere
conveyance of the artist's volition. In *Physics*, Aristotle explains that for
Plato:

> Every natural being . . . has within itself a beginning of movement and
> rest, where the "movement" is a locomotion, growth or decline, or a
> qualitative change . . . [whereas] not one product of art has the source
> of its own production within itself.[52]

Therefore, for Plato, art as *technē* has no existential value, as it is put
into production by human volition. It is simply a conveyance (medium)
that transmits the human will. In *Ion,* Plato compares the human will to
a magnet that in-forms not only the artwork, but also sensations, affections, and emotions:

> As I said earlier, that's not a subject you've mastered—speaking well
> about Homer; it's a divine power that moves you, as a "Magnetic"
> stone moves iron rings. (That's what Euripides called it; most people
> call it "Heraclean.") This stone not only pulls those rings, if they're
> iron, it also puts power *in* the rings, so that they in turn can do just
> what the stone does—pull other rings—so that there's sometimes a
> very long chain of iron pieces and rings hanging from one another.
> And the power in all of them depends on this stone. In the same way,
> the Muse makes some people inspired herself, and then through those
> who are inspired a chain of other enthusiasts is suspended.[53]

As Giorgio Agamben points out, Aristotle does not agree with Plato's view. For Aristotle, the fact that a piece of art is not self-caused means that the artist must disconceal the artwork's existence, thus making present what would otherwise remain absent. Aristotle therefore redefines *poiesis* as a process of creative intervention. For Agamben:

> [T]he Greeks used the word ποίησις [*poiesis*] to characterize τέχνη [*technē*], human pro-duction in its entirety, and designated with the name of τέχνίτης [*technítis*] both the craftsman and the artist. But this common designation does not in any way suggest that the Greeks conceived of pro-duction from its material and practical side, as a manual making; what they called τέχνη [*technē*] was neither the actualization of a will nor simply a constructing, but a mode of truth of ά-ληθευειν [*alátheia*] of the unveiling that produces things from concealment into presence.
>
> In other words, τέχνη [*technē*] meant for the Greeks "to cause to appear," and ποίησις [*poiesis*] meant "pro-duction into presence"; but this production was not understood in connection with *agere*, doing, but with γνώσις [*gnosis*], knowing.[54]

A piece of art as *poiesis*, therefore, has its own existential value that has been uncovered by the artist. It is put into production by the artist as *technítis*; after that, it assumes a life span on its own, independent of the artist's volition.

Therefore, by claiming that the photographic image is "formed automatically without any creative intervention of man," Bazin indicates that it is not brought into production by the human will. In other words, for Bazin, photography is not art. He can hence argue that: (1) photography is neither produced nor unveiled by any human volition and (2) it has no intrinsic existential value. Instead, its *existence* depends on that of the photographed being or object.

For example, Figure 4 is a sepia medium close-up of an uncle of my partner, John, named John Adams, when he was seventeen. The picture was taken in spring 1944 in a drugstore in Brooklyn, New York, when he was on leave from the army, shortly before he was sent to occupied France, where he died saving a wounded comrade on the battlefield. The portrait was taken with a low-quality camera, and the entire image is out-of-focus. Yet, I quickly bypass these formal qualities, imperfections, and blemishes produced first by the camera and then, later, through material deterioration. I almost immediately perceive it as being an

FIGURE 4. Portrait of
John Adams taken in Lower
Manhattan, shortly before he
was sent to occupied France in
spring 1944 (d. Amanvillers,
occupied France, September 11,
1944). Courtesy of John
Christiansen.

imprint of Adams as an existential whole. In this portrait, he wears a
slightly oversized leather jacket. Underneath, he wears a plaid shirt
with the top button open, thus revealing his white undershirt. Adams's
head is slightly lowered, yet his eyes stare directly into the lens. Cor-
respondingly, his crescent-shaped mouth is partly open with a smile, as
though the smile had yet to be completed or as though he were about
to say something. In fact, his somewhat lowered head seems to be arrested in the middle of an action. His strong nose sits in the middle of
his face, his eyes are wide open and brightly lit, and his thick eyebrows
frame the top of his eyes and give form to his tall forehead. His left ear
(on frame right) is hidden from the camera, whereas his right ear (on
frame left) juts out with a touch of humor. He has a young and handsome
face with an air of defiance. He wears a smoothly and immaculately
done Rockabilly hairstyle parted toward the left side of his skull. *He is
looking at you.*

No matter how deliberately this photograph is composed, the
image-itself is not willed by the photographer. Rather, it is mechanically
captured by the camera. The affective qualities—eroticism, nostalgia,
and desire—are conveyed not directly by the composition, but instead

by an implicit belief that this young man, who cannot possibly be "present," is indeed present—the presence of an absence. As Jean-Paul Sartre would argue, I bypass the materiality of the photograph and the formal composition that the photographer puts into it, so that I come face-to-face with a milieu in which I am with Adams.[55] In Simondon's terms: I am transindividuated with Adams as an anthropotechnical technicity-consciousness.

This is not to say that the photographer had no agency in the process of capturing this moment of existence in 1944. But their agency did not lie in their ability to bring this moment to life; rather, they exercised their skills to bring to light (to unveil, in another sense) a point-instant of existence, "snatch[ed] it from the flow of time," and mummified it.[56] It is in this light that Bazin argues:

> The aesthetic universe of the painter is different from the universe around him. His milieu encloses a substantially and essentially different microcosm. The existence of the photographed object participates, on the contrary, in the existence of the model in the manner of a fingerprint. Because of this, it is really added to natural creation—and vice versa—instead of substituting it with another.[57]

For Bazin, the ontological ground of the photographic image is not some nebulously defined reality. In Buddhist terms, one can say that the existences of the photographed being (in this case, Adams) and the inanimate object (his clothes, the setting, and the light) were contingent on a set of interdependent conditions that gave rise to the milieu (image) in 1944. Today, the same conditions, encapsulated in this photographic imprint, give rise to an image that recalls the existence of that moment. This *ontological relationality* between the layout of conditions in the past and that in the present is made possible by a technico-technological condition: the mechanical capability of the camera to capture an image without any creative intervention.

Bazinian ontology is therefore in accord with the axiom of dependent originations. In Buddhist terms, the shared (nominal) existential ground that gave rise to the physical body and life of John Adams in 1944 and to the photographic image with which I am transindividuated now can be regarded as the *ātmakatva* (body), that is, the self-nature of the photographic image. Adams's physical body in the past and the photographic image of his body in the present are the *lakṣanas* (forms) initiated from their shared existential ground (self-nature). Meanwhile, a layout of anthropotechnical conditions constitutes a process that Bazin famously calls "change mummified."[58] These conditions include the camera that the photographer held in 1944; it caused the production of an image (effect), which enables a fleeting moment in the past to be both preserved (seed conditions) and reactualized in the present (matching conditions). The relationalities between the seed and the matching conditions are karma. For Bazin, the invention of the photographic technology was motivated not by a will, but rather by an unconscious desire to conquer death. In Buddhist terms, it was motivated by a form of karma: an *upādāna* (attachment) to *bhava* (that which exists).

As Roland Barthes (1915–80) argues, once the camera shutter was triggered by the photographer in 1944, the existence of young John Adams, at that very moment, was already dead. In this photograph, what I take for granted as the presence of this young man—that John Adams *exists* in front of my eyes—is his absence. In other words, his photographic *presence* is merely a trace of a moment of his life that has been *dead* ever since the camera shutter was triggered. As I perceive this photographic image, his *life* in front of me is only a trace of his physical death, his youthful image signifies the passage of time passed since his demise, his muscular appearance serves as a testimony of his corporeal decay. As Barthes comments on Alexander Gardner's (1821–82) photograph of Lewis Payne (1844–65) in 1865, shortly before he was executed for an attempted assassination of U.S. Secretary of State William H. Seward (1801–72), "He is dead and he is going to die."[59] The sensations and affections associated with a photographic image, for Barthes, always carry a longing, nostalgia, or even mourning: *rāga* (avarice) for a time that I cannot possibly recover, *dveṣa* (anger or frustration) for a sense of absence, and *moha* (delusion) of taking what is effectively absent as presence. In other words, what Bazin calls existence is a perceptual-conceptual proliferation contingent on the existences and originations of sensations and affections. In the terms of Charles Sanders Peirce, these sensations and affections in-form a perceptual-conceptual relationship called indexicality (Thirdness), which gives the impression that the matching condition (the photographic image) is directly caused by the seed condition (the image of Adams in 1944).[60] Such *existence* and the ontology onto which it is projected are fundamentally empty, and such emptiness is in turn the ontological ground

of existence. In this light, the difference between existence and emptiness is—meontologically—ultimately empty, that is, the emptiness of
emptiness.

IMAGING AND IMAGINATION

In Simondon's terms, photography for Bazin is an anthropotechnical
transduction, whereas the li/technicity of the image-consciousness and
its formational process remain constant. Manovich's argument that
"*[d]igital cinema is a particular case of animation that uses live-action footage
as one of its many elements*" therefore identifies an ontogenetic, not ontological, shift. For him, in digital cinema, the "final images are constructed manually from different elements, and all the elements are
either created entirely from scratch or modified by hand."[61] If so, digital
cinema, as a *new* anthropotechnical transduction, is best understood as
a mode of mimesis in the Platonic sense: a *praxis* crafted by the human
hand and willed by its volition.

Manovich's claim is refuted by Thomas Lamarre on two counts. First,
Lamarre suggests that cel animation, as a technology and aesthetics
developed in the United States, strives to imitate live actions and forms
by shooting twelve picture frames per second (that is, holding each
frame for two film frames). Each picture frame is made up of a series of
cels that are stacked on top of each other on a stand; each contains a
component of a picture, such as the background, the bodies of the characters, and their eyes, mouths, hands, and other physical parts. These
components can then be replaced by the animator to create minute
movements, including movements of the lips that would correspond to
the spoken words. In this sense, movements are created not simplisti-
cally by connecting samples of a continuous movement linearly, but by
manipulating planes (cels) on an animation stand vertically, from one
temporal point-instant to another.

Historically, Japanese anime was developed during the 1930s when
the raw materials for cel-making—celluloid nitrate and camphor—were
largely exhausted by the war industry. To economize, anime artists
would use as little as one to three cels. Those cels that represent back-
grounds or even the outlines of the characters' bodies or faces would be
held for mere seconds. Then, the characters' mouths would alternate
between being open and being closed (two alternating cels) to indicate
lip movements. Bodily movements were sometimes not even animated.

Instead, anime artists borrowed techniques from the *manga* to convey rapid movements by using a montage of still pictures of a character's body arrested in actions, with a blurred background sketched with horizontal or vertical lines indicating the directions of their movements. Sound effects and music would then be added to enhance the impression of movement. For Lamarre, anime reveals to us how few audiovisual clues the human consciousness needs to give life to pictures that are barely animated in the first place. In fact, these pictures are perceived, animated, and given life *as* a consciousness precisely at what he calls the *blink* (as in the blink of an eye): a transient moment (split second) at which the sensory-perceptual system is not actively being stimulated (in Buddhist terms, emptiness), so that the process of perception and recognition can take place.[62]

Lamarre's second refutation of Manovich's argument is that animation is a process of transindividuations where a metastable milieu—the animated image along with the media ecology that renders such an image possible—is formed out of a layout of technical, biological, and psychic interactions. It is because on the one hand, animation/anime (or what Lamarre calls animetism) is not simply a technic that is subsumed under the cinematic (what Lamarre calls cinematism), that is to say, animation/anime is neither a kind of cinema nor being entirely unrelated to the cinema. Rather, it is a media ecology on its own, which has been more ontogenetically, economically, and industrially affiliated with television and video games than the cinema.

On the other hand, the process of animation is also not a purely technico-technological process, but an anthropotechnical one. In this process, a metastability (that is, the animated sequence's appearance as a continuous movement-cum-image; see the introduction to this book) is arrived at through an actualization of an avalanche of potentialities, which is in turn perceived and conceptualized as a sequence of awarenesses. The originations and existences of these awarenesses are dependent on the originations and existences of a desire to *know*, retrospectively and retroactively, those immediately contiguous awarenesses that were materialized before the present. The metastability is also driven by a desire to anticipate what is about to emerge. Our inability to focus on the *here and now* as *the way it is* animates our perception by giving these contiguous awarenesses an impression of unity, consistency, and continuity. For Lamarre, Japanese anime often makes use of

optical elements like flash frames, juxtapositions of cognitively disso-
nant colors, and manipulations of television's line-scanning process to
engage the viewers' affective intensities on a microperceptual level. At
the *blink*, these affective engagements become responsible for animating the image.[63] In Buddhist terms, what animates the image is therefore
karma, and the potentialities that make such a formational process
possible have always been in the *ālaya*-consciousness.

In this light, Christian Metz is apt to call the cinematographic image
an imaginary signifier: a sign (in the Symbolic order) that enables the
sentient body, in its "sub-motor and super-perceptive state," to configure a disorganized and incoherent field of sensory stimulants (the Real)
into an Imaginary order, with a set of codes that is in-formed by the
symbolic arrangement of the cinematic apparatus itself.[64] However, the
ālaya-consciousness does not require the body to be in a "sub-motor and
super-perceptive state" in order to initiate the imaginary. Karma compels us to perceive and conceptualize *imagination* as *image*, from one
kṣaṇa to another.

This statement, at first glance, does not seem to agree with Sartre's
understanding of imaging and imagining. For him, imagining is a mental
process, which conjures up a mode of reality in its totality. For instance,
in my personal imagination, John Adams the soldier photographed in
Brooklyn is a living being, with his individuality, subjectivity, and volition. Thus, the imagined Adams is always apprehended as a whole.
Meanwhile, the photographic imprint of Adams is two-dimensional,
arrested in action, and physically incomplete. However, by grafting my
imagination of Adams as a whole onto the photographic imprint, I bypass the imperfection of the imprint and instead apprehend an animated and existent image-consciousness of the young man.[65]

The Yogācāra philosopher Dignāga (whose work I have discussed in
the introduction and in the earlier part of this chapter) would argue
that Sartre locates imagination in the sixth (thought) consciousness,
where a mental consciousness-manifestation is in-formed by an avalanche of actualized potentialities from the *ālaya*-consciousness. This
mental consciousness-manifestation then functions as a technology of
recognition, so that the bare cognition of the photographic imprint is
recognized as an image-consciousness-manifestation (first consciousness). For Dignāga, what it means is that the operation of the *ālaya*-
consciousness enables the originations and existences of two modes of

consciousness-manifestation at once: an image and an imagination. They are two different forms, but they are structurally and ontologically identical. Dignāga calls this *dvirūpatā* (double initiation).[66] This notion is well illustrated in §32 of the *Diamond Sutra*:

All phenomena are like
A dream, an illusion, a bubble and a shadow.
Like a dew drop and a flash of lightning,
Thus should you view them.[67]

In other words, the perceptual-conceptual originations and existences of all forms, like the originations and existences of dreams and illusions, can be considered imaginations that are empty of existential values. Yet, we cannot help but give them an imagistic substratum and regard them as existent. Meanwhile, like a dewdrop or a flash of lightning, they are impermanent. Yet, we cannot help but perceive them as temporally continuous. The image-consciousness is neither an illusion nor an existent reality, neither not an illusion nor not an existent reality. The relationality between imaging and imagining is what Buddhist philosophy calls *tathātā*: thusness, or *the way it is*.

In film theory, this question was ruminated on by Pier Paolo Pasolini (1922–75) in his essay "Il cinema di poesia" ["Cinema of Poetry," 1965]. For Pasolini, the cinematographic image is apprehended as a piece of "brute reality," which is perceived and conceptualized as objective. Yet, the origination and existence of each semiotic unit in the cinema (imsign) is dependent on the origination and existence of a bare cognition that is prelinguistic (or, in Buddhist terms, prior to the origination and existence of both sensations and affections). Moreover, this bare cognition is coded by a signifying potential that is preconscious (in Buddhist terms, deposited in the *ālaya*-consciousness). If so, the cinematographic image is neither subjective nor objective (prelinguistic and preconscious) yet is at once subjective and objective (brute reality as an objectivized subjective). Pasolini considers a film itself to be an image-consciousness, which is made up not by syntagma, but by stylemes.[68] For him, a styleme refers to a set of interdependent relationships between objects, which, as Deleuze argues, is the cinema's proper register of primary articulation.[69]

As Olga Solovieva argues, a styleme is best understood as a point of referentiality, whose references (denotations and connotations) are

determined not only by its relationship with other stylemes synchronic-
ally and diachronically, but also by the relationship between the position
of the character's body, the camera position, and their relationalities in
the spatiotemporal coordinates of the image. For Solovieva, Pasolini
takes his cues from sign language, in which a hand gesture is not a stand-
alone sign, but in fact a point of referentiality. It relates the position of
the body of the addresser to that of the addressee, the position of the
hand to the rest of the body, and the position of the addresser/addressee
to the object to which it refers. In other words, what we recognize as a
piece of reality is constituted by a set of interdependent coordinates,
whose referentialities are always in a process of becoming.[70]

Stylemes are therefore manipulatable physically by changing the
positionalities between the objects and the camera, psychically by
changing the codes that configure the formational process of the
image, and technologically by foregrounding, concealing, erasing, or
inserting existing or new coordinates. Thus, the image as a technicity-
consciousness is modulated from one kṣaṇa to another, which renews
and conflates the boundary between imaging and imagining, and between self and other. As Thomas Elsaesser argues, such indiscernibilities
have often been written into the cinematic text as a subject of rumina-
tion and investigation since the early days of cinema.[71]

In the Euro-American context, Elsaesser was drawn to a mode of
narration that he calls the "mind-game film." He notices that since the
1990s, an increasing number of Hollywood as well as European films
either feature characters who are "being played games with, without
knowing it or without knowing who it is that is playing these . . . games"
with them, or else the "audience . . . is played games with, because certain crucial information is withheld or ambiguously presented." In these
films, the characters' mental condition is "extreme, unstable, or patho-
logical," yet their "'being in the world' [is] presented as normal." By
following the characters' pathologies, the film poses ontological and
epistemological questions by probing the human consciousness, often
in a way that is narratively disorienting. For Elsaesser, the mind-game
film instantiates a "'crisis' in the spectator-film relation" by experi-
menting with "spectator-address, in the face of technical, economic, or
demographic changes."[72]

For Elsaesser, the emergence of the mind-game film coincided with
a sociopolitical culture that had gradually moved away from linear

narrativity and a mode of subjectivity that were built on knowing and commanding the realm of the visible. Rather, memories and embodied experiences have been increasingly compartmentalized as modules that can be deposited organically or technologically as databases, from which one can revisit them, reembody them, rewrite them, and even reboot them as a process in which one's uncertainty of oneself can be acknowledged and worked through. For Elsaesser, the mind-game film provides the spectator a second chance to reboot their consciousness and their sensory-motor system, from which individuality, subjectivity, and agency can be reconfigured. As Elsaesser argues, these films correspond to Walter Benjamin's (1892–1940) observation of the two functions of the cinema: on the one hand, the mind-game film trains the spectators to acknowledge the erosion of sense-certainty and agency under our control-society; on the other hand, it prepares the spectators with strategies by which they can cope with, critique, or even rewrite their relationship with state power.[73]

Long Day's Journey into Night

Shortly before his visit to Beijing in 2019, Elsaesser discussed with me in New York the applicability of the term "mind-game film" to contemporary Mainland Chinese independent cinema, especially the works of Bi Gan. That director became known to the international film festival circuit with his second feature, Lubian yecan [Kaili Blues, 2015], which won both Best New Director in the 52nd edition of the Golden Horse Awards and the Swatch First Feature Awards of the 68th edition of the Locarno Film Festival. With such critical and commercial success, he secured a deal with his producer, Heavenly Pictures, for Long Day's Journey into Night. Eventually, he completed this project with Huace, the second largest media corporation in Mainland China. Born and raised in Kaili, a prefectural city and an ethnic Miao (Hmong) community in Guizhou (southwest China), Bi Gan graduated from the Communication University of Shanxi in 2012 having produced a short film called Jingang jing [The Poet and Singer, 2012], a black-and-white film about a murder in a remote town. The protagonists of these three films are not the same, though they are often read as transmigrations (or different embodiments) of the same consciousness (or character).[74]

In January 2020, film critics and programmers in the International Film Festival Rotterdam (IFFR) coined the term "the Nanfang xin *langchao*" (South China New Wave), which was instigated by the success of *Kaili Blues*. The festival featured a number of mind-game films made by directors who work in regions south of the Yangtze River, including *Chunjiang shuinuan* [*Dwelling in the Fuchun Mountain*, Gu Xiaogang, 2019], *Nanfang chezhan de juhui* [*The Wild Goose Lake*, Diao Yinan, 2019], *Huinan tian* [*Damp Season*, Gao Ming, 2020], and *Ta fangjian li de yun* [*The Cloud in Her Room*, Zheng Lu Xinyuan, 2020].

In all the festival's post-screening question-and-answer sessions, these directors insisted that their works were "realistic."[75] For them, those Chinese independent filmmakers who started their careers in the 1990s and the 2000s (including Jia Zhangke, Wu Wenguang, and Zhang Yuan) believed—and still do—that digital technology was simply a more economical and convenient version of celluloid film in its ability to capture reality. Such a technology enables filmmakers to use handheld cameras and long takes to convey a sense of *xianchang* (on-location-ness)—in other words, an embodied sense of *being there on the scene*.[76] The South China New Wave directors, meanwhile, seek to use digital technology to renegotiate the boundary between subject and object, and imaging and imagining. They use fluid, stabilized handheld cameras and carefully composed long takes that embody sensations and affections experienced by the actors, the characters, and the directors themselves. However, these long takes also objectify these subjective structures of feeling as *jing* (milieus). The spectator is then solicited to share a milieu not only as a bare cognition, but also as a recognition of those sensations and affections that in-form it. Meanwhile, editing is then regarded as a technic that connects the various milieus sensorially and affectively, instead of spatiotemporally and causally. It is in this sense that these directors' films can be understood as a storehouse (database) of potentialities, from which sensations and affections modulate into an avalanche of awarenesses: the film image—or, some may say, the post-cinematic image.

In terms of *playing games*, these new southern directors are not doing exactly the same thing as their Euro-American counterparts. They all agree that they sense a need for a reboot of one's physical, psychic, social, and technical consciousnesses by *presenting* the way in which sensations, affections, and memories are laid out in their disorganized, though mutually dependent, manner. Bi, Gu, and Zheng Lu all acknowledge that the Buddhist understanding of imaging and imagination in-forms their stylistic and aesthetic choices. For them, this consciousness reboot is necessitated by a sense-uncertainty among their generation, whose individuality, subjectivity, and agency are often performed under the prescriptions laid out by the party-state, a capital-driven and state-controlled postsocialist economy, and also one's family.

To illustrate how a contemporary Chinese independent mind-game film initiates a consciousness reboot, I turn to Bi Gan's *Long Day's Journey into Night*. This film can be seen as a reinterpretation of *Kaili Blues*, which in turn can be regarded as an extension of *The Poet and Singer*. In both *The Poet* and *Kaili Blues*, Bi Gan frames the films with §32 of the *Diamond Sutra* (quoted earlier in this chapter), thus offering the spectator a user manual to transindividuate with the film as a storehouse of potentialities as well as an avalanche of awarenesses.

Long Day's Journey into Night does not start with a citation of §32, though the *Sutra*'s message is configured as an enigma in the opening sequence. As a technicity-consciousness, the film begins with a close-up of a right hand and a forearm, which belong to a woman who is standing offscreen by the left of frame. This hand is holding a black microphone, which is pointing toward the woman. Her fingernails are painted red and she wears an elegant watch with a burgundy leather wristband. The bottom of her forearm is highlighted by a green light. In the background lies a black drum set against a wall washed over by a green light. This background is entirely out-of-focus, and the wooden floor at the bottom of the frame forms a patch of red in this predominantly green environment. This shot sets up the color scheme of the entire film: the complementary colors red and green. The film's dim lighting makes these two colors at once mutually distinct and indiscernible. The competition between these two optical wavelengths stimulates the anthropotechnical sensorium; yet such stimulation is dampened by the shadows and the shallow depth of field, thus producing a subtle fatigue in the spectator's eye muscles. Such fatigue, in turn, produces a comforting, sleep-inducing, and dreamlike electromagnetic field.

In the shot, the woman offscreen puts another hand onto the microphone stand and takes the microphone away toward the left of frame. This action motivates a zoom-in and tilt-up, which moves the phantom peripheral vision of the anthropotechnical consciousness away from the woman's body. On the soundtrack, a man's voiceover claims that whenever he sees *her*, he is certain that he is in a dream. As the camera continues to tilt up, it captures circles of blue and green lights drifting from the left of frame to the right of frame. The voice says that in dreams, his body feels weightless. He can even levitate! The camera then tilts up and drifts toward the left and gradually reveals more circles of red, blue, and green lights, until it reveals a spinning disco ball that emanates these lights in a close-up. As the camera continues to tilt up, it leaves the disco ball and shows a ceiling full of light circles, until the image fades to black. In the voiceover, the man wonders if his body is made of hydrogen. If so, his memories must be made of stone.

The film's opening enigma is therefore configured as a woman, whose identity is unclear both to the disembodied male voice and to the cinematic consciousness, and her body is also concealed from the anthropotechnical field of vision. According to this voice, the sight of this woman is supposed to be the only imagistic evidence that the man is imagining (dreaming), thus giving his dreamt reality an ontological consistency. Meanwhile, this dreamt reality is manifested as a cinematographic image-consciousness, whose existence—like the circulating circles of light in the room (which is probably a karaoke)—is transient and empty. This image is at once an objectivization of the male voice's subjective imagination and a subjectivization of an image, which is captured profilmically as a trace of an objectivized subjective reality. The camera's upward motion enables the consciousness to sense the weightlessness of the man's hydrogenic body, which, according to the voiceover, is best understood as a projection of an aggregate of concrete memories that awaits actualizations.

This enigma serves as an impetus that instigates the journey of the male protagonist, Luo Hongwu (Huang Jue), to search for this unknown woman. This journey is divided into two parts. The first part, which lasts seventy-nine minutes, is presented in 2D. It also serves as a storehouse consciousness (ālaya-consciousness), from which seeds are actualized as a virtual layout of images and events. The dominant condition that enables their actualizations is the cinema as a technicity-consciousness.

Those spectators who have watched *The Poet and Singer* would realize that these seeds were configured as this enigma through the protagonist's act of murder in the past. In fact, the first half of the film suggests that Hongwu killed his best friend, nicknamed Wildcat (Lee Hong-chi), in order to be together with Wildcat's girlfriend. Hongwu murdered his friend in a dark movie theater by stabbing Wildcat from the back; he then buried Wildcat's body in a mineshaft. Thus, these seeds were once actualized as sensations, affections, actions, and events that led up to the act of murder (seed conditions), and they are now reactivated as matching conditions under a new dominant condition: Hongwu's release from prison. In this first part of the film, the seed conditions and matching conditions do not unfold chronologically. Rather, they are concatenated into a sequence of random events based on these events' sensorial and affective affinities. Visually, the only indicators of their temporal relationships are the degrees of grayness of Hongwu's hair.

Shortly after the opening scene, this enigma is symbolically displaced to the absent figure of Hongwu's dead mother, Xiaofeng. This displacement is conveyed nonchalantly as Hongwu takes his last look at the restaurant owned by his recently deceased father. This scene unfolds in one take, with Hongwu being consistently framed in a medium close-up in the foreground of the frame, while it reframes him as he walks around the restaurant. In the background of the frame, out-of-focus, the new owner tells Hongwu that she plans to renovate the restaurant. Hongwu then asks her not to change the name, as it is the name of his mother, who disappeared when he was a child. At this point, Hongwu walks out of the restaurant and looks pensively at the shop sign with his mother's name on it. In the soundtrack, the sound of heavy rain motivates a cut to an abandoned and gradually flooding dormitory for workers, built in the 1950s.

In this scene, Bi Gan pays tribute to what he claims to be his favorite film, Stalker [Andrei Tarkovsky, 1979].[77] The scene begins with a medium to three-quarter shot of a younger Hongwu walking from the foreground of the frame in a damp room with decrepit furnishings, with a wooden electric switchboard lit by a bare lightbulb (yellow light) and two color-coded cables: red and green. This scene is shot in deep focus. In the background there are a gray brick wall and an inset window with a thick wooden frame that emanates green and blue lights. As Hongwu walks toward the background, wandering around an unlit ceiling lamp, wavering and intersecting lines of green and blue lights are reflected onto the wall, presumably by the water on the flooded floor (out of frame). The camera slowly dollies toward the background. When Hongwu notices the ceiling lamp, in a medium close-up, he screws in a lightbulb, which emanates a bright yellow light that gives form to the

FIGURE 5. In *Long Day's Journey into Night*, Hongwu screws a lightbulb into a lamp, which gives form to the showering rain leaked from the ceiling.

showering rain that has been leaking through the roof (see Figure 5). The film then cuts to a high-angle shot of the semiflooded floor as Hongwu walks past the camera and sits down on a metal trunk. His hand is holding an old clock that indicates nine o'clock. He then turns the clock to its back, opens the cover, and pulls out a small black-and-white photograph of a young woman. Her face, however, is obscured by a hole from a cigarette burn. Behind this old photo, someone has inscribed the name and phone number of a person: Tao Zhaomei.

This photograph of a young woman with a missing face therefore gives the film's enigma a body substitute, though the actual identity of the unknown woman and what she signifies remain unclear. What complicates matters is that this enigma is displaced from Hongwu's missing mother to his love interest in the past, named Wan Qiwen (played by Tang Wei), who was the girlfriend of Wildcat. When Wildcat died, Hongwu began dating Qiwen as a token of his friend's memory. Alternatively, one may also say that Hongwu killed Wildcat in order to take Qiwen as his girlfriend. The image-consciousness then initiates fragmented memories of Hongwu's romantic vignettes with Qiwen, and it gives a brief close-up of Wildcat devouring an apple when he feels depressed—a habit Hongwu picked up from Wildcat. These memories are then intercut with Hongwu encountering a young woman who resembles Qiwen (played by Tang Wei again), who begins to develop a relationship with Hongwu. Yet, as Hongwu acknowledges, Wan Qiwen is in fact the name of a Hong Kong television star from the 1980s, which suggests that this name—or even the person—could have been merely a placeholder of a je ne sais quoi. In this sense, this image-consciousness, which is rendered by digital technology, suggests that the connection between the (celluloid) photography (the mother's photo) and *reality* (memories of Hongwu) is unreliable, as it is a construction initiated by karma.

This first part of the film can be seen as an avalanche of awarenesses that is actualized from the seeds of an *ālaya*-consciousness, because a dominant condition (the cinematic technicity-consciousness) enables these potentialities to be imaged-imagined by Hongwu and the cinema itself. What is absent, however, is an ontologically consistent volition that organizes these spatiotemporally discrete moments into a coherent whole. In other words, these images are not attached to by a singular *manas;* rather, they are seed and matching conditions that are being put on display as *the way it is.*

In one sequence, Hongwu manages to locate a middle-aged woman in a prison, whom he believes to be Tai Zhaomei. In an over-the-shoulder medium close-up of this woman, the older Hongwu asks her if she is Zhaomei. After her denial, the camera dollies to the left slightly to offer a more-frontal view of Zhaomei's face. In this shot, Zhaomei is seen through a piece of wired glass. She wears a clean blue uniform and she sits against a nebulous green background under a pristine white light. She therefore appears to be an uncannily lifelike image in a damp, foggy, and dreamlike milieu. Suddenly, this woman speaks *as* Zhaomei and recounts a story of her and Qiwen breaking into a house in an attempted robbery, in which they found a room decorated as in a fairy tale. As they heard the owner of the house returning, they decided to steal one thing from it and run away. When they reached a wooded area, they found out that Qiwen had stolen a novel, which was the book that Hongwu is holding in the scene. This woman claims that she and Qiwen had read the whole novel, in which there was a poem. When one recites the poem, one can make spin the very room from which they escaped. This sudden shift in this woman's identity in the scene makes tangible how identities, memories, and histories are intersubjectively configured as perceptual-conceptual proliferations. In this image-imagination, all transindividuated beings are interbeings, and the image-consciousness is not owned by a single being. Rather, it is a *process of interbecomings*.

Toward the end of this first part of the film, the younger Hongwu visits Wildcat's mother (Sylvia Chang) in her hair salon. Here, Wildcat's mother looks content and relaxed, and she recounts how she taught Hongwu and Wildcat to dye her clients' hair. She laughingly tells Hongwu that no client would ever want to dye their hair pink. In the following sequence, Hongwu visits an abandoned town, which is going to be demolished the next morning: a transient image-imagination that is captured the moment before it disappears. There, he encounters a sex worker who tells Hongwu that he can visit her karaoke to look for the woman he seeks. But before the karaoke opens, he can go to the movie theater to watch a pornographic film. Hongwu then enters a movie theater (which recalls the very site at which Hongwu might have killed Wildcat), watching a film called *Long Day's Journey into Night*. Once he sits down, he puts on a pair of 3D glasses. As instructed by the usher prior to the screening, the spectators also put on their own. What follows in the next fifty-nine minutes is framed as both a film within a film and a dream (imagination) in 3D. This entire sequence unfolds in a single long take. It can be understood as an actualization of Hongwu's memories from the ālaya-consciousness as an imagination. Yet, such an imagina-tion is actualized, in all its reality and concreteness, as a continuous and three-dimensional image: an embodied and sensuous process of interbecomings.

This long take begins with Hongwu driving a minecart backward into the depths of a mineshaft (which could be the place where Wildcat has been buried), which opens into a cave. This cave is supposed to be located at the back of the cinema, where he cannot find an exit. In this cave, he meets a young man who wears the skull of a sheep as a mask. This young man takes off his mask and promises to take Hongwu down the mountain if Hongwu can beat him in a game of Ping-Pong. Hongwu beats the young man by using a technique he jocularly calls "spinning paddle." This young man asks Hongwu to name him, and Hongwu calls him Wildcat. "Wildcat" then shows Hongwu the exit and gives Hongwu a ride on his motorcycle. He also gives Hongwu a Ping-Pong paddle and tells him to spin it if he wants to fly. However, halfway down the mountain, the road is blocked. From that point, Hongwu takes an industrial-cable cradle to descend slowly into a pinball machine parlor and pool hall located on a cliff overlooking a village.

In the pool hall, Hongwu meets Kaizhen (also played by Tang Wei), and he tells her that she reminds him of Qiwen. Kaizhen ignores him at first and asks him to leave. As Kaizhen is about to close the pool hall, she is harassed by a group of teenagers who refuse to leave. Hongwu comes to her rescue. In revenge, the teenagers lock Kaizhen and Hongwu up in the pool hall as they depart. Hongwu then spins the Ping-Pong paddle. At this point, the camera becomes one with Hongwu's and Kaizhen's bodies by assuming their point of view. Their joint body levitates and flies slowly down into the village. When the camera lands, it separates itself from Hongwu and Kaizhen and resumes its role as an observer and a follower. This dream is therefore generated from the site where Hongwu buried Wildcat's body, and metaphorically, the traumatic memory of the murder. In it, therefore, Wildcat and Qiwen are resurrected and reembodied by the young man (as "Wildcat") and Kaizhen. Meanwhile, the motion of spinning, which is first shown in the opening sequence of the film as circles of light that spin around the karaoke and is then configured as a secondary enigma as a magical poem in the novel that Qiwen stole, is now literalized as the spinning paddle that enables Hongwu and Kaizhen to fly. But as the voiceover indicates in the beginning of the film, the moment the enigmatic woman is embodied and visualized, the resulting image is immediately given its ontological consistency—as an imaged imagination (objectivized subjective)—where his body is hydrogenic and his memories are the only substance that exists. And such ontological consistency and sense-certainty of the dreamt reality is confirmed by the image-consciousness's three-dimensionality and temporal continuity.

On land, Kaizhen is no longer with Hongwu. Hongwu then wanders into an open-air karaoke stage located in a carnivalesque public square with circles of red, blue, and green lights spinning all over it and the surrounding buildings. Thus, this public square can be considered a larger version of the karaoke in the opening of the film. Hongwu looks for Kaizhen in the square, and he eventually finds her backstage. In front of her vanity decorated with red fabric, Kaizhen tells Hongwu that she wants to show him a room that belongs to a married couple, which is decorated as in a fairy tale. Her verbal description of the room recalls

Zhaomei's depiction of the room where she and Qiwen had stolen the novel. However, Hongwu tells Kaizhen that he still wants to find Qiwen. He then leaves the backstage and returns to the public square.

There, he suddenly spots Wildcat's mother wearing a pink wig (a hair color she deemed ridiculous in the first part of the film) and a beige leather jacket. She appears to be distressed, and she lights up a torch from a bonfire roaring in the public square and waves the torch against a few karaoke customers. The camera then follows Hongwu on a gimbal, who follows Wildcat's mother down a meandering staircase until they reach an imposing metal gate. Behind the gate, there is a sport utility vehicle with its engine already running, on a road that leads straight to a dark background. Hongwu sees her shouting to a man on the other side of the gate. She begs this unknown man to take her with him, yet he ignores her and hops into the SUV. Hongwu walks up to Wildcat's mother and asks her why she is there, but she does not recognize Hongwu. Instead, she asks him to convince the unknown man to open the gate for her. Hongwu promises to help her, on the condition that she leaves him her most precious possession. She then leaves him the wristwatch that was worn by the unknown woman at the beginning of the film.

After this, Hongwu returns to the backstage area of the karaoke, where he sees Kaizhen again. She then takes him to an abandoned, half-demolished living room, which she claims to be the bedroom of the pair of lovers she mentioned, though it has been slated for demolition the next morning (like the town itself). This darkly lit room, which is both visually and sensually dampened by a wet and cold grayish green, evokes the memory of the leaking dormitory in the first part of the film. Here, Hongwu gives Kaizhen the wristwatch he has just taken from Wildcat's mother, which connects Kaizhen symbolically to the unknown woman in the beginning of the film (that is to say, the embodiment of the enigma). Kaizhen tells Hongwu that she once heard from someone that this room will spin if only one knows the password. Hongwu then recites the poem from the book he held when he visited Zhaomei, which makes the room spin. This act of spinning connects the mystical room that Zhaomei and Qiwen had once visited, the semiflooded dormitory, and this abandoned room together, thus confirming Qiwen and Kaizhen as being symbolic substitutes of the enigmatic woman. The camera then follows the rotating movement of the room and departs from Hongwu and Kaizhen. It finally stops at the backstage area of the karaoke, with a long shot of the vanity. On it, a Roman candle is burning with bright and colorful sparkles.

THE ENIGMA OF ENIGMA

What is the enigma in *Long Day's Journey into Night*? What does the film tell us about cinema as a technicity-consciousness?

As I mentioned earlier, Qiwen and Kaizhen are the symbolic substitutes of the enigma. In psychoanalytical terms, they are Hongwu's mother substitutes, who enable Hongwu to return to his infantile state of Oneness—a perfect sensorial and affective union with the mother's body. To complicate matters, Qiwen used to be Wildcat's girlfriend before his death. In this sense, Qiwen and Kaizhen serve as the symbolic displacements of Hongwu's dead friend. In the second part of the film, it is "Wildcat" who takes Hongwu out of the mine in order to search for Qiwen/Kaizhen, and it is a gift from Wildcat's mother that enables Kaizhen to assume her role completely as Qiwen's substitute at the end of the film. Configured in this enigma is therefore the trauma of his best friend's death—or his act of murdering his best friend. Therefore, the *mise-en-abîme* (deep structure) of this trauma is a *seed*—a memory and a sense of guilt—which is unnamable and unbearable: the enigma. This enigma functions to produce an avalanche of karmic impulses that instigates and propels the formational process of Hongwu's subjective imaginations, which are objectively imaged as an intersubjective sensorial and affective milieu: a process of interbecomings.

For the audience watching this film, which is typically composed primarily of film festival goers (including myself), the pleasure of engaging ourselves in this technicity-consciousness is generated not only by Hongwu's journey of disconcealing the enigma (which he never manages to do). It also trains the consciousness (or the anthropotechnical body) to be mindful of each phase of the formational process. In so doing, we can let this enigma be as *the way it is*. It is fine for us spectators that the enigma is not locatable, since by definition an enigma is unlocatable. But then, every *sati/smṛti* (awareness) that constitutes the overall technicity-consciousness is a manifestation of this enigma. In this sense, the enigma is nowhere to be found; yet it is everywhere. If we read the film as a sociopolitical symptom, we can see it as a rehearsal to a potential way to engage in (be *mindful of*) our sociopolitical enigma:

the *dispositif*. The *dispositif*, in our control-society, is nowhere to be found. Nonetheless, every formation is its manifestation.

One can argue that the mind-game structure of *Long Day's Journey into Night* would have been possible had Bi Gan shot it on 35 mm film. However, the often gravity-defiant camera movement throughout the film; the navigation of the camera not only between subject and object but also *amid* an affective milieu where the subject-object divide is indiscernible; the falsification of the direct relationship between the image and reality; and the long take that claims an *existence* on its own—all these aspects can be regarded as what Shane Denson would call discorrelated images (images that are no longer ontologically grounded in a subject-object correlation). For Denson, such discorrelation was perceived and conceptualized even before the emergence of digital technology, or, as Hui Yuk would argue, it might even have been a principle that was responsible for the emerging configuration of the digital.[78] Nonetheless, the constitution of such a (post-)cinematic image-consciousness and the desire to produce one are rendered possible by a digital *existence*. Such an existence can be regarded as an anthropotechnical ecology in which digital modes of operation have made tangible the tension between relational thinking and logic, on the one hand, and a belief in the Cartesian substrate-form/subject-object divide, on the other. As Thomas Lamarre argues, this is not to say that digital existence overdetermines ontology. Rather, technics, as a configurative component in a larger ontogenetic layout, *underdetermines* (that is, determines from *below* as an *infra*-structure) those ecological changes that produce an impression of an ontological shift. Such an impression is initiated by changes in our affective relationship with the larger ecological transductions.[79] And what actively rewrites—and is rewritten by—our affective relationship to these changes, I argue, is karma.

CHAPTER 2

THE KARMA-IMAGE

"In front of your eyes: Here and now." This motto was bequeathed to us by Sheng-yen (1931–2009), Dharma heir of the founders of the two oldest schools of Dzhiɛn/Chan/Zen: Liɪmtsèi Ng'iɛ̀hwen/Linji Yixuan (Rinzai Gigen, d. 886) and Dùngsh'ɛn Liɐngkèi/Dongshan Liangjie (Tōzan Ryōkai, 807–69).[1] In our ordinary lived experience, apprehending what lies in front of our eyes, *here and now,* is an impossible task. It is because the very temporal point-instant at which we become aware of the *here and now* is already a recognition: a contiguous matching condition that names and in-forms a memory of the preceding seed condition. If we are able to apprehend the *here and now,* we can become mindful of a bare cognition at a singular *kṣaṇa* (smallest unit of time), which neither refers to a seed condition in the past nor instigates a matching condition in the future. Such a *kṣaṇa* is therefore liberated from dependent originations. *Tathātā—the way it is—*is thus disconcealed.[2]

A Zen practitioner who wishes to train themself to apprehend the *here and now* usually encounters a conundrum. A sentient being who is mindful of nothing but a bare cognition at a *kṣaṇa* is supposed to dwell in *tathātā.* However, if this bare cognition takes place at a *kṣaṇa* prior to the existences and originations of sensations and affections, this *kṣaṇa* refers to a zero point-instant at which time has yet to be perceived and conceptualized. This *kṣaṇa* is therefore named a *kṣaṇa,* though it is not actually one *kṣaṇa.*[3] Yet, by saying so, a perceptual-conceptual differentiation between time (*kṣaṇa* as the smallest unit of time) and timelessness (*kṣaṇa* as a linguistic placeholder of "the negation of time") is

71

drawn. Such a differentiation insinuates that *time/timelessness*—as a structural difference—has an existential value; its existence is a fabric on which dependent originations take place. When such a *kṣaṇa-as-time/ kṣaṇa-as-timelessness* is actualized as a sequence of point-instants, dwelling in *tathātā* then means dwelling in a series of contiguous *kṣaṇas-as-time/kṣaṇas-as-timelessness*. If so, *tathātā* must be impermanent and nonself: it is merely a form among many others. Otherwise, the *kṣaṇa-as-time/kṣaṇa-as-timelessness* itself must be permanent, that is to say, the unmoved mover, which contradicts the axiom of dependent originations.[4]

This aporia initiates Gilles Deleuze's discussion of cinematographic movement and time. Following the understandings of time proposed by Immanuel Kant and Henri Bergson, time for Deleuze has no existential value.[5] For him, time is neither an object independent of the image nor a form; it is a perceptual-conceptual relationship constituted by the qualitative changes between objects.[6] Deleuze argues that before the 1940s, in the cinemas of the United States, Europe, and Japan, time was perceived and conceptualized in subordination to movement. The sociopolitical trauma and the human sense-uncertainty during the 1940s changed the way the anthropotechnical image-consciousness is informed.[7] Since then, the (anthropotechnical) body's sensory-motor system has no longer always made direct correlations between perception, affection, impulse, action, and reflection. Rather, it dwells in the relationality itself as a *pure optical and sound situation*. This relation instantiates not a qualitative change between objects, but rather the change itself as an actualization-reflection of the *durée* (duration), a pure potentiality from which temporalities are activated.[8]

In this chapter and the next, I maintain a conversation with Deleuze's *Cinema 1* and *Cinema 2*. While this chapter focuses on the movement-image, the following chapter rethinks what it means by the time-image. As Deleuze argues by the end of chapter one of *Cinema 1*, movement is an *expression* (manifestation) of duration, and the image is the expression itself. For him, "duration, by changing qualitatively, is divided up in objects, and objects, by gaining depth [becoming an impetus], by losing their contours, are united in duration. We can therefore say that movement relates the objects of a closed system to open duration, and duration to the objects of the system which it forces to open up."[9] If so, both movement and duration are expressions of *conatus* (*puissance*): a mode of existence's impetus to subsist, which is immanent in the mode itself and emanative to the whole.[10] In *Cinema 1*, therefore, Deleuze scrutinizes how the movement-image is in-formed in a process driven by this impetus to *image* and *imagine*.

In the Buddhist discourses, movement and time are considered two perceptually different, but conceptually identical, proliferations invoked by karma: impulses that configure the initiation-extinction of forms from one *kṣaṇa* to another, which function *like* codes that affect—and are affected by—the configuration itself. Karma is always at work and cannot be conceived otherwise. However, when one is mindful of the *here and now*—*kṣaṇa-as-time/kṣaṇa-as-timelessness*—the *lǐ*-technicity that renders possible the relationship between *affecting* and *being affected* is disconcealed. This insight into *lǐ*/technicity-*džǐ*/ consciousness is called *paññā/prajñā*.[11]

The cinematographic image is therefore best rethought in terms of both the karma-image and the insight-image. The karma-image is informed, at every *kṣaṇa* of its formational process, by the predisposed layout of power relations inscribed by karma. These inscriptions codify what Buddhist scholars call the five *khandhas/skandhas* (formal aggregates): forms, sensations and affections, perceptions, volition, and consciousnesses. In the cinema, volition (karma) propels sensations and affections to convert a bare cognition into a perception (recognition), thus putting into movement the formational process through the operation of the six consciousnesses. This process in turn impels the proliferation of karmic impulses.[12] The movement-image is, by default, a karma-image.

The karma-image can therefore be defined as the foundation of all those cinematographic images, where the formational process and the process of interbecomings operate with their *lǐ*-technicity largely concealed. Hence, most films that follow the classical Hollywood style (in itself a historically and conceptually contestable notion) belong to this category.[13] In this chapter, I use John Ford's *The Searchers* [1956] to illustrate how the karma-image operates as a process of interbecomings. By the insight-image, I mean a technicity-consciousness (as defined in the introduction to this book, an anthropotechnical body, together with the embodied mind and its associated milieu, that can sense, perceive, affect and be affected, and think) that is mindful of the *here and now*—or is mindful of itself. As I will discuss in the following chapter, some of the features of the insight-image correspond to those of the time-image. We can say that the time-image *can be* a mode of the insight-image. In this light, I do not propose to replace Deleuze's two terms by mine. My contention is, rather, that many readers of Deleuze focus on how he discusses the movement-image and time-image as *lakṣanas* (forms), while overlooking their *ātmakatva* (ontological ground) and *adhyavasāyas* (modifications of the self-nature of forms). For Deleuze, if the formational process of the cinematic technicity-consciousness drives—and is driven by—*conatus,* we must be mindful that such a process of interbecomings is a layout of relationalities. It means that as much as *we,* as spectators, are impelled by an attachment to this formational process and the way it has been habitually configured, we have an agency to make changes. As I shall demonstrate, by focusing on how karma operates in the formational process and how insight can initiate perceptual-conceptual changes, we are able to focus not only on what forms the image can assume, but also on *what cinema does and what we can do with the cinema.* We can therefore envision cinematographic images and modes of mediation that will instigate possible ethical, aesthetic, and political changes.[14]

TIME: A PARADOX

In *Kritik der reinen Vernunft* [*Critique of Pure Reason,* 1781 and 1787], Kant discusses the inseparability between time and imaging. For him, time is a "necessary presentation that underlines all intuitions." However, it is also a representation of change—for example, from presence to non-presence and from one spatial coordinate to another. For example, in early October, when I meditated in my lounge, a cool breeze from the outside gently brushed against my skin. My body generated a pleasant response to it, which instantiated a difference from the warm and humid sensation I experienced in August. This affection of mine initiated a mental image: that there was a difference between my affection in the fall and the one my body generated in the summer. This mental image enabled me to *sense* time. Yet, if I say that such a change took place *in time,* I am imagining time as a container in which such a change took place. In this sense, I regard time as the "formal a priori condition of all appearances": formation, transformation, and extinction of all phenomena. Nonetheless, as a sensuous image of the change itself, time does not *exist* independently from my intuition.[15]

For Kant, there is no such thing as time-in-itself. Rather, he posits that I deduce time from a process of differentiation based on my sensorial experience. However, in this process of differentiation, I come up with two mutually conflicting impressions. In one register, time is the condition of the formation of all phenomena, and all phenomena are formed out of causality (dependent originations). In other words, time is perceived and conceptualized as the fundamental condition on which causality is set in action. Thus, it is posited *outside* of causality. In another register, as a configurative element of all forms, time is formed, transformed, and extinguished by the process of causation. Hence, it is part of causality. In the cinema, we often (mis)construe the image as a layout of causes-conditions that *endure,* and time is thus regarded as the fundamental condition on which such endurance depends. Meanwhile, we hold on to a paradoxical belief that our sense of time emerges as we perceive and conceptualize the qualitative changes of a state of things or being.

As a perceptual-conceptual proliferation, time is therefore configured as a paradox. To complicate this matter, within this paradox, there is another one: that time is imagined as being at once impermanent and permanent. In the first chapter of *Cinema 1,* Deleuze reposes this quandary. We all know that a moving image is technically constituted by a sequence of immobile sections, which run up to eighteen frames per second in films made during the silent era, twenty-four frames per second for celluloid film with an optical soundtrack, 29.97 (NTSC) or twenty-five (PAL) frames per second on television, and up to 120 frames per second in 4K digital cinema. How then, do these immobile sections come to be perceived and recognized as an enduring movement?[16]

Up until the early twentieth century, this phenomenon was interpreted by philosophers and physicists as persistence of vision, which was first proposed by Aristotle.[17] Joseph and Barbara Anderson point out that this notion was already contested by early scholars who were interested in the motion picture, including Max Wertheimer (1880–1943) and Hugo Münsterberg (1863–1916).[18] Yet, it still found its way into film studies via two citations of Peter Mark Roget's (1779–1869) article "Explanation of an Optical Deception in the Appearance of the Spokes of a Wheel When Seen through Vertical Apertures" [December 9, 1824]: one by Terry Ramsaye (1885–1954) in his influential historical account of Hollywood, *A Million and One Nights* [1926], and the other one by Arthur Knight in *The Liveliest Art* [1957].[19]

Based on neuroscientific findings in the 1970s, the Andersons point out that the visual cortex processes real motion (that is, the qualitative change of an actual moving being or object) and apparent motion (or movement generated by optical illusions) differently. In the first chapter, I discussed more recent findings by neuroscientists. As the electrical signals from the photoreceptive cells in the retinas are transmitted through our visual cortex, the patterns of real motion are identified and configured in V3, whereas velocity and direction are defined in V5. The information processed in V3 and V5 will not be complete until V6 provides the information regarding self-motion (the motion produced by the perceiving body). Meanwhile, apparent motion is processed in V4, which determines the spatial relations between optical elements under the perceiver's attentive gaze.[20]

The Andersons argue that for Paul Kolers and J. R. Pomerantz, the short-range apparent motion produced by immediately contiguous sense data is processed in a way identical to that which processes real motion.[21] In other words, the motion perceived and conceptualized in the cinema is real motion, not because the spectator actually apprehends qualitative changes of—and between—objects, but because the visual cortex remains ignorant of the fact that there are no qualitative changes in the first place. In other words, our optico-neurological system is in-formed to ignore *the way it is* and instead chooses to process a sequence of motionless and impermanent forms as a mobile and enduring field of vision.

How does this field of vision come to be recognized as an image-consciousness? As Deleuze points out in the opening chapter of *Cinema 1*, for Bergson, a sequence of immobile sections does not immediately produce a perception and conception of time. Rather, it enables the human consciousness to perceive and conceptualize movement that endures in time (Bergson's first thesis of movement). Meanwhile, the consciousness perceives and conceptualizes this sequence as a mobile section—a movement-image—whose qualitative changes in a continuous process of becoming enable perceptual-conceptual relations to be in-formed (Bergson's second thesis). These relations, which help the operation of the consciousness to connect perception, affection, impulse, and action (the sensory-motor system), constitute a temporally continuous and existentially enduring milieu. Thus, Deleuze proposes the following understanding of the movement-image based on what he calls Bergson's third thesis:

$$\frac{\text{immobile sections}}{\text{movement}} = \frac{\text{movement as mobile section}}{\text{qualitative change}^{22}}$$

We are therefore confronted with a paradox of time: (1) on the one hand, time is fundamentally made up of impermanent and immediately contiguous conditions (modulations); (2) on the other hand, time is perceived and conceptualized as a continuous and enduring process of changes (mediation). Deleuze argues that the former is an illusion, whereas the latter is *the way it is*. In Mahāyāna scholarship, the former operation refers to time as *lǐ*-technicity, whereas the latter refers to time as *dzī*-consciousness. Contrary to Deleuze, neither technicity nor consciousness is *the way it is*.

NĀGĀRJUNA: KARMA, MOVEMENT, AND TIME

Mahāyāna scholars regard the *Fundamental Verses on the Middle Way* by Nāgārjuna (see also the introduction and chapter 1) as the definitive text on this subject. They turn especially to three key chapters: "Gatāgataparīkṣā" [On movement], "Karmaphalaparīkṣa" [On karma], and "Kālaparīkṣā" [On time]. The source of the debate is often traced back to SA-79 of the *Connected Discourses*, in which Śākyamuni Buddha seems to propose two mutually conflicting understandings of time— impermanence and permanence:

If neither the form of the past nor the form of the future has any existential value, the form of the present also has no existential value. Those disciples who have well understood this principle thus observe as such: they do not look back to the form of the past and they do not anticipate the form of the future. They therefore dislike the form of the present, distance themselves from longing, and attain the ultimate extinction of all forms, sensations and affections, perceptions, volition, and consciousnesses.

Thus, *bhikkhus* [you monks], if there is [no belief of the] form of the past, those disciples who have well understood this principle will all look back to [perceive and conceptualize] the past. Since there has been [a belief that there is] the form of the past, those disciples who have well understood this principle would [train themselves] not [to] perceive and conceptualize the past. If there is [no belief of the] form of the future, those disciples who have well understood this principle will anticipate the future. Since there has been [a belief that there is] the form of the future, those disciples who have well understood this principle do not anticipate the future. If there is [no belief of the] form of the present, those disciples who have well understood this principle will not generate a dislike of all forms, distance themselves from longing, and strive towards the ultimate extinction of all forms. Since there is the form of the present that exists, those disciples who have well understood this principle generate a dislike of all forms, distance themselves from longing, and strive towards the ultimate extinction of all forms, sensations and affections, perceptions, volition, and consciousnesses.[23]

The Sarvāstivādas point out that the first paragraph in this *sutta* suggests that in principle, the forms of the past, the future, and the present have no existential value. In other words, these three temporalities are best understood as perceptual-conceptual proliferations (impermanence). Meanwhile, the second paragraph has two meanings. First, since the present is defined as the extension of the past and it is then extended to the future, if a practitioner holds on to the present, this present has already suggested a retrospective regard to the past as well as an anticipation of the future (permanence). Thus, second, the solution is not to negate the relationships between the past, the future, and the present. Rather, the practitioner should acknowledge that these perceptual-conceptual proliferations exist (nominally) as a set of relationships, so that they can be mindful of their emptiness.[24] In Sarvāstivāda philosophy, therefore, time as consciousness is perceived and conceptualized as continuous (permanent), whereas their instantiations as temporalities (time as technicity) are discontinuous (impermanent).

In "On Karma" (see the introduction and chapter 1), Nāgārjuna seems to privilege the view that our impression of temporal linearity and continuity (permanence) is the result of a sequence of immediately contiguous conditions, whose originations and extinctions from one *kṣana* to another are perceptually and conceptually ignored (impermanence). Therefore, karma is best understood not as a potentiality left behind by an extinguished seed condition, which remains potent until it is delayed and deferred through a passage of time. Rather, a seed condition, which is originated and extinguished in one *kṣana*, is immediately followed by a contiguous matching condition ad infinitum (see Figure 2 in the introduction). Each matching condition can be seen as a modulation of the seed condition that has just been extinguished. It therefore takes on the appearance of a repetition, variation, inversion, or reversal of the initiating seed condition.[25] In this light, however, karma is a perceptual-conceptual proliferation. It is neither an enduring impetus nor a series of impulses, neither not an impetus nor not a series of impulses.

Using a similar logic, Nāgārjuna argues that movement, stasis, and the difference between them are fundamentally empty. Nāgārjuna's treatise is written in verses. The points he makes in these verses are listed and numbered according to his logical and rhetorical flow in the table in Figure 6. Pay attention to his method of reasoning. He works through a logical sequence to first deconstruct the notion that "movement is an enduring mobile section" (points 1–5). He then negates each of these points in reverse order (that is, from points 5–1) in order to deconstruct that "both movement and stasis are empty of existential value" (points 6–10). In other words, point 6 should be read as a negation of point 5 (and vice versa), point 7 should be read as a negation of point 4 (and vice versa), and so forth. As a result, the left column of the table and the right column of the table negate one another. The point is that both sides of the table are perceptual-conceptual proliferations. Hence, read the table in Figure 6 according to the numerical order. Then, compare the two columns and see how this process of mutual negation works.

Similarly, in "On Time" (see the introduction), Nāgārjuna first argues that the existence and origination of the future depend on the existence and origination of the past. If so, neither the future nor the past has any existential value. Meanwhile, if one considers the present as the interval between the future and the past, its existence and origination depend on the existences and originations of the future and the past. Thus, if neither the future nor the past has any existential value, the present also has no existential value. Moreover, if one considers these three moments as a continuous whole, the present is an extension of the past (the *future* of the past) and in itself an extension toward the future (the *past* of the future). In this case, the present has no existential value. If so, the future and the past also have no existential value. Both positions—impermanence and permanence—are logically absurd. Nāgārjuna then argues further:

Movement as an enduring mobile section	Emptiness of movement and stasis
1. Movement cannot be separated from the moving subject, for if we separate them, the form of movement and the form of the moving subject are then separated, which is absurd;	10. If there is neither movement nor stasis, there is neither the form of movement nor the moving subject, the same can be said about stasis.
2. If movement is perceived and conceptualized as an enduring process of becoming, there is no stasis; in other words, an image as a perception-conceptualization is movement;	9. But if there is no stasis, the perception and conception of a series of immobile sections are also absurd;
3. As moving positions are defined by movement, the space that these positions are traveled is a perceptual-conceptual proliferation produced by movement;	8. But if movement is an impression produced by a series of immobile sections, there are neither moving positions nor spatial coordinates;
4. If image is movement, and if movement is a perceptual-conceptual proliferation that is continuous, there is no point of initiation or extinction;	7. If a *kṣaṇa* cannot be considered a moving moment, it is absurd to say that there is such a thing as movement with a point of initiation and a point of extinction; if so, movement as a perceptual-conceptual proliferation is made up of a sequence of immobile sections;
5. If movement exists at the moving moment, then the past, future, and present are a continuous process of becoming constituted by a perpetual here and now;	6. But then, if movement does not exist in the past (having-moved) and the future (yet-to-move), the moving moment at a single *kṣaṇa* cannot be considered a movement;

FIGURE 6. Nāgārjuna's understanding of movement and stasis, summarized from Yin Shun, Zhongguan lunsong *jiangji* [Lectures on the *Mūlamadhyamakakārikā*] (1952; repr., Taipei: Zhengwen chubanshe, 2014), §2 (84–99).

Axiom: When we say that existence endures in time, we are suggesting that time is, by definition, an endurance in which a process of becoming takes place.

Proposition 1: If we then argue that our impression of temporal linearity and continuity is constituted by a sequence of immediately contiguous *kṣaṇas,* we are assuming that an endurance can take place at one transient *kṣaṇa.*

Counterargument 1: To say so, however, we are violating the axiom of dependent originations and the definition of endurance: that endurance depends on the relationship between a seed condition that comes before it (the past) and a matching condition that comes after it (the future).

Proposition 2: If we then propose that at this *kṣaṇa,* endurance is immobile, we are still violating these two axioms, as (1) we are suggesting that this immobile section exists without origination and extinction and (2) we are arguing that an endurance is a state of being, rather than a process of interbecoming.

Counterargument 2: Therefore, an immobile state of being cannot be understood as time.

Proposition and Counterargument 3: If we then argue that at this *kṣaṇa,* endurance is mobile, we are inadvertently surrendering the notion that time is discontinuous and impermanent in favor of continuity and permanence.

Conclusion: Therefore, what we call time is neither permanent nor impermanent, neither not permanent nor not impermanent.[26]

However, for Nāgārjuna, when we perceive and conceptualize qualitative changes in forms (*dži*-consciousness), we perceive and conceptualize temporal continuity and permanence. Meanwhile, when we perceive and conceptualize a movement that is constituted by modulating forms from one instant of origination-extinction to another (*lĭ*-technicity, which is the layout of causal relations itself), we perceive and conceptualize temporal discontinuity and impermanence.[27] In other words, we do not perceive and conceptualize time directly. Instead, we derive such perception-conception from modulations or mediations of forms. If so, the cinematographic image cannot represent time directly, and time and temporality cannot be *mediated*. Rather, time is an expression of mediation.

POTENTIALITY AND FORMATION

For Gilles Deleuze, if the image is movement, and if the form of movement, the moving subject, the moving positions it travels, and the passage of time in which it endures are inseparable, the movement-image must be studied as an overall technicity-consciousness. In such a technicity-consciousness, the relationships between external forms (objectivized subjective reality) and internal forms (the technical-sentient body) are in a perpetual process of interbecomings. Let us say that in the cinema, qualitative changes between objects are perceived and conceptualized as real movement. This first thesis of Bergson enables Deleuze to analyze how movement and time are perceived and conceptualized through framing and *découpage* ("editing" within a shot), by which movement and the spatial coordinates it travels are deterritorialized and reterritorialized.[28] However, when he begins to scrutinize *montage* (editing), Deleuze needs to circumvent a problem that is familiar to film scholars: that Euro-American cinemas during the "classical period" are organized into a somewhat standardized semiotic layout.[29] In other words, is there such thing as a cognitively innate or historically conventionalized paradigm, in which the image-consciousness is in-formed?

Christian Metz thinks so, and he calls the cinema a syntagmatic system. For him, a *langue* (language) is a system of differences, which, according to Ferdinand de Saussure (1857–1913), consists of infinite arbitrary relationships that are fundamentally empty. However, once they are instantiated as *paroles* (speeches), phonemes are in-formed, which are then articulated into syntagma. Certain syntagmatic relationships are then conventionalized as paradigms. Metz believes that the cinematographic image does not go through any double articulation (the conversion of phonemes into syntagma through morphemes). Hence, he insists not only that the smallest semiological unit in the cinema is already a syntagm, but that its articulation is never arbitrary. Although, strictly speaking, there is no such thing as a cinematic grammar, syntagmatic relationships are codified through conventions into paradigmatic relationships. For Metz, these paradigmatic relationships, which are exemplified by Hollywood cinema, are universal.[30]

It is important to note that David Bordwell calls this the classical mode of narration. For Bordwell, the cinema is not a language. Instead, cinematic narration is a style that is conventionalized industrially. These conventions are modeled on both our inborn (and universal) human cognitive process of perception and on a continual reconfiguration of such a process through our day-to-day social interactions. Within a mode of narration, the *mise-en-scène* is optimized to invoke a set of schemata—mental images—in the spectator's brain, which is used to organize the various narrational devices in order to recognize the image as a coherent whole. Since these responses are innate, sociocultural differences are mere variations of a universal set of cognitive operations. Industrially speaking, Hollywood captures this universal set, of which other regional cinemas can be considered variations.[31]

Both Metz and Bordwell therefore believe that a mode of operation (technicity) that is commonly found among human beings inevitably produces a singular exemplary consciousness (form)—Hollywood cinema. In so doing, they have universalized the exception and used such a universalized exception to define other modes of consciousness as exceptions. In political terms, their theories are acts of epistemic violence. Contrary to their belief, Deleuze's understanding of the cinema is closer to the Saussurian *langue* (technicity): a layout of relationalities that can be actualized as infinite layouts of *paroles* (instantiations). Such actualization is based on sociocultural and individual conditions that are often arbitrary. In other words, in the formational process of the image-consciousness, a potentiality to in-form can be actualized into infinite modes of existences (images). Meanwhile, a mode of existence is best understood as a process of interbecomings and transindividuations. Thus, the process itself both affects—and is affected by—a large number of conditions.

For Deleuze, therefore, asking how this technicity is in-formed is no trivial matter. If we regard the potentiality to in-form as an innate cognitive operation or a linguistic convention, we are taking away an individuated being or community's agency over the formational process, which is also a sociopolitical process of transindividuations and interbecomings.[32]

Deleuze believes that the potentiality to in-form is immanent in—and emanated from—the formational process itself. Strategically, such an argument posits the agency to in-form and reconfigure the formational process in the interbecomings (transductions) between the agent and patient of the formation. This is to say that *we*, as both agent and patient in the formational process, have the agency to make changes, except that we may be ignorant of such potentiality.

Deleuze conceptualizes this potentiality to in-form and be in-formed on Baruch (Benedict de) Spinoza's (1632–77) understanding of *conatus* (*puissance*) in *Ethica* [*Ethics*, written 1664–65, published 1667].

In his discussion elsewhere, Deleuze defines Spinoza's understanding of *puissance* as such:

> (1) The capacity to exist (that is, the possible existence involved in the essence of a finite thing) is a power; (2) Now, a finite being already exists necessarily (by virtue of some external cause which determines its existence); (3) If absolutely infinite Being did not itself exist necessarily, it would have less power than finite beings, which is absurd; (4) But the necessary existence of the absolutely infinite cannot obtain by virtue of an external cause; so that it is through itself that the absolutely infinite being necessarily exists.[33]

For Spinoza, a finite being is a mode of existence or a modification of substance. The power of a finite being to exist comes from its participation in substance, but it also means that such power is a modification of the necessity to exist of the infinite being. For Spinoza, this power is the essence (*fond* or depth) of being, which is the power to act and affect and the power to be acted on and affected:

> A mode's essence is a power; to it corresponds a certain capacity of the mode to be affected. But because the mode is a part of Nature, this capacity is always exercised, either in affections produced by external things (those affections called passive), or in affections explained by its own essence (called active). Thus the distinction between power and act, on the level of modes, disappears in favor of two equally actual powers, that of acting, and that of suffering action, which vary inversely one to the other, but whose sum is both constant and constantly effective.[34]

Deleuze therefore argues that the potentialities to in-form constitute what Henri Bergson calls the plane of immanence. Since the potentiality to in-form is immanent to the image-itself, the plane of immanence *is* the plane of existence of the movement-images:

> Th[e] infinite set of all images constitutes a kind of plane [*plan*] of immanence. The image exists in itself, on this plane. This in-itself of the image is matter: not something hidden behind the image, but on the contrary the absolute identity of the image and movement. The identity of the image and movement leads us to conclude immediately that the movement-image and matter are identical. . . . The

> *movement-image* and *flowing-matter* are strictly the same thing. . . . The
> plane of immanence is the movement (the facet of movement) which is
> established between the parts of each system and between one system
> and another, which crosses them all, stirs them all up together and
> subjects them all to the condition which prevents them from being
> absolutely closed. It is therefore a section; but, despite some termino-
> logical ambiguities in Bergson, it is not an immobile and instantaneous
> section, it is a mobile section, a temporal section of perspective. . . .
> And the plane is not distinct from this presentation of planes. This is
> not mechanism, it is machinism. The material universe, the plane of
> immanence, is the *machine assemblage of movement-images*
> [technicity].[35]

Let us think about this metaphorically for a moment. Imagine a
piece of celluloid film: a layout of silver particles (technicity or
substrate). When it is exposed to *all* images, it is a plane of absolute
luminosity: a plane of absolutely equal relationalities (form). However, when it is exposed to a specific set of conditions, a specific set
of relationalities is in-formed between those particles (technicity
or substrate), and certain images are obscured. As a result, a specific
form is now instantiated (consciousness). For Bergson, the plane of
immanence can be compared to a plane of absolute luminosity. Images are formed as movement diffuses light, thus producing layouts
of relative luminosities and obscurities. In other words, there is no
divide between substrate and form *until* their indiscernibility and
indistinction are obscured by movement: a process of affecting and
being affected.

When a layout of luminosities and obscurities is "related to a centre
of indetermination, it becomes *perception-image*." Deleuze borrows the
term *center of indetermination* from Bergson's *Matière et mémoire* [*Matter
and Memory,* 1896]. For Bergson, an individuated being (or, some say,
subject) is best understood as a "center of indetermination" on a plane
of immanence, whose "presence is equivalent to the suppression of all
those parts of objects in which their functions find no interest."[36] Hence,
though the perception-image can be roughly regarded as an image that
is initiated from an individuated being's subjectival position, it is
more appropriately understood as a site where the transindividuation between the subject and object is initiated out of an affect—an

instantiation of an impulse or energy to affect and be affected. Perception-image therefore includes a perception of the act of perception (for instance, as the camera/spectator observes a character seeing, by either including or excluding the object of being seen) and a perception of perception (for instance, a point-of-view shot and the shot/reverse-shot). The perception-image can transition into a potential to act (virtual action), whose actualization in-forms the action-image, including the form of action, the acting subject, and the self or other on which it is acted. Meanwhile, the interval between them, which determines the center of indetermination, is called the affection-image.[37] The terms perception-image, affection-image, and action-image do not refer to specific syntagma or narrational devices. Rather, they indicate qualitative changes within the movement-image, which may or may not correspond to the technical changes.

AFFECTS AND IMPULSES

Here, we must clarify the difference between and relationship between an "affect" and an "affection." As I pointed out, an affect instantiates an impulse to affect and be affected. Meanwhile, an affection—in the form of pleasure, displeasure, or indifference—arises when an affect initiates a transindividuation between internal and external forms. It turns a bare cognition into a recognition (objectivized subjective). If so, what we usually call an "affection" has two sides: an affect (an auto-affection prior to the differentiation between agent and patient) and an affection (an objectivized subjective response by the internal forms to the external forms they contact). An affect/affection therefore propels each moment of dephasing, transduction, and transindividuation in the image. How affects and impulses operate in the formational process is thus the most crucial point in Deleuze's argument.

Based on the theories proposed by Béla Balázs (1884–1949), Deleuze argues that the affection-image is best exemplified by the close-up and long shot, which do not always engage the sensory-motor system in an act of perception or action. Rather, they posit the anthropotechnical body momentarily in an *espace quelconque* (any-space-whatever). In such a space, the anthropotechnical body (center of indetermination) dwells in the contour of the space itself, whether it be a *décor,* the facial feature of an actor, a bare landscape, the minute movements generated by the affective intensities of an actor, or the subtle qualitative changes of a still life.[38] In other words, the anthropotechnical body posits itself in an interphase between transductions. Engaged in the acts of affecting and being affected by the process of transduction and transindividuation, the body awaits a reconfigured differentiation between the agent and patient in movement.

An affection-image does not transition into an action-image immediately. Rather, the action-image is triggered by an impulse-image. In the any-space-whatever, an impulse—an instantiation of *puissance*—is to be acted on by external things (patient) and to act from its own essence (agent). In the cinematic image-consciousness, *puissance* is initiated from the *monde originaire* (originary world) or, in Buddhist terms, a layout of empty relations. The overall image-consciousness (in textual terms, the *récit* or narrative) can be considered an instantiation of this layout of relations. A *pulsion élémentaire* (elementary impulse) is then best regarded as an instantiation of the *puissance* in a specific affective juncture, which serves as the *fond des milieux déterminés* (essence or driving energy of the determined milieus).[39]

If so, the overall movement-image and the operation of the sensory-motor system (meaning the entire film as a technicity-consciousness) are initiated by a series of impulses (within specific situations), which are themselves instantiations of the *puissance*. In classical (or even *pre*-classical) cinemas, the image-consciousness, as an overarching action-image, is often in-formed in accordance with two genericized relations: that of the situation-action-situation (SAS') or the action-situation-action (ASA').[40] For example, in the Western, a situation (S) is established and disturbed, which triggers an action (A) that seeks to restore or reconfigure this situation (S'). In a comedy, a series of actions (A) produces a situation (S), which requires further actions (A') to address and rectify it.

Yet, as an abstract drive, *puissance* cannot be expressed directly. Rather, an affection-image refers to an impulse—and vice versa—as a quality (Firstness).[41] For D. N. Rodowick, Deleuze's argument suggests that the affection-image requires the actualization of a possibility or quality (Firstness) in an actual state of things (Secondness):

> Therefore, powers-qualities can be signified in one of two ways: either through Secondness as actualized in a state of things, or for

themselves directly in the image. If expressed in relation to Secondness, Deleuze calls them "real connections"; if expressed as firstness,
he calls them "virtual conjunctions." In the former the affect is
excess. What cannot be fully expressed by an action or conflict is
experienced as a visceral response, according to the dynamics of
action and reaction in the sensorimotor whole. In the latter the
affect is abject in the sense of an objectless emotion or feeling. In
both cases affect produces a movement whose trajectory cannot be
precisely plotted.[42]

It is tempting to say that in the movement-image, affections and affects
are the responses to perception, which in turn puts action into motion.
However, for Deleuze, affections and affects act—and are acted on—as
both perceptions and actions. As Kañukurunde Ñaṇananda argues, according to the *Connected Discourses,* sensations and affections instigate the conversion of a bare cognition (an impersonal attention) to
a personal one, which is then named and informed as a recognition
(the objectivized subjective).[43] Therefore, sensations and affections are
the key in the formational process of every awareness that in-forms the
image-consciousness. In other words, there lies a virtual conjunction
in every *awareness,* not only in a specific state of things or being in the
movement-image.

Hence, classical Hollywood and European cinemas generally abide
by the following order (see Figure 7):

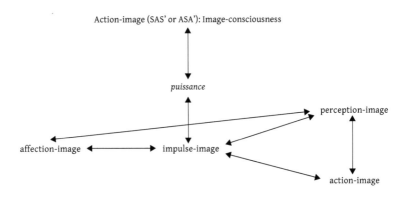

FIGURE 7. Deleuze's understanding of the movement-image

For example, *The Searchers* begins with a medium shot of the back of Martha Edwards (played by Dorothy Jordan, 1906–88) opening a door overseeing Monument Valley on the Utah-Arizona border (even though the film is set in Texas). In the beginning of this shot, the frame is almost completely dark. Even so, *puissance* has already set in motion the operation of the technicity-consciousness by actively in-forming the image as a mobile section. As the door opens, the silhouette of a woman and a doorframe are revealed, while a rock formation can be glimpsed in the background. The appearance of these forms rewrites how the *puissance* is actualized: from an impulse to see (in the dark) to an impulse to see the entire landscape of Monument Valley and then to identify who this human figure is. Hence, in the depth of forms, an impulse-image is at work, which compels the image-consciousness or anthropotechnical body to follow the movement of this human figure as she opens the door completely (see Figure 8). This impulse also motivates a camera movement—a tracking shot—from the interior to the exterior, as well as a bodily movement as Martha walks out of the house. These qualitative changes motivate a transition from a brief moment of pure impulse into a perception-image.

FIGURE 8. The opening sequence of *The Searchers:* Martha opens the door of her home onto Monument Valley.

As the camera follows Martha out of the house, it stops as she leans against a post on the terrace (see Figure 9, top). At this moment, a qualitative change occurs, as the image transitions from the perception-image (as we see Martha beholding Monument Valley) to an affection-image. The affect here is configured as an affective paradox: the sight of Martha, a motherly figure, generates a pleasing sensation and affection (beauty) as she beholds the grandiosity of Monument Valley, which initiates an overwhelming sensation and affection (sublime).[44] Notice that at this point, the subject-object position is still indiscernible, because the image is a perception of: (1) Martha perceiving; (2) the affective intensities that are actualized in the minute changes in Martha's hair and her body; and (3) the almost undetectable movements in the landscape. One of those movements is a figure riding a horse toward her, in a motion that follows her eyeline. This qualitative change enables the affection-image to transition into an action-image—via a renewed impulse to discern what is moving in the distance. Once the action is established, the image-consciousness cuts to a medium shot of Martha (see Figure 9, middle), thus showing her reaction to the action (horse-riding) and actualizing the impulse to see and explore. The image now transitions into a perception-image again. The image of Martha perceiving triggers the initiation of a sensory-perceptual link, which connects this shot to the following long shot: a closer view of the rider (see Figure 9, bottom).

The first three moments of this image can be considered what Deleuze calls *opsigns* (optical signs) and *sonsigns* (sonic signs) that rewrite—and are rewritten by—*puissance*. The actualizations of the *puissance*, as impulses, generate—and are generated by—perceptions, affections, and actions.[45] Figure 9, bottom, however, functions as a *lecto-sign*: in the movement-image, this means a sign that can be read. Notice that a carpet with a Native American design is hung in the foreground of the shot, which was not there in Figure 9, top. Hence, it is in-formed as a sign that invokes a set of relationships: that the Nʉmʉnʉʉ (Comanche) fighters are going to present themselves as an obstacle in the overall narrative. They will soon destroy the Edwards family and abduct their daughter, Debbie (Natalie Wood, 1938–81). The man riding the horse, Ethan Edwards (John Wayne, 1907–79), and Martha's adopted son, Martin Pawley (Jeffrey Hunter, 1926–69), will set out on many long journeys to search for Debbie. Meanwhile, Martin, who is one quarter Apache, will be distrusted by Ethan, thus making their journeys challenging. We

FIGURE 9. The opening sequence of *The Searchers:* Martha perceives the landscape of Monument Valley as Ethan approaches her house.

can pause and read this image as a semiotic unit because this part of the cinematographic image is also a relation-image (Thirdness): a "pure optical and sound image which breaks the sensory-motor links, over-whelms relations and no longer lets itself be expressed in terms of movement, but opens directly on to time."[46]

The interbecomings of these relationalities set up the film's overall situation, which will in turn propel a series of actions so that this initiating situation can be restored or reconfigured (SAS'). The *puissance* of the overall movement-image is instantiated as an impulse to search, which is renewed and reinstantiated from one awareness to another. What the movement-image searches for is a process of negotiation between a set of differences: (1) family safety versus individual freedom; (2) a secure patriarchal order versus its matriarchal alternative; (3) the White American sense of lawfulness, equity, and humanity as understood by the U.S. audience of the time versus (the excitement of) *physis* (nature); and (4) racial purity versus miscegenation. These differences are all inscribed onto Martha's act (she being the matriarch) of opening her family door into the wild in anticipation of the arrival of Ethan (the patriarch). It also opens the family to the potential invasion of the Numunuu: an invasion that will destroy the matriarchy and put into question the potency of the patriarch by means of miscegenation. *The Searchers,* as a movement-image, is therefore propelled by a renewal of this impulse to search from one *kṣaṇa* to another. If so, on the surface, the movement-image creates transitions between the perception-image and the action-image, a process that is occasionally intervened by real connections (affection-images). In the *mise-en-abîme,* sensations and affections—which drive impulses and are driven by them—convert bare cognitions into recognitions from one *kṣaṇa* to another.

KARMA

Baruch Spinoza's understanding of *conatus* and its Bergsonian variation, the *élan vital* (life force), are sometimes considered forms of mysticism.[47] The belief that there is an impetus that is immanent in—and emanated from—the formational process requires a leap of faith. As we have seen, in the *Fundamental Verses of the Middle Way,* Nāgārjuna demystifies the notion of a karmic impetus by illustrating that it is a perceptual-conceptual proliferation. However, Theravadin scholars would argue that in a world constituted by perceptual-conceptual proliferations, forms and the operation of the technicity-consciousness that produces them seem to both actively *tsiɛu/zhao* (vocate) and *kʌˇm/gan* (be vocated by) karma.[48] Hence, this *illusionary* impetus does exercise *real* power in the formational process.

In an attempt to define *puissance,* Deleuze cites Plotinus's (circa 204 or 205–270) discussion of Plato: "It is because *there is nothing in it* that all things come from it."[49] In other words, the impetus to vocate—and be vocated by—each phase of transduction in the formational process comes from the absence of such power. Meontologically, we can say that such an impetus *is* the emptiness of emptiness. If so, we come face-to-face with a conundrum: How does an impetus that does not exist in the first place play such an important role in the formational process?

The founders of the Yogācāra school, Asaṅga and his half brother Vasubandhu, hold two different views on such an aporia (previewed in the introduction). For them, what is at stake is that this *nothing* is not simply an absence of forms. Rather, it refers to a *kṣaṇa-as-time/kṣaṇa-as-timelessness* of nondifferentiation between presence and absence, and emptiness and existence. In this sense, as a layout of formless relationalities between mobile potentialities, this *nothing* is neither present nor absent, empty nor existent. As a *pure potentiality* (potentiality of potentiality), the same layout *is*—or, as some say, *functions as*—the impetus, which is manifested in all forms. The debate on karma that Asaṅga and Vasubandhu initiated has been historically considered one of the most philosophically challenging discussions in Buddhist philosophy. However, understanding this highly complex discourse allows us to address how the formational process operates relationally on a microtemporal/metatemporal and microperceptual/metaperceptual level, and how the operational principle or technicity initiates the substrate-form divide that underdetermines and obscures our ontological and epistemological investigations.

Asaṅga

Asaṅga bases his epistemology on two presuppositions: (1) while the potentialities (seeds) in the ālaya-consciousness are engaged in a series of contiguous modulations or a process of mediation, the layout of relationalities itself neither affects, nor is affected by, their movement; and (2) while modulations/mediation are/is represented as the six consciousnesses (as movement and time), *actualization-virtualization* is ontologically grounded neither inside nor outside—neither not inside nor not outside—time: the *kṣaṇa-as-time/kṣaṇa-as-timelessness.*

The differentiation between the seeds stored in the *ālaya*-consciousness and the *ālaya*-consciousness itself as a layout of relationalities is often confusing for scholars. One of the best illustrations of this difference can be found in the *Śūraṅgama Sūtra:*

> World Honoured One (foreign dust) [external sense data] is like a guest who stops at an inn where he passes the night or eats something and then packs and continues his journey because he cannot stay longer. As to the host of the inn, he has nowhere to go. My deduction is that one who does not stay is a guest and one who stays is a host. Consequently, a thing is "foreign" [external] when it does not stay. Again, when the sun rises in a clear sky and its light enters (the house) through an opening, the dust is seen to dance in the ray of light whereas the empty space does not move. I deduce that that which is still is the void and that which moves is the dust.[50]

Sense data (foreign dust) are impermanent forms that are perpetually in motion. These sense data, however, remain formless in the *ālaya*-consciousness until the operation of the six consciousnesses actualizes the dependent originations between the potentiality to perceive and conceptualize and the potentiality to generate signs. The dependent originations of these two potentialities constitute the internal forms (sensory-perceptual organs) and the external forms (a layout of moving dust). It is in this sense that the image is the *movement* of the dust, and such movement appears to be hosted by the space in which the dust moves. However, if this space is not a *thing*, but only a layout of the paths on which the dust travels, the existence and origination of the space depend on the existence and origination of the moving dust. This *host* (compare to the *langue*), which is the layout of the moving relationships between these particles, *actually* exists, but the self-nature of this host is its self-nature-less-ness. Meanwhile, the image in-formed by the moving dust (compare to *paroles*) exists nominally.

Fyodor Stcherbatsky argues that up until this point, the Yogācāra position is similar to Immanuel Kant's, as the layout of relationships is comparable to what Kant calls the transcendental plane. Meanwhile, the dust in the dark is comparable to the things-in-themselves, which are ungraspable until they are actualized in sensuous forms (the dust dancing in the light).[51] However, for Asaṅga, the *kṣaṇa-as-time/kṣaṇa-as-timelessness* at which the operation of the six consciousnesses is initiated lies neither inside nor outside—neither not inside nor not outside—time, even though the six consciousnesses perceive and conceptualize the actualized layout as a movement-image that endures in time. In other words, qualitative changes (a series of *kṣaṇas*) are manifestations of the *kṣaṇa-as-time/kṣaṇa-as-timelessness*. While these qualitative changes are perceived and conceptualized as a movement, the *kṣaṇa-as-time/kṣaṇa-as-timelessness* is neither mobile nor immobile and neither not mobile nor not immobile.

In order to understand this idea, let us return to the comparison between a layout of potentialities and a layout of dust particles in a dark room. When a ray of light penetrates into the dark (the initiation of the operation of the six consciousnesses), the dust is seen as "dancing" in the room. This is to say that once the six consciousnesses are put into operation at the *kṣaṇa-as-time/kṣaṇa-as-timelessness,* these potentialities are actualized as sensuous forms (in time). These actualized forms (dust dancing in the light) are therefore *neither different from nor the same as* the potentialities (dust in the dark), and *neither not different from nor not the same as* the potentialities. In Yogācāra terms, the six consciousnesses (a roomful of dust seen in the light) are the manifestations of the *ālaya*-consciousness (the room in the dark). In this sense, the *ālaya*-consciousness is neither transcendental (beyond the six consciousnesses) nor immanent (inherent within the six consciousnesses), neither not transcendental nor not immanent. Therefore, the difference and nondifference between the transcendental plane and the plane of immanence are perceptual-conceptual proliferations, not *the way it is.*[52]

In this light, when the qualitative changes in forms rewrite—and are rewritten by—the configuration of their relationalities, these formal changes affect—and are affected by—the corresponding potentialities and their relationalities. Meanwhile, the host, as a layout of *formless* relationalities, is neither moving nor unmoving and neither not moving nor not unmoving. Therefore, the layout of *potentially* changing configurations in the *ālaya*-consciousness is—or functions as—an impetus (on the technical level) that remains formless until it is actualized. As a pure potentiality from which time and movement are initiated, such a layout is neither permanent nor impermanent (*kṣaṇa-as-time/kṣaṇa-as-timelessness*). Yet, once *actualized*, it is perceived and conceptualized as a series of contiguous impulses, or an enduring *force* (or impetus on the formal level).[53]

Sarvāstivāda scholars believe that the existence and origination of this series of impulses depend on the existence and origination of a thought (an act committed by the sixth consciousness), or an action (an act committed by the body), or a speech (an act committed by the speech organs). After the extinction of the act, if a series of immediately contiguous conditions is initiated and extinguished, the karmic force is considered manifested. If the series of matching conditions are deferred and delayed, the karmic force is regarded as unmanifested (awaiting an opportunity to be manifested). In the *Abhidharma-samuccaya* [Compendium of Abhidharma], however, Asaṅga argues that action and speech are subordinate to thought, while a thought is subordinate to a *manasikara* (impulse). For him:

> What is a *manasikara* [impulse]? Its *ātmakatva* [ontological ground] is an impetus that is generated from an attachment [*manas*] to . . . a milieu [image] constituted by the interaction between the potentiality to perceive and conceptualize and the potentiality to generate signs.[54]

For Asaṅga, therefore, the *ālaya*-consciousness is a subset of a layout of *all* predispositions or possibilities (compare plane of immanence or luminosity), which is to say, all impulses. However, when *manas* attaches itself to a certain subset of dispositions and possibilities (*ālaya*-consciousness), this subset is manifested as the six consciousnesses: an avalanche of impulses. By the same token, the *ālaya*-consciousness, under the magnetic force of *manas*, now functions as an impetus that impels the formational and individuating process of a being. Its instantiation is the avalanche of impulses that configures the forms and the formational processes in accordance with these dispositions and possibilities. However, the *ālaya*-consciousness is not a closed subset. Rather, interrelated potentialities and impulses, like a roomful of dust, can travel across various subsets and initiate new processes of interbecomings. For instance, the *ālaya*-consciousness that constitutes an individuating process of a human being can overlap with the *ālaya*-consciousnesses of other individuating human and sentient beings. Thus, these individuating processes are dependently originated (transindividuations). Likewise, the karmic impulses that affect—and are affected by—these individuating processes are also dependently originated. In this sense, karma is constantly being reconfigured in a cosmic process of interbecomings.

Vasubandhu

In the *Abhidharmakośakārikā* [Verses on the treasury of Abhidharma], Vasubandhu proposes a similar theory. For him, impulses are formless relations that are stored in the *ālaya*-consciousness. However, these relations are themselves potentialities, which can either be generative (actively initiating immediately contiguous or delayed consequences) or nongenerative (remaining virtual until a new dominant condition emerges).[55] Thus, Vasubandhu expands Asaṅga's definition of potentialities to the configurative relationships between them. If so, the host itself is the empty *pure relationality* of all potentialities.

Vasubandhu's revision of Asaṅga's theory is subtle, though it has a serious meontological implication. For Asaṅga, the host, being an empty layout of relationalities, is a monistic creative impetus (a layout). Meanwhile, for Vasubandhu, if potentialities are to be considered the ontological *ground* of existences, the host would be the meontological *pure relationality*—the *lĭ*-technicity that *underdetermines* the relational configurations and pathways of all potentialities. In this pure relationality, which can be considered the emptiness of emptiness, the impetus is nowhere to be found. Yet, as a pure relationality, it is actualized as impulses (configurative relationalities) that are responsible for all modes of existence, based on the differentiations between substrate and form, subject and object, time and timelessness, and movement and nonmovement.

Dharmapāla (530–61) calls the host itself the *ultimate existence:*

> If someone follows the axiom of *śūnyatā* (emptiness), practices benevolent [thoughts, speeches, and acts], and attains the ultimate dignified fruit, they should arrive at a belief and understanding—that emptiness is the only actual existence. All the other existences are nominal ones that are transient manifestations of the Tathāgata [neither moving nor not moving, or Buddhahood]. As the Buddha says, there are two kinds of manifestations: emptiness and non-emptiness. If we have any doubts about non-emptiness, we can work through it logically by comparing it with emptiness. We will arrive at the conclusion that all forms are empty and their emptiness is unrepresentable and non-differentiable. They are ultimately *one:*

that is, they are formless. The nature of all forms is inarticulable in language, that is, it is unrepresentable. This nature is also not generated by the dependent originations of the potentiality to perceive and conceptualize and the potentiality to generate signs; it is not generated by dependent originations. Therefore, it is non-differentiable. Since all forms are generated out of these two kinds of dependent originations, this nature is formless. This ultimate emptiness is neither empty nor not empty. Therefore, it is formless and monistic (non-differentiated). But then, since formlessness is named a form, we can call this the ultimate form.[56]

Bhāviveka (circa 500–78), a self-proclaimed follower of Nāgārjuna, criticizes Dharmapāla for confusing emptiness with form:

If we observe the existence of a form that is formless, which is manifested as an uninterrupted whole, we should follow the axiom of dependent originations and observe its empty nature, until emptiness is no longer a form or manifestation. Rather, formlessness is form. Emptiness, by definition, means that there is no self-nature, or that its nature is empty. Based on this understanding, its form cannot be actual; rather, it cannot possibly exist. Based on the principle of formlessness, we can see that form and formlessness are one.[57]

Bhāviveka therefore argues that the ālaya-consciousness, as a layout of potentialities, is not the ultimate existence. Rather, it is the ultimate emptiness: neither empty nor existent, neither not empty nor not existent. But then, for him, this difference between ultimate existence and ultimate emptiness seems to be a semiotic and polemical one.

To resolve this question, Bhāviveka furthers his argument by calling his readers' attention to a conundrum. Nāgārjuna's argumentation is termed the catuṣkoṭi (four-cornered negation). Bhāviveka argues that it is unclear whether Nāgārjuna refers to: (1) a paryudāsa (implicative negation), which means that the doubly negated statement should be regarded as affirmative—that the ultimate existence or emptiness is at once empty and existent; or (2) a niṣedha (nonimplicative negation or existential negation), which means that this ultimate existence or emptiness is neither empty nor existent, neither not empty nor not existent.[58] Bhāviveka explains that an implicative negation refers to the intricately interdependent relationship between lakṣaṇas (forms) and śūnyatā (emptiness). Thus, it is the relationality between form and emptiness that is an impetus (substrate), even though this relationality is

empty of existential value (formless). Meanwhile, an existential negation suggests that the ultimate existence or emptiness, which is inarticulable in terms of the difference between existence and emptiness,
actively *functions as* an impetus (a form-producing formlessness), even
though it does so as a pure relationality (substrate). For Bhāviveka, both
arguments configure this layout as a monistic substrate. They fail to
understand the relationship between substrate and form *relationally*,
that substrate is neither different nor the same as form, neither not
different from nor not the same as form. Meontologically, the difference
between substrate and form, as far as this layout is concerned, is inoperative (that is, the difference between operative and inoperative is no
longer meaningful and purposeful).

   Scholars who follow the debate between Dharmapāla and Bhāviveka
call this *actual existence/ultimate emptiness* the Tathāgatagarbha: the womb
or storehouse from which *the way it is* is generated. The Tathāgatagarbha
is neither substrate nor form, neither not substrate nor not form; it is
neither form nor formlessness. Once manifested, it is instantiated as the
substrate of all forms *in relation to* all forms: the plane of luminosity.

   The Tathāgatagarbha understanding of image-formation therefore
matches Gilles Deleuze's notion of the movement-image: that the
movement-image is initiated out of the *puissance*. But then, "It is because
there is nothing in it that all things come from it."[59] Yet Deleuze's understanding of the *puissance* still implicitly posits this nothingness as a
monistic ontological ground (substrate). What Bhāviveka teaches us is
that this *puissance* or karma is not initiated out of nothing, but rather is
a pure relationality that is neither substrate/nothing nor form/some-
thing, neither not substrate/not nothing nor not form/not something.
Karma neither exists nor not exists in this pure relationality, but it is
everywhere in the operation of the six consciousnesses and is instantiated as the initiating impulse in every step of the formational process.
It *exists* and exerts real impact on the configurational changes of all
relationalities precisely because it is a perceptual-conceptual proliferation: the microtemporal/metatemporal and microperceptual/metaper-
ceptual force that constitutes our mode of existence. It also obscures
the pure relationality itself by differentiating form from substrate,
movement from time, and object from subject.

   Deleuze's understanding of the movement-image, in Buddhist terms,
is largely based on an image's *parikalpitah-svabhāva:* that is, its nature of

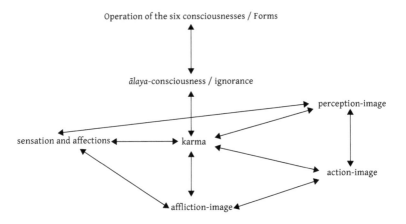

FIGURE 10. The karma-image

being initiated out of the dependent originations between internal and external forms via sensations and affections, perceptions, volition, and the consciousnesses. In Buddhism, this is called the *jñeyāvaraṇa* (obstruction of the ultimate emptiness, or actual existence, by taking forms as knowledge). For Yogācāra scholars, an image also has *paratantras-vabhāva:* the nature of its being initiated out of dependent originations, impelled by impulses.[60] When we ignorantly oblige ourselves to these karmic impulses or surrender our agency to karma, *kilesas/kleśas* (afflictions) are initiated: namely, avarice, frustration and anger, delusion, arrogance, suspicion, worry, sorrow, suffering, and anxiety. The movement-image is therefore a karma-image, and the karma-image affects—and is affected by—the affliction-image.

Reinterpreted in Buddhist terms, Deleuze's understanding of the movement-image can be remapped with karma being the microtemporal/metatemporal and microperceptual/metaperceptual driving force in the formational process (see Figure 10).[61]

THE KARMA-IMAGE AND THE AFFLICTION-IMAGE

How is the circulation between the perception-image and action-image instigated by a series of karmic impulses? As I mentioned earlier, Asaṅga argues that a *manasikara* (impulse) initiates an act of thinking, that is, the operation of the sixth consciousnesses, while a thought initiates an action or a speech.[62] Hence, in a virtual conjunction, sensations and affections vocate, and are vocated by, an impulse to initiate an act of thinking and a thought, *before* the image transitions to the perception-image or the action-image. Again, an act of thinking or a thought is by definition unmanifested, even though it can be expressed as a relation-image or reflection-image. The reflection-image refers to a "sign which, instead of referring to its object, reflects another (*scenographic* or *plastic image*); or which reflects its own object, but by inverting it (inverted image); or which directly reflects its object (*discursive image*)."[63]

For Asaṅga, this impulse can be subcategorized into:

1. The impulse-itself
2. The impulse to attach the six consciousnesses to the existence of the self, so that the movements of all the sense data can cohere into a form
3. The impulse to subjugate the operation of the six consciousnesses to the twelve *nidānas* and to the dispositions that encode—and are encoded by—a layout of actualized forms
4. The impulse to reconfigure the dispositions of these actualized forms, which will in turn recode the forms and their potentialities
5. The impulse to liberate the six consciousnesses from karma.[64]

In the cinema, the first kind of impulse—the *manasikara*-itself—can be understood as the initiation of an avalanche of awarenesses from one *kṣaṇa* to another. The second and the third kinds of impulses are responsible for generating attachment and longing, which in turn produce afflictions. The fourth kind can generate either attachment and longing, or a longing for detachment. Meanwhile, the fifth kind is an instantiation of an impetus to attain insight. The karma-image operates only on the first four kinds of impulses.[65]

These impulses appear to codify, and are codified by, those dispositions specific to the form of the sentient being and its body. For example, the human form and its formational process are codified differently from the feline form. In the context of the cinema, dispositions seem to underdetermine (that is, determines from *below* as an *infra*-structure; see chapter 1), and are underdetermined by, one's gender, sexuality, socioeconomic classes, historical and political conditions, and personal experiences from the past. Some of these dispositions are therefore *common,* since the ālaya-consciousnesses of a number of individuated beings can overlap and be transindividuated with one another; while others are specific to an individual. These dispositions underdetermine whether an impulse will produce a consequence contiguously (manifested), or a deferred or delayed consequence (unmanifested). The strength of a disposition depends on how strong the six consciousnesses are attached to by *manas*.[66]

Like sensations and affections, impulses and dispositions belong to the order of Firstness, which can only be expressed as virtual conjunctions or via a state of being (Secondness). As I argued in my previous film analysis, impulses are in operation as soon as the opening awareness is initiated in a film. In the case of *The Searchers,* as I suggested, the darkness that precedes the image of Martha's opening the door vocates—and is vocated by—an avalanche of impulses to discern this electromagnetic field of darkness by searching for what the previous awarenesses were. This retrospective search, however, is expressed as a protention: an anticipation of the introduction of light into the image. This impulse to search is then reproduced, repeated, and reconfigured from one *kṣaṇa* to another, which then becomes the foundational impulse of the formational process of the entire karma-image.

As Martha opens the door and reveals the silhouette of her body in the foreground overlooking Monument Valley in the background, the impulse to search is renewed as an instantiation of a set of symbolic differences (Thirdness). This act of thinking and thought are initiated by a disposition rested in the operation of the six consciousnesses: the potentiality to perceive and conceptualize and also the potentiality to generate signs. As Christian Metz argues, cinematographic denotation is always more-or-less motivated by dispositions.[67] For example, the form in the background would be immediately recognized not as any natural landscape, but as Monument Valley: a symbolic substitute or transference of *physis,* masculinity, freedom (from the law), the potentiality of encountering the *other* (Native Americans), danger of miscegenation, and even individual determination. In the same process, the silhouette of Martha is immediately recognized as home, femininity, obedience to the law, protection from the *other,* racial purity, and collective determination.

The impulses and dispositions that initiate the opening of this karma-image are centered on an attachment to the ego. The longing for a reaffirmation that these awarenesses are existent produces afflictions instantaneously. In other words, *impulses and dispositions are always expressed in afflictions.*

For example, in Figure 8, the camera is compelled to follow Martha out the door in order to permit a full view of the overall environment. Such a compulsion is motivated by an avarice to know, a frustration that the view has been partially obstructed, and even a delusion that a further movement will enable the body to command *all* that exists. The same dispositions are expressed in the shot/reverse-shot structure between the medium shot of Martha (see Figure 9, middle) and the long shot of Ethan (see Figure 9, bottom). They are also expressed in two of the subsequent shots in the film: (1) a medium shot of Martha, in which her husband, Aaron (Walter Coy, 1909–74) enters the frame from the left, exchanges glances with Martha as he stands beside her, and walks toward the camera with his gaze fixated on Ethan offscreen; (2) a long shot taken from the side of the house's front porch, where Lucy (Pippa Scott) and Debbie (Lana Wood) have also gathered to look. They are later joined by Ben (Robert Lyden, 1942–86). Although the Edwardses are perceived and conceptualized as the seers, their subjectivities are yet to be in-formed in the karma-image. Rather, the anthropotechnical body perceives and conceptualizes these seers, who are engaged in the act of perceiving.

Such subjectival indetermination, however, does not cease even when the film cuts to a long shot of Ethan approaching the house over Aaron's shoulder (after two intermediary inserts of the children). Then, the film cuts to a medium shot of Lucy and Ben, where Lucy exclaims, "That's your Uncle Ethan!" This exclamation inscribes an individuality and subjectivity onto Ethan's body. When the film cuts back to the over-the-shoulder shot of Ethan, who dismounts from his horse and walks up to Aaron, this subjectivity is further confirmed by the face of John Wayne, enhanced by his recognizability and his position in the frame—marked by the two famous peaks of Monument Valley in the background (see Figure 11).

This over-the-shoulder shot does not inscribe the anthropotechnical body's point of view (that is to say, the perception of the technicity-consciousness as a whole) onto either Aaron's or Ethan's body. Rather, the anthropotechnical body remains the primary perceiving body, whereas the entire milieu is apprehended as a layout of external forms. This example illustrates that a shot/reverse-shot structure does not automatically indicate a point of view and initiate any identification. It merely confirms that this milieu is karmically common between the

FIGURE 11. The opening sequence of *The Searchers:* Ethan walks up to Aaron, a moment of transindividuation.

anthropotechnical body and the operation of the six consciousnesses of all these sentient beings. In Figure 11, the cinematic technicity-consciousness begins to enable a *transindividuation* between the anthropotechnical body and Ethan's.

Such a transindividuation is rendered possible by afflictions. In Figure 11, a potentiality to generate afflictions is embedded in Ethan's costume: a worn-out Confederate Army uniform. This insinuates a possible conflict between Ethan and the law (of the Union) and a possible clash between his and the others' sociopolitical values. However, these dispositions introduced by Ethan's presence do not produce any immediate consequences. The first possible affliction is actualized that evening, when Ethan reveals that he is carrying a bag of gold and gives Lucy a badge that indicates his involvement in the Mexican campaign (1862–67). This sense of uncertainty of his history is aggravated when Captain Clayton (Ward Bond, 1903–60), who visits the Edwardses the next morning, suggests that Ethan fits the description of someone who has stolen gold during that campaign.

Our suspicion that Ethan is a criminal, our anxieties about his inevitable separation from his family and his land, or even about his persecution and possible execution, initiate a longing to attach to the image and the ego, thus propelling the cinematic technicity-consciousness as a whole (or the anthropotechnical body) to perceive and conceptualize this image as existent. However, these afflictions are largely displaced and delayed, from one scene to another, by the image's attention on the second affliction of the film: fear of miscegenation (discussed in the following section).

Our anxieties about Ethan's criminality and his inevitable separation from the Edwardses are not expressed as an affliction-image until the end of the film, when Ethan brings Debbie to the front terrace of the homestead of the Jorgensens (the Edwardses' neighbors). In this long shot, Ethan initially refrains from stepping onto the terrace, while the Jorgensens take Debbie into the house. As they walk toward the camera, the camera dollies back into the darkness of the house, thus reversing the movement of the opening shot of the film. Ethan is then seen stepping onto the terrace, but at the same time, Martin Pawley and his fiancée, Laurie Jorgensen (Vera Miles), walk past him and enter the house as well. Ethan is left in the middle of the frame outside the house, putting his left hand over his right arm (see Figure 12). Here, Wayne borrows this gesture from William S. Hart (1864–1946), who was one of Hollywood's first Western heroes but was largely forgotten by the time he died. Ethan then turns around and walks into the wilderness. In this sense, all the afflictions—anxieties, attachments, and sorrow—generated by Ethan's conditions are expressed and transferred to this final gesture.

FIGURE 12. The affliction-image of anxieties, worries, and sorrows

FEAR OF MISCEGENATION: SECOND AFFLICTION

The second affliction—fear of miscegenation—however, becomes the central drive that initiates the movements of the karma-image. In the second sequence of the film, the Edwardses are having dinner together.[68] Soon after they have started, the film cuts to a long shot of Martin riding a horse toward the house. This shot is framed by the door in a manner that invokes a symbolic comparison between Ethan (a war-torn patriarch who will no longer be part of the family) and Martin (an unbridled young man who will grow up and become a patriarch). When Martin enters the house, Ethan is taken aback by his appearance and suspects that Martin is a "half-breed." Martin confesses that he is one quarter Apache. Martha then explains that they took him in when he was a child because his parents were killed by the Texas Rangers. In this scene, Martin sits next to Ethan on the left side of a long table. However, the incommensurability between Ethan and Martin is expressed by the lack of any overlap between their milieus, as their respective consciousnesses are entirely separated by the camera's alternating between their medium close-ups. Their difference is then further demarcated by a lamp (see Figure 13), an object that obscures the contiguity between the spaces they occupy.

The anxieties about miscegenation and the attachment to racial purity are therefore expressed in this affliction-image. Yet, amid a family who was willing to take in Martin, the dispositions that in-form Ethan's impulses are not entirely in accord with those of the Edwardses. Here, such a disagreement configures another affliction: a frustration over this disagreement. Such afflictions, however, draw the attention of the technicity-consciousness as a whole (or the anthropotechnical body) to the milieu as a layout of causes and conditions, with a strong attachment to, and a longing for, finding out and knowing how these conditions are going to be actualized in the rest of the karma-image. In fact, this affliction-image demonstrates that such an attachment does not require the cinematic technicity-consciousness's dispositions to be in accord with the protagonist's, unless a spectator's dispositions are far stronger than the protagonist's. For instance, most spectators who do not agree with Ethan's racism will still be able to indulge themselves in the rest of the karma-image, whereas a Native American spectator may find it impossible to do so from this point on.

FIGURE 13. The affliction-image of the anxieties about miscegenation and an attachment to racial purity

This affliction-image initiates not only a movement on the overt level (the alternation between perception and action), but also a movement on the covert level, constituted by the initiations of the acts of thinking and thoughts. As Thierry Kuntzel (1948–2007) and Raymond Bellour argue, this covert level can also be regarded as the film's semiotic trajectory, marked by a series of delays, deferrals, transferences, and displacements of the afflictions crystallized here (that is to say, karma).[69]

For example, two sequences later, the Edwardses, who implicitly disapprove of the killing of the Nʉmʉnʉʉ warriors, will be invaded and themselves killed mercilessly. In this event, both Lucy and Debbie are abducted. While Lucy will be found raped and killed later, Debbie is believed to be living with the warriors. This invasion seems to justify Ethan's dispositions and his unconditional rage against the Nʉmʉnʉʉ warriors. His afflictions therefore initiate his impulses to undertake his obsessive search not for Debbie, but for the warriors who took her. The karma-image therefore takes the form of a series of episodes, which, as Viktor Shklovsky (1893–1984) argues, defers and delays the completion of this search.[70] His wrath is crystallized again in a search mission after Lucy's funeral. In this search, the party finds a burial ground of some unknown Nʉmʉnʉʉ warriors. The party members remove a stone that covers one of the graves. At the sight of the warrior's body, Ethan furiously shoots its eyes out, raises the stone, and throws it onto the corpse's head in order to crush it.

Ethan's rancor makes it difficult for non-white-supremacists and Native Americans to ever transindividuate with him under his conviction. The karma-image therefore propels—and is propelled by—a karmic force to look for an opportunity of reconciliation. This opportunity arrives when Ethan and Martin visit Scar (Henry Brandon, 1912–90)—before they confirm that Scar was the warrior who captured Debbie—who confesses that his own rage is driven by a search for retribution for the murder of his two sons by white Americans. This confession does not produce an immediate reconciliation between Ethan and Scar, though it enables the cinematic technicity-consciousness as a whole (or the anthropotechnical body) to catch a glimpse of the dependent originations between Ethan's karma and Scar's: a momentary window that opens into the layout of the karmic relationships as *the way it is* (relation-image and reflection-image).

This momentary insight, however, has the effect of differentiating the karmic force that drives Ethan to search for Scar and kill him (a malevolent karmic force that solicits a retribution in the future) from the karmic force that drives Martin to search for Debbie (a benevolent karmic force). In the following sequence, in a long shot, when Ethan and Martin are packing up their campsite on a riverbank, Debbie is seen running down a slope behind them toward a natural-earth crossing.

Martin runs toward the crossing in order to meet Debbie. In a series of shots/reverse-shots, Debbie uses (supposedly) *nɨmɨ tekwapɨ* (the Nɨmɨnɨɨ language) to ask Martin to leave, while Martin tries to persuade Debbie in English to acknowledge her memory of him. She eventually confesses in Martin's language that she remembers, though she has long given up her hope for her rescue. The film transitions to a perception-image of Ethan (a low-angle medium shot) walking slowly toward the camera, with his hand grabbing his pistol. When the film returns to the shot/reverse-shot structure between Debbie and Martin, she tells Martin that the Nɨmɨnɨɨ are her people now. This initiates an impulse in Ethan to pull out his pistol in his medium shot and an impulse in the anthropotechnical body to command the overall milieu by means of a 180-degree cut to a long shot of the riverbank (see Figure 14), where Martin uses his body to cover Debbie in fear that Ethan will shoot her. The difference between Ethan's malevolent karma and Martin's benevolent one is now fully expressed.

Although no reconciliation ever takes place between Ethan and Scar, and among the white settlers and the Native Americans, a displaced reconciliation is attained between Ethan's karmic force and Martin's. Yet this transference is not achieved until Martin sneaks into the

FIGURE 14. The confrontation between Ethan's malevolent karma and Martin's benevolent one

Numunuu village in preparation for the Texas Rangers' final invasion. In the tent, in the embrace of Martin's half-naked body, Debbie asks for her rescue. Their embrace invokes a longing both for the erotic sensation of being with a young white male body and for the *Heimlich* (familiarity) of an idealized and idolized kinship between two white bodies that are at once represented—perversely—as siblings and lovers.[71] Under such wholesomeness/eroticism, Debbie—as well as the cinematic technicity-consciousness as a whole—experiences a surging attachment to *whiteness.* This does not mean that the spectators become white supremacists. Rather, it means that the spectators—having been transduced as one with the cinematic technicity-consciousness—have subtly driven, and been driven by, a series of karmic impulses that carry the dispositions (*dispositif*) that long for a reaffirmation of the authority and economy of desire associated with whiteness. As Richard Dyer suggests, whiteness is a concrete set of power relations that is in-formed not only by a *structure of difference,* but also by the absence of any position from which differences are initiated.[72] In fact, whiteness is effaced by means of its instantiation as universal humanism: the benevolent act of rescuing Debbie from her captor.

A force initiated by a blind attachment to an impetus that is fundamentally empty—of which whiteness is a prime example—is karma. This is not to say that *The Searchers* fundamentally drives, and is driven by, racism and white supremacy. On the one hand, the karmic force, which initiates and propels the movement-image, generates a longing for the erotic pleasure and familiarity promised by whiteness. On the other, it puts on display, through Ethan's blind rage and the afflictions embodied by his final gesture (see Figure 14), the ignorance that propels a search under a conviction that is fundamentally empty.

THE PERSISTENCE OF THE KARMA-IMAGE

Many of the claims I have made in this analysis correspond to readings that can be arrived at via major strands in film theories: cognitivism and aesthetics, structuralism, poststructuralism, phenomenology, and Deleuzian philosophy, to name a few. This is because each of these methods accounts for an aspect of the human impulse to vocate, and be vocated by, the desire to *image* and *imagine.* Each method explicates on, or inadvertently reveals, how an impulse that initiates both the potentiality to perceive and conceptualize and the potentiality to generate signs is, in turn, driven by a layout of dispositions. It also demonstrates how we film spectators actively—knowingly as well as unknowingly—inscribe these dispositions onto all those perceptual-conceptual proliferations we take for granted as independently existent, without knowing or even acknowledging our interdependencies.

The karma-image has never been—and will never be—in crisis. This is because the attachment to the ego and the longing for imaging and imagining are always in operation—and cannot be conceived otherwise. Such an operation conceals *the way it is:* the fundamental emptiness of the impetus that gives us a sense of ontological consistency. Jacques Lacan (1901–81) calls this the unlivable Real.[73] In other words, the cinematographic technicity-consciousness has always been in-formed out of a need to disavow this ontological crisis. Hence, as long as we are indulged in karma and adhere steadfastly to the formation of the ego, and as long as we are not willing to take agency over our own ontological crisis, the karma-image will persist. Still, by understanding how karma operates and how it generates an *existence* in time-movement, we can bring to the fore the relationship between the consciousness and its technicity. By being mindful of the way karma configures and codifies such a relationship, we can actively rewrite this process of reconfiguration and initiate changes through this ongoing process of transductions and transindividuations.

CHAPTER 3

THE INSIGHT-IMAGE

What is an insight-image? How does a cinematic technicity-consciousness become mindful of the way it is? Again, as defined by Gilles Deleuze and Buddhist philosophy, technicity-consciousness is to be understood as the anthropotechnical body—together with the embodied mind and its associated milieu (the "film image")—which is capable of sensing, perceiving, acting and being acted on, and thinking.

The *point de départ* of this chapter is the time-image. A time-image, however, is not necessarily an insight-image. As D. N. Rodowick points out, the time-image does not guarantee an existential liberation or a site of political resistance.[1] Instead, by drawing the six consciousnesses' mindfulness to a pure optical and sound situation in which time—as an abstract relation—can be reflected on as though it were a sensuous form, the time-image often initiates an attachment to time-as-form.

In the first chapter of *Cinema 2*, Deleuze argues that in the cinema, a pure optical and sound situation can only be apprehended by contrast with a sensory-motor situation. He defines a sensory-motor situation as a "setting which is already specified and presupposes an action which discloses it, or prompts a reaction which adapts to or modifies it. But a purely optical or sound situation becomes established in what we might call 'any-space-whatever'. . . ." In the time-image, the "sensory-motor connections are now valid only by virtue of the upsets that affect, loosen, unbalance, or uncouple them. . . . No longer being induced by an action, any more than it is extended into one, the optical and sound situation is, therefore, neither an index nor a synsign." Instead, in the

113

time-image, there are *opsigns* and *sonsigns*, in which the difference between subject and object is indiscernible.[2]

Nonetheless, if a pure optical and sound situation is understood as
a sign, it should have already been mediated by a mental image. For
Charles Sanders Peirce, such a mental image (representamen) serves as
a reference that connects the sign to the object.[3] Thus, it is already a
recognition driven by karma, that is, an objectivized subjective that is
part and parcel of the sensory-motor system. But how does a karma-
image leave open the potentiality of initiating an insight?

Deleuze circumvents this problem in his chapter 2, where he privileges Pier Paolo Pasolini's im-sign as the fundamental semiotic unit of
the cinema: a pure optical and sound situation that is pre-grammatical
and pre-morphological, that is, being in the language of memories and
dreams (see my chapter 1). In a formational process, the potentiality to
generate an im-sign, and the potentiality to perceive and conceptualize
(image-imagine) it, are actualized from the unconscious—or, in Buddhist terms, the *ālaya*-consciousness. Yet, an im-sign does not immediately surrender itself to a series of karmic impulses to initiate sensations
and affections (as in a karma-image). Instead, the consciousness can
remain mindful of its own technicity. Therefore, while the im-sign has
been actualized as an image-consciousness (objectivized subjective *reality*), it can remain *open* as a layout of potentialities. It is in this sense
that these open im-signs are characterized by a "principle of . . .
indiscernibility: we no longer know what is imaginary or real, physical
or mental, in the situation, not because they are confused, but because
we do not have to know and there is no longer even a place from which
to ask."[4] The image-consciousness is therefore mindful of—and capable
of letting be—its own technicity.

In *Cinema 2*, Deleuze enumerates his observations on how European,
American, and Japanese cinemas—primarily since the 1940s—have
managed to use specific stylemes (stylistic units) to bring the technicity-
consciousness to mindfulness. He uses Henri Bergson's understanding
of time and temporalities and Peirce's semiotics to theorize how the
time-image upsets the sensory-motor operations and expectations until
the consciousness becomes mindful of the technicity of time. However,
Deleuze has yet to explicate on what exactly these stylemes do—at a
critical juncture in the formational process—so as to disconceal the
insight into the relationality between technicity and consciousness. In

this chapter, then, I argue that such disconcealment is rendered possible when the technicity-consciousness assumes an agency over its karmic operation. I do so by reconfiguring Deleuze's discussion of the time-image step-by-step through the Buddhist discourses of time.

As I shall illustrate, for Buddhist scholars and practitioners, what is at stake in this process is not time, but *consciousness-as-insight*. An insight-image disconceals not only the technicity of a consciousness in an existential and epistemological sense, but also in a political sense. At the end of this chapter, I analyze how Pema Tseden's *Tharlo* [2015] enables the image-consciousness to become mindful of the existential and political technicities and technologies that put *life* into a deindividuated, desubjectivized, and deautonomized position, and I examine how such an insight enables the consciousness to render such technics and powers meaningless.

RECOLLECTIONS, DREAMS, AND THE CRYSTAL-IMAGE

On a day-to-day basis, we rarely pay attention to the present. Rather, we live in circuits between recollections and anticipations. When I feel thirsty and want to drink some water, I seldom pay attention to the sensations and affections that in-form my thirst and my desire for water. Rather, a recollection of these sensations and affections habitually stimulates an impulse to simply grab a glass of water. By the time I grab the glass, I have already diverted my attention to the next sentence I am about to compose. Hence, we always think that a recognition is an image-consciousness of an object—a state of being with my desire to drink, a glass of water, and the act of drinking. Yet, what constitutes this recognition is both a recollection of the object and an anticipation of what we want or what will happen in the future. In *Matter and Memory*, Bergson calls this an automatic or habitual recognition.[5]

For Deleuze, every recognition in the movement-image is built on a recollection of the past, which stimulates an immediate anticipation of the future. Thus, Deleuze argues that automatic recognition "works by extension: perception extends itself into the usual movements; the movements extend perception so as to draw on its useful effects." As a result, "we constantly distance ourselves from the first object: we pass from one object to *another one,* according to a movement that is horizontal or of associations of images, but remaining on *one and the same plane.*"[6]

Meanwhile, if I turn my attention to a tree outside my window, the perception does not extend itself into associational movements. Rather, a relationship is formed between the subtle movements of the tree and of my perceiving body. The interdependent relationship between the moving object and the moving body constantly redraws my attention to the object itself, thus enabling me to refresh the object's contours and to relearn my relationship with it. In this form of recognition—which Bergson calls attentive recognition—the same object passes through various temporal planes.[7] In such a formational process, I become mindful of my consciousness as a pure relationality between the tree and my body, which is modulated from one moment to another.

As formational processes, both automatic and attentive recognitions endure over time. In an automatic recognition, the present is always concealed as a neglected interval between a retrospective regard to the past (virtual) and an anticipation of the future (virtual). In an attentive recognition, I let go and let be the circulation between my retrospection and anticipation. Therefore, despite the fact that the formational process of such a recognition endures in chronos, I become mindful that both virtual planes of existences (a temporal circuit) are reflections that are immanent in—and are emanated from—a relationality: an actualization *here and now*, which I usually ignore in automatic recognition.

In *Matter and Memory*, Bergson draws the schema shown in Figure 15 to illustrate the temporal relations that constitute an attentive recognition. In this schema, O represents the object as recognized *here and now* (actual). In an automatic recognition, this image will be in-formed as a circuit (A) between a recollection and an anticipation, which will produce an impulse to initiate another object. In an attentive recognition, circuit A reverts back to the object, thus in-forming circuit B. This circuit draws the consciousness's attention not only to the object *here and now*, but also to the technicity (the temporal circuit) that in-forms it. Such mindfulness—a mental capacity to reflect on the technicity-consciousness as *the way it is*—can be considered circuit B'.

As this process continues, circuits A–B–C–D can be regarded as circuits of recollection-anticipation *as* consciousnesses, whereas O–B'–C'–D' are the reflections on their operating technicities. Alternatively, we can say that A–B–C–D are the manifestations of O–B'–C'–D'. The farther these circuits ripple out, the more the technicity-consciousness becomes mindful of these relationalities. Based on his reinterpretation

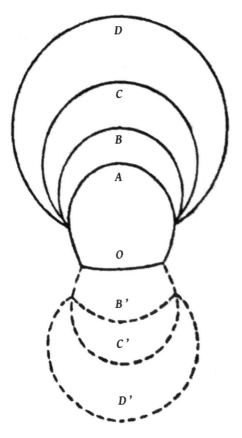

FIGURE 15. Bergson's first schema of time, in *Matière et mémoire. Essai sur la relation du corps à l'esprit* (1939; Paris: Presses Universitaires de France, 2019), 115

of Bergson's understanding of the dream image, Deleuze argues that *"the dream represents the largest visible circuit or 'the outermost envelope' of all the circuits."* In this outermost visible circuit, the recollection of the object is abstracted as a layout of pure optical and sound sensations and impulses. Such a pure optical and sound situation is a manifestation of an insight into the relationalities between sensations and affections, desires, frustrations, and impulses as a technical layout. For Deleuze, the manifestation itself is a "total dream image."[8]

This process of transduction, which constitutes the attentive recognition, can be regarded as the operating principle of the time-image. Deleuze calls its most fundamental cinematic instantiation a crystal-image. He borrows this term from Félix Guattari (1930–92), who compares the crystal of time as a *ritornello*: a musical refrain in a folk dance, to which the performer(s) would return repeatedly after the theme and each variation.[9] The refrain can be compared to the actualized *here and now* (0), to which the music insistently and repeatedly returns. Meanwhile, the theme and variations can be considered circuits of recollection-anticipation. Each variation is a manifestation of the relationalities (harmonic structures and melodic motifs) that constitute it, and each new variation instantiates a more profound and abstract derivation of these relations. These relations (sensations, affections, and impulses) gradually affect—and are affected by—the musicians, until the outermost audible circuit becomes a total *fantasia* out of the technicity-consciousness's own volition.

As a styleme, the technicity-consciousness of the *ritornello* or crystal-image operates on the technicity of these circuits until the *relationalities between these circuits* become forms. It is in this sense that the consciousness becomes a pure manifestation of its disconcealed technicity: it becomes mindful of itself.

DAYBREAK: THE INSIGHT-IMAGE AS AN ANTHROPOTECHNICAL TRANSINDIVIDUATION

In *Cinema 2,* Deleuze refers to the narrative pattern in *Le jour se lève* [*Daybreak,* Marcel Carné, 1939] as an example of what could have been a crystal-image. Gilles Deleuze complains that Carné is too eager to signal to the spectators the difference between the actual (present) and the virtual (recollections) by stylistic strategies, including dissolves and superimpositions. Moreover, for Deleuze, the film's "flashbacks" not only are unified by, but even stem from, a centralizing affective source: the anger expressed by François (Jean Gabin, 1904–76), which gives the film a *surlinéarité* (super-linearity).[10] For me, Deleuze's reading of the relationship between the actual and virtual in the film is far too *literal*. If we are engaged not only in the *récit*, but also in the *mise-en-scène* of the film, we will notice that the distinction between the present and recollections is not always certain. In fact, François's anger is the key to our understanding of how a cinematographic technicity-consciousness gradually becomes mindful of its own operation.

Daybreak is the story of a foundry worker named François, who kills Valentin (Jules Berry, 1883–1951) at the beginning of the film (offscreen). He then locks himself up in his studio apartment all night, awaiting the inevitable invasion by the police, who have already besieged him soon after his neighbors heard the gunshots. The film alternates between brief moments of François, in his mentally agonized state, defending his position in his apartment from the police's attempted invasions, and long flashbacks of his romantic relationships with Françoise (Jacqueline Laurent) and Clara (Arletty, screen name of Léonie Marie Julie Bathiat, 1898–1992). The narrative pattern therefore instantiates Henri Bergson's first schema of time.

As Deleuze argues, at first glance, the image unfolds with a seemingly clear sense of temporality organized around François's state of agony: that the man, who stays in the apartment in the present, reminisces about his romance with Françoise in the past through flashbacks.[11] In these flashbacks, François and the cinematic technicity-consciousness begin to suspect that Françoise has always maintained an intimate relationship with Valentin, an animal trainer who performs a dog act in a variety show. Meanwhile, Valentin's assistant, Clara, who works for Valentin under abusive and codependent conditions, falls in love with François. In the film, François is portrayed as a young, virile, honest, and masculine working man. In contrast, as Ben McCann and Richard Dyer argue respectively in their analyses, Valentin is mostly seen in the first half of the film, under the gaze of François, as a fragile, perfidious, and effeminate (some may even say homosexual) older fraud.[12]

The mendacity of Valentin, I argue, is a key prompting us to question the film's *surlinéarité*. It is first hinted at by the film via a collection of postcards of well-known scenic sites around Europe, pinned onto the frame of Françoise's vanity mirror. In a medium close-up, François examines these postcards closely and verbalizes his fantasies of spending time with her in these places. He then sits down next to her, at the edge of her bed, asking her whether she has ever been to these places. Françoise confesses that she has never been; but someone (Valentin) has told her about these places, to the extent that she can visualize them in her head and tell François their details. Later in the film, François learns from Clara that Valentin said the same thing in order to woo her. Meanwhile, Valentin himself has never been to those places.

Lying and being lied to are therefore experiences that mediate François's relationship with Françoise and Clara, the two women's relationships with Valentin, and eventually François's relationship with Valentin. In the film, lying can be understood in several registers: (1) lying as the fundamental relationality of which the time-image (consciousness) and its technicity (a layout of circuits of recollection-anticipation; see Figure 15 again) are its instantiations; (2) lying as a metaphor, in which Valentin, whose name invokes romance, mediates human relationships by means of lying; and (3) lying as an image: that the photographic image—consisting of the postcards and the cinematographic image itself—is not to be taken as evidence of lived memories; instead, it presents itself as a fantasy that is in-formed by the characters' shared lies.

Unlike Deleuze, I propound that once the technicity-consciousness as a whole (that is, the anthropotechnical body, together with the embodied mind and the associated milieu) becomes mindful of lying as the fundamental condition of the formational process, the temporal relations between the *object* (O in Figure 15; the murder in the film) and the circuits of recollection-anticipation (or we can call them temporal circuits; A–B–C–D and O'–B'–C'–D' in Figure 15) are no longer ones between the actualized present and flashbacks (virtual images). Rather, each temporal circuit is in-formed out of a deeper understanding of the implicit acts of lying that these optical and sonic situations come to instantiate. In each temporal circuit, François is driven deeper and deeper into his afflictions. As a result, he becomes increasingly affected by—rather than actively affecting—the karmic impulses that propel the overall technicity-consciousness. Meanwhile, in each circuit, François and the other characters are transindividuated anew, a process that makes their subject-object relationships increasingly indiscernible.

This process of transindividuation is clearly *expressed* (Thirdness) in a pivotal scene in a bar. In this scene, Valentin initiates a drink with François. The scene begins with a high-angle long shot of the bar room, in which François and Valentin sit at a table in the background on the left of frame, and the camera is positioned on the right side of the table. Then, the camera crosses the 180-degree line and observes the two men from the left side of the table, yet this switch is *hidden* with a cut on action (the two men sitting down). Their conversation is conducted in a series of over-the-shoulder shots/reverse shots (see Figure 16, top and bottom). During the first half of the conversation, Valentin tells François that he can do whatever he wants with Clara, but that he should stay away from Françoise, because she is his (Valentin's) own daughter.

Valentin's plea to François, however, is suddenly interrupted by the sound of a trumpet playing a tune he normally uses in his show. In a

FIGURE 16. The bar scene from *Daybreak,* in which Valentin asks François to stay away from Françoise

medium close-up over François's shoulder, Valentin stops speaking and looks up. The film then cuts to a long shot of a trumpeter playing outside the bar (see Figure 17, top). This shot intercedes not only the conversation between the two men but also the point-of-view of the image. As the film cuts back to the table, the camera is now positioned on the right side of the table, and the rest of the conversation, in which François questions Valentin's claim to be Françoise's father (both François and Françoise are themselves orphans) and his sense of duty as a father, is conveyed by a series of shots/reverse-shots from this angle (see Figure 17, middle and bottom).

This 180-degree reversal, through a deliberate visual and sonic interruption, sends a subtle but unsettling sensual shock to the technicity-consciousness as a whole (or the anthropotechnical body), as it is drawn to the indeterminability between subject and object. With this perspectival switch, neither François nor Valentin is the narrational agent. Rather, they are both agents and patients in a formational process that affects—and is affected by—the karmic impulses to falsify.

If the technicity-consciousness (or image-consciousness) as a whole, especially the spectator's body and the embodied mind as well as the filmic-machinic body and its embodied mind, came to believe in the beginning of the film that the image itself (that is, the *récit* or narrative) alternated between François's actualized present and his recollections, this scene disconceals the technicity (karmic impulses to lie) of the image-consciousness's own formational process. At this moment, the *consciousness becomes mindful of its own technicity.* Bear in mind that the karmic impulses to lie are not only François's or Valentin's, but also *ours* (the spectators') and the film's as a process of becoming. In Buddhist terms, these impulses lie in the *ālaya*-consciousness of the technicity-consciousness as a whole. For example, when we *engage* in the film and become one with it as an embodied experience, we lie to ourselves that the image-consciousness is existent and also that we are ignorant of our own act of lying. As *our* overall anthropotechnical body is ignorant of the fact these lying impulses are actively in-forming its process of becoming, every phase in its transduction (transformation) and every transindividuation between the spectatorial body, the machinic body, and the bodies of François and other characters *instantiates* a lie. In this sense, metaphorically, the postcards pinned onto Françoise's vanity are like seeds that are stored in the *ālaya*-consciousness. Each of them is a

FIGURE 17. The bar scene from *Daybreak*, in which a
180-degree reversal puts into question the subject-object
relationship between François and Valentin

potentiality to lie as well as a potentiality to generate a sign (image) based on an act of lying.

If the film is to be seen as a layout of circuits of recollection-anticipation around the murder as the initiating object (see Figure 15 again), each circuit in the film is therefore an actualization of an avalanche of seeds (the potentialities to lie and the potentialities to turn lies into reality); the actualized form is simultaneously virtualized and reconfigured as seeds. On the one hand, the dependent originations between the actual and the virtual pull François's body and its embodied mind deeper and deeper into his karmic indulgence—and eventually propel him to commit suicide. On the other hand, they seem to be able to pull the spectatorial and filmic-machinic bodies and their embodied minds out of their own karmic indulgence, as these reindividuated consciousnesses become mindful of their own technicity and François's ignorance of its perniciousness.

Deleuze's comments on the relationship between the actual and virtual can therefore by pushed further if we read them not as clearly demarcated segments in the *récit,* but instead as a *relationality* that is mutually dependent:

> [I]n Carné, in *Daybreak*, all the circuits of recollection [again, see Figure 15] which bring us back each time to the hotel room, rest on a small circuit [here, Deleuze is referring to O in Figure 15 as the originating temporal circuit], the recent recollection of the murder which has just taken place in this very same room. If we take this direction to its limit, we can say that the actual image [A–B–C–D] itself has a virtual image [O–B'–C'–D'] which corresponds to it like a double or a reflection. In Bergsonian terms, the real object is reflected in a mirror-image as in the virtual object which, from its side and simultaneously, envelops or reflects the real [O]: there is "coalescence" between the two. There is a formation of an image with two sides, actual *and* virtual. It is as if an image in a mirror, a photo or a postcard came to life, assumed independence and passed into the actual, even if this meant that the actual image returned into the mirror and resumed its place in the postcard or photo, following a double movement of liberation and capture.[13]

Notice that Deleuze sees both the scenes in the hotel room (A–B–C–D; pay attention to Figure 15) and the flashback sequences (B'–C'–D') as temporal circuits that ripple out of a singular point-instant (the murder: O). This point-instant takes place in the beginning of the film offscreen and is therefore inaccessible to spectators. While Deleuze considers such inaccessibility the film's liability, we can see it as an even more direct expression of the temporal schema. The enigmatic point-instant (O or the murder) can be regarded as the only image/nonimage (an *absented* image) that is actual, from which every temporal circuit is a manifestation that envelops and conceals it. The entire cinematographic image, including the so-called "presents" in the hotel room (A–B–C–D) and the so-called flashback sequences (B'–C'–D'), is best understood as *reflections* of this actual point-instant. These reflections constitute a layout of circuits of recollection/flashback-anticipation/ François's anticipation to his death.

By using Buddhist vocabulary to push further Deleuze's analysis of *Daybreak,* we can locate a mechanism within the crystal-image. In the film, in the overall image-consciousness, the spectatorial-filmic/ machinic bodies and their embodied minds become mindful of their own technicity, while François's consciousness becomes increasingly ignorant of its own karmic indulgence. In other words, the degree of *awakening* of the spectatorial-filmic/machinic consciousness and François's degree of ignorance are inversely proportional to one another. In Deleuze's reading of the film, he complains that the film indulges the spectatorial-filmic/machinic consciousness in François's anger so much that awakening would be impossible. For me, such an awakening is possible, but not *automatic* for two reasons.

First, in spite of the filmic/machinic consciousness' ability to dis-conceal its own technicity, the karmic impulses that initiate the increasingly perturbing temporal circuits (that is, the narrative itself) are still being actively deposited in the *ālaya*-consciousness of the image-consciousness as a whole precisely through the process of narration. In other words, the karmic impulses that take control over François's consciousness can likewise take control over the spectatorial consciousness and the filmic/machinic one. In this sense, *Daybreak* can be, as Deleuze argues, a perfectly cohesive movement (karma)-image. In formalist terms, the film itself continues to have the ability to enable the spectators to empathize with François and indulge in his afflictions. Second, once the technicity of the formational process (the outward rippling temporal circuits in Figure 15) is disconcealed and is appreciated as *form,* there is no guarantee that the spectators will not develop an attachment to time as a sensuous form and go on to develop a karmic indulgence in its formational process.

Therefore, the time-image does not guarantee an insight. An insight into the technicity of consciousness requires two necessary conditions, which are made possible by—but are not the direct results of—the disconcealment of the image's temporalities. First, when the spectatorial consciousness, the filmic/machinic consciousness, and a character's consciousness of the cinema are dephased and transduced into a unified technicity-consciousness (in phenomenological terms: the cinematic experience as a whole), their configurative elements affect—and are affected by—one another. While in the karma-image, these configurative elements collectively affect—and are affected by—karmic impulses and stay in a relatively stable relation, in the insight-image, a mindfulness of these impulses produces modulations between them. The spectatorial, filmic/machinic, and the character's consciousnesses may be transduced, transindividuated, and dephased into interdependent, yet potentially nonsynchronous, relationalities.

Second, as the Buddhist philosopher Asaṅga argues (see my discussion in chapter 2), to arrive at an insight requires an avalanche of karmic impulses that propels the consciousness to liberate itself from karma.[14] In other words, the sensual shock in the bar scene in *Daybreak* can disconceal the image's technicity only when the liberating seeds in the spectator's *ālaya*-consciousness are mature and strong enough to be actualized. Therefore, an insight-image, as an anthropotechnical transindividuation, requires a spectator's readiness to instigate and assume their agency over it.

THE CONE: ITS INSIDE AND ITS ENVELOPE

In his explication on the crystal-image, Deleuze uses a terminology that resonates with the Yogācāras and the Tathāgatagarbhas:

> The crystal-image has these two aspects: the internal limit of all the relative circuits [of recollection-anticipation], but also outer-most, variable and reshapable envelope, at the edges of the world, beyond even moments of the world. The little crystalline seed and the vast crystallizable universe: everything is included in the capacity for expansion of the collection constituted by the seed and the universe. Memories, dreams, even worlds are only apparent relative circuits which depend on the variations of this Whole. They are degrees or

modes of actualization which are spread out between these two extremes of the actual and the virtual: the actual and *its* virtual on the small circuit, expanding virtualities in the deep circuits. And it is from the inside that the small internal circuit makes contact with the deep ones, directly, through the merely relative circuits.[15]

What Deleuze describes here is very similar to the Tathāgatagarbha: an empty layout of relationalities between all potentialities (what Deleuze calls a seed) and their manifestations. The outermost envelope, for Deleuze, is the plane of immanence; for the Tathāgatagarbhas, it is the plane of luminosity. Perceptually and conceptually, at the *here and now* (O in Figure 15), each temporal circuit appears to be a relationality between a recollection and an anticipation. This is the way time is manifested as the six consciousnesses: that the present (O) is experienced as an interval in a circuit between the past and the future (A–B–C–D and their reflections B'–C'–D'). Technically, the *here and now* (O) is a temporal/atemporal instant at which an avalanche of seeds (for Deleuze, the seed) is actualized as these various temporal circuits, as well as their revirtualization and return to this originating instant (O). O is therefore a zero point-instant, that is, the *alaya*-consciousness, which has no past, no future, and no present; yet it is precisely the storehouse (or in a Deleuzian term: crystallization) of all the potentialities that constitute all pasts, all futures, and all presents—the *plane* of luminosity. In this sense, what Deleuze calls the outermost envelope (the actualization of all potentialities as a plane of luminosity) *is* the innermost seed (the virtualization of all forms)—and vice versa.

As I illustrated with *Daybreak,* while the temporal circuits push François deeper and deeper into O, they seem to pull the spectatorial and the filmic/machinic consciousnesses out of it. These circuits are therefore best reschematized three dimensionally as a cone, which is Bergson's second schema of time (see Figure 18). In this cone, S stands for the present, which is what we usually call the "present" as a state of things or being (the plane at the bottom of the schema). It is best understood not as a point, but as the smallest temporal circuit between actualization and virtualization. This smallest temporal circuit is a modulation of a *previous* temporal circuit (A"–B"), which is in turn a modulation of another temporal circuit (A'–B') ad infinitum. Each of these circuits "contains all our past as this is preserved in itself (pure

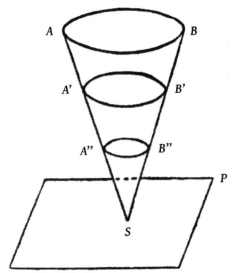

FIGURE 18. Bergson's second schema of time as illustrated in Deleuze, *Cinéma 2. L'image-temps* (1985; repr. Paris: Éditions de Minuit, 2017), 108 note 21; originally in Bergson, *Matière et mémoire*, 181

recollection)."[16] Thus, each circuit serves as a potentiality (virtuality or memory). S, as a *recognition* that we experience as the present, is therefore an actualization of all our previous memories-cum-potentialities.

In the movement-image, a recognition (S or the "present") is therefore a reinstantiation of another circuit of actualization-virtualization or recollection-anticipation (A'''–B''') ad infinitum. Thus, a series of reinstantiations (imagine S1, S2, S3, S4 . . .) gives the impression that a state of being or object moves spirally deeper into this cone. For Deleuze, the crystal-image disconceals the relationalities between these circuits. If we see the cone as the crystal-image (the overall image-consciousness), the character's consciousness is completely unified with the cone as it goes deeper and deeper into the cone. In fact, he lives as the cone. When a sensual shock in the image-consciousness triggers a transindividuation between the human (spectatorial)-machinic consciousness and the character's, they become interrelated but nonsynchronous. While the image-consciousness as a whole (of which the human-machinic and the character's consciousnesses are a part) continue to spiral down *as* the cone, the human-machinic consciousnesses simultaneously posit themselves in the outermost envelope (the plane of luminosity), thus attaining an insight into the technicity that constitutes the cone.

In *Cinema 2*, Deleuze is unclear about where lies the outermost envelope in the cone (Figure 18). Let us find out what he means by rethinking the cone in the Tathāgatagarbha terminology. We should return to the analogy of a roomful of dust (see chapter 2) in the *Śūraṅgama Sūtra*. Imagine a layout of moving dust that is open to other layouts ad infinitum. Each dust particle is a seed (potentiality), which does not exist until it is actualized. Meanwhile, the paths these particles travel—that is, their interdependent relationships—constitute the space that contains them (the room). This space can be understood as the only actual existence, whose self-nature is its self-nature-less-ness. However, this empty space does not exist without the dust particles and their movements, and the layout of dust is an instantiation of this space. Thus, the space that is neither going nor moving (the Tathāgatagarbha) is neither different from nor the same as the layout of moving dust (*ālaya*-consciousness).[17]

According to Hoi-yan (1886–1978) and Yuanying (1878–1953), at the *here and now,* the six consciousnesses are put into operation. We can imagine a dark room that is full of dust (a layout of dust), and the *operation* of the six consciousnesses is like a spotlight (a cone-shaped beam) that illuminates a sub-layout of dust within this layout. We are now effectively turning Figure 18 upside down. This spotlight is *manas* (volition), which claims this sub-layout as *my ālaya*-consciousness. Under this spotlight, these moving particles are actualized as a layout of conditions (forms, or in this case, dancing dust). The reconfigurations (modulations) of these forms are then perceived and conceptualized as karma, which drives—and is driven by—circuits of recollection-anticipation that spiral up this conic beam.

In the karma-image, therefore, the technicity-consciousness is the conic beam. In other words, *as I become one with the machinic consciousness and the character's consciousness in the cinema, I live as the cone.* As part of this layout of dust particles, the moment-to-moment reconfigurations of the layout of dependent originations (the changing configurations of the dust particles) are perceived and conceptualized not as a whole, but instead *lived* as circuits of recollection-anticipation that spiral up the light (consciousness as a temporal flux). In this process, as I spiral up the conic beam together with other dust particles (that is, my associated milieu; or in the cinema, the film itself), the present is misrecognized as a passing interval between the past and the future on my *path of life.*

In the insight-image, I continue to live as the cone, but the sensual shock also enables me to posit *myself*—together with the filmic/machinic consciousness, in this case—at the light source (the *here and now*). I am now in a position (the light source) where I can see the cone completely. From this perspective, the cone as a whole is a layout of all relationalities that constitutes the *cone-as-life*. Disconcealed as a *cone* of luminosity that opens to a cosmic layout of relationalities, what I used to perceive and conceptualize as a movement of spiraling up the conic beam is merely an illusion. This so-called (upward) *movement* is a process of becoming, in which those relationalities that constitute the cone (of which I am a part) are being reconfigured by karma (in the way illustrated in Figure 2 in the introduction). At the *here and now*, what I used to call *I* is merely a form that has been transindividuated with other forms out of the perpetually changing pattern of aggregation and dissipation of the dust particles. This so-called *I* is therefore part of this overall consciousness (the conic beam), which is now consciousness of its own technicity (the way it is in-formed) and of its relationalities with other consciousnesses (the cosmic layout of dust).[18] In the embodied cinematic experience (again, to borrow a term from phenomenology), in the crystal-image, I continue to engage in the film as a process of becoming, but I am also capable of grasping the karmic force that is impelling this process.

As Thich Nhat Hanh argues, awakening to the technicity of consciousness or illuminating its *reality* is not some mystical or magical revelation. It simply refers to a mindfulness of the *here and now*.[19] In the second half of *Cinema 2*, Deleuze points out that in a pure optical and sound situation, *I* am no longer distracted by recollections and anticipations. Rather, *I* am mindful of the *here and now*, from which a layout of intricate dependent originations is initiated. At this *here and now*, there is no *I*, but only relationalities. The body, mind, and vision that are often called *I* are constructed (by *manas*) as a placeholder of the *here and now*. This construction seems to give *me* a sense-certainty, but what it does is to conceal the technicity from being illuminated.[20] The actual differentiation between the past and the future—and the emptiness of such differentiation—cannot be clarified until the consciousness is mindful of its technicity: by positing itself at the *here and now* that constitutes the pure difference between the past and the future (see Figure 19).

FIGURE 19. Bergson's third
schema of time; in Deleuze,
Cinéma 2, 109 note 22

THE TECHNICITY OF TIME: SLOW CINEMA
AND GRADUAL AWAKENING

Deleuze calls this understanding of time Bergson's third schema (see
Figure 19). What Deleuze identifies in the crystal-image is therefore a
specific insight into the technicity of time:

> What constitutes the crystal-image is the most fundamental operation
> of time: since the past is constituted not after, the present that it was
> but at the same time, time has to split itself in two at each moment as
> present and past, which differ from each other in nature, or, what
> amounts to the same thing, it has to split the present in two heteroge-
> neous directions, one of which is launched towards the future while
> the other falls into the past. Time has to split at the same time as it
> sets itself out or unrolls itself: it splits in two dissymmetrical jets, one
> of which makes all the present pass on, while the other preserves all
> the past. Time consists of this split, and it is this, it is time, that we *see
> in the crystal.* The crystal-image was not time, but we see time in the
> crystal. We see in the crystal the perpetual foundation of time,
> non-chronological time, Cronos [*kairos*] and not Chronos. This is the
> powerful, non-organic Life which grips the world.[21]

Giorgio Agamben defines Cronos (*kairos*) as "the time it takes for
time to end," which is a measure of time in depth. He refers to an event
in the Práxeis Apostólōn (or Acts of the Apostles), in which Saul, later
renamed Paul, is being vocated (called) by the Messiah on his way from
Jerusalem to Damascus. Saul is blinded by the sight of the Messiah, who
appears to him as a bright light. After three days, his eyesight is restored
by Ananias of Damascus. According to Judaic scholarship, the point-
instant at which Saul is vocated by the Messiah, he is called into the end
(depth) of time. When he is asked later by his disciples and rivals how
he can explain the fact that after he has been vocated, he can return
from the end of time and carry out his praxis (acts) on earth, his answer
is *hos mē*: being called *as not* being called. If we use our analysis to push

Agamben's reading further, we can say that on his way to Damascus, Saul is suddenly being called to the *here and now*, where he apprehends the technicity of time (Cronos). Yet the technicity does not stop operating, which is instantiated as a consciousness that endures chronometrically. With a mindfulness of the relationality between Cronos and Chronos as neither different nor the same, neither not different nor not the same (*hos mē*), his praxis is the time it takes for time to end.[22]

In chapter five of *Cinema 2*, Deleuze proposes two kinds of time-image, which correspond to two ways of arriving at insight understood by Zen practitioners: *dziĕmnguò/jianwu* (gradual awakening) and *tuànnguò/ dunwu* (sudden awakening).[23] Gradual awakening is arrived at when the chronosign is extended into lectosigns and noosigns. In a karma-image, a lectosign refers to a hermeneutic field. In the time-image, however, it means something else:

> What the past is to time, sense is to language and idea to thought.
> Sense as past of language is the form of its pre-existence, that which
> we place ourselves in at once in order to understand images of
> sentences, to distinguish the images of words and even phonemes that
> we hear. It is between which we choose according to actual auditory
> signs which are grasped in a confused way. Similarly, we place
> ourselves initially in the idea; we jump into one of its circles in order
> to form images which correspond to the actual quest. Thus chrono-
> signs are continually extended into lectosigns and noosigns.[24]

A lectosign therefore refers to a sense-formation that converts a bare cognition into a recognition. In the same way, a sense-formation converts a sequence of phonic relations (syntagm) into an image-consciousness. Meanwhile, the noosign refers to a thought-formation, which is initiated by an impulse and is therefore a direct expression of that impulse. This kind of time-image corresponds largely to what we now call slow cinema, in which the slowness or even near-stasis of the image enables the anthropotechnical body to stay mindful of its own formational process. This kind of image requires a process of *studying* the image not by intellectual reasoning, but instead by a mindfulness of the body's sense and thought engagements from one moment to another. In Zen Buddhism, this is called gradual awakening.

It is important to note that Deleuze's understanding of the present is different from Buddhism's. In Deleuze's formulation of the crystal-image, he follows Bergson's conceptualization in *Matter and Memory* and regards the present as a crystallization of a set of memories and one of the *pasts* that will constitute part of the future (see Figure 18 again). This is the reason why living the present (S in Figure 18) is living the duration (the entire cone in Figure 18). Nonetheless, as Thomé H. Fang argues, Bergson's argument falls into the trap of suggesting that memories not only continue into the future, but also *determine* it.[25] For Fang, the Yogācāra concept of the *ālaya*-consciousness as a layout of potentialities that actualizes-virtualizes potentialities (memories from the past) addresses precisely this logical flaw committed by Bergson. It is because in the consciousness's process of becoming, memories and their relationalities do not accumulate and *overdetermine* the constitution of the present. Instead, they are *underdetermined* and rewritten by a constantly changing set of causes and conditions.[26]

As Tiago de Luca and Nuno Barradas Jorge argue, the term "slow cinema" did not become popularized among Anglo-American film programmers until 2010. This term indicates cinema that employs long takes, slow movements, or even (relative) stillness to enable the spectators to sense the duration in which an image is formed.[27] For Mary Ann Doane, the *seed* for slow cinema has been configured in the temporality of the cinematic image or apparatus. She argues that the "linear, irreversible, 'mechanical' temporality of the cinematic apparatus already constituted a major source of anxiety at the time of its appearance insofar as cinema's recording of time becomes immediately characterized by a certain indeterminacy, an intolerable instability. The image is the imprint of a particular moment whose particularity becomes indeterminable precisely because the image does not speak its own relation to time."[28] In this sense, slow cinema is best understood as a metacinematic contemplation—gradual awakening—of the relationality between the cinematic consciousness and its technicity. It achieves such gradual awakening by enabling the image to speak its own relation to time through an active engagement in its own temporal indeterminacy at the *here and now*.

In the Theravādin tradition, gradual awakening can be attained by means of *satipaṭṭhāna/smṛtyupasthāna* (mindfulness) in four domains: (1) *kaya* (body); (2) *vedanās* (sensations and affections); (3) *citta* (consciousness); and (4) *dhammās/dharmas* (forms and their emptiness). Methodologically, *satipaṭṭhāna* begins with a technique known as *ānāpānasati/ānāpānasmṛti* (mindfulness of breathing), which forms the basis of all methods of Buddhist meditation. The principle of *ānāpānasati* can illuminate how an insight-image initiates a process of gradual awakening:

> Breathing in long, he discerns, "I am breathing in long"; or breathing out long, he discerns, "I am breathing out long." Or breathing in short, he discerns, "I am breathing in short"; or breathing out short, he discerns, "I am breathing out short." He trains himself, "I will breathe in sensitive to the entire body." He trains himself, "I will breathe out sensitive to the entire body." He trains himself, "I will breathe in calming bodily fabrication." He trains himself, "I will breathe out calming bodily fabrication." Just as a skilled turner or his apprentice, when making a long turn, discerns, "I am making a long turn," or when making a short turn discerns, "I am making a short turn. . . ." In this way he remains focused internally on the body in and of itself, or externally on the body in and of itself, or both internally and externally on the body in and of itself. Or he remains focused on the phenomenon of origination with regard to the body, on the phenomenon of passing away with regard to the body, or on the phenomenon of origination and passing away with regard to the body. Or his mindfulness that "There is a body" is maintained to the extent of knowledge and remembrance. And he remains independent, unsustained by (not clinging to) anything in the world. This is how a monk remains focused on the body in and of itself.[29]

Being mindful of our breathing enables the consciousnesses to be mindful of the most fundamental karmic impulse that keeps one alive: the impulse to breathe. Since this impulse is deposited in the *ālaya*-consciousness, to which *manas* attaches itself, being mindful of such an impulse enables us to see how our sense of being is hinged on the presence of a karmic force that seeks to rebuild *manas* from one breath to another. The point, however, is not to reject these impulses. Rather, in the exercise, we are to embrace them and accept them as *the way it is.* By being mindful of every act of inhalation and exhalation, we come to realize that we exist neither in the past nor in the future, as the consciousness of the past is ungraspable and the consciousness of the future is ungraspable. If so, the consciousness of the present, the *here and now* of our existence, is fundamentally empty.

Apichatpong Weerasethakul's *Sleepcinemahotel,* an installation he constructed for the International Film Festival Rotterdam (IFFR) in

FIGURE 20. Apichatpong Weerasethakul's *Sleepcinemahotel;* photograph
by Victor Fan

2018, is a prime example (see Figure 20). During the festival, guests can
reserve for twenty-four hours a room (an open space) in the hotel: a
large metallic structure built in the ballroom of the Postillion Convention Centre. In the hotel, guests can rest in their own beds, take walks
around the installation, or lounge around on cushions. They are also
free to behold a moving image projected onto a circular screen at the
end of the ballroom. The image is composed of a montage of archival
footages and Apichatpong's original images. The montage projected
onto this screen is by no means slow. Yet, as the image does not follow
any apparent temporal, causal, or logical relationships, it compels the
consciousness to engage in the *here and now* of its becoming. Moreover,
as an extended cinema, what is at stake is not only the moving image
projected onto the screen, but also the embodied experience as the
guests are transindividuated with other beings and objects in a layout
of perpetually changing relationalities.

In *Sleepcinemahotel,* the guests are supposed to experience the time
it takes for the image to unfold (officially 360 hours; for an individual

guest, twenty-four hours) not by staring at the screen, but by navigating between the image on screen and their daily activities: going to other screenings, relaxing in their rooms, using the bathroom, chatting with friends, or working on their emails. Even when the guests go to sleep, they can still navigate between the image on the screen and their dream image. Occasionally, they may also notice that other guests and their dream images are synchronously transindividuated with the projected image on screen and the cerebral energies that flow between the bodies during their sleep. In such a milieu, the distinctions between the watching-dreaming subject and the object being watched and dreamt of, and between the perception-image in which they live (actual) and the watched-and-dreamt images (virtual), are often indiscernible and interchangeable.

In this process of becoming over the course of a day, the guests *slowly* become mindful of the almost undetectable transformations between boredom, exhaustion, invigoration, pleasure, displeasure, anxieties, and peace. The guests become mindful of the initiation and endurance of each thought, speech, and action that triggers these subtle changes: "I know I am sleeping; I know I am eating; I know I am brushing my teeth; I know every part of my body is engaged in this anthropotechnical milieu." In this state of mindfulness, the anthropotechnical body endures in chronometric time as a perpetual initiation-extinction of circuits between recollections and anticipations. Yet, posited at the *here and now,* the consciousness is mindful of its own technicity and the overall process of interbecomings.

Meanwhile, the montage projected onto the circular screen has no unity, coherence, or logicality. It can only be apprehended as an avalanche of awarenesses that appears on the screen, one awareness after another. In one register, these awarenesses are analogous to a sequence of bare cognitions actualized from the seeds of one's *ālaya*-consciousness. In another register, the lack of temporal, causal, and logical associations among them enables the consciousness to become mindful of the initiation and extinction of each moment. Through a process of watching the montage attentively (as in a meditation) and nonattentively (as one of the anthropotechnical operations), the consciousness becomes gradually awakened to its own technicity.

What makes *Sleepcinemahotel* cinematic, curiously, is not the moving image projected onto the screen. In this overall milieu, this moving image is simply one mode of anthropotechnical transductions. In this overall technicity-consciousness, the organic human body is the locus of anthropotechnical transindividuations. And in this process of gradual awakening, these organic configurations slowly take control of an agency in the process of image-formation—that is, over its own karmic impulses. In other words, this installation brings to the fore that what makes the cinema *cinematic* is not a specific technico-technological medium (as for example celluloid film or digital technology), but rather the *relationality* between technicity and consciousness.

SUDDEN AWAKENING

Meanwhile, the second kind of time-image, for Deleuze, is attained when the relationalities between pure optical and sound situations are configured as a conundrum. The technicity-consciousness needs to confront each situation as a present: present of the past, present of the future, and present of the present. At one moment in the formational process, the consciousness suddenly lets the conundrum be and accepts each present as an exception (Cronos) that stands for duration itself:

> [C]an the present in turn stand for the whole of time? Yes, perhaps, if we manage to separate [the present] from its own actual quality, in the same way that we distinguish the past from the recollection-image which actualized it. If the present is actually distinguishable from the future and the past, it is because it is presence of something, which precisely stops being present when it is replaced by *something else*. It is in relation to the present of something else that the past and the future are said of a thing. We are, then, passing along different events, in accordance with an explicit time or a form of succession which entails that a variety of things fill the present one after another. It is quite different if we are established inside one single event; if we plunge into an event that is in preparation, arrives and is over; if for a longitudinal, pragmatic view we substitute a vision which is purely optical, vertical, or, rather, one in depth. The event is no longer confused with the space which serves as its place, nor with the actual present which is passing: "the time of the event comes to an end before the event does, so the event will start again at another time . . . the whole event is in empty time that we anticipate nothing happens," and it is in empty time that we anticipate recollection, break up what is actual and locate the recollection once it is formed. On this occasion there is no longer a future, present and past in succession, in

accordance with the explicit passage of presents which we make out.
Adopting St Augustine's [354–430] fine formulation, there is *a present of
the future, a present of the present and a present of the past*, all implicated
in the event, rolled up in the event, and thus simultaneous and
inexplicable. From affect to time: a time is revealed inside the event,
which is made from the simultaneity of these three implicated
presents, from these de-actualized *peaks of present*.[30]

Here, Deleuze's reference to St. Augustine is based on his reading of
the third chapter of *Matter and Memory*. However, Thomé H. Fang argues
that the notion of the present as the *here and now* corresponds more
closely to William James's (1842–1910) concept of the specious present.
James borrows this notion from E. R. Clay (pseudonym of E. Robert
Kelly), which can be considered a bare cognition (a sense datum) that is
dependently originated by a layout of conditions in the past; yet it is the
only temporal point-instant that *exists*. James argues that what we call
the present is a recognition that belongs to the past: a fictionalization
of the specious present.[31] For Fang, Bergson would have never agreed
with James, since Bergson's insistence that the past *continues* to be part
of the present renders James's specious present logically unsound.[32]
Meanwhile, as Nāgārjuna argues (see chapter 2), if the present is dependently originated, this (specious) present is empty of existential
value. It is in this sense that Deleuze's understanding of the present of
the present deviates from Bergson, and it would be more similar to what
Buddhist scholars would call emptiness.

For Deleuze, this kind of time-image is best seen in the works of
Alain Robbe-Grillet (1922–2008) and Alain Resnais. In *L'Année dernière à
Marienbad* [*Last Year in Marienbad*, 1961], an object is proclaimed and
erased: the Man's (Giorgio Albertazzi, 1923–2016) claim that he met the
Woman (Delphine Seyrig, 1932–90) in Marienbad a year ago and that
they formed an intimate relationship together—or, some say, he raped
her. Despite the Woman's insistence that she had never met him before,
the Man persistently presents her with what he claims to be photographic evidence of their previous encounter. From time to time, a Second Man (Sacha Pitoëff, 1920–90) would intervene, who beats the Man
every time they play a game together.

In the film, the image *leaps* between the present, in which the Man
obstinately pursues the Woman, and the recollections or fantasies

(anticipations) of their encounter(s), affair(s), and rape(s). Set in a Baroque hotel, characters are arranged in enormous spaces, where their bodies are often merged into the ornate *décor* and the mathematically designed columns, windows, and plants. Very often, when one body moves at one static spot or across the frame, other bodies will remain still, thus turning each scene into a stylized any-space-whatever: a pure optical and sound situation.

Robbe-Grillet's equally mathematical writing reduces the dialogues into simple statements, which often have the effect of abstracting what the characters say from temporal connections, if not altogether from spatial and logical ones. In the novel, Robbe-Grillet even dictates how the camera should navigate around the space, how a scene should be seen in a temporally reverse order, and how transitions between temporal leaps should be erased and interrupted.[33] As a result, the image does not *travel* from one plane to another in association with the object. Rather, each scene is a *present*—present of a recollection, present of an anticipation, and present of the present—actualized by the technicity-consciousness. Furthermore, by narrating the way the camera narrates these events, Robbe-Grillet turns cinema's technics and technicity into form (the literary text and the cinematic image-consciousness); meanwhile, form is turned into its technics and technicity (the operational process of the cinematic technicity-consciousness).

Therefore, in the image, the relationships between subject and object, and between virtual and actual, are indiscernible, while the differentiation between permanence and impermanence is rendered inoperative. Deleuze argues that "we constitute a sheet of transformation which invents a kind of transverse continuity or communication between several sheets, and weaves a network of non-localizable relations between them. In this way we extract non-chronological time."[34] In this sense, time—as a formation—is abstracted as a *subject/object* of contemplation.

The complex technical manipulations that produce various temporal leaps, causal dissociations, and formal juxtapositions in *Last Year in Marienbad* do not put the anthropotechnical body into a process of mindful contemplation. Rather, the image-consciousness is configured as a conundrum with temporal, causal, and logical incongruities, each being instantiated as a sensual shock to the anthropotechnical body.

Brian Massumi points out that both Gilles Deleuze and Félix Guattari call such a sensual shock a "microperception":

[N]ot smaller perception, it's a perception of a qualitatively different kind. It's something that is felt without registering consciously. It registers only its effects. According to this notion of shock, there is always a commotion under way, a "something doing" cutting in, interrupting whatever continuities are in progress.[35]

In Zen, this is called sudden awakening. For Lıɪmtsèi practitioners, an affect that is initiated-extinguished at a kṣaṇa is ungraspable. However, when the lǐ-dǐ (technicity-consciousness) becomes mindful of itself, the here and now—which occupies the interval between feeling and thinking, bare cognition and recognition, affecting and being affected—is suddenly disconcealed. Instead of meditation, a Lıɪmtsèi practitioner is often given a h'uàidəu/huatou (watō, or a logical puzzle that cannot be immediately answered).[36] For instance, both Sheng-yen and Thich Nhat Hanh encourage their disciples to ask the question: Who is meditating?[37] To say that "I am meditating," I am adhering to the existential value of myself, the act of meditation, and the internal and external forms of meditation. To say that "Nobody is meditating," I am adhering to emptiness as form. By performing catuṣkoṭi (four-cornered negation; see chapter 2) to induce or deduce the answer logically, I will still need to find out whether ultimate emptiness is to be understood as an implicative or nonimplicative (existential) negation.

A puzzle therefore always aims to initiate a search for the Tathāgatagarbha, known in Zen Buddhism as dzùsièng/zixing (jishō; self-nature, which is nature-less). As Bhāviveka argues (see chapter 2), as a negation of negation, the Tathāgatagarbha is neither implicative nor nonimplicative, neither not implicative nor not nonimplicative. We have therefore arrived at the limit of what logical reasoning can do. Moreover, logical reasoning requires the practitioner to arrive at a conclusion. However, if self-nature (or self-nature-less-ness) is always manifested, here and now, as all forms, it is not an unknown to be arrived at, but a technicity (lǐ) that has always been there (dǐ).

Yet our karmic impulses always compel us to search for an answer as though it were an unknown (puzzle), rather than being mindful of its present with its presence being concealed by these impulses. In practice, when the ālaya-consciousness is preoccupied by the seeds to locate this answer, the presence of the answer (self-nature) will reach its maximum degree of concealment. At this point, a subtle sensual shock can immediately (without mediation) trigger a reconfiguration of a singular karmic impulse, which enables the consciousness to *abduce* the answer—by suddenly grasping the key to a process that can unlock self-nature meontologically. According to Charles Sanders Peirce, *abduction* is a process of disconcealing the meontological ground of a logical puzzle by first acknowledging the limits of induction and deduction. Then, a meta-analytical conclusion can be drawn, from which the differentiation between logicality and illogicality arises.[38]

As an image-consciousness, *Last Year in Marienbad* is therefore configured as a conundrum that grows increasingly puzzling in the formational process. The anthropotechnical body may feel lost or even threatened by its inability to induce or deduce temporality, causality, and formal relations as in a karma-image. However, when the body reaches the limits of induction and deduction and is able to accept and become mindful of each present as *the way it is*, it becomes *open* to affect—and be affected by—one of the many sensual shocks that has been built into the image. It takes only one of these shocks to crumble the technicity-consciousness's penchant to seek the answer of the puzzle. Once such longing is dismantled, *lǐ*-technicity is disconcealed as a layout of pure relationalities that has always been present. At this *kṣaṇa*, the human configurations are suddenly retransindividuated with the machinic components. These human configurations then posit themselves at the *here and now*. From this vantage point, all the relationalities that constitute the *ālaya*-consciousness are disconcealed and manifested as forms. Thus, as an image-consciousness, *Last Year in Marienbad* is: *lǐ*-technicity-as-*dʑì*-form and *dʑì*-form-as-*lǐ*-technicity.

FROM CONSCIOUSNESS TO INSIGHT

When a consciousness (*dʑì*) becomes mindful of its technicity (*lǐ*), it is called *prajñā* (insight). In both Yogācāra and Tathāgatagarbha scholarship, insight is to be understood transitively (insight *of* something) as well as intransitively (insight *as* something). In the *Discourse on the Perfection of Consciousness-Only*, Hwendzàng argues that a consciousness habitually seeks *āśraya* (shelter) in the *ālaya*-consciousness as a layout of karma-driving/driven and affliction-generating/generated seeds. An insight into the *lǐ*-technicity (insight of something) enables the consciousness to initiate a *parāvrtti* (reversal) by seeking shelter in the layout itself: pure relationalities (*lǐ-džì*).[39] The term "reversal" refers to the idea that insight is not something to be attained. Rather, as *lǐ*-technicity, it has always been there. Thus, being mindful of insight means that consciousness has *returned to the way it is*. Posited at the *here and now, džì*-consciousness remains operative as insight (*lǐ-džì*, or insight as something).

When the first five consciousnesses (of the eyes, ears, nose, tongue, and body) are converted into an insight, they are collectively known as the *kṛtyanuṣthānajñāna:* mindfulness of what must be performed.[40] Here, *what must be performed* refers to the technicity of karma. In the *Mahāprajñāpāramitāśāstra* [*Great Treatise on the Perfection of Wisdom*], Nāgārjuna argues that such an insight operates on a mindfulness on four points:

1. That all sentient beings *endure* in time (permanence), and endurance is marked by life and death (impermanence);
2. That life and death are forms initiated by karmic impulses, which produce afflictions;
3. That good and evil are not absolute values, as they merely produce different degrees of afflictions within the existential parameter of a mode of being;
4. The beingness of a sentient being is generated from *manas*, which develops an attachment to the five aggregates as *life*. Life and the five aggregates are perceptually and conceptually different (not the same), yet their difference is based on their nominal existences (not different). Whether they are the same or different does not matter on the level of their actual existence (pure relationalities).[41]

In this light, as an insight into the technicity of karma, mindfulness of what must be performed disconceals not only the technicity of a life's existence (biological existence) but also its ethical relationships with other beings and within its living environment (political existence), as well as the desires, frustrations, and delusions that arise in the process of interbecomings (psychical existence). Pema Tseden's *Tharlo*, I argue, illustrates how such an insight-image disconceals the existential and political technicities of a consciousness.

Pema is a film director of Tibetan descent. After graduating from the Beijing Film Academy in 2004, he made a number of feature films set in his home region of Amdo, including *Lhing vjags kyi ma ni rdo vbum* [*The Silent Holy Stones*, 2005], '*Tsol ba* [*The Search*, 2009], *Khyi rgan* [*Old Dog*, 2011], *Yangdar* [*The Sacred Arrow*, 2014], *Tharlo* [2015], *Jinpa* [2018], and *Dbugs lgang* [*Balloon*, 2019]. Because of his politically precarious position as a Tibetan filmmaker living in Beijing, Pema has chosen to work within the official censorship system of the People's Republic of China (PRC), and he has always been careful with not endorsing any one political position. Yet, because of this, his works sometimes disappoint or even irritate those spectators and critics who expect his work to offer political solutions. Meanwhile, he is regarded by some of his fellow filmmakers, critics, and academic scholars as a pioneer in the creation of a "Tibetan cinema."[42]

Most critics' and filmmakers' responses to Pema's work hold a common underlying assumption: that as a Tibetan filmmaker, he has the responsibility to speak for and represent Tibetan life. For example, the film director Tenzing Sonam argues that Pema makes a conscious effort to "Tibetanize" his image by eliminating all Han-Chinese characters from the screen.[43] Similarly, the scholar Tsering Shakya argues that through the "harsh and damaged landscape," Pema represents the "contemporary reality of nomads on the Tibetan plateau," with their "Spartan homestead" now encircled by barbed-wire fence, which in turn serves as a "metaphor . . . for confinement and for state of encroachment on local lives."[44]

Such a presupposition has been challenged by other scholars.[45] Dan Smyer Yu, for example, complicates this position by arguing that Pema's cinema demonstrates the inconsistencies, illogicality, and disturbing dislocation of the Tibetan spatial and psychological orders, a process that destabilizes the boundary between tradition and modernity—both being considered as formational processes that are actively negotiated in the film image.[46] Like Smyer Yu, Yau Wai-ping proposes that Pema's films are best "read as palimpsests"—that is, as textual layers that are always engaged in a perpetual proliferation and deferral of differences such as "tradition and modernity, the spiritual and the mundane, and [that] draw attention to the unfixity of the self and the diversity of perspectives."[47] Meanwhile, Anup Grewal argues that Pema's films "reveal the multiple, and often marginalized locations of particular Tibetan regions, like Amdo, within different economic, political and cultural configurations." For Grewal, by setting his films in specific landscapes where "cultural, political and economic situations" and their contestations are encapsulated, Pema demonstrates not only the contestations themselves, but also how they are structured into "positions of marginality."[48]

Therefore, in his work, Pema offers neither a political address nor a solution—at least explicitly. Rather, his films put into question what "Tibetan subjectivity" means, by rendering inoperative the very notion of subjectivity. He does so by converting the cinematic technicity-consciousness to the mindfulness of what must be performed—a point where an individual is desubjectivized, from which new relationships between individual and collective can be retransindividuated.[49]

Pema is incredibly sensitive to how the technicity-consciousness that constitutes the human body has always been transduced and trans-individuated with various technologies of recognition. In her discussion of Sinophone literature, Shih Shu-mei defines technologies of recognition via Teresa de Lauretis's study of Michel Foucault's notion of the *dispositif*, as the "constellation of discourses, institutional practices, academic productions, popular media, and other forms of representation that create and sanction concepts." This constellation therefore encompasses various media: literature, orature (including songs), photography, cinema, and various digital technologies. Shih regards these media as "mechanisms in the discursive (un)conscious—with bearings on social and cultural (mis)understandings—that produce" the opposition between the agent of recognition (for instance, the nation-state, a capital, or the "West") and its object (for instance, bare lives, consumers, and the "rest of the world").[50] The process of both gradual and sudden awakenings in *Tharlo* is tied to a synchronic layout of historically diverse and mutually competing technologies of recognition.

Tharlo portrays an eponymous protagonist (played by the popular comedian Shide Nyima) as a shepherd with a ponytail who is capable of reciting from memory a speech in Mandarin by Mao Zedong (1893–1976). He goes to the police station in order to apply for an identity card. A police officer, Dorje (Tashi), finds his memory admirable and he asks Tharlo to go into town to take an ID picture. In town, the photographer asks him to get a haircut, whereupon he meets and falls in love with Yangtso (Yang Shik Tso), a young hairdresser who claims herself to be charmed by Tharlo's rustic masculinity. Tharlo makes a date with Yangtso that evening at a karaoke bar. Not being able to sing the

Mandopop favored by Yangtso, Tharlo chants a Tibetan folk ballad for her, though he cannot remember the lyrics. After that, he has a fit of coughs that can only be alleviated by drinking hard liquor. He then spends the evening with Yangtso.

The next day, Tharlo returns to the village and passes his days in solitude herding his sheep and listening to the radio in order to learn the lyrics of the ballad. One evening, he has a fit of coughs again and he becomes inebriated, thus neglecting to take notice of the wolves outside. Next morning, he finds some of the sheep dead. The sheep owner comes to collect the carcasses and humiliate Tharlo. As a result, Tharlo sells all the owner's sheep and takes the money to Yangtso, in the hope that together they would spend it on traveling to Beijing. Yangtso agrees to flee with him, on the condition that she shaves his head. That evening, they attend a hip-hop concert performed by Dekyi Tserang, which he does not enjoy. The next morning, Tharlo finds out that Yangtso has fled with his money. As he returns to the police station, Officer Dorje hands Tharlo the ID, but urges him to take another picture with his bald head. Dorje asks Tharlo to perform his recitation of Mao's speech in front of the other officers, but Tharlo cannot remember anything. By the end of the film, Tharlo rides his motorcycle on his way home. However, halfway through his journey, he stops in front of a mountain lined by monstrously huge transmission towers, drinks a bottle of hard liquor, ignites a stick of dynamite, and holds it in his hand until it explodes.

ANTHROPOTECHNICAL INTERBECOMINGS

As a cinematographic image, *Tharlo* is in-formed as a mirror. If we see the film as a narrative structure, it is what Thierry Kuntzel and Raymond Bellour would call perfect symmetry, with each syntagm (scene) being articulated twice: once in the first half of the film and the second time in the second half. Each syntagm focuses on how a technology of recognition desubjectivizes Tharlo and retransindividuates him with other beings and technologies that constitute the environment. The mirror is expressed not only as the film's narrative structure, but also as a physical object (technology) that puts into question the differentiations between actual and virtual, subject and object, and permanence and impermanence.

Tharlo begins with a black screen, over which a voice is heard reciting in Mandarin Mao's essay "Wei renmin fuwu" ["Serve the People,"

September 8, 1944], which was collected in 1964 into the *Mao Zhuxi yulu* [*Quotations of Mao Zedong*], or the "Little Red Book." Yet such recitation is defamiliarized by the absence of any intonations. The sound-image is therefore momentarily divorced from any concepts, which compels the technicity-consciousness to apprehend it as a bare cognition. The ear consciousness tunes into the series of phonations and becomes hyper-aware of the act of listening. It also gradually comes to accept these phonations as *the way it is.* Their originations and existences, from one moment to another, depend on the originations and existences of the potentialities to hear, the potentialities to generate sonsigns, and the ears.

In this sense, the sound-image enables the technicity-consciousness or anthropotechnical body to be mindful of cinematic sound as a tech-nology of recognition. Furthermore, the way this recitation is delivered is remarkably close to the way a *mantra* is recited. As a technology of recognition in Vajrayāna schools of Tibetan Buddhism, the recitation is always carried out in Pāli or Sanskrit, without necessarily the reciter's knowledge of the words' meanings. Hence, a reciter is supposed to focus on the act of initiating a phonation, one after another, and on the rhythm formed by the phonetic sequence. This way, the consciousness is at once mindful of the present (the initiating impulse that triggers each phonation) and mindful of the rhythm (flux of impulses). Thus, the reciter becomes mindful that existence is neither permanent nor im-permanent, neither not permanent nor not impermanent.

A few seconds into the recitation, a visual image arises, which can be named and identified as a close-up of a baby goat being carried in a messenger bag, and a human hand is feeding it with a milk bottle. As the words "Mao Zedong" arise in the soundtrack, the technicity-consciousness is finally able to identify the content of the recitation as a passage from "Serve the People." Yet, the significance of the recitation is distracted by the sight and sound of the kid sucking milk. In other words, the eye consciousness and the ear consciousness are still seeking a technology—*manas*—to synchronize this sense-formation into a whole.

Such synchronization is finally rendered possible when the film cuts to a medium shot of Shide Nyima (see Figure 21). Like John Wayne in *The Searchers*, Shide's stardom in music and television provides the technicity-consciousness a recognizable sign to initiate empathy. Yet,

FIGURE 21. Tharlo recites "Serve the People" by Mao Zedong in *Tharlo*

Shide's weathered and down-to-earth appearance—as opposed to his usually urban and fashionable one in real life—signals to the anthropotechnical body that his performance should be separated from his public persona. In this shot, Shide faces the camera straight-on and occasionally looks into the camera lens. In a long take, the camera remains in this position without any movement through his entire recitation—and thereafter. As the Hong Kong film scholar Lam Nin-tung would argue (see chapter 5), with the absence of any changes in action within the frame, the technicity-consciousness or anthropotechnical body begins to *you* (drift, journey, or navigate) between the image's *pingyuan* (horizontal distance), *gaoyuan* (distance in height), and *shenyuan* (distance in depth).[51] On the horizontal plane, Shide recites Mao's quotation as though it were a mantra, which continues to enable the consciousness to stay mindful of the indiscernibility between the permanence and impermanence of existence. At the far end of the frame's depth, the words *wei renmin fuwu* (serve the people) are inscribed onto the wall. These words enable the thought consciousness to name the passage as Mao's essay.

Meanwhile, a subtle sound of boiling water draws the technicity-consciousness's attention to a kettle offscreen, which constantly emits steam into the frame. Such sound activates the nose consciousness to become mindful of the smell, temperature, weight, and even density of the air inside the room. Finally, Pema uses the highest resolution available (4096×2060), thus rendering the black-and-white photography with a crystal-like surface (luminosity), a dense texture, and a detailed gradation between the darkest and the brightest surfaces. In my conversation with him in Hong Kong, Pema admits that the use of black-and-white photography in this film was not meant to imitate celluloid photography. Rather, it was to intensify the image's tactility, which can only be rendered digitally. This turn heightens the perceptual and conceptual contrast between the image's lifelike concreteness, unity, and permanence, and its fundamental emptiness—as pure (digital) relationships.[52]

Reciting the *Quotations of Mao Zedong* is a socialist technology of recognition inscribed onto Tharlo, which was used during the Cultural Revolution (1966–76) to interpellate a *life* as a political subject. As Chris Berry points out, in this opening image, Tharlo's recitation recalls a collective memory of the past that the party-state has been consciously trying to put under erasure by postsocialist neoliberalism since the late 1990s.[53] However, the way this recitation is conducted highlights the failure of this technology to perform. Rather, it enables the technicity-consciousness to crystallize the indiscernibility between a virtual image (pure memory) of this technology and its actual rendition as a pure performance.

After his recitation, Tharlo moves to the left of frame, while Dorje enters from the right of frame and praises Tharlo's memory and performance. In this conversation, two issues are being brought up. First, Tharlo is in the police station in order to apply for an ID card (imprinted with an embedded memory chip that contains his biometrics). As Berry suggests, since its introduction, the ID card has been used by the Beijing government to monitor and restrict the geographical movements of ethnic minorities, and checkpoints were even set up on roads to control these movements (these are not shown in *Tharlo*). Therefore, Tharlo is here to surrender an older technology of recognition (his own name and body) and to replace it with a newer and digital form of recognition. In this memory chip, digital technology is employed not only as an instrument of surveillance, but also as a storage of Tharlo as a set of biometric data. Such a technology enables the party-state to desubjectivize and manage him as a biopolitical life. Nonetheless, Tharlo cannot understand the logic of this new technology. Unable to recall his own birthname, he prefers people calling him "Tharlo" ("Ponytail"). For him, as long as he knows who he is, that should be enough.

A second issue arises when Tharlo discusses the Mao quotation with Dorje, revealing that he confuses the subject of the quotation: it is either (1) Zhang Side (1915–44), who died in a kiln on September 5 as he participated in a local movement during the Sino-Japanese War (1937–45) in order to build a sustainable economy in Yan'an (Yenan), the capital of the Chinese Communist Party (CCP) government of the time; or it is (2) Sima Qian (145–86 B.C.E.), a historian whose words are being included in Mao's quotation. Tharlo's confusion arises with the last phrase of the quotation:

> All men must die, but death can vary in its significance. The ancient Chinese writer Szuma Chien [Sima Qian] said, "Though death befalls all men alike, it may be weightier than Mount Tai or lighter than a feather." To die for the people is weightier than Mount Tai, but to work for the fascists and die for the exploiters and oppressors is lighter than a feather.[54]

Tharlo's confusion also extends to a question: Why would dying for the people be considered a death that is "weightier than Mount Tai," whereas dying for the "exploiters and oppressors is lighter than a feather"? As Pema proposes, this question is cited in the film as a variation of the first remark from the *Great Treatise on the Perfection of Wisdom*. It is configured as the enigma of the entire film: that all sentient beings endure in time (permanence), and endurance is marked by life and death (impermanence).[55]

This scene is mirrored toward the end of the film as Tharlo returns to the police station after Yangtso has disappeared. In a long take, which is framed almost identically as Figure 21 (see Figure 22), Tharlo enters the police station not to report Yangtso, but to report himself for having succumbed to his desire. Notice that this image is digitally flipped as a mirror image of the one in the opening shot. Thus, while the human figures are still identifiable, the words on the wall are flipped horizontally and they lose their valence as linguistic signs. Hence, while the technicity-consciousness has no problem identifying the human figures and the objects in the room as actual, the wall falsifies the image and proclaims both its virtuality and its digital (empty) *existence*. In this

FIGURE 22. The mirror image of Tharlo reperforming the recitation

light, the difference between virtual and actual, as well as the difference between existence and emptiness, are both indiscernible.

Without knowing that Tharlo has stolen his employer's sheep and sold them, Officer Dorje tells Tharlo that the police cannot help him. Meanwhile, he tells Tharlo to take another photograph with his bald head and to recite "Serving the People" for his colleagues, which Tharlo fails to do. His failure is rendered not only by his inability to recall certain phonations, but also by his complete loss of rhythm. Thus, the recitation has lost its power as a technology of recognition. Tharlo then tells Dorje that he now understands what the final phrase of the quotation means, as he is now destined to die a heavy death, which is, ironically, "lighter than a feather." In this sense, heaviness and lightness are relative measurements. What counts is that Tharlo's death will be brought about by his untamed surrender to the karmic impulses that constitute his desire. This corresponds to the second remark in the *Treatise:* that life and death are forms initiated by karmic impulses, which produce afflictions.

The film maintains the one-scene-one-take technique as its dominant styleme, which means that actions in Tharlo's mundane reality are experienced by the technicity-consciousness as an expression of duration. These actions include waiting in the photo studio for Tharlo's turn to take his ID picture; waiting on the street to kill time; having his hair cut; singing in the karaoke; tending sheep; listening to the radio to learn a ballad; having Yangtso shave his head; buying groceries; and attending the hip-hop concert. Slowness is instrumentalized in the film as a technology to engage the spectator's technicity-consciousness in the present: "I know Tharlo is waiting. I know Yangtso and Tharlo are singing. I know Tharlo is tending sheep." At each present, the technicity-consciousness is mindful of itself as a body-formation that is neither the subject who observes nor an object that is being seen, but instead is an interval that is instantiated by impulses, thoughts, actions, and speeches. This body is in-formed as soon as the first awareness that constitutes the image is initiated, and it will die—as all sentient beings who are driven by afflictions will die—as soon as the image perishes.

In the film, Tharlo visits the photo studio twice. As Yau Wai-ping observes, the studio is spatially divided into the waiting room, where Tharlo awaits his turn to take his ID photo, and a dais, on which a young couple is having their wedding pictures taken. These two sections of the location are divided by the camera cutting on the 180-degree line. Yet, in this case, the editing does not indicate a subject-object relationship between the seer and the seen. Rather, the straight-on angle and flat-space composition turn these two sections into mirror images of each other, making the virtual and the actual indiscernible.[56] As the couple is having their pictures taken, the photographer's assistant changes the backdrops (photos printed on plastic curtains) from Potala Palace in Lhasa to Tiananmen Square in Beijing, and then to the (still standing) Twin Towers in Manhattan. The couple also changes from modern Tibetan to modern American-styled costumes. These changing backdrops and costumes will be echoed later by Yangtso mentioning her dreams to go to Beijing and New York with Tharlo's money, an aspiration that is—like these backdrops—nothing but make-believe. They also enable the technicity-consciousness to be mindful of the performativity of the image: that all forms are—by default—make-believe.

Meanwhile, Tharlo also visits Yangtso's salon twice. His first visit is entirely shot as a reflection from the salon's mirror, which covers almost the entire film frame. This technology of recognition is made visible, once again, as the technicity-consciousness is mindful of the everyday-ness of their conversation and actions (shampooing and blow-drying) in real time, while the subtle flares and double reflections on the mirror serve as reminders that the image has been flipped horizontally—that

FIGURE 23. Tharlo's second visit to the salon

the technicity-consciousness has misrecognized the virtual as the actual. In the background, photographs and posters of television and film stars from Hong Kong and Taiwan in the 1980s turn the salon into a crystal-image image, where an image of the present and images of the past coexist.

On Tharlo's second visit to the salon, the camera is placed in front of the hairdressing counter (see Figure 23). On the left of frame, a mirror reflects the image of Tharlo sitting on a barber chair while Yangtso stands behind him and tends his hair. On the right of frame, another mirror reflects the image of the rest of the salon, whereas in the middle of the frame, there lie Yangtso's equipment and a poster of young Brigitte Lin, one of the most popular film stars from Taiwan in the 1980s.

Up until this point, the awakening process of the technicity-consciousness has been gradual and accumulative. This scene, however, sends a sudden sensual shock to the anthropotechnical body. Having been beaten up and humiliated by the sheep owner, Tharlo suddenly appears in Yangtso's salon with an obscenely huge pile of banknotes: the money from the sale of the sheep he has stolen. The money is placed in front of the mirror as the only *actual* object that matters. In this sense, every thought-formation, every action, and every speech in the film is a misrecognition mediated by stolen capital—along with the desire for a second chance to live and a wish to be free, based on a belief that such capital will bring about one's emancipation.

This sensual shock continues when Yangtso agrees to flee with Tharlo, on condition that he allows her to shave his head. For spectators who are familiar with the story of Delilah asking Samson to do the same in the Sefer Shoftim [Book of Judges] in the Torah, their technicity-consciousness would become aware that Tharlo is about to be emasculated and betrayed. Even without this knowledge, the act of shaving Tharlo's head has the effect of depriving him of his very namesake (ponytail), his *real* identity (this has been his "ID card"), and his subjectivity (his rustic masculinity and association with the rural). Yet, Yangtso does not emasculate Tharlo or change him in any way. Rather, he made this change himself when he sold the sheep, an act that was driven by a desire for monetary capital and for Yangtso, his frustration and anger toward the sheep owner and toward himself as someone who has already been rendered impotent under capitalism, and a delusion that stealing money and fleeing with Yangtso will bring him freedom.

The sensual shock of this scene, however, is even more complex than this. Stealing the property from his owner in exchange for money is unforgivable under capitalism. Yet, as someone who has been economically exploited all along, Tharlo is committing a socialist act of rebellion by taking ownership of his exploiter's property and recuperating his rightful share. This is the kind of rebellion the People's Liberation Army encouraged the Tibetan peasants to do during the invasion from 1950 to 1951. It is also the message advocated by a propaganda film on Tibet titled *Nongnu* [*Serf*, Li Jun, 1963], which, as Pema claims, was shown to all Tibetan children when he was growing up. The film effectively reverses this colonial trope by demonstrating that (1) the trope has been reversed by the CCP all along under postsocialist neoliberalism, that what was seen as a socialist rebellion is now considered a capitalist crime; and (2) such an act of rebellion further desubjectivized Tharlo by reducing him to a biopolitical life (that is, an *animal* life that is deprived of individuality, subjectivity, and agency), who, under the contemporary technology of surveillance, is a nameless prisoner of himself everywhere he goes. This is a moment in which the human, the machinic, and the character's consciousnesses in the technicity-consciousness are retransindividuated. On the one hand, Tharlo goes deeper and deeper into his karmic indulgence. On the other hand, posited at the *here and now*, the spectatorial and the machinic consciousnesses become mindful of the whole image-consciousness's technicity.

At this point, the third remark in the *Treatise* is revealed: that good and evil are not absolute values, as they merely produce varying degrees of afflictions within the existential parameter of a mode of being.

One can argue that the sequences shot in and around Tharlo's house in the countryside and on the roads that connect the town and the country are not mirrored. Thus, Berry and Yau both regard *Tharlo* as a negotiation between tradition and modernity.[57] However, Tenzing argues that the stunning—almost prototypical—Tibetan landscape captured by the camera is always marked by transmission towers, whereas open lands are circled—mostly by Han-Chinese landowners—by wired fences in preparation for development.[58] In fact, while Tharlo keeps claiming that he owns the sheep he herds, as though he were a cowboy roaming the land of the free, he is living in the deserted land both owned—and abandoned—by the sheep owner. Almost all the sequences in which Tharlo is shown herding his sheep and going on with his solitary living are accompanied by a subtle voice singing the same ballad he tried to sing in the karaoke through a shortwave radio: another abandoned technology of recognition during the socialist era. His trajectory from forgetting the lyrics of the ballad to learning and mastering them in the countryside mirrors his trajectory from remembering and performing Mao's quotation to losing his ability to do so. These technologies of recognition, after all, no longer matter. In fact, the differences between life and death, something and nothing, time and timelessness no longer matter—as they are all fundamentally empty.

SUBJECTIVITY-DESUBJECTIVITY

In film and media philosophy, we often presume that a fully individuated, subjectivized, and autonomized being enters the cinema, where such individuality, subjectivity, and autonomy (agency) are performed, put into crisis, and restored. In Yogācāra and Tathāgatagarbha scholarship, subjectivity is a manifestation of *manas,* which is dependently originated from one moment to another. In the karma-image, *manas* maintains its ontological consistency through performance, crisis-management, and restoration; in the insight-image, its technicity is left *open* as the way it is.

As I argue in *Extraterritoriality* [2019], individuality, subjectivity, and autonomy are colonial privileges. In the case of *Tharlo*, one may ask: What is Tibetan subjectivity? How can a Tibetan subject individuate themself out of a milieu of sense-data that constantly requires an extra effort to cohere, and how can one possibly name such subjectivity when there is no name and epistemic space for it? This comes down to the very fact that a colonized life (1) is not a politicized subject; (2) is not a complete object; (3) cannot be both a subject and an object; and (4) cannot be neither a subject nor an object. It always occupies a position that is *extra-territorial*. The desubjectivized life does not form any interdependent relationship with any geopolitical or psychic territories, yet it is configured as the *différance* from which all territorial differentiations and names are engendered.[59]

As Agamben argues, since the Euro-American understanding of individuality, subjectivity, and autonomy is our global political default, and since the official and neocolonial Chinese and Indian understandings of these values are often measured with and against their Euro-American counterparts, *politics* renders a desubjectivized life unlivable. It is in this sense that colonized, occupied, marginalized, and ostracized lives are—literally—*nobody*.[60] Politics is configured in a way that these lives are precarious and dispensable labor by people who live in a prison they build for themselves, where emancipation *is* enslavement. This can be regarded as biopolitical desubjectivity.

What the insight-image can do, however, is to disconceal the technicity of *manas*. In so doing, it reveals that politics—especially under postsocialist neoliberalism—has been operating on a reversal of our understanding of desubjectivity. The difference between subjectivity and desubjectivity is a construction in the first place. Hence, rendering such a difference inoperative is the first step toward an emancipation from politics and from our ignorance that existence has any existential value. This corresponds to the last remark in the *Treatise*: the beingness of a sentient being is generated from *manas*, which develops an attachment to the five aggregates as *life*. Life and the five aggregates are perceptually and conceptually different (not the same), yet their difference is based on their nominal existences (not different). Whether they are the same or different does not matter on the level of their actual existence (pure relationalities).

In the closing scene of *Tharlo* is a medium shot of Tharlo on his motorcycle, with his back against the camera. In the background, the majestic mountains seem to be unmoving; but on closer observation, their forms and appearances change as the light arises and annihilates from one frame to another. After finishing half a bottle of liquor, he takes out a stick of dynamite from his messenger bag and raises it in the air. The film then cuts to a black frame with the sound of a dynamite explosion at the interstice between the image and its absence. This can certainly be read as a suicide. However, the detonation takes place precisely at the very point-instant from which the differentiations between something and nothing, and time and timelessness, are initiated. In this sense, this explosion is the ultimate mindfulness of what has to be done, from which the illusive notion of subjectivity and its annihilation are both suspended. As Mao said in his 1944 essay, "All men must die, but death can vary in its significance."[61]

CHAPTER 4

CINEMA ECOLOGY

Insight is a layout of pure relationalities. In the karma-image, consciousness affects—and is affected by—an avalanche of karmic impulses under *manas* (volition). In this case, consciousness runs on autopilot. It operates as a process of self-becoming driven by desires and afflictions. In the insight-image, consciousness becomes mindful of its own technicity (dependent originations-emptiness). On the one hand, the karmic impulses that in-form the process of self-becoming continue to spiral up the conic beam of existence (see chapter 3 and my discussion in relation to Figure 18) as forms. On the other hand, posited at the *here and now,* this reconfigured consciousness (insight) is mindful of its own formational process as a layout of pure relationalities: a process of interbecomings.[1]

The insight-image therefore enables the consciousness to perceive and conceptualize itself in relational terms. But then, why does relational thinking matter?

When I say that the karma-image runs on autopilot, I mean that the formational process is driven (piloted) by an attachment to the perceptual-conceptual *existence* of *rūpas* (forms), *puruṣa* (spirit or agency), *puggala/pudgala* (individuality), *citta* (a disembodied mind), *māṇavaka* (ignorance as self-nature), *kartṛkaraṇe* (seeking shelter in agency), and *vedanās* (affections as self-nature).[2] These are collectively taken as the ego. In the cinema, transindividuation is therefore seen as a perpetual process of differentiation between self and other. At each *kṣaṇa* of the formational process, I see myself as either an agent or a patient. As Ching-kung argues, power relations in a reality in-formed by karma are by default asymmetrical.[3] This is the reason why scholars such as Vivian Sobchack, William Brown, and Shane Denson suggest or argue that those media ecologies and modes of digital existence, where this agent-patient relationship is no longer secure or discernible, should be reclassified as post/super-cinema(tic).[4] Nonetheless, in Buddhist philosophy, even in an ecology where the difference between agent and patient is indiscernible, there still lies a subtle but impactful hierarchical—and often politicized—difference between transindividuated beings.

Thinking relationally enables the consciousness to be mindful of the technicity on which power relations operate. If the reality we live in is in-formed by dependent originations, one act of karmic reconfiguration can instigate a cascade of interpersonal, social, or even cosmic changes. As Brian Massumi urges us: think ecologically. In an ecology, where configurational elements affect—and are affected by—one another, one micro-decision or action is bound to affect the entire layout of relationalities. Corporate and state powers have understood such technicity all along, and this is the way sociopolitical transindividuations have always been working. We are simply not awakened to the idea that we can *exercise* an agency over it.[5]

According to Mahāyāna philosophy, relational thinking enables the consciousness to attain—and return to—the four *brahmavihārās* (heightened states of mind): *mettā/maitrī* (benevolence), *karuṇā* (compassion), *muditā* (empathy), and *upekkha/upekṣā* (equanimity).[6] These four *brahmavihārās* underline what we may call a Mahāyāna ethics, which are considered both the paths toward—and the results of—mindfulness. However, how relationalities are reconfigured on these paths and how Buddhist understandings of relationalities can be compared to their Euro-American counterparts are subject to debates.

In this chapter, I turn to some current discourses of relational thinking in film and media studies and propose to use the four *brahmavihārās* as a method to rethink cinema ecologically. I argue that relational thinking reveals what we do in the cinema (identification), what the cinema does (negotiating powers), how the power asymmetry between the human and machine is configured, and most importantly, how we can instigate changes. By the end of the chapter, I will have illustrated this idea by analyzing contemporary *tongzhi* (comrade) or queer cinema in

Mainland China as a media ecology, with special attention to three films: *Xing xing xiang xi xi* [*Star Appeal*, Cui Zi'en, 2013], *Huoxing zonghezheng* [*Martian Syndrome*, Kokoka, 2013], and *Canfei kehuan* [*Deformity Sci-fi*, Kokoka, 2013].

PHENOMENOLOGY

In cinema studies, relational thinking is an aporia. In the beginning of *Les structures de l'expérience filmic* [*The Structures of the Film Experience*, 1969], Jean-Pierre Meunier, based on the works of Maurice Merleau-Ponty (1908–61) and Angelo Hesnard (1866–1969), argues that cinematic identification is best understood not as a relationship between two individuated subjects. Rather, it is an interpsychic connection that takes place on a level prior to individuation and subjectivization.[7] In this sense, identification is not a process in which a pre-constituted subject becomes one with a pre-constituted object. Rather, it is a process of transindividuation, in which the divides between the self and other, subject and object, and spectator's body *in here* and image *out there*, are initiated.

Then, drawing on the work of Jean-Paul Sartre, Meunier reminds us that what we sense and perceive as an individual in the image is the presence of the absence of the said individual whose image was captured by the camera in the past.[8] Identification therefore requires the spectator to: (1) "presentify" in a home movie, that is, make present the absence of someone we have known all along; (2) "personalize" in a documentary, that is, give personality to an individual who has been reduced by the documentary to a representation of a larger social group; and (3) "affectivize" in a fiction film, that is, establish affective connections with an imagined character who has no existential value in our lived reality.[9]

Between these two registers of understanding, there is an aporia. The understanding of identification, according to Merleau-Ponty and Hesnard, presumes an interdependent relationship between the spectator and the image. The transindividuation of these two parties renews itself at each moment of identification and each temporal point-instant of sense-perception. In this light, each party does not exist in its own right. The understanding of identification according to Sartre, however, presupposes the temporal permanence of a sentient body, which enables each sensory-perceptual point-instant to take place. It is this sensory-perceptual process that makes present the absence of the image, thus allowing the spectator to presentify, personalize, and affectivize the image.

Meunier's shift from the first register to the second is symptomatic of a philosophical struggle outlined in the beginning of Henri Bergson's *Matter and Memory*. We cannot say that there is a permanent world out there that constitutes the mind in here (materialism), or that there is a permanent mind that projects a world out there (idealism). This is because our ability to sense and perceive, and what we do sense and perceive, are interdependently related, that is, they arise and are extinguished in relation to each other. Nevertheless, despite our knowledge of this, it is extremely hard to theorize identification without imagining a temporally and existentially permanent self. Yet, if understood this way, identification is ultimately not an intersubjective process, but an idealistic one, that is, the image is a milieu initiated from this *self*.[10]

In other words, thinking relationally is a counterintuitive process. As Sobchack argues, in Meunier's own analysis of the structure of identification in the home movie, he suggests that we cannot actually presentify someone who maintains an undeniable temporal, spatial, or even existential distance from us. Rather, in the home video, the viewer "is confronted with the void and remains suspended, without any possible outlet or any real signification." We come face-to-face with our "self-presence," an evocation of a past that is fundamentally irremediable.[11]

However, must cinematic identification be driven by a karmic impetus to maintain the ego? In her own intervention, Sobchack argues, "the cinema makes visible and audible the primordial origins of language in the reversibility of embodied and enworlded perception and expression."[12] In the cinema, the seer and the being seen do not always form a "dialectical reversal" between one another. Merleau-Ponty calls this *chiasmus:* that they are "two aspects of the reversibility which is the ultimate truth."[13] A film is, in this light, "an act of seeing that makes itself seen, an act of hearing that makes itself heard, and an act of physical and reflective movement that makes itself reflexively felt and understood." As the camera perceives and as its body moves, it expresses what it perceives. Meanwhile, I (the Eye) perceive(s) the perception and the perceiving process expressed by the camera as my embodied experience. Sobchack argues:

The cinema thus transposes what would otherwise be the invisible, individual, and intrasubjective privacy of direct experience as it is embodied into the visible, public, and intersubjective sociality of a language of direct embodied experience—a language that not only refers to direct experience but also uses direct experience as its mode of reference. A film simultaneously has sense and makes sense both for us and before us. Perceptive, it has the capacity for experience; and expressive, it has the ability to signify. It gives birth to and actualizes signification, constituting and making manifest the primordial significance that Merleau-Ponty calls "wild meaning"—the pervasive and as yet undifferentiated significance of existence as it is lived rather than reflected upon. Direct experience thus serves double duty in the cinema. A film presents and represents acts of seeing, hearing, and moving as both the *original structures of existential being* and the *mediating structures of language*. As an "expression of experience by experience," a film both constitutes an original and primary significance in its continual perceptive and expressive "becoming" and evolves and regulates a more particular form of signification shaped by the specific trajectory of interests and intentions that its perceptive and expressive acts trace across the screen.[14]

Gilles Deleuze raises doubts on Merleau-Ponty's notion and its applicability to the cinema: "What phenomenology sets up as a norm is 'natural perception' and its conditions. Now, these conditions are existential coordinates which define an 'anchoring' of the perceiving subject in the world, a being-in-the-world, an opening to the world which will be expressed in the famous 'all consciousness is consciousness of something.'"[15] In Buddhist terms, Merleau-Ponty's understanding of intersubjectivity is still founded on subjectivity: an attachment to the self.

Nevertheless, for Sobchack, the camera body and the organic body, in their reversibility and immediacy, perceive and express not in a mutually adoptive and adaptive relationship, but instead as an *intentional* one. This is to say that a *consciousness of something* (for example, *my consciousness*), as a mode of existence, is always a representation and an expression of its intentionality toward what it posits as the object. Therefore, the *relationality* between subject and object is a processual whole. In other words, like Deleuze, Sobchack replaces the question of identification by drawing our attention to the relationality between the organic and technical bodies that coalesce into an operation. The resulting embodied experience thus enables direct experiences that are otherwise private and inarticulable to be directly shared by all the participating bodies. And their shareability is rendered possible by their im-mediacy (unmediated by technics, including language). In this sense, Sobchack's understanding of the cinematic language is remarkably similar to Pier Paolo Pasolini's im-sign: the same presupposition held by Deleuze himself (see chapters 2 and 3).

Both Sobchack's and Deleuze's arguments reveal that what we do in the cinema (identification) is what the cinema does (negotiating power relations). But as Sobchack argues, in post-cinema (including animation and videogame), animated and simulated camera movements, angles, and compositions that begin with a human subject's point of view often transition into a machinic's or digital being's without reaffirming the spectator's or user's subjectival integrity.[16] Denson calls this a discorrelated image: an image in which the chiasmic correlation between subject and object is no longer binary and stable. In this book, we have seen these examples in *Long Day's Journey into Night* and *Tharlo*. For Denson, in the discorrelated image, human existence is often subsumed under digital existence.[17] In other words, relational thinking is contingent on how we perceive and conceptualize the relationality between the human and the machine. If that is the case, we need to first abandon the differentiation between the human and the machine, as these two perceptual-conceptual frameworks are dependently originated.

HUMAN AND MACHINE

In "Psychosociologie du cinéma" [Psychosociology of cinema, 1960], an unfinished manuscript, Gilbert Simondon perceives and conceptualizes the cinema not as a technological instantiation, but as a layout of psychosociological relations that are concretized as an anthropotechnical ensemble:

> The cinema is a psychosociological reality because it involves a human activity in group, and an activity that supposes and provokes representations, sentiments, voluntary movements; this activity supposes and produces an interindividual relation in which the individuated intercedes not only as a unity, but also as a bearer of a bundle of significations, intentions: tendencies that are actualized in the cinematographic situation in a way they could not come to be known earlier in the entire human duration of time. Being discovered and

being a construction of man by himself, a realization of a historicity
that is not only factual, but also a reserve of virtualities and *puissance*
of auto-creation, such is the signification of the test to which the
cinema submits humanity by a new mode of consciousness and
knowledge, appreciation and representation. Returning from reality of
man to knowledge of man, from gesture to the consciousness of
gesture, with a certain deadline and a definite formalization that
effaces or reinforces electively such and such aspects, augments or
reduces such and such dimensions, the cinema is a certain regime of
man's relationship to himself, as an individuated and as a group, to
himself and to others.[18]

For Simondon, therefore, cinema as a technology instantiates not only
a layout of interindividual relationships that constitutes the social, but
also a transindividuated being's relationship to themselves and to others.
In addition, the technology also instantiates a consciousness's relationship to its technicity in a process of transindividuations. In this process,
consciousness operates as a "reserve of virtualities and *puissance*"—or
in Yogācāra terms, an *ālaya*-consciousness.[19] Hence, Simondon argues
that a technical object is not to be considered as a utensil enslaved to
human beings. Rather, it is "like a condensed human effort, in waiting,
being an available virtuality, a potential action." In this sense, "it is really like a social being, and it does not constitute a supplement of the
soul (that it cannot *be*), but a supplement of the society and the power
of action: the human-machine couple is a concrete ensemble." For
Simondon, such an ensemble makes possible "modes of being and
thoughts, types of social structure" that would otherwise be impossible
without it as a reserve of potentialities.[20]

But then, why are the human and the machine fundamentally coupled? How does such an understanding of anthropotechnics enable us
to better negotiate power relations?

As I mentioned before, the intervention of sensations and affections
in the formational process in-forms a differentiation between internal
and external forms. As a result, the operation of the six consciousnesses,
which is an abject process, is turned into an objectivized subjective
experience.[21] Bernard Stiegler, based on Immanuel Kant's understanding of consciousness, calls this process tertiary retention: the projection
of a reproduction (secondary retention, that is, recognition) of an apprehension or intuition (primary retention) onto an exterior medium

(consciousness or technic), which in turn serves as the substratum that promises the interiority and integrity of the ego as a continuous flux.[22]

For Stiegler, the technicity of consciousness is what Walter Benjamin calls *Reproduzierbarkeit* (reproducibility).[23] Such reproducibility is in turn driven by a protention: a sense of inadequation that unity and continuity cannot be completed without a tertiary retention. As a process of reproduction, consciousness performs and proliferates the differentiations between subject and object, interiority and exteriority, and human and technic. It is also manifested and experienced as temporality:

> [C]onsciousness is a flux constituted through articulations of primary and secondary retentions and protentions. As anticipations of the unity of conditions of the flux still to come, these protentions currently arising (apprehensively) from the flux of the past (through reproductive imagination) are also what project the synthesis of recognition. This assures the accumulation of all these points of view and of touch, of external sense in general, as (cinematic) *rushes* constructing the unity of a selfsame flux, adequate to itself at the conclusion of its unfolding, differentiated from the projective protention of precognitive recognition.[24]

Bernard Stiegler therefore argues that consciousness is by default cinematic. It is constituted by a projection (exteriorization) of an internal reproduction (objectivizing the subjective) and a (re)interiorization of this image as the ego (subjectivizing the objective). Thinking relationally is counterintuitive because consciousness *is* a process of differentiation between subject and object. He agrees with a position raised in the 1950s by Theodor Adorno (1903–69) and Max Horkheimer (1895–1973): that human consciousness is industrializable as the cinema, television, and the internet. Historically, such industrialization has been instrumentalized in order to consolidate the United States' global domination.[25] For Stiegler, Hollywood and Silicon Valley have been doing so by means of tertiary retention: the projection of the *I* onto an external medium as the *We* as well as the interiorization of the *We*—the universalized image of the United States *as* humanity—as the *I*.[26]

Technics and Time therefore reiterates an understanding of the *dispositif* as a process in which all biological lives participate voluntarily because their consciousnesses are hard-wired to do so. For Stiegler,

anthropotechnical transduction and transindividuation anticipate a
new metastable phase's incorporation into the power relations that the
layout perpetuates and promises to maintain.[27] However, in so doing, he
falls prey to what Peter Sloterdijk calls *cynical reason,* which is configured as a paradox. On the one hand, by acknowledging that human
beings are by default technical beings, we must acknowledge that the
human and the machine are transindividuated. On the other hand, by
suggesting that human consciousness has its own technicity, which is
hard-wired to be mechanically reproduced and then reinternalized by
the consciousness, Stiegler returns to a cynical notion that human beings are enslaved to technics and technology.[28]

Sloterdijk therefore argues:

> Cybernetics, as the theory and practice of intelligent machines, and
> modern biology, as the study of system-environment-units, have
> forced the questions of the old metaphysical divisions to be posed
> anew.
>
> Here, the concept of objective spirit turns into the principle of
> information. Information enters between thoughts and things as a
> third value, between the pole of reflection and the pole of the thing,
> between spirit and matter. Intelligent machines—like all artifices that
> are culturally created—eventually also compel the recognition of
> "spirit." Reflection or thought is infused into matter and remains
> there ready to be re-found and further cultivated. Machines and
> artifices are thus memories or reflections turned objective.
>
> The statement "there is information" implies therefore that there
> are systems; there are memories; there are cultures; there is artificial
> intelligence. Even the sentence "there are genes" can only be
> understood as the product of the new situation wherein the principle
> of information is successfully transferred into the sphere of nature.
>
> Such a reconceptualization of reality diminishes the interest in
> traditional notions of theory, such as subject/object relation. Even the
> constellation of "I" and "world" loses much of its luster, not to
> mention the worn-out polarity of individual and society. But above all,
> the metaphysical distinction between nature and culture withers.
> This is because both sides of the distinction are only regional states of
> information and its processing.[29]

For Sloterdijk, therefore, if we work within the logic of cybernetics, all
states of things and beings are instantiations of information. Yet, to say
that "there is information" implies that these individuated states of

things or beings have always existed and endured as technicities-consciousnesses, and that information is always information *of* something. The point is that these states of things and beings are media that retain, convey, and process information *as* something. What cybernetics—and today, digital existence—demonstrates is that states of things or beings are manifestations of a layout of pure information. In our control-society today, there is no biopolitical life. Rather, anthropotechnically, we are instantiations of a matrix of relationships (data). Governmentality is therefore carried out as a management of such relationships as pure technicity.

AFFECTS

Nevertheless, information is not something. It indicates the relationalities or potentialities that can be retrieved and actualized as something. In this sense, Sloterdijk has not departed significantly from Stiegler. For Sloterdijk, there is a singular technicity (operational principles) that in-forms any state of anthropotechnical things or being (the human consciousness and the machine): information-matter (potentiality-actualization). For Stiegler, a technical medium reproduces the technicity of the human consciousness. For both of them, such technicity runs on autopilot and cannot be conceived otherwise. In this light, our anthropotechnical milieu (or plane of existence) operates on a perpetual process of transindividuations that maintain a certain balance between power relations. These power relations, as Michel Foucault demonstrates, are inevitably configured and manifested as biopolitics. All these theories rehearse and reiterate the substrate-form divide in European logical reasoning.

If we put these ideas side-by-side with Yogācāra Buddhism, we can say that for Sloterdijk, the divide between the human and the machine is a perceptual-conceptual proliferation initiated by the karmic operation in the *ālaya*-consciousness. In this sense, in the *ālaya*-consciousness itself, there is no divide between human and technics. Meanwhile, we can say that for Stiegler, the cinema is a reproduction of the *ālaya*-consciousness.

My comparative reading here reveals two blind spots in their arguments. First, if the process of actualization-virtualization is activated by karmic impulses, it does not need to run on autopilot. The consciousness can assume an agency over this process once it arrives at an insight into how each impulse affects—and is affected by—this process of becoming. Second, as Foucault argues, the *dispositif* is the layout of power relations, not the states of things or beings that instantiate these relations. Therefore, each transindividuating process rewrites not the status (stasis) of each individual, but rather the relationalities that affect—and are affected by—how things and beings are transindividuated. In other words, one microperceptual change will trigger a macro revision of the overall layout—albeit the rippling effect of such a revision may seem intangible at first. Affects operate—and can be rendered inoperative *as not* operative—precisely because substrate and form are neither different nor the same, neither not different nor not the same.

Brian Massumi therefore argues that a microperceptual change takes place on the level of affect. In *Ethics,* Baruch Spinoza defines *affectus* in the following way:

1. The human body can be affected in many ways by which its power of acting is increased or diminished, and also in other ways which make its power of acting neither greater nor smaller....
2. The human body can undergo many changes, and yet retain the impressions, i.e. the traces, of objects ... and consequently the same images of things....

   Our mind sometimes acts, but sometimes is passive; namely in so far as it has adequate ideas, so far it necessarily acts, and in so far as it has inadequate ideas, so far it is necessarily passive....
   From this it follows that our mind is liable to more passions the more inadequate ideas it has, and conversely that it performs more actions the more adequate ideas it has.[30]

Affect is therefore the interstice between being affected and affecting, and between feeling (a bodily impression) and thinking (idea). If the idea is inadequate, it produces passions (potentials to act), whereas if the idea is adequate, it produces actions. However, Spinoza adds immediately: "The body cannot determine the mind to thinking, nor can the mind determine the body to motion or to rest, or to anything else (if there is anything else)."[31] It is because only *conatus* can propel the formational process of a thought (an act of thinking) or movement, through its instantiations as impulses.[32] Hence, affect can be understood as an activator of potentialities and possible conditions, from one moment of *living* to another.[33]

But how do we become mindful of affects? As I discussed in the previous chapter, the *Mahā Satipaṭṭhāna Sutta* suggests that we first observe our breathing intently. When the consciousness is mindful of every moment in the act of inhalation-exhalation, the present is no longer experienced as an interval between the past and the future, but as *the way it is.* For the Theravādins, this enables the consciousness to be mindful of the body as a "sack" that encloses organs, muscles, and bones that are connected by tendons, nerves, and blood vessels. Rather than being dictated by a *self,* these components perform their functions as the way it is, though these functions—and their forms—are attuned and adjusted ecologically.[34]

The *Sutta* then recommends the practitioner to be mindful of the *vedanās* (sensations and affections) generated by the body: being pleasant, unpleasant, or neither pleasant nor unpleasant.[35] In order to do so, the consciousnesses must first become mindful of the sensorial stimulations each perceptual organ receives: the light that hits the retinas; the minute magnetic energies that compose a sonic field; the olfactory stimulations that enter the nose; the subtle tastes at different parts of the tongue; the tactile sensations and temperature differences that envelop the skin of our entire body; and psychophysical stimulations.[36] The practitioner will arrive at a *sudden* awareness that at the *here and now,* internal forms (the perceptual organs) and external forms (sense data that stimulate these organs) are inseparable. Their boundary and their dependent originations are initiated by *vedanās:* each being a subtle affective stimulus in which feeling and thinking are interchangeable.

After this, the practitioner should proceed to observe how each instant of feeling-thinking gives rise to the first five consciousnesses: of the eyes, ears, nose, tongue, and body. Each instant of affective intensity instantiates the potential to perceive-conceptualize and the potential to generate signs, and their actualizations into internal and external forms. Such an instant or process *is* the consciousness.[37] The sixth consciousness (of the mind) operates with the other five consciousnesses and coordinates such an operation ecologically under the seventh consciousness or *manas.* Every configurative component, element, and tissue in this ecology is an actualized potentiality, and these potentialities are actualized microperceptually at each interstice between feeling and thinking.[38]

Affect is therefore not a thing, not even a feeling or thinking, but a *relation* between feeling and thinking that is instantiated as a relation between forms and the sensory-perceptual abilities (consciousnesses).[39] As I mentioned in the previous chapter, Massumi—based on Gilles Deleuze and Félix Guattari—calls a sudden insight into such a relation a "microperception."[40] This concept corresponds to the Zen understanding of *tuầnnguồ* (sudden revelation) and to Charles Sanders Peirce's notion of abduction.[41] Erin Manning puts this idea into her choreography. She calls each beat of her performance an event, an "actual occasion" that "foreclose[es] momentarily the potential for recombination." Between events are intervals, which she calls "refrains." Such refrains reopen potentialities that can reterritorialize the body as "molecular and molar composites" that puts into creation renewed spatial relationships and *embodied* durations. Each refrain is therefore an affective insight: a return or reflection of the creative process itself.[42]

REFLECTION INSIGHT

This insight into relationality is called *pratyaveksanāprajñā* (reflection insight). *Pratyaveksanā* refers to a reflection (mindfulness) of the operation of dependent originations (as in *pratya* or conditions), from one moment (*kṣaṇa*) to another. It also refers to a mode of interbecoming that is based on *care-for*, a notion that resonates with Martin Heidegger's Dasein (being-there; *In-der-Welt-sein* or being-in-the-world; and *Mitsein* or being-with). In *Sein und Zeit* [*Being and Time,* 1927], Heidegger argues that Immanuel Kant's understanding of "I" as *res cogitans* means that the *I* is a logical substratum—ὑποκείμενον (*hypokeimenon*)—that binds all together, which is to say the consciousness itself. Heidegger therefore calls it the εἶδος (*eidos*) or form of representation, which "makes everything representing and everything represented be what it is." Therefore, *I* is best understood as Being-present-at-hand, or put simply, the "Reality of the *res cogitans.*"[43]

Nonetheless, on a day-to-day basis, *I* is not understood as Being-present-at-hand and Being-in-the-world (*in-der-Welt-sein*). For Heidegger, the "everyday interpretation of the Self . . . has a tendency to understand itself in terms of the 'world' with which it is concerned. When Dasein has itself in view ontically, it *fails to see* itself in relation to the kind of Being of that entity which it is itself."[44] In other words, when we say *I,* we often *overlook* the very Being-in-the-world that is Dasein itself; instead, *I* look for *they-self* to authenticate *I*. In this sense, Dasein, which is *authentically itself* and has its *self-constancy*, falls *"factually into non-Self-constancy."*[45] This failure or fall therefore compels *I* to project the Being of Dasein, on which (*das Woraufhin*) the possibility of Dasein's totality can be interpreted and discerned (what Stiegler calls tertiary retention). The structure of *care* is therefore a resoluteness or a determination to strive toward what Dasein can potentially be (*Sein-zum-Tode* or Being-toward-death), yet this anticipation is Dasein's *immer schon* (always-already), as its totality has been merely in concealment all along.[46]

Imamichi Tomonobu (1922–2010) argues that there is a structural resemblance between Heidegger's understanding of care and Zen Buddhism's. If we understand Dasein as the Tathāgatagarbha, the ultimate emptiness or existence that is an instantiation of—and is instantiated by—*all potentialities,* it is indeed the *hypokeimenon* of all forms or modes of existence (*eidos*). The Tathāgatagarbha is always concealed, as it is the emptiness on which the layout of interdependent relations between these potentialities is projected. But then, emptiness is not a thing; it simply refers to the existential/nonexistential quality of the layout itself. Thus, the layout (*ālaya*-consciousness) and its *hypokeimenon* are neither different nor the same, neither not different nor not the same. On a day-to-day basis, when I say, "*I care*," I project the Tathāgatagarbha as a Being that is to be achieved, even though it has always been there all along.[47] As the Sixth Elder of Zen, Hwèinəng/Huineng (638–713) exclaims after he has finished hearing the *Diamond Sutra: Hagi dzìɪsièng pŭən dzìɪ kɪotsɪok?/Heqi zixing ben zi juzu?* (*Nanzokisen, jishō wa hon'yori gusoku serukotoo?;* Who would expect that self-nature [the Tathāgatagarbha], in itself, has always been adequately there)?[48]

However, *pratyaveksanāprajñā* (reflection insight) does not refer to this form of care: one that is locked within *manas.* If the Tathāgatagarbha has always been *already there,* the form of care driven by an anticipation is a mere performance driven by afflictions and anxiety, as well as a failure to understand that: "the past mind is ungraspable, the present mind is ungraspable and the future mind is ungraspable."[49] In the *Śūraṅgama Sūtra,* when Ānanda asks whether the Tathāgatagarbha lies within causation (that is, it is identical to the layout of forms) or outside causation (that is, its form-giving ability is self-causing), Śākyamuni Buddha answers:

Therefore, you should understand that the existence of the essential, wondrously understanding, enlightened . . . awareness [the Tathāgatagarbha] is not dependent for its existence on causes and conditions, nor does it exist in and of itself. Nevertheless, one cannot say that it does not exist in and of itself, nor can one say that it is independent of causes and conditions. Statements that account for its existence cannot be negated, yet one cannot say that they cannot be negated. Such statements cannot be affirmed, yet one cannot say that they cannot be affirmed. What is entirely beyond all defining attributes—that is the entirety of Dharma.[50]

What is being abduced in this passage is a reserve of potentialities that are nondifferentiated and nondifferentiable, yet, once actualized, they are manifested as a layout of differences (forms). Care must therefore be exercised mindfully *here and now,* and it can only be done so by attending to the relationalities between forms. This is because these relationalities are the instantiations of emptiness. Massumi argues that Heidegger's understanding of care as being structured as Being-toward-death is symptomatic of anxiety. For Gilbert Simondon, anxiety is generated when the preindividuated formative field is mistaken as the subject's interiority, which is both impossible and unimaginable.[51]

As I mentioned in the beginning of this chapter, care is considered in Buddhism to be an engagement with benevolence, compassion, empathy, and equanimity. In meditation, a practitioner can train themself by scanning the life of an enemy or a loved one, and by engaging their consciousnesses in this person's life from the moment of their birth until the present. The practitioner is not to think and analyze the experience. Rather, the practitioner is to be mindful of the subtle affective changes that in-form this experience.[52] Usually, the practitioner would experience benevolence, as they perceive and conceptualize what they scan as the experience of the other.

Then, as they experience the afflictions, suffering, and hardship this person goes through, they subjectivize these sensations and affections as compassion. Soon, scenes of other people who are related to this person would emerge: the romance between their parents, private moments experienced by their friends, their first romantic encounter, and so forth. Thus, a life is no longer perceived and conceptualized as a self-sustained and linear trajectory, but as an ecology of relations. Life cannot be imagined without death, and both are forms that instantiate a karmic relationship. When compassion becomes overbearing, the practitioner needs to accept the ecology as *the way it is,* thus enabling empathy to be developed. Meanwhile, equanimity can be achieved when the practitioner is able to let go of the idea of life as a duration, and instead engage themself in and only in the present.

IDEOLOGY AND IM-MEDIATION

In political relationalities, where lies ideology? How does ideology in-form—and be in-formed by—the technical configuration of the cinematographic consciousness? Eventually, what is the medium specificity that enables the cinematographic consciousness to attain—and arrive at—a reflection insight?

Let us revisit a set of definitions we have established thus far. The cinematographic image is, by default, in-formed by a layout of karmic impulses. A karmic impulse actualizes the potentiality to perceive and conceptualize and also the potentiality to generate signs. This impulse, in itself, is actualized as an affect. The karmic impulse that harnesses and actualizes those potentialities in the *ālaya*-consciousness (or, in Henri Bergson's terms, memories) in order to initiate a *present:* what Brian Massumi calls ontopower.[53] When an ontopower operates in its state of concealment and triggers the differentiation between internal and external forms, the divide between self and other appears to be unquestionable. Meanwhile, the sense of attachment initiated by *manas* firmly adheres to the existence of such a divide. Such an attachment in turn produces afflictions out of inadequation: avarice, frustration and anger, and delusion. Consciousness is therefore perceived and conceptualized as a layout of power relations.

In *Die deutsche Ideologie* [*The German Ideology,* Karl Marx (1818–83) and Friedrich Engels (1820–95), 1832], consciousness is configured as an awareness of a set of relationships—between human and nature and between capital and labor—that are codified and determined by a superstructure. A worker therefore reproduces and interiorizes ideology as the relationalities that constitute their consciousness; they then project these relationalities as an awareness exterior to their lived experience (see Bernard Stiegler's tertiary retention).[54] In classical Marxist film and media theories, therefore, an ideology appears to be a superstructure that the consciousness adopts and reproduces through a cinematic experience.[55]

However, as Massumi points out, the *dispositif* is a layout of processual power relations. Bodies are then given form as traces and inscriptions of these power relations.[56] As Judith Butler argues, subjectivity is
both an inscription and a performance. It is best understood not as an
internal formation that envelops the beingness of an individual. Rather,
it is an expression of those power relations that a biopolitical life lives
through, as such life comes to believe that it has managed to be individuated by encapsulating these inscriptions as its interiority.[57] In this
light, Gilbert Simondon calls this an encapsulation of the preindividual
inside the individuated, and the anxiety this process creates obliges the
individuated to externalize what is un-internalizable as *ideology*.[58] As
Massumi argues, what we call ideology—exteriorized and projected as
a technology of recognition—is in-formed by every instant and instance
of our participation in these power relations. In other words, the lived
power relations are the ideology—and we all *willed* it to its formation.[59]
Thomas Lamarre therefore argues that ideology is best understood not
as a superstructure that overdetermines the configuration of a techno-
social ecology, but as an infrastructure that underdetermines every
refrain.[60]

As Mouloud Boukala argues, modern film theorists including Jean-
Louis Baudry, Christian Metz, and Jacques Aumont have made it clear
that *dispositif* is a relational process.[61] In spite of their clarifications, there
is still a tendency for us to pay attention not to the relationalities themselves, but to the power formation that seems to operate *on* us from
above. In *Technics and Time*, Stiegler calls this process Epiphylogenesis.
What he means is that consciousness operates as the cinema, and what
we call the cinema is a technical instantiation of the consciousness. Teleologically, the consciousness projects its technicity as the ideology,
which is reproduced and instantiated as various media formations. These
formations, as technical consciousnesses, in turn instill, reproduce, and
internalize ideology as the human technicity-consciousness.[62]

By saying so, Stiegler has disconcealed an aporia: (1) the medium
specificity of the cinema is its reproducibility, which is the technicity
that constitutes consciousness; and (2) since all media formations are
based on reproducibility, what we have historically called the cinema
has no medium specificity. However, if we rethink this aporia in Mas-
sumian and Buddhist terms, we may arrive at a different conclusion. By
focusing on the forms that conceal the relationalities they instantiate,

we invest our energy into the *media* and how they mediate the power relations they form among themselves. Instead, we should investigate the process of mediation (transduction) and how media are in-formed not as coherent and unified systems, but instead as relationalities that are being rewritten and reinstantiated from one moment to another.

In *The Lumière Galaxy* [2015], Francesco Casetti therefore argues that the question "What is cinema?" is better understood as "Where is cinema?"[63] For Casetti, a cinematic layout (assemblage) requires: (1) an ensemble of products; (2) "a set of rules for constructing these products on a narrative, stylistic, or grammatical level, which, despite its change over time, represents a reference point for the production process"; and (3) a form of production that either conforms to or challenges these rules. He calls the intersection of these three domains an "imaginary archive" that "enacts a language." In the process of consumption, cinema "is an experience that implicates sight and hearing within a circumscribed situation." Then, the cinema, as an environment, is always "*embodied* (connected to the body) and *embedded* (connected to a culture)." Such an environment is also "always *grounded,* which is to say that it takes place in precise, physical spaces," be that a movie theater, on a mobile device, on a personal computer, or even on social media.

Finally, for Casetti, the cinema is also driven by *symbolic needs,* that is, needs to use storytelling as a device to confirm and reconstruct the spectator's sense of *being human.* This anthropological dimension of the cinema is rendered possible through: (1) *negotiation,* which is what Stiegler calls tertiary retention; (2) *suture,* that the image, which is made up of discrete pieces of audiovisual fields, is made unified and coherent as a flux as the spectator's gaze is locked into the gaze of the "absent subject," which the cinema always implicitly addresses; and (3) *selection,* that the process of negotiation and suture inevitably involves a process of selection, which actualizes a number of potentialities while abandoning others. Finally, all these processes will converge and return to a mode of *recursivity,* or what Stanley Cavell would call automatism: the establishment of a discourse that retrospectively and retroactively gives the cinema a definition.[64] Alternatively, Hui Yuk regards recursivity as a principle or technicity that impels a recursive assemblage of relationalities.[65]

What Casetti describes can be considered a media ecology that we would historically regard as the cinema. What underlines each domain of his definition, I argue, is karma. What Casetti calls an imaginary archive is best understood in Pasolini's terms as a reserve of im-signs, or in Buddhist terms, the *ālaya*-consciousness. Under a set of causes and conditions, these relationalities are instantiated as the anthropotechnical technicity-consciousness, that is, the psychic, physical, and social bodies that constitute what we call the cinema. As instantiations, media formations are by default embodied, embedded (in culture), and grounded (in a physical space).

However, Casetti's understanding of the cinema becomes contestable when it comes down to the three symbolic needs. As Erin Manning argues, each event can be understood as a selection, which momentarily suspends the actualization of those potentialities that are yet to be realized. But then, as I have discussed, digital modes of existence (and, some say, post-cinema) are more productively understood and engaged not as a form of suture, but rather as a process of transindividuation. In fact, as I argue in chapter 2, even in the karma-image, there is no identification (suture), but only transindividuation. In this sense, negotiation needs to be reconsidered not as a mode of reproduction, but as a mode of coproduction (or cocreation). However, such a coproductive-cocreative force (ontopower) is not always harnessed democratically and relationally by transindividuated beings for what Markos Hadjioannou would call an *ethical* purpose.[66]

Ontopower is therefore frequently harnessed by the karmic impulses as a way to preempt the consciousness from being mindful of its own technicity. Preemption is attained precisely by means of tertiary retention: the reproduction and projection of such recursivity as ideology. This projection is often seen either as a sociopolitical technicity that codifies every aspect of the transindividuated being's psychic, physical, and social lives, or as a threat, terror, or force of evil against which a transindividuated being's freedom (from ideology) must be defended. In other words, there is no ideology.[67] There are only recursive karmic impulses that strive to preempt the consciousness from being mindful of itself. This process is by no means specific to the cinema as a medium.

Massumi uses an example to illustrate his point. On April 15, 2011, *The Guardian* published his first journalistic article, titled "The Half-Life of Disaster," which analyzed how the tsunami in Japan and Hurricane Katrina in New Orleans were reported in mass and social media. In both instances, Massumi argues, the disasters were reported as horror: an *affect* that has its own existential value. Such an overwhelming horror convinced the readers that any individual or collective efforts to initiate changes would be inconceivable. To counter such an existential threat, the Japanese and U.S. governments both violated their own constitutions and deployed their national security guards domestically to rescue lives and preempt local unrests. In both countries, such a state of exception has been normalized, as national security guards have been deployed, with increasing frequency, to preempt, manage, or suppress both lawful and unlawful protests as well as to collect private information for the purposes of preemption and persecution.

Massumi observes that, once archived as a tertiary retention in mass and social media, the horror's (of both events) potency to effect changes was reduced exponentially in a matter of two weeks. Meanwhile, Massumi notices that the feedback section of his article, which is supposed to function as a public sphere, contains posts that are entirely disengaged from the article's subject matter. Most readers state and reiterate their beliefs and defend them as their own existential values. These are not negotiations of private opinions. Rather, each reader uses other readers' comments as platforms of im-mediations: they respond to their own affective engagements, which are entirely driven by *manas*. He therefore argues that perhaps there is no such thing as a public sphere—and there has never been one.[68]

What we call ideology is therefore a reproduction and projection of a seemingly insurmountable fear of the unlivable preindividual, or a state of nondifferentiation between self and other. Such a state of nondifferentiation, ironically, is *the way it is:* the plane of absolute luminosity and the source of infinite creativity. Yet, the potentiality of letting be the technicity of consciousness is considered a threat by an individuated being, as the beingness of such a being is founded on an attachment to a metastable phase in a larger process of becoming. As fear is projected as something that has its own existential value, a creative potential that can initiate changes is imagined and imaged as a threat against such metastability. To conquer such an existential crisis, fear has always been considered a just cause of political persecution, violence, and genocide—only that what used to be considered a historical or communal exception is our day-to-day reality.

MISAPPREHENSIONS, FEARS, AND QUEERNESS

Yogācāra and Tathāgatagarbha scholars argue that fears are generated by four *viparyāsas* (misapprehensions or perceptual-conceptual inversions): *śuciviparyāsa* (misapprehension of our impure body as pure), *sukhaviparyāsa* (misapprehension of those afflictions produced by sensations and affections as happiness), *nityaviparyāsa* (misapprehension of impermanence as permanence), and *ātmaviparyāsa* (misapprehension of nonself as self). Any challenges to these misapprehensions are to be considered as ontological threats to our existence and must therefore be preempted.[69]

As a perceptual-conceptual proliferation, conventional reality and the ecology that sustains it operate on a process of misapprehension. An insight into such technicity enables the consciousness to become aware of the karmic impulses or affective power that it can actively rewrite with a mindfulness of the nondifferentiation between purity and impurity, happiness and afflictions, permanence and impermanence, and self and nonself. For us, however, the idea is fearful that there is no difference between purity and impurity, happiness and afflictions, permanence and impermanence, self and nonself. Our *manas* is there to conserve our sense of purity, happiness, permanence, and self and further to preempt any threats that are considered alien and alienating.

In cinema and media studies, queer scholars were among the first group of intellectuals who realized the ethical and political impasses brought about by the discipline's adherence to the divides between the center and margin, the empowered and disempowered, normativity and exception, subject and object, and self and other. In order to challenge these divides, we need to first acknowledge that they, together with the *ideology* that codifies them, are not systems in which we operate. Rather, they are effects of reading and writing, and of looking and being-looked-at, in a mediating process, from one moment to another. In this light, each affective instant is a potentiality that can disconceal the technicity of our transindividuated consciousness(es) and can persuade us to confront our fears of differences.

For Teresa de Lauretis, queer theory emerged toward the end of the 1980s, in the middle of the AIDS crisis, out of a political need for using queer visibility as a strategy to challenge the self-perceived purity, happiness, permanence, and self-consistency of heteronormative subjectivity. Yet, by entering the heteronormative discourse without questioning how power relations in-form—and are in-formed by—the discourse itself, queer activists and intellectuals soon found themselves operating with the same technicity as the heteronormative consciousness they sought to critique. By letting such technicity operate on autopilot, they became patients—not agents—of ontopower.

For de Lauretis, relationalities are constantly reconfigured by affects. An affect encapsulates and releases the narcissistic (the navel gazing-examination of the self and the reflective attention to the self as the other), intransitive (how a subject-object relationship is fostered), transitive (relationality), and active but not transitive (reconstruction of subjectivities).[70] As Earl Jackson Jr., argues, the subject is an "effect of signification" that is "socially constructed and discursively realized" in a way that neither the "mechanisms of its constructions nor its discursive formations ever totalize or even fully stabilize the subject." Hence, it is "out of their indeterminacies, overdeterminations, contradictions, and signifying excesses and insufficiencies that agency emerges." For Jackson, these signifying exceptions instantiate potentialities that are not recognized by the heteronormative discourse. Yet, they remain operative as creative affective engagements: ontopower.[71]

Nonetheless, as early as 1989, Kobena Mercer and Richard Fung pointed out that the demand for self-(re)presentation, energized largely by Anglo-American gay white males, not only desubjectivizes queer lives of color, women, and trans people, but also turns them into technologies of recognition that help to construct a *queer normativity*.[72] Moreover, as queer scholars began to study queer histories, cultural productions, and activisms outside North America and Europe, they have also brought to the fore queer theory's own Euro-Americancentrism and postcolonialism. Even though the technicity of consciousness remains the same, the technologies of recognition and exclusion are culturally and historically specific, which require different affective engagements and reconstitutions.

For example, as Petrus Liu argues, when queer theory was translated, disseminated, and discussed in Mainland China, Taiwan, Hong Kong, and other Sinophone regions, activists and scholars immediately found that the mode of heteronormative exclusion was—and still is—configured differently in China and in the Sinophone communities, due to their historical differences.[73] As Tze-lan Deborah Sang and

Giovanni Vitiello point out respectively, during most parts of the Ming (1368–1644) and Qing (1644–1911) dynasties, there was a firm divide between reproductive and nonreproductive kinships and affections. Reproductive kinships were largely instituted as family and communal affairs, whereas nonreproductive ones—including same-sex relationships and desires—were regarded as private matters so long as they did not interfere with reproduction. However, by the late nineteenth century, European notions of sexuality (as a medical category) and normativity (as a sociopolitical and moral category) were disseminated by missionaries and medical practitioners throughout Asia, thus making what we now call homophobia a sign of modernity and progress.[74]

These two conflicting notions—same-sex affections and nonnormative sexualities—still coexist in Mainland China, Hong Kong, Taiwan, and other Sinophone regions today. First, there is a consensus that same-sex affections are private matters so long as they do not interfere with either reproduction (on the familial level) or public morality and *hygiene* (on the social level). Such a consensus can sometimes create a false impression that nonnormative sexualities are tolerated in private. By contrast, bullying and harassment at school, work, home, and church, as well as in legal matters, are common experiences of the lesbian, gay, bisexual, transgender, queer, intersex + (LGBTQI+) community. Legally, homosexuality between men was decriminalized in colonial Hong Kong in 1991, with an age of consent set at twenty-one (versus sixteen for heterosexual individuals), and on the Mainland in 1997. After the handover of Hong Kong to the People's Republic of China (PRC) in 1997, the Special Administrative Region government has insisted that LGBTQI+ rights do not require legal protection.[75] In the Republic of China itself, there has never been a law prohibiting homosexuality, though homophobia was institutionalized in Taiwan under Chiang Kai-shek's (1887–1975) military regime (1945–75).

Second, since the late-1990s, the queer movements in North America and Europe sometimes operate on the neoliberal presupposition that as a productive consumer, a person living a queer life should have the right to determine that person's own relations with other producers and consumers. This logic coincides with a belief circulated in urban Mainland China during the 1990s, advocated by the writer Wang Shuo and his supporters: that liberalism enables each individuated consumer to make decisions that would maximize their collective freedom, thus economic reforms would inevitably lead to political democratization. As Jason McGrath points out, this belief was crushed by the Tiananmen Square crackdown in Beijing in 1989, followed by Deng Xiaoping's (1904–97) southern tour in 1992. These developments confirmed the Chinese Communist Party's (CCP) policy of building a market economy regulated, supervised, or even directly owned by the party, with increasingly tightened political surveillance.[76] In the PRC, therefore, the term *fenhong jingji quan* (pink economy) has a *double entendre*: (1) an economy built for the benefit of middle-class queer-normative professionals, many of whom were educated overseas with the monetary and cultural capitals to consume a Euro-American queer lifestyle; and (2) an economy capitalized on by corporations that are run by the party-state, which uses queer consumption as a façade to prove contemporary China's cosmopolitanism and cultural liberalism.

Third, queer activists often lost sight of relationality in their struggle for self-(re)presentation, a dimension from which people who inhabit a postsocialist neo-Confucian milieu cannot possibly escape.[77] Neo-Confucianism today is a postsocialist invention, which emerged in the 1980s as a *return* to family values, heteronormative gender roles and performances, and the accumulation of family capital at the expense of individual interests in order to safeguard the financial security of future generations. Neo-Confucianism then was institutionalized by the party-state as the *shehui zhuyi hexie shehui* (socialist harmonious society), a national policy adopted by the Sixteenth Central Committee of the CCP on September 19, 2004, according to which media should promote the formation of a public consensus by generating affects that would allow the spectators to *gongming* (resonate) their sensoria with each other by means of patriotism and nationalism.[78] Even though such a policy had not been systematically carried out in Hong Kong until 2020, neo-Confucianism had gradually taken hold through mass media and social media that had both been increasingly attuned to the Beijing consensus.[79]

Whether we be intellectuals or activists, we may have the insight to point out that postsocialist neoliberalism is fundamentally at odds with queer politics, queer cultural productions, and queer creativities. Yet the technicity of our consciousness—to misapprehend impurity as purity, afflictions as happiness, impermanence as permanence, and non-self as self—persuades us to conserve these illusions by submitting ourselves to a preexisting topos that seems to have always guaranteed these values to all willing participants. We let karma run on autopilot. The more we do, the more we come to believe that there is an insurmountable, impregnable, and undefeatable—and therefore, fearful—stasis.

TONGZHI CINEMA AS A MEDIA ECOLOGY

In Mainland China, Hong Kong, Taiwan, and other Sinophone regions, the term *tongzhi dianying* (*tungzi dinjing* in Cantonese or "comrade cinema" in English) is commonly used to designate films, video art, and other media about queer subject matters. On a day-to-day basis, the term *tongzhi* is used interchangeably with the term *ku'er* ("queer") in Mainland China and the Sinophone. The nomination *tongzhi* was originated in the Mainland during the revolutionary era (1921 or 1949–76) and was appropriated toward the late 1980s by the Chinese and Sinophone lesbian and gay communities, for several reasons. First, as people under oppression, lesbians and gay men considered themselves comrades who fought for a common objective. Second, the term *tongzhi* contains the word *tong*, which signifies *tongxing'ai* (same-sex love), a term coined in Japan during the late Meiji (1867–1912) and early Taishō (1912–25) periods to translate the German clinical term *Homosexualität*. While the German nomination classifies same-sex intercourse as a form of sexuality, its Japanese-Chinese translation connotes intimacy, camaraderie, and kinship. Third, by calling each other *tongzhi*, members of the LGBTQI+ communities playfully turn a term that used to be associated with political violence (especially during the Cultural Revolution in Mainland China, 1966–76) into one that signifies communal bonds and liberation.[80]

Tongzhi cinema has always been part and parcel of the larger interregional (that is, global or transnational) and intraregional (that is, Sinophone and inter-Asian) queer cinema. As Karl Schoonover and Rosalind Galt argue, there is something fundamental about the cinematographic image and apparatus that "pushes against the reification of meaning, as it keeps the signifier in motion, never fixing terms of relationality."[81] Thus, *tongzhi* cinema, like queer cinema in general, challenges the heteronormative mode of meaning production and discourses by destabilizing those social codes that bind a signifier to a signified (or a form to its values).[82]

For example, by destabilizing the relationship between the signifier/ form (*tongzhi*) and its signified/values (political violence/alternative kinship and liberation), the act of calling oneself *tongzhi* engages one to see these various signifieds or values as a palimpsest.[83] It makes palpable that alternative kinship and liberation are necessary because of the historical violence that the heteronormative society—maintained and managed by party-state power—has constituted one's condition of marginalization. Moreover, the term *tongzhi* foregrounds an intricate relationship between the private and the public by suggesting that individual sexual freedom must be fought for by reinventing kinships and rewriting the larger layout of political relationalities.

Neo-Confucian technologies of recognition (including education, mass media, social media, governmentality, and postsocialist neoliberal economy) harness every biopolitical life's direct affective engagement in relationality—as in *care-for-the-others*—as an ontopower. In other words, censorship, harassment, detention, imprisonment, and persecution are justified by the party-state's acting on behalf of the *people*. Biopolitical violence is therefore seen as an act to care for the purity, happiness, permanence, and ontological consistency of the larger social ecology. What *tongzhi* filmmakers do is to disconceal the technicity of consciousness that sustains this political metastasis. They do so by enabling the consciousness to be mindful of how each misapprehension is acknowledged as the only acceptable norm because *the way it is* is too frightening to imagine. A new kinship based on *care-as-the-way-it-is* can be configured out of a shared insight into such technicity.

Independent *tongzhi* cinema emerged in the PRC in the early 1990s. Since then, the Beijing-based filmmakers and festival curators have maintained an uneasy relationship with the city government. Despite the fact that the party-state gradually acknowledged the legitimacy of independent filmmaking in Mainland China between 1995 and 1999, the State Administration of Radio, Film, and Television (SARFT, now called the National Radio and Television Administration) has considered explicit representation of queer sexuality and nonnormative gender identities as grounds for denial of a license for distribution in mainstream movie theaters and broadcast television.[84]

In 2001, the first Beijing Queer Film Festival (BQFF) opened in the South Wing of the Peking University Library. It showcased six medium-budget fiction films, including Zhang Yuan's *Donggong xigong* [*East*

Palace, West Palace, 1995], Liu Bingjian's *Nannan nünü* [*Men and Women,* 1999], and Stanley Kwan's *Lan Yu* [2001].[85] Even though the festival received an acknowledgment from SARFT, the university's projectionist interrupted the screening of *East Palace, West Palace* and decried it as a moral corruption. The projectionist's complaint brought the festival to the attention of SARFT and the Beijing city police. Since then, subsequent editions of the BQFF were forced into exile in independent art galleries, foreign embassies, cafés, artist communes, and other venues, as the city police constantly interrupted screenings and discussion sessions by accusing them of breaching sanitation regulations or endangering public safety.[86]

As Bao Hongwei argues, the presence of state surveillance and intervention inspired festival curators Cui Zi'en, Fan Popo, and Stjn Deklerck to turn their attention from studio-style fiction films to Beijing-based documentary films and experimental fictions that use cinema as a form of direct audience engagement. In addition, these festival organizers chose their sites of exile strategically to signal their positionality vis-à-vis the city of Beijing and the party-state. For example, the second edition of the BQFF took place in the Songzhuang art village outside the city, under the auspices of the Li Xianting Foundation and the Beijing Independent Film Festival (BIFF). The following year, however, the festival curators moved the screenings back to galleries, cafés, and community centers in Central Beijing to reoccupy the urban center. Yet these strategies also signaled to the city government that the BQFF considered itself not only a cultural event, but also a mode of political activism, which triggered an even higher level of police intervention and surveillance through the internet and cell phones. As a result, the seventh edition of the festival mobilized a series of overseas servers to stream the films online, and in one event, the festival attendants boarded a train from Beijing to Dalian to watch a film distributed by USB sticks during their journey.[87]

Chinese independent *tongzhi* cinema is therefore not only a collection of films, but also a process of rewriting the power relations between the *tongzhi* creative community and the party-state by rethinking (1) how media can be appropriated, repurposed, or enlisted in a way that can affect—and be affected by—the configuration of a community in relation to the party-state power and (2) how geographic sites and locations can be re-spatialized to foster a sense of community not as a static formation, but as a mobile process of becoming that is constituted by a set of constantly changing relationalities.

We can therefore consider independent *tongzhi* cinema as what Brian Massumi would call a media ecology. There has always been a media ecology, including the cinema, television, and the internet. However, what these filmmakers do is to rewrite the modes of affective engagements between them, the spectators and participants, and the party-state. In such a process of rewrite, the metastability of the media ecology transduces into a destabilized phase, where new transindividuations arise between the biopolitical beings and the technological formations with which they work and coexist. The result is a microclimate. However, a microclimate is a critical point of convergence of anomies: a site of activated creative potentialities that await a layout of dominant conditions to rewrite the entire ecology.

On April 1, 2017, the PRC implemented the *Dianying chanye cujin fa* (Law to expatiate the [development of] the film industry). Article 26 of the law made it illegal to create, exhibit, and distribute independent films either in Mainland China or abroad (including Hong Kong and Taiwan) without obtaining a government permit.[88] The party-state's urgency to legislate against independent cinema testifies that a microclimate, no matter how minuscule, is perceived and conceptualized as a threat to the purity, happiness, permanence, and ontological consistency of the larger social ecology for which the party-state is supposed to *care*.

DEINDIVIDUATION, DESUBJECTIVIZATION, AND DEAUTONOMIZATION

It is important to remember that queer film festivals in other cities did not face the same level of challenge as the BQFF. For example, the ShanghaiPride Film Festival (SPFF) has enjoyed mainstream publicity and corporate sponsorship. In a way, being one of the four direct-controlled municipalities in the PRC (the others being Beijing, Tianjin, and Chongqing), a level of governance immediately below the central government, the city government of Shanghai enjoyed a high degree of administrative autonomy. In the eyes of that government, the SPFF has helped promote Shanghai's image as a culturally liberal and cosmopolitan space, as well as a significant site of major business opportunity and queer-friendly tourist attraction.[89] In other words, must *tongzhi*/queer recognition/self-recognition be a radical revision of the existing media and social ecologies?

In an online panel discussion in 2020 at "Queer" Asia, a London-based cultural and research group, I argued:

> Neoliberalism operates as a paradox. On the one hand, it encourages innovations and venerates "radical newness" as a sign of its progres-siveness. On the other hand, it takes away the means and agency from individuals to instigate radical changes. It does so by channeling our ontopower for preemptive measures. Under neoliberalism, we are encouraged to think inside the box by imagining radical changes within the "system," thus turning these radical changes into an impetus to encourage productive consumption and preemptive measures. Alternatively, we seem to face one remaining option: to think outside the box by dismantling the system.
>
> But then, we often fail to recognize that there has never been a box in the first place and the box is put there—by our own desire and fear—and is designed for us only.[90]

Individualities, subjectivities, and agencies are produced in every *act*, and every act instantiates a potentiality to enact and be enacted. As I pointed out in the panel, "The term 'queer' was originally proposed as an act of defiance, so that we can be mindful of each act as a potential-ity to make radical changes. Yet, when the term is used on a day-to-day basis in consumption, the ontopower of being queer has been preempted."[91]

In other words, every thought, act, and speech affects—and is affected by—a karmic impulse, which rewrites the technicity of the entire consciousness. As Cui Zi'en argues:

> I think the process of deconstruction itself is a new outcome, not that something new and different will arise and replace the deconstructed ones. If I kick this table here and it falls apart, the ruin is already a new outcome. . . . Actually, this so-called deconstruction is not deconstruc-tion. It's really my own innovation. The system we are confronted with is so big that every independent innovation on our part is read against it.[92]

Both Petrus Liu and Bao see Cui's own cinematic works as examples of how radical queerness can be conducted through seemingly individual and microscopic, but socially nourishing labors of deconstruction.[93] As a graduate of the Beijing Film Academy, Cui is a thinker in queer politics and aesthetics. In his work, Cui enables the consciousness to be mindful of the impact of microperceptions in the rewriting of an overall ecology. He demonstrates how individual films—as acts of defiance—can inspire independent *tongzhi* filmmakers to rethink what queer creativity can do under a system that operates on preempting such creativity.

Cui's film *Star Appeal* can be seen as an analogy of how microperception and ontopower operate. In the beginning of the film, a young man Xiao Bo (played by Yu Bo) and his friends pick up a young, naked, male hitchhiker, who claims himself to be a Martian. Xiao Bo then brings the hitchhiker home and names him E.T. In the first half of the film, Xiao Bo spends a lot of time with E.T. and teaches him language, mathematics, geography, and even history. As E.T. remains naked, Xiao Bo and his girlfriend, Wen Wen (Zhang Xiwen), also dress up E.T. and teach him social etiquette. Meanwhile, E.T. insists on remaining naked and waves his arms up and down as though they were wings, which he claims will take him back to Mars.

In the first part of the film, therefore, Xiao Bo and Wen Wen try to humanize and civilize E.T. However, as Xiao Bo teaches E.T., the anthropotechnical consciousness becomes mindful of the fact that each piece of knowledge is being presented as an act of differentiation: differences between a vowel and a consonant, one and zero, China and Japan, human and Martian, and human and animal. Such a system of differentiation, however, baffles E.T. In the second sequence of the film, for example, E.T., Xiao Bo, and his friend Xiao Jian (Hou Jian) gather on an empty field. E.T. turns his face toward the sun and tells his earthling companions that this is the way he absorbs nutrition. Xiao Jian, however, argues that on earth, only plants absorb nutrition through photosynthesis. But then, Xiao Bo seems to be convinced that perhaps we need to rethink how our natural and political ecologies operate in ontogenetic and interdependent terms.

The sequence in which Xiao Bo teaches E.T. how to become human consists of two static long takes. The first one is a long shot of their bed from a high angle, which reduces the sense of depth in the image. As in the rest of the film, the image is shot through a navy-blue filter, which reduces both the luminosity (light contrast) and temperature (color contrast) of the image and defamiliarizes the objects and beings by giving the overall milieu an aquatic quality. In the shot, Xiao Bo wears a blue T-shirt and a pair of dark blue shorts, while the bed is covered by a blue-and-white checkered sheet. The overall *mise-en-scène* therefore posits all the objects and beings on an equalizing plane of existence. In this shot, Xiao Bo gives E.T. a bottle of cologne and tells him to use it in order to cover his body odor. E.T.'s nudity, the proximity of the two men's bodies on the same bed, and the discussion of body odor all build up a sense of intimacy in the environment. In spite of Xiao Bo's reiteration of the difference between an earthling and a Martian, the anthropotechnical consciousness perceives and conceptualizes them as two biological lives that are intimately dependent on each other, liberated from those linguistic and epistemic differences that Xiao Bo is about to teach E.T.

Meanwhile, in the second shot, the camera is positioned on the side of the bed, which captures Xiao Bo and E.T. lying on their stomachs next to one another, as Xiao Bo gives E.T. his lessons. Again, this is conducted in a single long take. The film's penchant to use a one-scene-one-take style posits the consciousness in a series of pure optical and sound situations, thus severing the correlation between the body's sensory-motor functions and the process of image-formation. On the one hand, the consciousness continues to drive—and is driven by—an avalanche of karmic impulses. On the other hand, it is also conscious of its own becoming in a shared space with Xiao Bo and E.T., where observers are also the observed: *I know I am* being-with *these two biological lives; I know we are imaging-imagining together.* The consciousness therefore becomes mindful of the dependent originations of all the beings and objects that constitute it and how it is configured as a process of differentiation.

As the film progresses, to Wen Wen's chagrin, Xiao Bo falls in love with E.T. Two-thirds into the film, the *ménage à trois* visits a seashore on a sunny day. The three lovers walk down the top of a seawall. E.T. is ahead of Wen Wen and Xiao Bo, and he stands at the edge of the wall, naked, facing the sea, and waving his arms as though he were waiting to be delivered back to Mars. As Wen Wen and Xiao Bo walk down the seawall, the handheld camera does not follow them as an observer. Rather, in one take, it is discorrelated from these characters' perspectives and assumes the position of a fourth party in this outing and navigates between their bodies and the bodies of other visitors. Eventually, the camera "sits down" next to Xiao Bo, while E.T. waves his arms in the background. In the middle ground, Wen Wen addressees both Xiao Bo

FIGURE 24. The image as a layout of pure relationalities in *Star Appeal*

and the camera and asks him and *us* to make a decision between her and
E.T. (see Figure 24). In response, Xiao Bo replies that he does not see any
need to do so.

In this one-scene-one-take sequence, whose shot duration and camera mobility are made possible by digital technology, the (discorrelated
and *dividuated,* that is to say nonindividuating and nonindividuated)
image can be considered a layout of pure relationalities.[94] There are observers and observed, agents and patients, subjects and objects, though
these positionalities are initiated and extinguished interdependently
from one moment to another. The consciousness is therefore mindful of
its technicity and the shifting relationalities that affect—and are affected
by—each moment of karmic initiation-extinction. Narratively, E.T.'s arrival has rewritten the overall ecology of romantic relationships and kinships, a revision that Wen Wen cannot accept. The film does not invite
the consciousness to make any moral judgment on such a revision. Rather,
at this critical juncture, Xiao Bo and Wen Wen can both exercise their own
agencies over their relations to this changing ecology. In so doing, E.T.,
Xiao Bo, and Wen Wen are transindividuated as part of this new ecology
and they make their decisions intersubjectively.

Toward the end of the film, E.T. tells Xiao Bo that he was sent from
Mars to teach earthlings how to live with one another. Thus, the film

can be seen as a user manual for us to image-imagine a *tongzhi* utopia. As a film, *Star Appeal* does not create any opportunity for "identification." Rather, all the beings that constitute the technicity-consciousness as a whole relate to one another by means of (1) benevolence, or an unconditional care based on the fact that differentiation is a perceptual-conceptual proliferation; (2) compassion, or an ability to feel the way all sentient beings feel as the consciousness becomes mindful of how karma generates afflictions; (3) empathy, or a peaceful understanding of how all sentient beings must feel; and (4) equanimity, or a mindfulness of the technicity of sensations and affections. In this sense, the discorrelation brought about by digital existence becomes a moment of reflection (or refrain) that stimulates a potentiality of coproduction and cocreation.

POETRY OF CINEMA REBOOTED

Between 2004 and 2014, the Beijing police continued to harass and shut down the BQFF and its ally BIFF. As an attempt to "clean up" Beijing in preparation for the 2008 Olympics, the city government also cracked down on *weiquan* (civil rights) advocates, lawyers, nongovernment organizations (NGOs), and numerous protest movements. Such a crackdown exacerbated after the Olympics. Then, by the time Xi Jinping became president in March 2013, queer artists and activists believed that a wholesale shutdown of politically sensitive independent films was imminent.[95] In September 2014, the Beijing police raided the Li Xianting Foundation and confiscated its hard drives containing all the entries of the BIFF. Since 2014, Chinese independent filmmakers have increasingly turned to media corporations and multinational private investors to make higher-budget films under the dictates of party-state censorship. Until 2021, LGBTQI+ subject matters had been permitted either as elements within a film's broader narrative or as demonstrations of China's being an increasingly open and progressive society.[96]

For the independent *tongzhi* filmmakers, what is at stake is not how deindividuated, desubjectivized, and deautonomized lives can be transindividuated, intersubjectivized, and interautonomized as political subjects, but rather how they are implicated in this process of deindividuation, desubjectivization, and deautonomization within a juridical mechanism to which both the state and the depoliticized lives subscribe.

By understanding its agency in this karmic process of becoming, the technicity-consciousness or the anthropotechnical body (that is, the sentient body of the spectator, the embodied mind, and the associated milieu as a whole) may become mindful of the technicity of deindividuation, desubjectivization, and deautonomization not as a means of re-individuating and resubjectivizing themselves, but instead as a form of liberation from individuality, subjectivity, and autonomy.

Of all the contemporary Beijing-based queer films, Kokoka's works stand out as prime examples of this new mode of intervention. What strikes most viewers about his films is his unrestrained visual style, one that defies ideas such as narrative logic and elegance in camerawork and editing. Kokoka is the pseudonym of Xue Jianjiang. He began his career as an amateur filmmaker, after dropping out of school at the age of fifteen. Hence, at first glance, it is tempting to call his style "amateur." Nevertheless, his stylistic unrestrainedness is so consistent that it must be understood as a poetics in its own right.

His film *Martian Syndrome* is about a young gay man who seeks refuge in his own home against his suitor. The young man calls a friend to keep him company while living under his suitor's threat. During the course of the film, the young man claims that both he and his suitor are Martians. According to the young man's confession, they met on the outskirts of Beijing and the young man took his suitor in. His suitor promised that he would adjust to his life on earth financially and emotionally, but the suitor turned out to be a liar. The young man kicked his suitor out of the house and accused his suitor of harassing him. The young man's friend talks to the suitor and threatens to call the police, yet the suitor claims that it is the young man who keeps inviting the suitor back into his house.

The entire film is shot with a night-vision camera on a two-hour-long digital video (DV) tape, with minimal cutting between the young man and his friend inside the house and the suitor outside. The camera mostly stays in a third-person observational position, with the three characters occasionally looking directly into the camera. In the final half hour, the film interrupts these long takes by cutting back to some of the earlier moments in the film to reveal the inconsistency between the young man's testimonies and the suitor's. In the end, the young man and his suitor have a talk through a screen door. Their conversation reveals that their relationship is codependent and sadomasochistic, as the young man willingly forgives the suitor and acknowledges his pleasure of going through the ritual cycle of being harassed, then shunning and condoning him.

It is tempting to read *Martian Syndrome* as a sequel to Cui's *Star Appeal*, with the interdependent relationship between Xiao Bo and E.T. deteriorating to be a codependent one. Nonetheless, Kokoka is less interested in creating a visual metaphor than in engaging the audience in a structure of feelings of "desperation, confusion, fear, and nihilism" under public surveillance and party-state power.[97] As Kiki Yu argues, "*Martian Syndrome* documents the isolated selves in a public space. These selves narcissistically expose themselves [in front of the camera], and they also unrestrainedly unveil the personal secrets of those people around them at a zero-degree distance." For Yu, the film is symptomatic of the young generation of gay men's desire to seek family relationships and protection in a society that actively deprives them of the opportunity to do so.[98]

For me, the young men in *Martian Syndrome* are not seeking family relationships. Rather, the film makes tangible those sensations and longings that are often mutually conflicting and inconsistent. Unlike Cui's E.T., who is gradually ostracized by the earthlings as his mutual attraction with Xiao Bo becomes increasingly visible, the young man and the suitor in *Martian Syndrome* are victims of one another's sadomasochistic desires. In the beginning of the film, for example, the young man speaks to the cameraperson (Kokoka himself) about his predicament. Through the lens of the camera, the young man nervously seeks safety and protection in the dark, groping for his cigarettes, and exposing his vulnerability. Yet, this night-vision camera makes the consciousness mindful of public surveillance (a mode of state-controlled digital existence), of which it is partaking in the formational process. By occasionally addressing the camera, the young man, his friend, and his suitor not only perform for the camera voluntarily and put into question the truth-value of their performed testimonies, but also actively implicate the technicity-consciousness in the process of surveillance as it monitors the process of their negotiation. The technicity-consciousness becomes mindful that the young man's state of vulnerability has been performed for the camera as a narcissistic erotic display.

Throughout the film, the young man begs Kokoka and his friend to stay and keep him company. The longer *we* stay with the young man and listen to his complaint about his suitor, the more we begin to witness and experience his fear of loneliness, his nihilistic view of being different in a hostile urban environment, and his confused feelings toward submitting himself to his suitor's harassment. Shot in a summer night, the young man and his friend remain bare-chested. To comfort the young man, his friend caresses his chest in an erotic manner, thus suggesting that though the young man's codependent and self-abusive relationship has generated his anxiety and fear, he is ultimately drawn to it because it gives him sexual satisfaction. Toward the end of the film, the young man talks to his suitor through a screen door. The young man explains to his suitor that violence and harassment cannot solve any problems (see Figure 25). Immediately after he has made this statement, Kokoka cuts to the footage from an earlier part of the film, in which the

FIGURE 25. The young man tells his suitor that violence is not the solution to his problem. The subtitles read: "Nobody fear fighting, but no one wants it. Only gets trouble." [Nobody is afraid of getting into a fight. But who really wants to fight? Fighting will only bring trouble to us.]

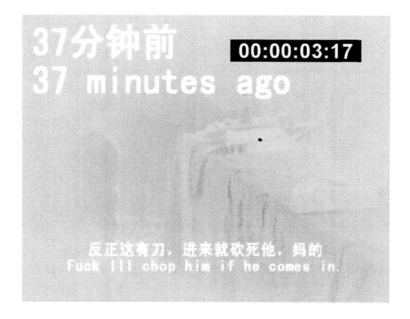

FIGURE 26. The film cuts to an earlier part in which the young man confesses to the camera that he wishes to exercise violence against his suitor: "Fuck!!! I'll chop him if he comes in."

young man confesses to the camera that he wishes to chop his suitor to pieces (see Figure 26).

Interestingly, the film's "flashbacks" function precisely as a digital technology of surveillance, which offers an instantaneous reference to verify the truth-value of the young man's statement. These flashbacks therefore initiate a sudden awareness not only of the violence of party-state surveillance, but also of the masochistic pleasure and comfort of submitting oneself to party-state power so as to live in a state of self-effacement and normativized anonymity. The consciousness also becomes mindful of how the party-state apparatus preempts queer radical changes by turning same-sex desire into a commodity of consumption, one that drives—and is driven by—gay men whose sexuality becomes a pure inscription of consumerist comfort and pleasure. It is in this sense that there is no ideology, but only an infrastructure of fear and anxiety of which every biopolitical life participates via a digital existence that *turns itself into* an ecology of (self-)surveillance.

Kokoka's other film, *Deformity Sci-fi,* is set in a post-apocalyptic village outside Taiyuan, the capital of Shanxi. The film can be understood as a coming-of-age story about a teenage gangster who seeks pleasure in extreme physical violence. After his father dies of tuberculosis, the boy grows up into a young man, and he moves to Taiyuan and joins a small gang from which he seeks camaraderie. Being unable to enter into any heteronormative relationship and having been driven out of his home by the police, the young man tries to return to his hometown. But his trip is interrupted as he takes a break along the river, where his Martian mother appears in the sky and condemns him to eternal banishment from family life and manhood.

In one register, *Deformity Sci-fi* follows an Oedipal/post-Oedipal logic. In the beginning of the film, the teenage gangster goes home to visit his dying father. The father spits out some phlegm onto a tissue and asks the son to ingest it as a contract of agreement that the son will take care of the mother after his death (see Figure 27). In this fictional ritual, the father accuses the son of killing him because of the son's ruthlessness and unruliness. This promise is never fulfilled. On the contrary, the son abandons his family and joins a gang in Taiyuan. This ritual is transferred from the kinship between father and son to an

FIGURE 27. In *Deformity Sci-fi,* the father asks the son to ingest his phlegm as a contract of agreement.

alternative kinship between other men, as the young man is asked to drink a cup of water after his "brother" in the gang has spat into it. Throughout the film, the young man constantly seeks camaraderie and companionship through exchanges of blood, urine, filth, phlegm, and other bodily fluids with other gang members, as though these abject and corporeal mediations would enable him to revisit not only the trauma of his father's death, but also his drive toward abandoning or even killing his father. Symbolically, this ritual of male-to-male bonding constantly reminds the young man and the anthropotechnical consciousness of his act of "patricide." By repeating this ritual, same-sex bonding becomes simultaneously an act of rebellion against the father and heteronormative kinship, and a rite of passage in which an alternative kinship is fostered out of acts of violence. This sadomasochistic quest for male bonding through acts of violence bars the young man from forming any heterosexual romance. In the end, the young man is killed by an omnipotent Martian mother who spits on his face from heaven.

The narrative logic is not immediately apparent on the first viewing of the film. This is because, formally, the film is composed of a seemingly aleatory selection of styles that consistently defies any type of visual or narrative logic: ranging from breathtaking static shots of the scenery of the countryside to unstable handheld shots that observe and capture scenes from angles and perspectives that are not motivated by any narrative logic; from long takes to montage; and from straight-on camera angles to turning the camera upside down. The effect of this *systematically eclectic* style is akin to what Pier Paolo Pasolini would call a free-indirect discourse.

Pasolini argues that a "free-indirect discourse" in the cinema is one in which "the author penetrates entirely into the spirit of his character, of whom he thus adopts not only the psychology but also the language."[99] For him, the classical Hollywood shot/reverse-shot, by cutting into the subjective views of the characters from an establishing long shot, and by framing these subjective views within the narrative cause-and-effect logic, puts the characters' subjectivities within the filmmaker's or the camera's. Instead of doing this, Pasolini believes that by juxtaposing shots that appear to be highly objective not by means of cause-and-effect logic, but rather by means of affective connections, the consciousness will begin to give up trying to read the film prosaically.

Rather, as when one reads a poem, one's consciousness will grasp the overall image as an affect. As Gilles Deleuze argues, each shot or im-sign functions like a harmonic, and the spectators are engaged not in the appreciation of every single note but instead in taking in the sum effect of all the harmonics as a piece of music or an affective experience.[100]

In a free-indirect discourse, im-signs are no longer organized into syntagma or stylemes. Rather, they are put together in accordance with their affective connections. Therefore, at each moment of the formational process, the consciousness remains mindful of how each karmic impulse affects—and is affected by—the layout of relationalities. Such a layout transduces from one phase to another, as beings and objects are transindividuated from one moment to another, without any preconceived grammar or logic. The one consistent feature of all the images is their situatedness—neither subjective nor objective, but rather an abject milieu, or what Deleuze calls a pure optical and sound situation. The sum effect of these abject im-signs is a direct engagement of the consciousness in the reserve of fear, anxiety, desire, and pleasure. In this case, the portable digital camera liberates the film from (1) stylistic consistency by allowing stylemes to be initiated from one moment to another out of the interstices between feeling and thinking from one sequence to another and also from (2) a subject-object binary correlation in favor of an embodied and endworlded experience of transindividuations among these young men through their corporeal and mental sufferings.

By forcing the consciousness to come face-to-face with the abject experience of witnessing phlegm, blood, and urine exchanged between the father and the son and among the gangsters, the film etches the traumatic experience of wanting to fit in and growing up through ritualistic endurance of disgust, and through constant alienation and ostracization from heteronormative social values and kinship. At the same time, the film remains mindful of the karmic impulses that drive—and are driven by—these traumatic affects. In the end, it fosters a direct engagement between the spectators and the characters—as a technicity-consciousness—through their empathy and equanimity.

ECOLOGY AND RESTORATION

Martian Syndrome and *Deformity Sci-fi* both exemplify a new form of queer cinematic experience that refuses to ground itself in any form of subjectival positionality. In so doing, the (post-)cinematographic image embodies a highly subjective sensorium of someone who has lived through such experiences of physical and social violence. Yet, as a series of pure optical and sound situations, the consciousness also posits itself at each initiating instant of their traumatic affects and becomes mindful of how each instant drives karma and is driven by it.

This new form of queer cinematic strategy puts into question the party-state power and heteronormative social values to which members of the LGBTQI+ community subscribe and under which they are rendered precarious. In other words, there is no ideology and no system, but there are only conflicting senses of fear, alienation, nihilism, anxiety, self-hate, and sadomasochism. By actively driving—and being driven by—these afflictions, queer lives have continued to subject themselves to and are subjected by party-state violence and surveillance. These films enable the consciousness to be mindful of the human condition as *the way it is* (empathy and equanimity). Being mindful of such technicity is the first step toward rewriting the karmic impulses *here and now*—and, with it, the consequences they can produce in the overall sociopolitical ecology.

CHAPTER 5

IN-AESTHETICS

Buddhist aesthetics, in cinema studies, has always been associated with the curtain shots of Ozu Yasujirō, the poetic realism of Mizoguchi Kenji (1898–1965), the slowness of the quotidian yet precarious life embodied in the image of Tsai Ming-liang, and the blurring boundary between sleep-consciousness and waking-consciousness in the media ecology of Apichatpong Weerasethakul (see chapter 3). These directors were and are very open about their respective affiliations with Buddhism, and the scholarly discourse of their works also engages in the profundities and specificities of their philosophical frameworks.[1] Nonetheless, for nonspecialists who regard these works as the sole representations of Buddhism in cinema, Buddhist aesthetics can be easily misconstrued in terms of a number of clichés: slowness, emptiness, nonhappening, banality of the everyday, ascetic disengagement from life, and as Paul Schrader famously puts it, transcendentalism.[2]

From the perspective of art history, the notion of *Buddhist aesthetics* is an oxymoron, and most of the qualities I have just mentioned do not correspond to Buddhist philosophy in the first place. As Richard Gombrich argues, aesthetic judgment is understood as an indulgence in form, which is not mentioned anywhere in the Pāli canon.[3] In the *Connected Discourses,* Śākyamuni Buddha only encourages his disciples to seek refuge in nature, where a practitioner can be mindful of the transience of forms and the relationalities between them.[4]

Historically, there has never been such a thing as a unified Buddhist aesthetics. Since the 1890s, art historians have surmised that the earliest Buddhist art was aniconic, based on the Sarvāstivādin belief that Buddhahood is unrepresentable.[5] Thus, Alfred Foucher (1865–1952) argues that anthropomorphic representations of the Buddha were an Indo-Greek hybridization during the Greco-Bactrian kingdom (250–130 B.C.E.; nowadays Afghanistan) and the Indo-Greek kingdom (180–10 B.C.E.) in the Indian subcontinent.[6] This theory, however, was rejected by Foucher's contemporary Ananda Coomaraswamy (1877–1947), who criticizes Foucher for imposing the historiographical framework of Judaic-Christian art onto its Buddhist counterpart.[7] By the 1990s, Susan Huntington argues that some of the aniconic artefacts studied by Foucher were holders or containers of *cetiya* (relics); thus, the absence of any iconographic representation was supposed to be supplied by the corporeal fragments of the Buddha.[8]

Artistically, these artefacts were modeled on the styles popular in the Indian subcontinent. Between the third and sixth centuries, culturo-linguistic practices and values, including those associated with Buddhism, were translated and introduced into Northern China through Turkic scholars. Early Indo-Turkic translators and Chinese intellectuals borrowed the vocabulary and conceptual frameworks from Taoism in their discussions of art and aesthetics. Meanwhile, some of these concepts, reconfigured under Buddhism, *returned* to Taoism.[9] Thus, some of these theoretical discourses, which would then be debated, critiqued, and revised under the label *Liuchao yifeng* (legacies of the six dynasties), are grounded equally in both philosophical lineages.[10]

During this period, some artists in Tibet actively combined in their works local Mahāyāna, Tantric, and Bön styles with Nepalese and Chinese elements.[11] During the *Dang/Tang* dynasty (618–907), Japanese and Korean artists developed their own aesthetic values while maintaining a close conversation with Sinitic practices and intellectual debates.[12] Processes of cultural dephasing and transductions with local, colonial, intraregional, and interregional exchanges have taken place in the Indian subcontinent itself, as well as in Afghanistan, Myanmar, Thailand, Vietnam, and other parts of Southeast Asia.[13] In short, reducing Buddhist aesthetics—if any—to a few cinematic clichés ignores the complexity and diversity of the histories of Buddhist arts and cultures and the colonial history that codifies these clichés in the first place.

In this chapter, I start by clarifying how certain aesthetic choices came to be defined as Buddhist through the lens of the colonial discourse, and how these choices can be more properly contextualized within the larger East Asian Buddhist philosophical debates. I then rethink what is meant by a Buddhist attitude toward art, by conversing with the *Avataṃsaka Sūtra*. This *sūtra* describes how, once the ultimate emptiness/existence has been disconcealed for Śākyamuni Buddha, the cosmos is im-mediately in-formed by the dharma bodies (emptiness) of the Buddhas, bodhisattvas, and other enlightened sentient beings. These *bodies* perceive and conceptualize layouts of relationalities as wondrously pure, dignified, and glorious forms, which in turn serve as offerings for Śākyamuni Buddha.[14] The cosmological view of the *Avataṃsaka Sūtra* is sometimes mistaken as a transcendental aesthetic. These wondrous treasures and heavenly bodies are best read as the presence of all forms, that is, pure luminosity, which are instantiations of emptiness. Only when the emptiness of emptiness is disconcealed can the nondifferentiation between forms and emptiness be abduced as *the way it is.* The supreme treasure, content, dignity, and glory are neither transcendental nor immanent, and the cosmological view presents not so much an aesthetics, but rather what I call an in-aesthetics: the emptiness on which aesthetic judgment is based.

In this chapter, I use the word "in-aesthetics" in a way both different from, and similar to, Alain Badiou's definition of "inaesthetics." For Badiou, inaesthetics is "a relation of philosophy to art that, maintaining that art is itself a producer of truths, makes no claim to turn art into an object of philosophy." The term "describes the strictly intraphilosophical effects produced by the independent existence of some works of art." Needless to say, Buddhist philosophy would never subscribe to the notion that a work of art has any existential value or to the idea of truth(s).[15] However, like Badiou's understanding of inaesthetics, a Buddhist attitude toward art sees an artwork not as a praxis that is separate from philosophy.[16] Rather, art is seen as a process that can illuminate the emptiness of emptiness, and this process can do so because as an embodied experience, it is in-formed out of dependent originations. Thus, the artwork as a technicity-consciousness instantiates the very relationality between existence and emptiness. But what it reveals is neither *truth* nor *untruth,* neither not truth nor not untruth, but simply: *the way it is.*

The methodology I use in this chapter differs slightly from the ones I used in previous chapters. Since Buddhist aesthetics has had a long history in Asia, I pay attention not only to its theories and methods, but also to its histories and historicities. Hence, this chapter engages in a philosophical discussion via a reexamination and rehistoricization of the key debates in East Asian Buddhisms mainly from the mid-nineteenth century to the twentieth century. At the end of the chapter, I demonstrate what is meant by in-aesthetics through reevaluating both the history of reception of Ozu's cinema and some of his own works.

CALIFORNIA ZEN, SHAKU SOYEN, AND SUZUKI DAISETZ

The popular Euro-American (mis)understanding of Buddhism as a tran-scendental religion has been largely informed by what Inken Prohl calls "California 'Zen.'" As Prohl argues, by the 1950s and 1960s, the Beatniks and the Love Generation considered Zen as a lifestyle: a holistic, rela-tional, ascetic, and spiritual self-cultivation alternative to the rising notion of consumerism. The irony was that this lifestyle was brokered, marketed, and consumed by countercultural figures, intellectuals, and, later, established institutions and corporations as a commodity.[17] Yet, such understanding also in-formed how cinema scholars from that generation studied and analyzed Japanese cinema.[18]

The emergence of California Zen can be traced back to a series of intraregional and interregional cultural exchanges under competing modes of colonialism among North America, Europe, Japan, and China. As R. John Williams points out, Buddhism was introduced into the United States through its promulgation by Japan in the World's Colum-bia Exposition in Chicago in 1893. It was branded as a mode of modern existence, or, more properly, called *technē,* an alternative to *Western* modernity.[19] For the visitors to the Chicago Expo, Buddhism offered an epistemic space that explained how the human comes into being as part of technical-environment-cum-nature. Japanese art and technology, which were packaged in that exposition as holistic, organic, spiritual, and beautiful, yet mechanically precise and functional, were presented as an antidote to the cold, intimidating, mathematical, and inhuman conceptualizations of art and technics in modern Europe and North America, where human beings were pitted against nature on the one hand and the machine on the other.[20]

As Williams argues, Anglo-American understanding of Buddhism and Asia as *technē* has been intricately bound up in the discourse of

Orientalism on the one hand and nationalism on the other. On September 11, 1893, the World Parliament of Religions opened in Chicago. The convention was attended by the Zen master Shaku Soyen (1860–1969), who gave a speech titled "The Law of Cause and Effect, as Taught by Buddha," read in English by John Henry Barrows (1847–1902).[21] He then read a short intervention called "Arbitration Instead of War" in Japanese. Both texts survived in their English translation done by one of his students at the University of Tokyo, Suzuki Teitarō Daisetz (1870–1966). In his speech, Soyen urges delegates from Europe and the United States to expand the coverage of the international law to East Asia and further to acknowledge Japan and China as nation-states. He does so by putting Buddhism, Christianity, and Confucianism on equal footing, and by regarding their common pursuit of truth as a universal human aspiration:

> Our Buddha, who taught that all people entering into Buddhism are entirely equal, in the same way as all rivers flowing into the sea become alike, preached this plan in the wide kingdom of India just three thousand years ago. Not only Buddha alone, but Jesus Christ, as well as Confucius, taught about universal love and fraternity. We also acknowledge the glory of universal brotherhood. Then let us, the true followers of Buddha, the true followers of Jesus Christ, the true followers of Confucius, and the followers of truth, unite ourselves for the sake of helping the helpless and living glorious lives of brotherhood under the control of truth. . . .
>
> You must not say "Go away," because we are not Christians. You must not say "Go away," because we are yellow people. All beings on the universe are in the bosom of truth. We are all sisters and brothers; we are sons and daughters of truth, and let us understand one another much better and be true sons and daughters of truth. Truth be praised![22]

As John Thompson argues, it is unclear what changes Suzuki has introduced into the translation of Soyen's speech. Soyen was trained as a Rinzai (Liìmtsèi) priest, who became master of Engaku-ji in 1892 and chief abbot in 1889. Asian delegates at the Chicago conference included the Hindu monk Swami Vivekananda (1862–1902), the Theravādin priest Angarika Dharmapala (1864–1933), and the Confucian scholar and diplomat Peng Guangyu (known as Pung Kwang Yu). In Chicago, Soyen fostered a lifelong friendship with the philosopher Paul Carus (1852-1919), who invited him back to the United States in 1905-1906, where he stayed in San Francisco. It was there that he began teaching Rinzai practices, including *kōan* (*kung?àn/gong'an*): telling stories of how Zen masters arrived at—and returned to—their insights by revealing only the logical puzzles they tried to solve, while leaving the puzzles intact for the practitioner to mull over.[23]

Thompson argues that Soyen's sermons in Japanese are in accord with the Rinzai line of thinking. What made him outstanding in the U.S. context was his evangelical ambition. As Margaret Dornish points out, Suzuki produced several *super-signs* (see the introduction) that would have a long-lasting impact on the Euro-American reception of Buddhism: (1) that sudden insight is to be considered a theory of mysticism; (2) that *prajñā* is best understood as a spiritual awakening; and (3) that *tathātā* is the transcendental truth. These were gambits that enabled Soyen's—and later, Suzuki's—Christian followers and Euro-American philosophers alike to draw parallels between Buddhist and Judaic-Christian epistemic spaces.[24]

Yet Dornish argues that these views are more typical of Suzuki's early works than his later interpretations. Suzuki went to study with Carus and he stayed in La Salle, Illinois, in 1897. At that time, Carus had already known Soyen, and he was fascinated with reading Buddhism through the lens of Baruch Spinoza.[25] Suzuki's reliance on Spinoza to interpret the Tathāgatagarbha, which he calls the *anupalabdha* (Unattainable), becomes increasingly evident in his later works:

> The Unattainable, so termed, subsists in its absolute right and must now be taken hold of in a way hitherto unsuspected in our intellectual pursuit of reality. The intellect is to be left aside for a while, in spite of a certain sense of intellectual discomfort, so that we may plunge into that nothingness beyond the intellect, as if into a threatening abyss opening up at our feet. The Unattainable is attained as such in its just-so-ness, and the strange thing is that when this takes place the intellectual doubts that made us so uncomfortable are dissolved. One feels free, independent, one's own master. Experiences at the level of intellection are restrictive and conditioning, but the "inner" self feels the way God felt when he uttered, "Let there be light." This is where zero identifies itself with infinity and infinity with zero—if we call that both zero and infinity are not negative concepts, but utterly positive.[26]

A casual reading of Suzuki may lead to a mistaken notion that the Unattainable is transcendental. Nonetheless, in his later works, Suzuki clarifies that *anupalabdha* is immanent:

> Reality is all-inclusive, there is nothing that can be outside of it. Because it is all-inclusive, it is the fullness of things, not a content-free abstraction, as the intellect is too frequently apt to make it. It is not a mere aggregate of individual objects, nor is it something other than the objects. It is not something that is imposed upon things stringing them together and holding them together from the outside. It is the principle of integration residing inside things and identical with them.[27]

Yet this subtle difference between transcendence and immanence might not be apparent for those readers in the Euro-American countercultural movements, who had neither training in philosophy nor access to the Buddhist canons. Such a cross-cultural misunderstanding has since then underlined the Euro-American misconception of Buddhism as a transcendental religion.

THE KYOTO SCHOOL AND PURE LAND

The impact of Suzuki's work can be seen in the debate among him and his contemporaries who were based in Kyoto during the 1920s and 1930s. His language also affected how Buddhist aesthetics was defined in cinema studies. The core of this debate is the definition of Jōdo (Dzièngthǔo/Jingtu, or Pure Land). According to the two versions of the *Sukhāvatīvyūha Sūtra* [*Infinite Life Sutra* and the *Shorter Sukhāvatīvyūha Sutra*], Śākyamuni Buddha tells the story of a bodhisattva named Dharmākara (literally, Storehouse of Dharma), who takes a vow under Lokeśvararāja Buddha, that when he attains Buddhahood, his Pure Land—named by him as Sukhāvatī—will welcome anyone who recites his Dharma name, Amitābha, repeatedly until this person's *ālaya*-consciousness has reached a state of absolute mindfulness. Sukhāvatī is described in these two *sūtras* as a glorious realm constituted by heavenly treasures and dignity, where every practicing bodhisattva has already achieved the *anuttarasamyaksambodhi* (ultimate mindfulness).[28]

As I mentioned in the beginning of this chapter, when the Tathāgatagarbha is disconcealed, the nondifferentiation between forms and emptiness can be abduced as the way it is. In such a state—or more properly speaking, nonstate (we can call this "state/nonstate") — of insight (formerly consciousness) is pure technicity (dependent originations-emptiness). It is a plane of absolute luminosity where the differentiations between potentialities and actualities, and forms and emptiness, are rendered inoperative. In absolute mindfulness, each awareness is initiated not by a karmic impulse, but by an insight that exercises full agency over itself. Therefore, according to the *Avataṃsaka Sūtra*, absolute mindfulness is manifested as a Pure Land: a milieu of supreme treasure, content, dignity, and glory (a plane of absolute luminosity). What we call conventional reality is a perceptual-conceptual "version" of the same manifestation, which is obstructed and distorted by sensations, affections, and afflictions.[29]

Pure Land Buddhism has a long history, based on the two *Sukhāvatīvyūha Sūtras*, and became popularized by Hwèihʉeˇn/Huiyuan (Eon, 334–416) in China and the Sinosphere in 402.[30] The founder of Thenthʌi/Tiantai (Tendai) Buddhism, Th'ièngiˇ/Zhiyi (Chigi, 538–97), based on the *Avataṃsaka Sūtra*, proposes the idea of *ʔiɨtnèm samtshen/ yinian sanqian* (*ichinen sanzen*): that one thought-impulse in-forms an awareness that constitutes the *tri-sahasra-mahā-sahasra-lokadhātu* (three thousand billion universes).[31] Based on Th'ièngiˇ's idea of *ʔiɨtnèm samtshen*, Shinran (1173–1263) of Matsuwakamaro argues that Pure Land can be arrived at the *here and now*. His belief is called Jōdo Shinshū or Shin Buddhism.[32]

We often imagine an arrival in Pure Land as a "going toward" — that is, a state of being that is to be achieved by a subject through an ontological investigation. Nonetheless, if the Tathāgatagarbha is *the way it is* and *the way it has always been*, Pure Land is a state/nonstate of pure technicity from and to which the consciousness returns: a process of desubjectivization/resubjectivization through a meta-ontological investigation. For the Kyoto school philosophers, what is at stake in Shin Buddhism is the recognition that the ultimate emptiness (emptiness of emptiness) is not an existential nihility. Rather, it is a source of life and the ultimate reason for care.

Based on this idea, Tanabe Hajime (1885–1962) argues that every ontological investigation requires a metanoetic one: an investigation into how the mind and the ontology it constructs are restricted by the limitations of reason. For Tanabe, an ontological investigation is based on an objectivized subjective position, which means that an ontological

ground is always limited by the technicity of the consciousness as a
process of subject-object differentiation:

> Contrary to what [Immanuel] Kant mistakenly supposed, in arriving
> at a definition of metaphysics as subjective through his critique of
> human knowledge, it is impossible for the subject to be considered as
> the transcendental ground of the object, while the object—within the
> subject-object opposition—is firmly established by means of the
> subject's formal independence. In truth, subject and object stand in
> a dialectical relationship in the sense that each mediates itself by
> making the other mediate it. This is the structure of active reality
> whose essence, we may say, consists in "subject-*qua*-object" and
> "object-*qua*-subject."[33]

Tanabe points out that Martin Heidegger has identified the ground
from which the subject-object duality is initiated as the emptiness of
the ground. He argues, "Heidegger terms this sort of 'not' (*Nicht*) an
'existential nihility' (*Nichtigkeit*), and considers the nihility of the
ground as the fundamental guilt (*Schuld*) of one's being (Dasein)." Here,
Schuld can also be understood as "fault," a fundamental misapprehension of emptiness as that which exists. In this sense, *Schuld* is comparable to what the Theravādins would call *avijjā/avidyā* (ignorance). For
Heidegger, the "awakening to consciousness of this guilt is called conscience, and the resolve to preserve conscience, the freedom of one's
being." In this light, what Heidegger calls conscience is insight: a consciousness's agency (freedom) over itself.

However, for Tanabe, Heidegger fails to recognize that absolute
nothingness is not simply an existential nihility. Rather, it is the layout
of pure relationalities between all potentialities. Therefore, Tanabe argues that Dasein is also a "principle of absolute transformation," that
is, "being-*qua*-emptiness."[34] It is in this sense that he considers metanoetics as *zangedō* (way of repentance), that is, a way of caring-for all sentient beings as *the way it is* (equanimity). For him, *zangedō* is best
understood not only as an *ōsō* (going toward) Pure Land, but also as a
gensō (returning from), so that *care-as-the-way-it-is* can be carried out in
forms as in emptiness.[35]

In a similar vein, Nishitani Keiji (1900–90) believes that the human
intellect is initiated from *eidos* (form or representation), which takes its
own parameters as a technology of self-recognition. Hence, what we

take as an episteme is no more than *technē*—a form of knowledge limited by the maximum field of imagination we have. For him, however, *"it is the field of emptiness (śūnyatā) or absolute nothingness—or what may perhaps be called the None in contrast to, and beyond the One—which enables the myriad phenomena to attain their true being and realize their real truth."*[36] Here, Nishitani emphasizes that in the Tathāgatagarbha, emptiness *is* existence. It is not a state that one seeks to attain, but *the way it is* that is manifested in all forms.

Meanwhile, Suzuki also turned to Shin Buddhism as a way to rethink ethics. His vocabulary then becomes the critical paradigm in the study of Japanese aesthetics in both Europe and North America. For Suzuki, Pure Land instantiates the relationship between *hō* (Dharma, the absolute self or the Tathāgatagarbha) and *ki* (air, subtle energy, or the relative and conceptual self-form, which is a Taoist concept).[37] In the studies of *karesansui* (a garden composed of sparingly placed rock formations and a substrate of pebbles that are combed with a wavy pattern) the "empty" space of the garden is often interpreted as *hō*. Such emptiness initiates a *ki* that flows around the garden, which enables the consciousness to perceive and conceptualize forms (the "waves") that are relative to the beholder's subjectivity. In this sense, the seated beholder is not an immobile observer. Rather, their consciousness flows and wanders with *ki*.[38]

Suzuki's notions find their way into the analysis of Ozu Yasujirō's cinema conducted by Donald Richie (1924–2013) and Noël Burch. In their works, Ozu's curtain shots (shots of inanimate objects that often precede, intercede, or follow a scene, which perform relatively little narrational functions) are interpreted as *hō*, which instantiates the ultimate emptiness from which *ki* is initiated. *Ki* then serves as the impetus that puts into motion the formational process (narration). Likewise, Mizoguchi's long takes through an empty landscape are often regarded as *hō*, which sweep up the *ki* in the milieu until the camera arrives at a human or ghostly form, whose transient existence is merely an illusion originated among other things and beings in the environment.[39]

Strictly speaking, Suzuki never proposed a Zen aesthetics. The relationship between *hō* and *ki* explains how the formational process can be conceptualized. In this process, the internal forms of the beholder and the external forms (of the art) can be considered as transient instantiations of *ki* from one moment to another. Each moment affects—and is affected by—a karmic impulse, which is instantiated as sensations and affections. Thus, in an artistic or meditative experience, consciousness becomes mindful of the fact that the existence of each form is empty and that what it apprehends as reality is a perceptual-conceptual proliferation. I call such an attitude of observation "in-aesthetics," because it: (1) seeks not to make any judgment on *aisthēta* (perceptible things), but rather to disconceal *tathātā* of the perceptual-conceptual process; (2) seeks to refrain from any aesthetic judgment based on sense-perception; and (3) seeks to engage in the process of actualization-virtualization by navigating between *ōsō* (going toward) and *gensō* (returning from) the Tathāgatagarbha.

BUDDHIST RENAISSANCE

As I mentioned in the introduction of this book, Taoist vocabulary and concepts were being borrowed by early Indo-Turkic translators of the *sūtras* and *śāstras* as early as the Han dynasty (206 B.C.E.–220 C.E.).[40] Between the Song (960–1279) and Ming (1368–1644) dynasties, academic scholars also developed a study called *lixue* (the study of *li*, aka neo-Confucianism) by syncretizing Taoism (as a *ti* or ontological ground), Buddhism (as *xiang* or form), and Confucianism (for *yong* or sociopolitical application).[41] Such syncretism was considered a productive discourse until a debate between two scholars, Yang Wenhui (1837–1911) and his disciple Ouyang Jian (Ouyang Jingwu, 1871–1943), revealed its logical inconsistency.

Yang grew up in a bureaucratic family in Peking (Beijing). In 1861, he joined the Zongli yamen (Foreign Office) and moved to Hangchow (Hangzhou). In 1862, he bought a copy of the *Mahāyānaśraddhotpādaśāstra* [*Awakening of Faith in the Mahāyāna*, attributed to Aśvaghoṣa (circa 80–150 C.E.)] in a bookstore and decided to devote the rest of his life to Buddhist study.[42]

As a diplomat, Yang visited Great Britain and France in the 1870s and 1880s, where he met the Shin scholar Nanjō Bunyū (1849–1927), who helped him recuperate *śāstras* that were left out by the 1733–38 edition of the Chinese Buddhist canon compiled during the reign of the Qianlong Emperor (1733–96). In 1878, he established the Jinling kejingchu (Jinling Sutra Publishing House) and hired the Yokohama-born monk Su Manshu (1884–1918) to teach Sanskrit and English. In 1894, he collaborated with the Baptist missionary Timothy Richard (1845–1919) to translate the *Awakening of Faith* into English.[43] Seminars organized at the publishing house were convened, attended by, and visited by leading intellectuals of the time, including Ouyang, Liang Qichao (1873–1929), Wang Guowei (1877–1927), Feng Zikai (1898–1975), and Thomé H. Fang (1899–1977).

According to Tanxu (1875–1963), as the violence of wars, political turmoil, and economic collapse came hand-in-hand with colonialism, Buddhist philosophy offered an alternative mode of modernity for scholars as well as an equal playing field for their intellectual exchanges with scholars in Japan, Europe, and North America. It also provided its practitioners with a way to cope with the transience of life in these political crises.[44] Besides academics, clergy including Yinguang (1862–1940) of Pure Land Buddhism, Taixu (1890–1947) of the Linji school, Xuyun (1840–1959) of both Linzi and Dzaudùng/Caodong (Sōtō) Zen, and Tanxu (himself) of Tentai revived textual analysis, historiography, and logical studies through publications, seminars, and university lectures.[45]

Despite Yang's friendship with Nanjō, he was critical of Shin Buddhism. For Yang, the Shin understanding of imminent Pure Land is based on Dharmākara's eighteenth vow: that anyone who follows the five precepts (no killing, stealing, excessive sexual indulgence, lying, and drinking) and invokes his name repeatedly will attain absolute mindfulness. The Shin Buddhists therefore ignore his two subsequent vows:

19. That Amitābha, Avalokiteśvara, and Mahāsthāmaprāpta will appear in a practitioner's consciousness by the time they are ready to go to Pure Land; and
20. That the formation of Pure Land is a result of the practitioner's nurturing of the purifying seeds in their *ālaya*-consciousness (or planting those seeds in Pure Land). These seeds in turn give rise to the perfect and dignified forms.

Although Shinran's understanding of imminent Pure Land makes logical sense in light of Zen's understanding of sudden insight, his theory places an emphasis on the practitioner's faithful invocation of Amitābha's name, rather than the reconfiguration of the *ālaya*-consciousness. In so doing, Amitābha is treated as the ultimate agency of enlightenment.[46]

For Yang, the invocation of Amitābha is a method by which the practitioner can become mindful of the consciousness's technicity, which is
well-explicated in the *Awakening of Faith:*

> *Śūnyatā* [emptiness] is fundamentally different from the polluted
> phenomenon [form]. It instantiates a difference from all perceptual-
> conceptual forms, as it is initiated from the absence of any illusory
> thought at a given point-instant. Therefore, *tathātā*-as-self-nature is
> neither form nor non-form, neither not form nor not non-form; it does
> not exist nor not-exist simultaneously; it is neither monistic nor
> dualistic, at once monistic and dualistic. In sum, for all sentient beings
> whose illusory minds initiate one thought after another, from one
> instant to another, [*śūnyatā*] instantiates a fundamental difference and
> a plane of existence that cannot be called *śūnya* [empty]. However,
> once they no longer exercise their illusory minds, there is no *śūnyatā*.
> *Śūnyatā* refers to the fact that the phenomenal manifestation has no
> foundation. It is the nonillusory reality and the real mind. Absolute
> permanence, nonpollution, and satisfaction are called non-*śūnyatā*,
> which is not that which exists. Unless one departs from the plane of
> perceptual-conceptual existence, one cannot substantiate this
> non-*śūnyatā*. The mind that arises and is extinguished is the mind that
> is initiated from *tathātā*, which is neither unified with nor different
> from [the mind] initiated from the *nidānas* or the *ālaya*.[47]

In other words, the *citta* (absolute mindfulness) is subdivided into two
departments: (1) the Tathāgatagarbha, that is, the non-*śūnyatā;* and
(2) the *ālaya*-consciousness, from which the conventional reality is
in-formed according to the technicity of dependent originations-
emptiness. For Yin Shun, this passage betrays a neo-Confucian ontol-
ogy/meontology: (1) the *ātmakatva* (*ti* or self-nature) here is non-*śūnyatā;*
(2) *lakṣanas* (*xiang* or forms) are constituted in accordance with the technicity of dependent originations-emptiness in the *ālaya*-consciousness;
and (3) the *adhyavasāya* (*yong* or function) of the *ālaya*-consciousness is to
perform the formational process.[48]

The use of the three neo-Confucian concepts of "self-nature,"
"forms," and "function" as an ontological framework to interpret the
Awakening of Faith and the *Śūraṅgama Sūtra* was first suggested by Ouyang. In 1904, Ouyang met Yang in Nanking (Nanjing) on his way back
from his public office examination in Peking. Although there is no

reliable record of their conversation in this meeting, historians today deduce from Yang's notes that Ouyang questioned the authorships of both the *Sūtra* and the *Śāstra*.[49] For Ouyang, these works' ontological framework betrays that they were written—not translated—during the Song dynasty (960–1279) by neo-Confucian scholars. Yang defended their Indian origin by referring to the neo-Confucians themselves, who claimed that they borrowed the concept of consciousness from these texts.[50]

For Ouyang, if absolute mindfulness is subdivided into two departments, karmic impulses will not be deposited in the Tathāgatagarbha. Yet, as the ontological ground of the *ālaya*-consciousness, karma must be generated from the Tathāgatagarbha. If so, either: (1) these affliction-inducing impulses are contained within the Tathāgatagarbha—the emptiness of emptiness—which makes the Tathāgatagarbha impure and nonempty; or (2) the Tathāgatagarbha is a transcendental and monistic ground, a concept that is fundamentally at odds with Buddhism.

Yang's posthumously published letter to his friend Degao reveals his reply to Ouyang, which leans toward the second argument:

> *Tathātā* is being enwrapped by dependent originations. It does not change, even though it lets dependent originations be. In it, there exists a consciousness driven by karmic ignorance. As it lets dependent originations be without changing, its self-nature is pure, even though karmic ignorance exists in it.[51]

After Yang's death in 1911, Ouyang followed Yang's will to serve as the manager of the Jinling Publishing House, though he rebelled by establishing his own institution: the Zhina neixueyuan (China Inner Studies Institute, or CISI).[52] Under his supervision, the corrected edition of Hwendzàng's *Discourse on the Perfection of Consciousness-Only* and the Chinese translation of the *Yogācārabhūmi-Śāstra* [*Treatise on the Foundation for Yoga Practitioner*, attributed to Asaṅga], which Yang recuperated from Japan, were both printed by the CISI.[53] For Ouyang, these two texts do not suggest that the Tathāgatagarbha is a monistic or transcendental formation that contains karmic impulses; rather, as the self-nature of forms, *being-nothing*, because it is a layout of processual relationalities, performs the function of producing forms. If so, the "Tathāgatagarbha" is a term that designates an *ālaya*-consciousness that no longer drives—and is driven by—karma, but rather by insight.[54] Ouyang therefore argues that the transcendental notion of the Tathāgatagarbha is a Taoist inflection.

Ouyang's research gained support from Liang Qichao and Ouyang's student Lü Cheng (1896–1989).[55] Lü's idea resonates with Tanabe Hajime's. For him, the Tathāgatagarbha Buddhism developed in India emphasizes that the self-nature of self-nature is nothing. Thus, an insight into this nothingness of nothingness indicates a "going toward," a mindfulness of the inseparability between śūnyatā-lakṣaṇā (emptiness-form). Meanwhile, the notion of *citta* proposed by the *Awakening* indicates a "returning-to" what has always been there—the *lǐ*-technicity of consciousness—which betrays its neo-Confucian origin.[56]

Thomé H. Fang contends that neither Ouyang nor Lü grasps the aporia raised by Tathāgatagarbha scholars. For him, Chinese Mahāyāna Buddhism has always been built on a Taoist ontological and epistemological framework.[57] For Fang, this is most evidently seen in the (mis)translation of śūnyatā (negation of existence or emptiness of something) and *bhava* (existence) into *khung/kong* (emptiness as something) and *hǐǔ/you* (having or existing-in-something). The logic behind the original Pāli and Sanskrit terms is a matter of affirmation versus negation. Meanwhile, *khung* comes from the *Laozi* [*Tao Te Ching*], which designates *dao* (Tao) as the emptiness of emptiness, from which *ziran* (nature)—that is, the mathematic codes in which *fa* (forms)—are constituted. And for the *Laozi*, the substance of forms is *qi*. Meanwhile, the concept of *you* is taken from the *Zhuangzi* [*Chuang Tzu*], which argues that the self-nature of all forms is Tao—the nothingness of nothingness.[58]

Fang points out that both Yogācāra and Taoist scholars wrestle with the question of meontology. He cites Friedrich Nietzsche (1844–1900) by arguing that once Zarathustra has arrived at the stage of *Übermensch,* he returns to humanity with empathy and equanimity—what Nietzsche calls the "eternal return."[59] This idea of meontology is known to be the major difference between the Mahāyāna notion of bodhisattvas, who are supposed to return to form by engaging themselves in relationalities with equanimity, and the Theravādin notion of the *arahant/arhat,* who are supposed to dwell in emptiness. Historically, when Hwendzàng introduced Yogācāra Buddhism in the *Discourse on the Perfection of Consciousness-Only,* he implies that enlightenment is a state of nothingness that can be attained by rendering the *ālaya*-consciousness inoperative. In other words, he omits the entire debate on the Tathāgatagarbha from India. Thus, the writers or translators of the *Awakening* needed to supplement what had been deemed missing in Chinese Yogācāra studies by drawing on the Taoist notion of meontology. It was a historically roundabout and culturo-linguistically syncretic process of addressing an aporia that had been debated by the Yogācāra scholars in India during Hwendzàng's lifetime.[60]

WANG GUOWEI AND *JINGJIE*

While Buddhist philosophers have regarded syncretism as a liability ever since the Buddhist Renaissance, it has been seen as a productive discourse in the formulation of Buddhist aesthetics. The scholar who initiated an interest in formalizing a Taoist-Buddhist-Confucian aesthetic was a philologist, Wang Guowei. Wang entered the imperial academy in 1892. After his graduation, he chose not to enter the bureaucracy. Instead, he became a proofreader at a Shanghai newspaper called *Shiwu bao* [Current affairs post]; he also studied Japanese, German, and English. He was sent by the government to the Tokyo School of Science in 1901, though he returned to China in 1902 and became an instructor in the humanities at the Kiangsu Normal Academy. In 1907, he was hired by the Ministry of Rites (which oversaw education) in Peking, though he fled to Kyoto after the 1911 Revolution and stayed there for five years. He was hired by Peking University in 1922 and then Tsinghua University in 1925 to teach. Sadly, he committed suicide without any clear reason on June 2, 1927.[61]

In one of his earliest essays on aesthetics, "Kongzi zhi meiyu zhuyi" [The aesthetic education of Confucius, 1904], Wang argues that for both Immanuel Kant and Arthur Schopenhauer (1788–1860), aesthetics is considered a *Bildung* (formation or education), which is in accord with the Confucian understanding of poetry as stated in the *Lunyu* [*Analects*]: "Poetry can stimulate affections, put you in a state of contemplation, consolidate a community, express discontent, serve your father who lives near you, and pay respect to your lord in a distance."[62] Yet, Wang sees the art not simply as a biopolitical technology of recognition, but also as a *jingjie* (milieu): an image-consciousness. He argues that Schopenhauer inherits Kant's notion of aesthetic judgment, which entails the beholder to view an artwork as a purposeless form. In so doing, the beholder's "consciousness is no longer considered an individuated self, but a pure desireless [deindividuated] self." This is what Schopenhauer calls a return to the will.[63]

As Ñāṇājīvako argues, Schopenhauer's view can be understood in Yogācāra terms as a storehouse of potentialities. What the will does is to activate these potentialities in an eternal flux, thus enabling existence to manifest itself as a perpetual process of becoming. For Schopenhauer, this process drives—and is driven by—desire, which operates *in ignōrantia*. Like the Theravādins, Schopenhauer argues that ignorance produces a perpetual craving for permanence and continuity. Thus, the will engages in an endless cycle of birth and death, and formation and extinction.[64]

Wang therefore argues that the will is emptiness, which is in turn grounded in the emptiness of emptiness. Thus, he paraphrases the *Awakening of Faith* to explicate on Schopenhauer: "When there is no desire, there is no emptiness; there is then neither hope nor fear. When we see an exterior object, we do not form any beneficial or detrimental relationship with it; rather, we see it as a pure external object—a milieu of pure beauty." He then argues that this is what the scholar Su Shi [1037–1101, himself a Zen practitioner] calls "consigning *yi* [*ideation* or the process of becoming of an idea-formation] to the object."[65] However, Wang prefers the Taoist scholar Shao Yong's (1011–77) interpretation:

A cultivated human being can become one with the *qing* [sensations, affections, and desires] of all things, since he can practice *fanguan* [reverse observation]; *fanguan* refers to the process of seeing not from the perspective of the self. Seeing not from the perspective of the self is seeing from the perspective of the object. If they can see an object from the perspective of the object, where lies the self in the process?[66]

Wang's ruminations in that essay would be further developed in his most celebrated book, *Renjian cihua* [On human lyrics, 1910]. In the book, Wang argues that the most important element in lyrics is *jingjie*, which can be constructed out of either *lixiang* (enticing an imagination or idea, that is, ideation) or *xie* (description). There are two kinds of *jing*: with a self and with no self. He then argues: "A *jing* with no self can be attained in quietude-in-itself, while a *jing* with self can be attained in a quiet state within movement. Hence, the former is [equivalent to Kant's understanding of] beauty, whereas the latter can be considered the sublime." For him, according to Taoism, all things in *ziran* (nature) are interrelated and inter-constrained. When a realist describes reality, they inevitably make creative decisions that go against these natural relations. Hence, an artistic milieu, in accordance with Zen, refers not only to the objects in it, but also to the affective processes of becoming: content, anger, sorrow, and joy. In fact, the interdependent relationships between objects are instantiations of these affects. What the thirteenth-century critic Yan Yu (1191–1241) regards as the *shenyun* (essence or soul) of art, a concept originated from Taoism, is the idea of *jingjie* in Buddhism.[67]

In §26, Wang argues that the process of aesthetic judgment mirrors the process of attaining or returning to insight, which involves three phases:

> Yesterday, the westerly withered the jade trees; Alone, [I] climb up to the top of a tall building, commanding a panoramic view of all the paths leading to the edge of the world: this is the first *jingjie*. [My] belt has become gradually loose, [yet] in the end, [I have] no regret; for that person, [I] am reduced to an emaciated figure: this is the second *jingjie*. Having searched for them a hundred or even a thousand times, [I] turn my head around and suddenly realize: that that person, here and now, has always been under that burning streetlamp by the fence: this is the third *jingjie*.[68]

The first *jingjie* is initiated by a sudden insight into the transience of existence, as the "westerly withered the jade trees" overnight. In response, I "climb up to the top of a tall building" alone in order to gain a panoramic view of an entire network of intersecting paths that constitutes *my* world. This *jingjie* drives—and is driven by—a desire for knowledge in-formed by *manas*. The second *jingjie* drives—and is driven by—a desire for the other, to the extent that the self is constituted by the existence, need, and well-being of the other (benevolence), and that the self affects—and is affected by—their mutual afflictions: that is, compassion and pathos. The third *jingjie*, triggered by a sudden insight that the pure relationality that in-forms the difference between the self and the other, is not something to be attained, but the emptiness of emptiness that has always been there.[69]

Wang's three *jingjie* are comparable to a *gātha* (verse) that is attributed to Tshɛngngʉɐn H'æŋgsi/Qingyuan Xingsi (660–740):

> A mountain is seen as a mountain, a river is seen as a river;
> A mountain is seen not as a mountain, a river is seen not as a river;
> A mountain is seen still as a mountain, a river is seen still as a river.[70]

For Tshɛngngʉɛn, when a practitioner has arrived at—or returned to—insight, a mountain and a river are seen as objects that have their own existential values. Then, through reason, the practitioner comes to an understanding that the mountain and river are forms that have no existential values, with an attachment to the perceptual-conceptual differentiation between form and emptiness. Finally, with a sudden insight, the practitioner becomes mindful that such differentiation is empty—that *tathātā*, the pure relationality between form and emptiness, has always been there.

We can therefore say that in-aesthetically, the first two *jingjie* refer to two kinds of karma-image. Meanwhile, the third *jingjie* refers to the insight-image: a consciousness that is mindful of its own technicity.

CHU KUANG-CH'IEN: BUDDHISM AND PSYCHOANALYSIS

During the 1930s, Chu Kuang-ch'ien (1897–1986) introduced psychoanalysis into this line of thinking. Between 1925 and 1933, he studied literature and the humanities at the University of Edinburgh. He then audited courses at University College London and was also registered as a student at the Université de Paris. Eventually, he received his doctoral degree at the Université de Strasbourg with a thesis on psychoanalysis and aesthetics. He then returned to China in 1933 to teach and was eventually hired by Peking University in 1952.[71]

While he was in Strasbourg, Chu turned his doctoral thesis into a general-interest book for secondary-school students, called *Tan mei* [On beauty, 1932], and his thesis was eventually published as an academic monograph titled *Wenyi xinlixue* [Psychology of art and literature, 1936].[72] In *Psychology*, Chu claims himself to be a follower of Benedetto Croce (1866–1952). However, as Mario Sabattini (1944–2017) argues, though Chu and Croce both refer to aesthetic judgment as a mode of intuition, Chu's understanding of this process is closer to Kant's.[73] In fact, in *Psychology*, Chu uses Kant's definition of affects as his *point de départ*. For Kant:

> Affects are specifically different from passions. The former are related merely to feeling; the latter belong to the faculty of desire, and are inclinations that make all determinability of the faculty of choice by means of principles difficult or impossible. The former are tumultuous and unpremeditated, the latter sustained and considered; thus indignation, as anger, is an affect, but as hatred (vindictiveness), it is

a passion. The latter can never, in any circumstances, be called
sublime, because while in the case of an affect the freedom of the mind
is certainly hampered, in the case of passion it is removed.[74]

In other words, affect for Kant is *intuitive*, whereas passion is in the
order of recognition. In *On Beauty*, Chu illustrates this with a concrete
example. When a carpenter looks at an old cypress, they see a piece of
raw material that serves a purpose. When a botanist observes the cypress, they regard it as a specimen of a living organism. Nevertheless,
when an artist contemplates the same tree, it is now a form that serves
no purposes. This form does not exist in its own right; rather, it is a *jing*
(milieu) of affective relationalities (for example, dignity, ruggedness,
strength, and vibrancy). For Chu, to say that the cypress is a projection
of the beholder's affections suggests that these feelings come from the
beholder's body alone, with or without the sight of the cypress. Meanwhile, to say that these feelings are initiated from the cypress implies
that the presence of the beholder is unnecessary.[75]

Therefore, Chu argues that the *jing* is an instantiation of a flow of
affects on an intuitive impression. What propels—and is propelled
by—such a formational process is *Einfühlung* (empathy), translated as
yiqing zuoyong: affective transference.[76] In this light, there is neither an
agent nor a patient in this process of becoming. Chu enlists Sigmund
Freud's (1856–1939) notion of the unconscious to explicate this process
of identification:[77]

What we have learned . . . may be summarized as follows. First,
identification is the original form of emotional tie with an object;
secondly, in a regressive way it becomes a substitute for a libidinal
object-tie, as it were by means of introjection of the object into the
ego; and thirdly, it may arise with any new perception of a common
quality shared with some other person who is not an object of the
sexual instinct. The more important this common quality is, the more
successful may this partial identification become, and it may thus
represent the beginning of a new tie. We already begin to divine that
the mutual tie between members of a group is in the nature of an
identification of this kind, based upon an important emotional
common quality; and we may suspect that this common quality lies in
the nature of the tie with the leader. Another suspicion may tell us
that we are far from having exhausted the problem of identification,
and that we are faced by the process which psychology calls "empathy

[*Einfühlung*]" and which plays a major role thanks to the possibilities
that it opens up in penetrating the soul of people foreign to our ego.[78]

To elaborate on the idea of *Einfühlung*, Chu borrows Pan Guangdan's
(1899–1967) study of narcissism based on both Freudian psychoanalysis
and Zen Buddhism. Pan argues that narcissism consists of two components: *zilian* (desire for the self) and *yinglian* (desire for a reflection).
When Narcissus sees a reflection of his own image in a body of water,
these two levels operate inseparably. On one level, when Narcissus beholds his own image, the reflection presents to him nothing but a form.
Such an encounter initiates a sudden insight into the technicity of
(mis)recognition: that his own form and the image in the water are
impermanent instantiations of an affective relationship. Such an affective transference between the self and the reflection initiates a compulsion for the self to become one with the reflection out there, forgetting
that such an image is already a projection of his own consciousness onto
a technical medium (compare Bernard Stiegler's tertiary retention; discussed in chapter 4).[79] For Pan, therefore, identification is part of the
operational process of the consciousness, which requires its projection
and externalization onto a technical medium, provided also that it must
internalize it and reunite with it as a subjectivized objective. Thus, identification drives karma and is driven by it.

Chu, however, departs from Pan's analysis. For him, when an artist
beholds the cypress, the beholder's body and the form of the cypress
are in-formed out of an affective *gongming* (resonance). In such a formational process, the forms of the agent and the patient remain the same,
yet they are technically undifferentiated—a process he calls *wu wo tong
ti* (the object and I are one).[80] In such a *jingjie*, the consciousness lets be
the distance between the form of the beholder's body and the form of
the beheld body, with a mindfulness of their technical *in-difference.*[81]
Again, I call this the insight-image.

ZONG BAIHUA: ART AS A SPATIAL CONSCIOUSNESS

Chu's understanding of the *jingjie* as *wu wo tong ti* is further developed
by Zong Baihua (1897–1986) into a concept called *kongjian yishi* (spatial
consciousness). He does so by introducing the Taoist concept of *qi* (air
or subtle energy; what Shaku Soyen calls *ki*), *yun* (essence), *sheng* (en-
gendering), and *dong* (movement). According to Taoist philosophy, a *jing*

(what Soyen calls *hō*) is in-formed out of a circulation of subtle energies. These subtle energies drive—and are driven by—sixty-four mathematic combinations of natural elements. The configurative *qi* becomes the essence of a form. In this process, both the beholder's body and the *jing* are instantiations of an enduring movement. Thus, movement is the image and the image is movement.[82]

Zong grew up in an intellectual family and received a modern (Europeanized) education in the prosperous region south of the Yangtze River. In 1919, he became chief editor of "Xuedeng" [Light of learning], the literary supplement of the Shanghai-based *Shishi xinbao* [*China Times*] and grew to be an ally of the socialist writers Guo Moruo (1892–1978) and Tian Han (1898–1968). In 1920, he went to Germany and studied philosophy in the Goethe-Universität and Humboldt-Universität. In 1925, he was hired by the National Northeast University (renamed National Central University in 1927 and National Nanking University in 1949) to teach aesthetics, a post he held until he moved to Peking University in 1952.

In "Lun wenyi de kongling yu chongshi" [On emptiness-spirituality and fulfillment-concreteness in art and literature, 1947], Zong ruminates on two seemingly conflicting definitions of beauty raised by Zhou Ji (1781–1839): "When one first studies lyrical writing, one asks for emptiness, as it is upon emptiness that the spiritual energy constitutes movement; once one has achieved a formal style, one asks for concreteness, since it is upon concreteness that forms can be filled with energies."[83] Zong then defines emptiness-spirituality as:

> a *kṣaṇa* at which the self is forgotten, which is what we call *jingzhao* (quiet reflection) in aesthetics. The starting point of quiet reflection is the emptying of all, so that the *citta* no longer has any worries or obstacles [from accessing insight], and that we can sever all interdependent relationships with all current businesses and affairs. At this moment, with this *kṣaṇa* of insight, we can observe ten thousand phenomena in quietude. These phenomena dwell, as the way it is and being where they are supposed to be, in a mirror, as a plane of crystalline luminosity. Their individuated, self-fulfilled and concrete, immanent, and free *life* manifests itself. In other words, when we observe all forms quietly, they manifest themselves as the way it is.[84]

For Zong, emptiness-spirituality is not to be conveyed either through the use of empty spaces in a painting or through the employment of empty placeholders in a poem. Rather, as Wang Guowei argues, painters and poets have a penchant to conceal and insinuate the actual object, being, or view that is supposed to be the center of attention behind a *ge* (obstacle): a curtain, tree, rock, lake, or mountain. Such spatialization between the beholder and the object is not supposed to entice the beholder to know more. Rather, it is supposed to enable the consciousness to become mindful of its own technicity by focusing on the object's process of becoming, not its actualized form. Zong calls this technique *ziyuan* (self-distancing).[85]

Emptiness-spirituality is the ontological ground from which fulfillment and concreteness are generated. According to the *Ershisi shipin* [Twenty-four poetic criticisms, historically attributed to Sikong Tu (837–908)]:

> As the vital *khìi/qi* (energy) emerges from a distance, it never touches a spark of ashes (of death). *Dzìmgiɛn/ziran* (plane of existence) comes into being intricately [out of nothingness]: Who can give form to it and tailor it?[86]

The *Twenty-Four Poetic Criticisms* refer to the Thenthʌi idea of *khungthiung mièuhiŭ/kongzhong miaoyou*: that existence is initiated intricately out of the liminality between emptiness and existence.

In the early nineteenth century, Zhou Ji critiques the European notion of mimesis for failing to maintain the rule of self-distancing. For Zhou, concreteness is to be achieved by a few brushstrokes that lay out a milieu in its *pingdan* (flatness and flavorlessness), which serves as a layout of affective relationalities. This roughly sketched layout enables a beholder's consciousness to be in-formed with concrete details. They can look down into a lake from a cliff and watch a school of fish swimming. They can hear the laughter of a child walking hand-in-hand with their mother and also feel the happiness and anger of an audience who is watching a play, even though none of these details are depicted in the painting. The form sketched on the canvas therefore serves as a mirror—*citta*—from which the consciousness is in-formed in accordance with the affective energy that flows around it.[87]

In "Zhongguo shihua zhong suo biaoxian de kongjian yishi" [The spatial consciousness manifested in Chinese poetry and painting, 1949], Zong tries to cohere and formulate these arguments into what he calls a national aesthetics. Zong's effort needs to be understood as wartime and postwar attempts by Chinese intellectuals to define the terrain of *guoxue* (national studies). The term he proposes is called *kongjian yishi* (spatial consciousness).

Not surprisingly, Zong constructs such Chinese aesthetics by defining it against the Quattrocento. Based on Zou Yigui's (1686–1772) study of the Dutch paintings he saw in the trading ports, Zong argues that European understandings of perspective as a mathematical matter turn painting into a *gongjiang* (technic).[88] He cites Shen Kuo's (1031–95) *Mengxi bitan* [The written talks of Shen Mengxi, 1086–93], which argues that ink-wash paintings often employ the technique of *yi da guan xiao,* which means seeing a landscape from the perspective of someone who reduces it to a layout of miniatures in a process of becoming. For Shen, a landscape should be a journey through a number of stations. Each station serves as a spatiotemporal miniature, which we can call a scene.[89]

Zong then argues that unity is achieved by *qi, yun, sheng,* and *dong*—that is, by inviting the beholder to navigate in the milieu, which instantiates a mobile layout of affective relationalities. When the consciousness travels from one scene to another, the beholder shifts from one affective and physical distance to another, as the beholder's body and the state of things or being are originated dependently out of a *yishu de yizhi* (artistic will): the emptiness in which all creative potentialities are deposited and initiated.[90] In this sense, the affective *qi,* from one station to another, becomes the *yun* (essence) of form, which in turn *sheng* (engenders) *dong* (movement) as an image.

In this light, a painting is best understood as a mobile spatial consciousness actualized from the emptiness of emptiness as a source of potentialities. Zong cites a musician, Hei Khang/Ji Kang (223–63): "[I] look down and up at will,/as [I] navigate through the *thàihwen/taixuan.*"[91] The term *thàihwen* refers to Tao as an absolute (*thài*) mystery (*hwen*), a *state/nonstate* that is neither empty nor existent, from which creativity and conservation, and becoming and stasis, are initiated. Zong defines the *thàihwen* as the meontological ground of art, which he further defines by citing the *Yijing* [*I-ching*]: "An onward journey indicates that there is a return journey in sight; [navigating between those relational poles generated by the *thàihwen*], the boundaries of the universe [are being drawn and redrawn]."[92] In other words, a painting is in-formed out of the consciousness's navigation between these relation-alities, a process of ideation in which affects are spatialized.

As Yan Yu argues: "Like a tone that lingers in emptiness, a form that lingers within a form, the moon in the water, an image in a mirror: lan-guage is finite, whereas the *yi* [ideational process] it instantiates is a storehouse of infinite potentialities."[93] Therefore, Zong concludes that as a spatial consciousness, art *"inclines more toward a musical jingjie, one that is infiltrated by the rhythm of temporality. Nonetheless, such rhythm is not in-formed by a set of mathematical relationships, but by the technicities* [rela-tionalities] *between potentialities."*[94] In this sense, Zong argues that *xu* (emptiness) and *shi* (concreteness) are not formal matters, but relation-alities. For Zong, spatialization drives—and is driven by—*tui* (pushing), a *qi* that propels and is propelled by the formational process of idea.[95]

LAM NIN-TUNG: CINEMA AS A SPATIALIZING CONSCIOUSNESS

In the early 1980s, the Hong Kong film scholar Lam Nin-tung (1944–90), who graduated from the Università di Bologna, visited Zong in Beijing. During his stay in Italy, he had penned an unpublished article called "Zhongguo dianying lilun yanjiu zhong youguan gudian meixue wenti de tantao" [On the investigation into classical aesthetics in the study of Chinese film theory, written 1981]. Lam compares Zheng Junli's (Djen Jon Lee, 1911–69) film *Kumu fengchun* [*Spring Comes to the Withered Tree*, 1961] to a horizontal scroll painting. He argues that in such a painting, "the painter organically weaves images of different forms into a per-petual flux by means of a mobile gaze. When our gaze moves along the scroll, the image is instituted by a horizontal movement in a way similar to the cinema."[96]

Lam cites the production designer Han Shangyi (1917–98) as writing that the mobile *mise-en-scène* of a film must create:

the effects of *yibu huanjing* [a change of milieu as the spectator takes each step, one after another], *fenghui luzhuan* [an unexpected turn as the spectator saunters around one peak after another], *bubu rusheng* [entering into the climax step by step], *chujing shengqing* [initiating affects as each milieu is initiated], *jianwu siqing* [enabling the sight of each object to be associated with a set of affects]. . . . The overall *mise-en-scène* and the movements of the characters should bring forward those changes in the past and the anticipations of the future, the changes of light and color, and the changes between three-dimensionality and flat space.[97]

For Lam, what Han calls *yibu huanjing* is best understood as *you* (navigating or journeying). For him, therefore, *Spring Comes to the Withered Tree* and many other Chinese films are not composed out of narrative causality or spatiotemporal contiguity. Rather, a film is best understood as a spatializing consciousness, a movement in which states of things or beings are instantiations of affective changes.

Lam argues that a cinematographic image is initiated out of a *jingyun* (mirror-essence), a term coined by the cinematographer Nie Jing (1921–85). For Nie, a mirror-essence can be divided into *qiyun* (energy-essence), a circulation of subtle energy initiated by camera movement, and *dongyun* (movement-essence), that is, movement itself. The energy-essence and movement-essence of each shot should be part of an energy flux that was carried forward from the past and is pushing toward the future. A narrative is *sheng* (engendered) by an alternation between milieus that are directly associated with the plot and those that take the consciousness away from it. Performing within these milieus, an actor should maintain a distance between themself and the character, so that the *shen* (spirit) of the character is embodied—without being taken over by—the actor. The consciousness is then at once drawn into the formational process, while maintaining a mindfulness of its technicity.[98]

In 1982, Lam drafted an essay called "Zhongguo dianying de tedian" [The characteristics of Chinese cinema], in which he first coined the term *jing-you* (mirroring-navigating), which consists of a *mu-you* (navigating gaze) along with a *xin-you* (navigating mind).[99] What he means, however, is not entirely clarified until he penned the article "Zhongguo dianying de kongjian yishi" [The spatial consciousness of Chinese cinema, 1983]. In this article, Lam argues that the cinematographic image is a spatializing consciousness in-formed by a mobile *qi* (subtle energy). In the cinema, this process of spatialization is intervened by the camera, whose *jing* (lens or mirror) actualizes such navigation in framing, camera movement, and editing. In other words, the camera embodies the navigating gaze, which drives—and is driven by—the navigating mind.[100]

Lam is sometimes accused of being a cultural essentialist.[101] None-theless, he argues that it is impossible to locate a *Chinese* aesthetics in the cinema. For him, cinema's technology and form have always been determined by Euro-American directors and spectators. Therefore, Chi-nese filmmakers in Shanghai during the 1920s and 1930s and Cantonese filmmakers in Hong Kong in the 1950s had to engage in a "process of mutual separation and mutual connection between two spatial theories: *shixue jiegou* (optical structure) [in Euro-American aesthetics] and *lingxu jiegou* (structure founded on emptiness) [in Chinese aesthetics]."[102] Simi-lar to Jean-Louis Baudry before him, Lam argues that the penetrative gaze and the sociopolitical consciousness it carries were built into the camera obscura during the Quattrocento. Such gaze and consciousness were then adopted in Euro-American cinema.[103]

To complicate matters, the popularity of Dutch painting in the in-ternational trading ports in Southeast China and Southeast Asia during the eighteenth century inspired Chinese artists to adopt the Euro-American optical structure and reframe it in local terms. For example, Nian Xiyao (1678–1738), in his seminal work *Shixue* [The study of vision, 1729], rearticulates the optical structure in the critical language of Lu Ji (261–303).[104] For Nian, a Dutch painting can be described in accor-dance with Lu's "Yan lianzhu" [Performing a sequence of pearls]: "When you look at a mirror, it does not have any thickness; when you observe it, it is as deep as a bottomless pool."[105] Lam argues that this line of culturally syncretic spatial thinking was remediated by the spatial structure and ideological construct of the Euro-American camera, which became the aesthetic basis of Chinese cinema.

Nonetheless, Lu's understanding of depth is not entirely the same as the Quattrocento painters.' What Lu refers to is not depth (in an ob-jective reality), but *yuan* (distance) between the mind and the percep-tion. As argued by Guo Xi's (1000–1087) in "Linquan gaozhi: Shanshui xun" [On the way woods and streams are best placed within a landscape of mountains and water]:

> A mountain exists in three distances. Looking up to the top of the mountain from its foot is called *gaoyuan* [distance in height]. Catching a glimpse of the back of the mountain from its front is called *shenyuan* [distance in depth]. Commanding a view of the peaks in the distance from the peaks nearby is called *pingyuan* [flat distance]. The forms of

gaoyuan should be bright and clear, the forms of *shenyuan* should be layered and shadowed, and the forms of *pingyuan* should be both bright and shadowed. The force of *gaoyuan* should be rugged, the idea of *shenyuan* should be multilayered, and the idea of *pingyuan* should be both dashing and fusing, misty and dimly discernible. Regarding human figures in these three distances: those that are placed in *gaoyuan* should be clear and immediately graspable; those that are placed in *shenyuan* should be tiny and fragmented into points; those that are placed in *pingyuan* should be both dashing and withdrawn. Those that are clear and graspable should not be short; those that are tiny and fragmented should not be tall; while those that are dashing and withdrawn should not be large. Such are the three distances.[106]

Based on Guo's discussion, Lam argues that the Euro-American idea of analyzing a film based on camera distances (for instance, close-up, medium shot, long shot) only addresses the image as an object. He adds to these categories three modes of spatial consciousness: *jinjing* (close milieu), *zhongjing* (middle milieu), and *yuanjing* (distant milieu). These distances are not stases within an immobile composition. Rather, they are *yijing* (ideational milieus) engendered by *qing* (affective changes) as the consciousness *you* (navigates) from one temporal instant to another. Lam points out that such a vocabulary has been used by directors Zhang Shichuan (1889–1953 or 1890–1954), Hou Yao (1903–42), Sang Hu (1916–2004), Djen Jon Lee (1911–69), and Li Jun (1922–2013) in their own film analyses.[107] As Zhang recalled, "When I shot *Nanfu nanqi* [*The Newly Weds*, 1913], I only employed one camera distance, the long shot, in order to induce a milieu that is neither too far nor too close."[108]

Lam argues that Chinese filmmakers have a preference for the middle milieu, instantiated by the use of the static long shot or the three-quarter shot with staging that privileges the center of the frame. It is because such a distance can be considered an optimal point of negotiation between different affective energies. For Tsuong P'iæng/Zong Bing (375–443), the paintings of his contemporary Th'iɐng Siɛu/Zhang Xiao are usually "no more than three square *tshuàn/cun* [about 1.72 square inches], yet it gives the beholder an impression that its ink reaches a height of a thousand *ngìm/ren* [about 7,000 feet] and a width of a few *tshhiɛk/chi* [about a few feet]; it allows the beholder to sense the bodily impact of traveling a hundred *lï/li* [Chinese miles]."[109] For Lam, within the confines of a square cinematographic frame, filmmakers need to foster a sense of *kong* (emptiness), *da* (immensity), and *kuo* (breadth). They do so by positing the consciousness at the middle milieu, from which forms and ideas that are too far or too huge for the frame can be imagined.[110]

Lam calls such an understanding of the cinematographic image a *youdong de kongjian yishi* (mobile spatializing consciousness). In such a spatializing consciousness, the frame does not delimit the spatial boundary of the dramatic stage. Instead, it allows the anthropotechnical body to navigate, thus in-forming the close, middle, and distant milieus freely in a process of becoming. In other words, if Gilles Deleuze sees framing as a technique of deterritorializing and reterritorializing space, Lam Nin-tung sees the anthropotechnical consciousness as a moving and changing *phasiation* in which these territorialities are replaced by relationalities. It is in this sense that the cinema is best understood as a *jingjian* (mirror-reflection)—the emptiness of emptiness from which states of things or beings are imagined and imaged out of a processual layout of affective relationalities.[111]

OZU AS A BUDDHIST DIRECTOR: RECEPTION HISTORY

Lam Nin-tung's attempt to construct a Chinese cinematic aesthetics brings us back to the starting point of this chapter: that there is no such thing as a Buddhist aesthetics. In his—and his predecessors' discussions—we can see how Buddhist philosophy can help us develop a relational understanding of the formational process of the cinematographic image along with its meontology, epistemology, and ethics. Yet, as a philosophy that identifies the generation of sensations and affections as a point of epistemological concealment, it does not lend us a framework to examine why we find an artwork beautiful or sublime. It does suggest that an artistic experience (insight-image) enables the consciousness to become mindful of its own technicity and of how forms drive—and are driven by—affective relationalities.

Theravādin scholars acknowledge that stages of mindfulness bring about certain positive sensations and affections: (1) that empathy initiates *pīti/prīti* (rapture); (2) that relaxation generates *passaddhi/prasrabhi* (tranquility); (3) that entering mindfulness brings about *samādhi* (concentration); and (4) that absolute mindfulness produces *upekkha/upekṣā* (equanimity).[112] These sensations and affections are not initiated by a contact between internal and external forms, but rather by the consciousness's mindfulness of its own technicity. These are considered stages of *nibbāna/nirvāṇa* (release from and extinction of) dependent originations-emptiness with formal residues. These pleasing—and sometimes overwhelming—sensations and affections are best understood as releases, which, like all forms, must be let go. It is in this sense that these are not aesthetic judgments, but instead are in-aesthetic degrees of mindfulness that the consciousness has attained or to which it has returned.

For example, Ozu Yasujirō has been regarded by film historians as the quintessential Buddhist director. Yet, scholars who are interested in defining Ozu's Buddhist aesthetics put their emphasis on his formal strategies, which are technical means for Ozu to achieve an insight-image. These forms themselves have very little to do with Buddhism in the first place.

For Paul Schrader, the cinema of Ozu, like those of Robert Bresson (1901–99) and Carl Theodor Dreyer (1889–1968), strives to achieve a "common film form" that transcends the "film-makers' personalities, culture, politics, economics, or moralities. It is instead the result of two universal contingencies: the desire to express the Transcendent in art and the nature of the film medium."[113] For Schrader, the filmic medium has the unique ability to express what is inexpressible.[114] In short, Ozu's image is universal because it is transcendental (or spiritual). Schrader derives his understanding of Buddhism from the works of Donald Richie and Suzuki Daisetz, who, for a very specific reason that I have explained, defined Buddhism as a transcendental religion.[115]

Although Richie's studies predate Schrader, his monograph on Ozu was published only in 1974, which was considered an effort to ground the study of Japanese cinema within the context of Japanese culture. From our perspective today, however, Richie's understanding of Ozu's stylistic traits as fundamentally Japanese has been criticized as a form of cultural essentialism. In a seminar he gave at Yale University in 2006, he defended his position by illustrating how, historically, Japanese art has privileged vertical positions, flat space, a visual orientation from right to left, a construction of rhythm based on identity, repetition, and an intent focus on empty intervals.[116]

In his book, Richie attributes Ozu's style to the aesthetic concept of *yūgen* (or *mono no aware*), the use of a word or image to invoke the profound relationality between the world as a *saṃsāra* (cycle) driven by afflictions, and the emptiness on which such relationality is projected. While *yūgen* has a syncretic Taoist-Buddhist-Shinto origin and while it may well be one of Ozu's formal technologies, that does not explain the technicity of the formational process of Ozu's image. Moreover, Richie's purpose is not to interpret what Ozu's understanding of Buddhism is, but instead to explain how the use of *yūgen* instantiates his "Japanese-ness." Richie offers eyewitness accounts of how Ozu employed these aesthetic strategies in his direction, which are corroborated by his own interview with Ozu as well as Ozu's storyboards and his markups on his screenplays.[117] What this book illustrates is that cultural essentialism is always well-justified by archival documents and the investigator's lived experience. In fact, it was jointly *believed* by both Richie and Ozu as a technology of (self-)recognition.

Richie's effort was therefore not entirely different from that of Noël Burch's 1979 book *To a Distant Observer*. For Burch, Ozu's cinematic forms constitute a counter-cinema in the eyes of a U.S. filmmaker who lives in France—revealing a self-sustained system generated within the specific cultural and industrial conditions of Japan, seemingly indifferent to Hollywood.[118]

The use of Ozu's cinema and his *Buddhist aesthetics* as a Euro-American technology of recognition was criticized by Japanese writers. In 1984, Hasumi Shigehiko retorted that both Schrader and Richie define Ozu's cinema as a lack (for example, the lack of camera movement and the lack of anything really happening in the narrative) by positing it against the Hollywood norm. In so doing, they use Ozu's work as a means to conceal their own lack (in other words, as a cultural fetish), as though their look were free from any power relations. Hasumi suggests that we read Ozu's work as a system of semiological differences: eating and not eating, laundry and no laundry, open windows and closed windows, and so on. For example, by chasing the semiological structure of eating/not eating, we can see how Ozu's films operate intertextually and how the changing power relations in the larger society rewrote the codes of their symbolic relations.[119]

For instance, in Ozu's *Otona no miru ehon—Umarete wa mita keredo* [*An Adult's Picture Book View—I Was Born, But...*, 1932], food and nutrition take a centrality in the film in association with wealth and power. As the children realize that their father is not as socially and economically powerful as their bullies' father, they hold a hunger strike, despite the fact that they both love their mother's cooking.[120] Their decision is both humorous and poignant, as they naïvely believe that by choosing not to eat and putting their own well-being under threat (a strategy they learn from mass media), they can persuade their father to make changes. Yet, the spectators also realize that the father has no agency over his own position under capitalism, and they observe that it is painful for him to see his children launching this protest. The symbolic difference between eating and not-eating is therefore codified not only within the text's domestic setting, but also within the larger political struggle between the left and the right under the militarist government.

When the film was remade as *Ohayō* [*Good Morning*, 1959], this symbolic structure is textually transferred to a fight over the parents' ability to own a television set. This time, the hunger strike is replaced by a silence strike (to refuse saying "good morning" to the parents), thus displacing food/survival/power onto communication/familial harmony/right of consumption. The subversive hunger strike against capitalism in *I Was Born, But...* is now translated into a demand for the parents' acknowledgment of their children's rightful participation in capitalism. In other words, Schrader's and Richie's reduction of Ozu's work to a reflection of "Japaneseness" and Buddhism overlooks the sociopolitical complexities that it seeks to critique and negotiate.

In 1984, Satō Tadao (the pseudonym of Iiri Tadao), who is considered a more broad-church critic and was frequently quoted by Richie, argued that Ozu's cinema originated from the *shōmin eiga* (petit urbanite film) produced by the Shochiku studio during its Kamata era (1895–1936; during which the studio was located in this suburb of Tokyo). Its inspiration was the slapstick comedy of Charlie Chaplin (1889–1977). Satō argues that Ozu manages to "unify and organize [Japanese] customs, via film techniques, into perfect forms and types. For those foreigners who cannot possibly savor the subtleties of such customs, the tension, order, and humor embodied by these forms and types can attain a [transcultural] understanding."[121] Although Satō's statement still carries the tenor of cultural essentialism, the notion of "customs"—as opposed to "culture"—suggests that Ozu's work is founded on the social praxis of its time.

For David Bordwell, therefore, what Richie, Schrader, and Burch regard as Japanese culture and what Satō considers "customs" are best understood as the *materials* to which Ozu's *forms* refer. For Viktor

Shklovsky and Yuri Tyniyanov (1894–1943), forms are abstracted from the larger pool of sociopolitical, cultural, and industrial materials specific to the time of the artwork's production, and forms also serve as references to these materials.[122] Based on Satō's studies, Bordwell argues that Ozu drew his materials primarily from art, photography, popular culture, and Hollywood cinema, and also adopted some widely known frameworks from Buddhist art that made up the overall landscape of Taishō Japan. For Ozu, what mattered the most during his Kamata period (1920–36) was the excitement of urban modernity, as well as the broken promises of sociopolitical liberation and opportunities for the young generation that were made during the Meiji era (1868–1912).[123]

In my own research into Ozu's diaries written before the Pacific War (1941–45), I find his writing demonstrates a young man's fascination with Hollywood cinema, the individualism and youthful aspirations that it advocates, and its sense of humor and satirical sensibility toward social ills. Trapped within Shochiku's tight production schedule, Ozu and his cohorts in the studio had to develop a highly systematic way of shooting and editing without much room for camera movement and formal variations that Hollywood studios could employ. Thus, certain traits in Ozu's later work were being used in most Shochiku films during the silent era: the consistent use of low-angle shots, 180-degree cutting between characters who sit around a standardized urban room on tatami mats, and the spare use of transitions. What Ozu did was to perfect this system after the war into an authorial signature.[124] But as Jinhee Choi argues, perhaps such an authorial signature is not a retrospective summary of what Ozu's work does, but instead a stylistic sensibility—what she calls "Ozuesque"—that both defines, and is defined by, later directors' paths toward their own authorships.[125]

OZU AND IN-AESTHETICS

For David Bordwell, therefore, Ozu Yasujirō's aesthetics is grounded in Hollywood and Tokyo's urban modernity, and Buddhism was merely one piece of material among many. In this sense, Bordwell would probably agree that there is no such thing as a Buddhist aesthetics in the cinema, but at most a Buddhist attitude. Yoshida Kiju's controversial book *Ozu Yasujirō no han eiga* [*Ozu's Anti-Cinema*, 1998] takes this one step further. Based on Ozu's last words to Yoshida, that "Cinema is drama, not accident," and also on his earlier statement that "directors are like

prostitutes under a bridge, hiding their faces and calling customers,"
Yoshida sees Ozu as a studio filmmaker who has always found the world
chaotic. Meanwhile, commercial cinema assaults this already-chaotic
world by turning such a chaos into drama and sensations. Yoshida therefore argues that Ozu regards his cinema as "an act of penance for the
sins of his camera's assault on the world." He does so by adopting an
anonymous, indifferent, and empty look on our world and by making
the same film over and over again. He therefore makes visible not only
the transient and vicious cycle in which we willfully and ignorantly
engage, but also how the cinema has allowed the spectators to wallow
in their own ignorance.[126]

In my view, Yoshida's understanding of Ozu is the only work that
comes close to locating where we can *begin* to examine Ozu's Buddhist
attitude, even though Yoshida simply considers such an attitude as a
cynical one. One thing we can take from Yoshida's study is that Ozu's
cinema has never indicated that there is an exception lying somewhere
beyond the everydayness that constitutes his image. Rather, his image
is a direct engagement in the chaotic, nonsensical, and purposeless suffering and joy of the everyday. It invites us to be mindful of every moment as *the way it is*.

In *Cinema 2*, Deleuze probably offers the most philosophically engaged analysis of Ozu. He points out that in *Banshun* [*Late Spring*, 1949],
there is a scene in which Noriko (Hara Setsuko, 1920–2015) and her father, Somiya Shūkichi (Ryū Chishū, 1904–93), sitting in their hotel room,
have a conversation about her impending marriage. In this dialogue,
Noriko asks for her father's forgiveness, as she will no longer be able to
stay home to take care of him. Shūkichi tells his daughter not to worry,
as this is only a matter of life. By the end of the scene, they switch off
the light and go to bed. The film then cuts to a medium close-up of
Noriko in bed with a smile, followed by a long shot of a vase set against
a window. In this shot, we only see the foliage of a tree moving slightly
outside the window. After that, the film cuts back to the medium close-
up of Noriko, who stops smiling, turns away from the camera, and then
turns back to her original position with tears in her eyes (see Figure 28).

This vase shot is a "breathing moment" after an affectively intense
and emotionally charged conversation between daughter and father.
Satō would argue that Figure 28, top, is best understood as the ending
of the conversation, at which Noriko is content with the blessing her

FIGURE 28. The "vase" scene from *Late Spring*

father gave her. Then, Figure 28, middle, offers the anthropotechnical consciousness a moment at which it can reflect on what really happened in this conversation: the inevitable sacrifice of a father's life, at his old age, for the sake of his daughter's happiness. Someday, Noriko, as a mother, will do the same for her children. Human beings are therefore delusively engaged in a cyclical flux of life, as though their sufferings were inevitable and permanent. Yet, the permanence of such a cyclical flux is also impermanent, because one generation will be born, will grow old, and will inevitably die. The realization that time is impermanent, and therefore life is suffering, drives Noriko—and probably the spectator—to tears, as in Figure 28, bottom. In this light, Burch is apt to suggest that Figure 28, middle, serves as a "pillow shot," a sliding signifier (known in the haiku as a "pillow word") that interrupts what effectively is a single shot (Figure 28, top and bottom) by shifting the affective tonality of the image.[127]

Built on these interpretations, Deleuze argues that in these three shots:

> There is becoming, change, passage. But the form of what changes does not itself change, does not pass on. This is time, time itself, "a little time in its pure state": a direct time-image, which gives what changes the unchanging form in which the change is produced. . . . The still life is time, for everything that changes is in time, but time does not itself change, it could itself change only in another time, indefinitely. At the point where the cinematographic image most directly confronts the photo, it also becomes most radically distinct from it. Ozu's still lifes endure, have a duration, over ten seconds of the vase: this duration of the vase is precisely the representation of that which endures, through the succession of changing states.[128]

For Deleuze, therefore, Figure 28, middle, is a pure sound and optical situation, which enables the consciousness to become mindful of its own technicity: the technicity of time. It is in this sense that *Late Spring* can be considered a mode of insight-image.

What makes Ozu's insight-image different from the Euro-American examples Deleuze analyzes is that insight is not arrived at by any deliberate technical or formal manipulation. Rather, insight is attained—or returned to—out of banality. As Bordwell, Satō, and Yoshida all point out, as a Shochiku director, Ozu's films were meant to be family dramas that provided entertainment to the suburban middle class.[129] This is also the reason why most of his films are set in middle-class suburbia. If most of Ozu's formal signatures are common narrational strategies adopted by other Shochiku directors, his films can be seen as rearticulations of the Hollywood family drama with his studio's specific styles. Even his curtain shots or pillow shots (as in Figure 28, middle), which may not be immediately interpreted as part of the narrative's causality, always stay on the level of a scene's overall banality.

In other words, to understand the vase in *Late Spring*, we need to engage in the vase as a vase—and nothing more. It is when we are capable of being fully mindful of the existence of the vase—*here and now*—and come to a mindfulness that such an image-consciousness is ungraspable in the past and in the future, that it refers to nothing other than itself, that we can abduce an insight into the karmic impetus that initiates the image and the drama. Noriko's tears are shed not out of compassion and pathos for her father or an empathy between her and her father, but out of equanimity: that all sentient beings are driven by ignorance of ignorance. It is neither beautiful nor sublime. Rather, it is best understood as a *release* with formal residue.

In *Tōkyō monogatari* [*Tokyo Story*, 1953], the transition between the first and second sequences of the third act is marked by a scene of release. By the end of the first sequence, at night, Hirayama Tomi (Higashiyama Chieko, 1890–1980) dies in a coma, with her husband, Shūkichi (Ryū), daughter-in-law Noriko (Hara), and all her children but one—Keizō (Ōsaka Shirō)—with her. In the morning, Keizō finally arrives. Noriko realizes that Shūkichi has left the house. The film then cuts to a long shot of a road in front of a ceremonial hall of a monastery on top of a slope commanding the view of the harbor of Onomichi (see Figure 29, top).

The hall is located on the right of frame and the road is marked by a pair of stone lanterns in the middle ground. Those spectators who are familiar with the architecture of a Japanese monastery will know that the cemetery is next to this building. In this shot, Shūkichi stands in front of the lantern on the right of frame, facing the view of the harbor toward the left of frame. Meanwhile, Noriko runs from the foreground of the frame toward him. As Lam Nin-tung would argue, objects are placed on the two extreme ends of the frame, thus indicating a larger milieu around what is being captured by the camera and then drawing

FIGURE 29. The morning after Tomi's death in *Tokyo Story*

the consciousness's mindfulness to the middle milieu. Meanwhile, this mobile attention is pushed by Shūkichi's gaze, the pointed tip of the roof of the ceremonial hall, and the horizontal lines of the electrical wires in the background to the left of frame. Although what he looks at is never revealed in this sequence, the glimpse of the harbor in a *pingyuan* (horizontal distance) enables the consciousness to conjure up a panoramic view of the entire harbor.

As Noriko comes close to Shūkichi, the film cuts to a closer view (still in long shot) of the two figures standing next to the lantern on the right of frame. Noriko, facing Shūkichi, tells him that Keizō has arrived. Shūkichi simply says, "I see." He then remarks, "It was a beautiful sunrise." Noriko then turns around and faces the left of frame (see Figure 29, bottom) and beholds the same view that is physically concealed from the consciousness. Once again, the three vertical lines formed by the lantern, Shūkichi's body, and Noriko's initiate a rhythm that pushes the consciousness to this unseen view. Meanwhile, the electrical wires in the background tilt up, thus opening a space toward the sky. Here, the consciousness is grasping not only the image of Noriko and Shūkichi's perceiving bodies, but also a perception-image of the overall milieu of the harbor—and of the intricate and mobile relationalities that in-form it.

Noriko, Shūkichi, and the anthropotechnical consciousness at large are supposed to be grasping the same physical milieu, based on their shared karma and the meontological ground in relationalities. But then, each individuated consciousness is driven by slightly different karmic impulses that enable them to *see* different milieus. Later in the film, Noriko will confess to Kyōko (Kagawa Kyōko) that she is not as morally righteous as what Tomi had thought her to be, that, like everyone else, she is driven by her ego and desire. Earlier in the film, we have seen Shūkichi getting drunk in a bar, complaining about his children, and letting loose his desire and self-centeredness. Moreover, this bar scene is accompanied by the offscreen sound of the "Gunkan kōshinkyoku" ["March 'Man of War!'"], the Japanese Navy anthem that invoked the country's colonial history and Shūkichi's participation in it as a soldier in the 1940s.

In Figure 29, the anthropotechnical consciousness is in mourning, which is a form of attachment both to the existence of the self and to the milieu as a possession of the self. In other words, every sentient body that partakes of this milieu is driven by karma, and the image-consciousness is an instantiation of that karma. Hence, there is nothing transcendental in this moment—and nobody is letting go of anything.

The turning point of release comes when Shūkichi casually says, "It is going to be another hot day." He then turns around and walks toward the camera. In one register, what he says can be interpreted as "After all, this is another day." A *resonance* arises and permeates through this overall milieu: a grief that life goes on, which is in itself driven by suffering. Such resonance can be regarded as an empathy initiated out of compassion. In another register, this image-consciousness is initiated out of an avalanche of karmic impulses that is initiated and that perishes from one instant to another, which gives form to the processes of individuations and transindividuations. These karmic impulses initiate sufferings. However, this karmic-driven formational process and the milieu that comes into being are the manifestations of *the way it is.* By engaging in the *here and now,* life and death—together with selfishness and selflessness, desire, frustration, and delusion—can be taken as *the way it is.* The most intricate and wondrous *assemblage of relations* between forms and emptiness is always manifested as a layout of forms in its utmost banality. Meanwhile, banality itself is a manifestation of the most wondrous and dignified *set of relations* between forms and emptiness.

IN-AESTHETICS AND AESTHETICS

As a philosophy that ruminates on the technicity of image-formation and the role that sensations and affections play in human apprehension, the idea of a Buddhist aesthetics, as I remarked at the beginning of this chapter, is an oxymoron. The historical debates that I have outlined throughout illustrate that the concepts and frameworks of Buddhist philosophy have compelled philosophers to focus on meontology, ontology, epistemology, and ethics. Any attempts to build a Buddhist aesthetics inevitably return to these problems. These efforts have only identified formal strategies and technologies that are based on specific cultural and historical conditions, as well as on a syncretic understanding of key Buddhist ideas and concepts. Alternatively, they fall into the trap of cultural essentialism, or even Orientalism.

A Buddhist attitude toward an artistic experience can be called in-aesthetics. To recapitulate, in-aesthetics: (1) seeks not to make any judgment on *aisthēta* (perceptible things), but instead to disconceal the *tathātā* of the perceptual-conceptual process; (2) seeks to refrain from making any aesthetic judgment based on sense-perception; and (3) seeks to engage in the process of actualization-virtualization by navigating between ōsō (going toward) and *gensō* (returning from) the Tathāgatagarbha.

Buddhism has long been part of East Asia's process of cultural formation. Hence, we cannot fight Orientalism by simply writing Buddhist sensibilities and values out of our discussion. However, a Buddhist attitude toward art is not a matter of formal manipulation, and it is certainly not reducible to a handful of narrational clichés. Rather, an engaged Buddhist reading of an artwork or a film must be conducted in-aesthetically, that is, by addressing how the consciousness arrives at insight and returns to it. Some insight-images involve elaborate formal manipulations, while others, like Ozu's cinema, enable the consciousness to become mindful of the technicity in its very banality.

In-aesthetics and aesthetics are not mutually exclusive. Having an in-aesthetic attitude toward the cinema does not preclude spectators' making an aesthetic judgment. No one will stop us from appreciating an Ozu film for the pleasing or overwhelming sensations it generates. An aesthetic judgment evaluates the image as a consciousness, whereas in-aesthetics traces the *you* (navigation) between consciousness and technicity. The forms manifested by a mindfulness of their relationship are neither beautiful nor sublime, but instead are mindful, equanimous, and dignified.

CINEMA AND NONVIOLENCE

Cinema—as an anthropotechnical consciousness and in its various technological, corporeal, psychical, and sociopolitical instantiations—always operates on and within violence. As Laura Mulvey identifies, the process of subjectivization-objectivization im-mediately constitutes and *enframes* a power asymmetry in the form of a scopophilic regime.[1] Scopophilia is usually associated with *skopein* (to look at), even though it involves from the beginning the entire sentient body as a field of affective intensities. A case can be made that post-cinema allows modes of embodied engagement and transindividuation that can rewrite this power asymmetry. However, as a formational process, post-cinema still hinges on an attachment to the self and an attachment to the other as a fundamental condition.

The subject, operating under the magnetism of *manas,* comes to believe that it stands outside of all relationalities. Such a position enables the subject to watch and listen to what happens to and with the *other;* to generate olfactory, tactile, and thought sensations and affections as the other; and ultimately to care for the other with benevolence, compassion, and empathy. In so doing, however, as Giorgio Agamben argues, the subjectival position is made sacred: untouchable and severed from any relationality.[2] It *enjoys* the sights, sounds, sensations, and thoughts of violence under the impression that it plays no part in affecting violence or being affected by it. The truth is: subjectivization-objectivization is by default an act of violence to the overall technicity of the

241

consciousness. It merely defers and delays the technological, physical, psychical, and sociopolitical harm to the subject. As a technological transduction, the mechanical apparatus that came to be called the cinematograph (among other variations) toward the end of the nineteenth century emerged out of a gradually shifting process of bio-depoliticization-politicization. As Norbert Elias (1897–1990) and Pierre Bourdieu (1930–2002) argue respectively, the rise of the bourgeoisie and colonialism drove—and were driven by—a transference of the corporeal orientation and locus of knowledge-building from touch (proximity) to sight (distance).[3]

In the *Spectator* [1711–14], Joseph Addison (1672–1719) and Richard Steele (1672–1729) regard politics and art as a singular scopophilic regime, where a civilized spectator manages the divide between the subject and object. As a manager, they project their own excessive desires and afflictions onto others. Through the others' bodies, these desires and afflictions can be rehearsed and actualized in conflicts performed for their pleasure in nature, among the lower classes, and in the colonies.[4] The transference from touch to sight is therefore a process of relocating the affective intensities of and moral responsibilities for violence from the manager's body to the managed. It is one way to understand what Agamben means when he claims that violence is the norm and that normativity is a state of exception.[5]

As Thomas Elsaesser argues, early cinema took years to reach this metastable phase.[6] As Tom Gunning points out, "cinema of attractions" relied on corporeal stimulations, sensual shocks, and intersubjective boundary-crossings through physical immersions and direct addresses to the spectators.[7] Meanwhile, Charles Musser argues that these strategies enabled a predominantly working-class (often immigrant) audience in the cities to trespass established social relations.[8] Elsaesser refers to what he calls the "rube film," exemplified by Robert Paul's (1897–1943) *The Countryman's First Sight of the Animated Pictures* [1901] and Edwin S. Porter's (1893–1941) remake *Uncle Josh at the Moving Picture Show* [1902]. In these films, a rube who is unable to manage his excessive sensorial excitements and urge of immersion climbs up to the theater stage in an attempt to enter the screen. However, both rubes' attempts inevitably fail, and they are reined in by other spectators.

For Elsaesser, the rube film is symptomatic of the cinema's struggle to arrive at its metastable phase, that is, toward its formation as a

scopophilic regime. On the one hand, the rube film educates the spectators to distance themselves from violence (in the form of movement) by
managing their own excessive affective intensities. On the other hand,
it self-reflexively engages the spectators in the regime's active policing
of those affects that are fundamental in creativity, defiance, and innova-
tion.[9] For Gilbert Simondon, what society deems excessive affective
intensities are preindividuated impulses that drive—and are driven
by—the sustenance of an overall technicity. What we call the norm is a
critical point of convergence of *anomies*—exceptions that fail to harness
those creative energies that remain preindividuated. When normativity
is defined and measured by an aggregate of individuated anomies, these
preindividuated impulses become excessive and overbearing.[10] As Brian
Massumi would have argued, cinema's scopophilic regime preempts any
of these potentialities (ontopowers) from being actualized.[11]

In an online lecture given for the Whitechapel Gallery in 2020, Judith
Butler argues that it took a virus for us to attain an insight into the
technicity of biopolitics.[12] On October 24, 2019, 45 days before the first
wave of the global coronavirus (COVID-19) pandemic, two countries, the
United States and the United Kingdom, were deemed by the Global
Health Security Index as the most readied economies to manage an
outbreak. Yet they both failed to respond to the situation during the
actual outbreak. Such failure was mostly due to their leaders' unwillingness to treat senior patients, people of color, and individuals with
chronic diseases because of cost-effectiveness.[13] Mask-wearing, an *Asian*
method that was proven to be effective during the severe acute respira-
tory syndrome (SARS) outbreak in 2002–2004, has been widely dismissed
as ineffective partly due to most developed economies' unwillingness
to invest in personal protective equipment and partly due to a conviction that Asia as a whole is an exception: an embodiment of the virus.[14]

During and after the first wave, China, India, the United States, and
most European countries furloughed or dismissed workers who were
under casual contracts (known in the United Kingdom and the Com-
monwealth as zero-hour contracts, that is, contracts that do not specify
any minimum number of working hours).[15] In the United Kingdom, the
higher education sector revealed that in order to export their services to
Chinese, East Asian, and Southeast Asian students, universities took out
loans that required them to run on profit only. Thus, many U.K. universities needed to furlough employees while maximizing the permanent

contract instructors' teaching hours and administrative responsibilities, at the expense of the quality of teaching, research outputs, and student experiences. Meanwhile, on-campus teaching was implemented with inadequate plans to safeguard students' and staff's safety, so that these institutions could attract customers to rent their residential facilities.[16]

During the pandemic, the murder of George Perry Floyd Jr. (1973–2020) in Minneapolis reanimated and globalized the Black Lives Matter movement, which triggered President Donald Trump to send federal agents to suppress the resulting protests in Portland and other U.S. cities.[17] Protests in Hong Kong for democratization and against Beijing's direct political intervention and surveillance were violently suppressed by a police force that was trained by the U.S. federal government. The protests resulted in the arrest and disappearance of more than five thousand individuals, an emigration wave (both voluntary and involuntary) that is expected to displace up to 600,000 Hong Kongers to the United Kingdom as well as the passing of a National Security Law that legalized the surveillance and punishment of speeches and acts against China not only by Hong Kong residents in the city but by all "lives" in the world.[18] Millions of Uyghurs in their homeland within China have been sent to "reeducation" camps, where they were either under torture, enforced sterilization, chemical or physical execution, or forced to work under contracts of top Euro-American corporations.[19] Muslims as well as queer and trans people in India have been taken prisoner and stripped of political and civil rights under the current regime.[20] These acts of violence represent only the tip of the iceberg in our global biopolitical milieu.

David Fleming and Simon Harrison, largely based on the models proposed by Jean Baudrillard (1929–2007) and Paul Virilio (1932–2018), argue that our current impasse is a result of decades of postsocialist-neoliberal reconfiguration of our milieu into a simulacrum that drives—and is driven by—the desire to consume. This impetus to consume is actualized by a mega technicity-consciousness, which he calls the *shi*-nema (cinema of potentialities that perpetually remain unactualized): an assemblage of power relations that configures our milieu into an image-consciousness that *exists* for the sole purpose of performing consumption.[21]

To complicate matters, most desktop or mobile browsers and social media apps use cookies and other inter-/intra-site information-sharing devices to locate a user's internet protocol address, garner their consumption data, index their desires, and share their information with corporations and government agencies. These devices were introduced to personal technological environments invented for commercial purposes during the late 1990s. However, in the first decade of the 2000s, government departments and agencies began to collect these data as archives of their citizens' biopolitical identities. Major social media sites are open about their use of algorithms and artificial intelligence to help their customers—corporations and government agents—access the information they need.[22] The result, as we now know, is the ease of government and corporate control of communal opinions by feeding specific sets of data to these differentiated markets, which has the effect of polarizing their users' political opinions and affiliations, as well as dismantling an effective and functional public sphere (if a public sphere has ever existed).

Butler, following the line of thoughts of historical and contemporary acts of nonviolent civil disobedience, argues that nonviolence is best understood as a "practice that not only stops a violent act, or a violent process, but requires a form of sustained action, sometimes aggressively pursued."[23] This accords with the understanding of violence in Buddhist thought. Yet, it does not represent the full picture of how Buddhist philosophy envisions radical changes. For one, unleashing an onto-power is, by definition, an act of violence. We may not perceive that wearing a mask is an act of violence, as it is considered to be our social responsibility to do so. However, for someone who regards it as a threat, it is a form of violence to their civil liberty. In a karma-driven reality, radical changes are, unfortunately, always brought about by some form of violence that rewrites relationalities by force. The key is, as Butler argues, what nonviolence can be.

To define nonviolence, the Theravādins usually refer to the "Daṇḍavaggo" chapter (§10.129–34) of the *Dhammapada:*

> All tremble at the rod [punishment]. All fear death. Comparing others with oneself, one should neither strike nor cause to strike.
>
> Whoever, seeking his own happiness, harms with the rod other pleasure-loving beings experiences no happiness hereafter.
>
> Whoever, seeking his own happiness, harms not with the rod other pleasure-loving beings, experiences happiness hereafter.

Speak not harshly to anyone. Those thus addressed will retort.
Painful, indeed, is vindictive speech. Blows in exchange may bruise
you.
　　If, like a cracked gong, you silence yourself, you have already
attained Nibbāna: no vindictiveness will be found in you.[24]

The notion of nonviolence understood in the *Dhammapada* is therefore a utilitarian one. The presupposition of these verses is that in a conventional reality driven by karma, every sentient being strives to achieve happiness. In our effort to subsist in pleasure, it is inevitable that we will harm other sentient beings in both acts and speech. In so doing, we forget that what we are harming is not simply another sentient body or psyche, but also the overall relationality of which our consciousnesses are technical instantiations. Hence, if we do not see any immediate consequences or retributions, it is only because they have been transferred to the overall ecology, so that they appear to be deferred and delayed. Therefore, in fear of these consequences, we should refrain from harming other sentient beings.

However, here are two points of contention in the *Dhammapada*. As Michael Jerryson argues, these verses acknowledge that violence is an existential norm.[25] Yet, curiously, they put their focus on the performances of violence in acts and speech, without addressing the thought impulses that drive and are driven by them. The implication is that in order to preempt violence, a practitioner should arrive at—and return to—an insight into the technicity of consciousness: that the body is impure, that sensations and affections produce sufferings, that the consciousness is impermanent, and that forms have no self-natures. These verses therefore fall short of suggesting whether violence can be justified when committed supposedly for the purpose of removing an individual's or community's obstacle in their path toward mindfulness, or for preempting and stopping others from inflicting harms on themselves and others.

The Theravādin understanding of nonviolence is therefore criticized for being passive and ascetic. Historically, the *Dhammapada* verses have been mobilized by militant Buddhists in Thailand, Myanmar, India, and Sri Lanka to justify nationalism, militarism, and ethnic cleansing, a trend that has gained support since the 2000s.[26] In Sri Lanka, the Sinhalese Buddhist nationalists have justified military violence by citing §25 of the *Mahāvaṃsa,* a fifth century epic poem that chronicles the

Battle of Vijithapura: an expedition led by Dutugamunu (reign 161–37 B.C.E.) to overthrow the Tamil king Ellālan (reign 205–161 B.C.E.). The *Mahāvaṃsa* opens with three (legendary) visits of Śākyamuni Buddha to Sri Lanka, who allegedly sanctions the use of violence to turn it into a center of Buddhist faith. These visits are not recorded anywhere else in the Pāli canon.[27]

Mahāyāna scholars associate the discussion of violence with the six *pāramī/pāramitā* (perfections): *dāna* (letting go), *sīla/śīla* (discipline), *khanti/kṣānti* (patience and receptivity), *viriya/vīrya* (diligence), *jhana/dhyāna* (concentration), and *paññā/prajñā* (insight).[28] In the *Diamond Sūtra*, Śākyamuni Buddha argues that a practitioner should let go of the impression that the subject, object, and any acts, speeches, and thoughts that connect them have any existential values. In so doing, they can perceive and conceptualize all forms in relational terms. An act of giving (giving things such as wealth, pleasure, or even one's own body) is named an act of giving, even though there is neither a giver, nor a receiver, nor an object to be transacted, nor an act of giving. Rather, it is an active engagement in the revision of an ecology for all beings. In this light, disciplines—including no killing, stealing, excessive sexual indulgence, and hurtful or ungrounded speech—are observed neither for a fear of consequences nor for others' benefits. Rather, they are manifestations of an insight into relationalities.

Meanwhile, patience and receptivity do not refer to passive tolerance and acceptance. Instead, they refer to a mindfulness of, and therefore, an active engagement in, affects. In the *Sūtra*, the Buddha refers to the time he (in one of his previous transmigrations) was punished by Kaliṅga-rāja in a brutal act of vivisection. He was mindful of how physical pains and mental afflictions (especially hatred) affect—and are affected by—the overall formational process and layout of relationalities. By focusing on and engaging himself in the *here and now* of his affective impulses, he was able to preempt and let go of the formations of his mental afflictions along with their karmic perpetuation.[29]

Yinguang, based on the *Avataṃsaka Sūtra*, argues that Śākyamuni Buddha's suggestion here is to preempt a cause, not a consequence, from becoming.[30] On many occasions, Thich Nhat Hanh has both discussed and illustrated how this works. For example, if someone says something hurtful to me, my karmic reaction is to retort on the spot. Yet a retort, no matter how logical or reasonable it is, will inevitably be appropriated by the other person to strengthen their argument. It will also produce afflictions. This is because a heated argument is not based on reason, but on an unconditional surrender to affective intensities. Moreover, an argument is always a performance to myself and to others, which drives *manas* and is driven by it.

Thich Nhat Hanh's recommendation is to be mindful of our breathing, so that I am reminded of the technicity of the consciousness and the emptiness of forms. When I pay attention to my breathing, I am gradually focusing on my biological mechanism of self-sustenance, thus allowing me to disengage myself from the immediate assemblage of causes and conditions that constitutes my state of anger. Gradually, the karmic impulses that initiate my process of becoming no longer operate on autopilot. Instead, I gradually engage myself in and know clearly the karmic impulses that are responsible for *my* consciousness's initiation and extinction from one moment to another. By engaging myself in and knowing the generation and extinction of these impulses, I gradually become mindful of how each awareness functions as an assemblage of causes and conditions, which will inevitably produce consequences. I can then begin to take agency to ensure that these causes and conditions are initiated out of mindfulness, instead of letting my impulses run on autopilot. I can then make microperceptual choices between causes and conditions that would produce further mindful awarenesses and causes and conditions that would produce afflictions. To return to my example, the person who has verbally or physically harassed me may have the impression that they are "winning" by means of violence.[31] However, I know—and in public spaces, some people may come to realize—that intolerance and irrationality are manifestations of insecurities, anxieties, and afflictions. This in turn nurtures the seeds in our *ālaya*-consciousness(es) that strive for the preservation of our ecology through insight.

Today, many global atrocities seem to tell us that our natural, sociopolitical, and economic ecologies are beyond repair. This mode of nonviolent engagement is hardly convincing for individual lives and the lives of families who are now being taken to labor camps and prisons, being asphyxiated by the police, being physically mutilated by transphobes and homophobes, or facing the uncertainties of governmental terror. Elections around the world repeatedly demonstrate that this sense of hopelessness has convinced working classes that any proposals of reparation based on international collaboration, shared responsibility, human compassion, and trust have already failed. Instead, some of those people put their faith in populist leaders who promise them their self-subsistence at the expense not only of the socially othered, but also of their neighbors, children, and various loved ones.

The belief that our ecologies are beyond repair stems from an attachment to the consciousness as a manifestation. This is what Bernard Stiegler calls tertiary retention: the projection of my perception onto an external medium. In other words, the world is perceived and conceptualized as a karma-image. As Stiegler argues, in this part of the formational process, the "I" is projected as a collective "We," which we internalize as the "I." This karmic "I" therefore holds on to the conflicting beliefs that "I" am an individual; but "I" am responsible for "Us" and "Our" future. This "I" inevitably finds the collectivized "We" (what Gilbert Simondon calls the preindividual) overbearing, unimaginable, untamable, or even undesirable. As a result, "I" either find it overwhelming to resolve "Our" problems or "I" stop caring.[32]

The Simondonian preindividual or the Buddhist understanding of the state/nonstate of nondifferentiation is not a collective of lives that are manifestations of differentiations and individuations. Rather, it refers to the *here and now,* the very *kṣaṇa* that affects—and is affected by—the formation of a cause (relationality). Each *kṣaṇa* can be considered a potentiality that can ripple out to a layout of cosmic relational changes. "I" do this at every *kṣaṇa,* even though most of the time, "I" let it run on autopilot. Sheng-yen therefore argues that in Zen practice, the goal is not to *empty* the "I," but rather to return to this preindividuated "I," the very *kṣaṇa* at which the modality of becoming is determined. "I" cannot change the past or the future, but "I" can be mindful of the *here and now* that constitutes this "I."[33]

By focusing on the past and the future, we often overlook the impact of a single act of nonviolence. When we choose to disengage ourselves from an act of abuse, we often feel an unbearable sense of guilt that we have failed to engage in the past. For example, if I walk away from someone who harasses me on the street, I may go home, and then look back to that moment of my disengagement and blame myself for not fighting back. I would feel vulnerable and may even feel shameful for my vulnerability. Meanwhile, I would forget to keep an eye on what positive potentialities that momentary disengagement can yield. The consciousness that "I" call "the World" is ungraspable in the past or the future. It is in the *here and now* that I can make radical changes. "I" may feel impotent when I choose to disengage myself in an act of violence in the heat of the moment, but this past instant (my disengagement from this act of violence) is now stored in the *ālaya*-consciousness as a seed, a potentiality that awaits its actualization. I cannot simply *wait* for this seed to be actualized. Rather, I need to actively nurture it, through constant engagements in thoughts, speeches, and acts from one *kṣaṇa* to another, engagements that make radical changes not only in "Me" but also in all the relationalities that constitute every preindividuated "I."

How can "I" survive in an ecology that has already failed, and how can "I" make microperceptual changes that can repair "Our" technicity-consciousness? In the following pages, I turn to Christian Petzold's *Transit* [2018] as a user manual for making microperceptual changes.

Petzold started making experimental films during his study at Freie Universität Berlin in 1988. After his graduation, he studied filmmaking at the Deutsche Film- und Fernsehenakademie Berlin under Harun Farocki (1944–2014) and Hartmut Bitomsky. Petzold's feature films were often made in collaboration with Farocki (including *Transit*), and they demonstrate a strong belief in the value of using the cinema as a medium of political engagement. They do so by positing the anthropotechnical consciousness in a mode of indiscernibility between the past, present, and future, and also between illusions and realities. By using such a strategy to perform the lived experience of precarious lives, these films enable the consciousness to abduce how their biopolitical existences affect—and are affected by—a political norm that is in itself a state of exception. If so, precarious lives are posited—both by the political left and the political right—as an exception of exception.

Transit is an adaptation of a novel by Anna Seghers (1900–83) based on her personal experience in Marseille in 1940, before she fled occupied France to Mexico the following year. The plot follows a twenty-seven-year-old narrator (named Georg in the film; played by Franz Rogowski), who escaped from a concentration camp in Rouen on his way to Marseille. However, it is unclear for what reason he was interred. In Paris, the narrator's friend Paul asks Georg to deliver a letter to an author named Weidel. On arriving at the hotel where Weidel stays, the narrator finds out that Weidel has committed suicide. Weidel left some letters to his wife in Marseille as well as an incomplete novel manuscript. The narrator then goes to Marseille, where émigrés from Germany spend hours in cafés and at the U.S. Consulate waiting for their transit visas through the United States to Mexico. As the narrator brings Weidel's manuscript to the Mexican Consulate, he is mistaken for Weidel himself. He is then given a transit visa and an arranged passage to Mexico. Meanwhile, he falls in love with a woman who wanders in and out of the cafés and the U.S. Consulate like a specter. She turns out to be Weidel's wife, Marie. The narrator arranges a transit visa for her without her knowing that such an arrangement was made with his assumed identity as Weidel.[34]

The film adaptation follows Seghers' plot closely. However, its *mise-en-scène* indicates that the narrative takes place at once in 1942 and in contemporary France. Narrative details allude to today's modes of antiterrorism, preemptive policing, xenophobia, and Islamophobia set in France's contemporary cityscapes. While interior décors and costume are stripped of their historical specificities, props that include passports and visas, letters, ocean liner tickets, radios, and electrical fans are largely historical. The film can therefore be seen as a temporal palimpsest. In one register, Marseille's seemingly timeless buildings and institutions serve as a setting of an ecology of interdependent power relations, which gives form to a group of biopolitical actors that rehearses the same cycle of events simultaneously in 1942 and today. In other words, the same layout of karmic impulses initiates an identical layout of dependent originations in the past and the present, which drives—and is driven by—these actors' desires, frustrations, and delusions.

In another register, this palimpsest is also *ours*. For Elsaesser, a palimpsest performs the process of the larger society's collective erasure of a historical past (Nazism in the 1940s) and a repeated performance of the said trauma. Elsaesser calls this a *parapraxis*—the failure to perform and the performance of failure. In a parapraxis, the image-consciousness, which provides a parallax view of two actualizations of the same potentialities, is symptomatic of the larger sociopolitical failure to engage in its own traumatic past. The image therefore performs the said failure by making tangible a traumatic past that cannot be thoroughly erased, as well as a repeated performance that is exercised on those traces of erasure that continue to haunt the present.[35]

Olivia Landry argues that despite this film's dealing with the uncertainty, violence, and horror of precarious lives in waiting, it leaves open the potentialities that these lives await to fulfill while engaging in the beauty of waiting. Her analysis is based on Siegfried Kracauer's (1889–1966) study of the "anteroom" in Weimar Germany (1918–33), in which intellectuals did not necessarily *wait for* someone or something to happen. Rather, the act of waiting becomes an intransitive and aesthetic experience. She then pushes Kracauer's argument further:

> [Martin] Heidegger articulates an unambiguous affirmation of waiting in his dialogical "Zur Erörterung der Gelassenheit: Aus dem Feldweggespräch über das Denken" [Towards an Explication of *Gelassenheit: From a Conversation on a Country Path about Thinking*, 1944–45] which he describes as that exercise which leads to "Gelassenheit" or equanimity, a transcendent opening up to meditative thought. It comes with a single caveat: Waiting (warten) should not be confused with awaiting (erwarten)—that is, waiting is not a transitive experience. The action of waiting does not demand a direct object, for it is without end or definite object.[36]

What Heidegger refers to is similar to the last stage of *satipaṭṭhāna,* when a meditator engages in the act of waiting as *the way it is.*

Nevertheless, Heidegger's distinction between *warten* (intransitive) and *erwarten* (transitive) assumes that a subject can fully engage in the act of waiting and can attain equanimity by being released from the object for which they wait. His notion therefore presupposes that individuality, subjectivity, and autonomy (agency) are the fundamental conditions of existence. In *satipaṭṭhāna,* however, the meditator should first arrive at a mindfulness that the body, affections and sensations, and consciousness are all forms that are fundamentally empty, thus rendering purposeless the differences between individuation and deindividuation, subjectivization and desubjectivization, and autonomization and deautonomization.

Politically, as I argued in chapters 3 and 4, biopolitical lives who occupy—and are occupied by—an exception of exception are, by default, deindividuated, desubjectivized, and deautonomized. In the eyes of those lives who attach themselves to the normativized exception, these precarious lives are *nobody:* they are not individual subjects with agencies. It is in this sense that there is nothing for which they are waiting. For them, life is the *here and now*. Moreover, if states of things or beings are moment-to-moment instantiations of dependent origina- tions, *erwarten* is not a stasis. Rather, life is always in transit: a process of drifting in which relationalities can be reconfigured *here and now*.

In my analysis here, I turn to Georg's transindividuations with four characters: Weidel; Marie; Heinz's young son, Driss; and an unnamed German Jewish woman. I want to see how Georg and the cinematic con- sciousness exercise microperceptions to instigate relational changes.

Weidel never appears in the film. Yet, he haunts the consciousness as a voiceover. This voiceover initially emerges as Georg and his friend Heinz (who is dying of an inflammation of a wound on his leg) settle down in a cargo container on a freight train to Marseille. This voiceover is read by Matthias Brandt, son of the former German Chancellor Willy Brandt (1913–92; in office 1969–74). At first, the voiceover seems to be describing the predicament of Georg and Heinz. But soon, the film shows Georg reading Weidel's manuscript, which indicates that these lines are taken from the unfinished book. Through Georg's reading, these words are also embodied by Georg, as though they were his own creation.

As I mentioned earlier, Georg eventually assumes Weidel's identity as he is mistaken as Weidel in the Mexican and U.S. Consulates in Mar- seille. There, Georg was put to the test thrice. In his visit to the Mexican Consulate, the Consul asks Georg to verify his identity by naming his wife. Georg cannot recall her name at first. Then, Weidel's voice is heard on the soundtrack (by extension, in Georg's mind), which enables him to say "Marie." In his first visit to the U.S. Consulate, the Consul is in- quisitive about Weidel's belief in communism and his possible involve- ment with the U.S. Office of Strategic Services. Knowing that "Weidel" is going to stay quiet, the Consul mocks him for being an armchair revo- lutionary by drawing a verbal picture of Weidel's future idyllic bour- geois life in Mexico as a retired fiction writer. Suddenly, Georg, who has been reserved in the interview, retorts with a personal conviction (as though he were Weidel) that perhaps the Consul himself should retire to Mexico and become a writer.

In his second visit to the U.S. Consulate, during which he picks up Marie's visa, the Consul asks Georg/Weidel what he has last written. Georg looks pensive. The sound of a train moving on tracks emerges. The film then cuts to a high-angle shot of a pair of train tracks filmed from a moving freight train. The tracks occupy the upper third of the frame as the image moves parallel to them. Over this geometrically parallel image, Georg *becomes* the parallel of Weidel, as he recites a short story about a man who has just recently died and is supposed to register in hell. After having waited for ten years, he asks someone for help, and this person says, "But, sir, this *here* is hell." In his recitation, it is unclear whether Georg creates this story by himself or recites this story from his memory of Weidel's manuscript. The short story is not only an allegory of his own situation in Marseille as a purgatory for refugees, but also a reference to him and other refugees as biopolitical lives who are—in the eyes of the normativized exception—already dead. For the normative community, their dead bodies wander around in this unlivable purgatory, who must be removed and exterminated in order to put the failure of the ecology under erasure.

In these three visits to the Consul, both Georg and Weidel are transindividuated, or rather dependently originated, out of their shared conditions of exception. Through Weidel, Georg is also engaged in a process of transindividuation with Marie. Georg first encounters Marie when he is looking at the map of Marseille located on top of a metro station. Initially, the film shows Georg's back in a medium close-up as he studies the map, while Weidel's voice describes one's sense of alienation in the city. Suddenly, the film switches to a black-and-white, high-angle long shot of the station's entrance area with Georg in it, from the perspective of a close-circuit television camera. On the soundtrack, Weidel comments that in the city, you are aware that everybody stares at you, yet "you don't exist in their world."

These comments sum up the logic of a control-society: that every biopolitical life is being watched by other biopolitical lives, either physically or via media, to ensure that the normativized power relations are maintained. Nonetheless, such surveillance ascertains that these lives are nobody. At this point, a young woman in a coat enters from the bottom of the right of frame and runs toward Georg (at the center). The film then cuts on action to a medium close-up of Georg's profile as she approaches him and taps his shoulder in anticipation. Once he turns around and looks at her, she looks disappointed and runs away from him.

During the first hour of the film, this chance encounter is performed repeatedly as Georg spots this young woman in the café where he and other émigrés eat and socialize, in the lobby of the U.S. Consulate, and on the street. On some occasions, she passes by him without noticing him; on others, she taps his shoulder and then looks disappointed like the first time they met. These repeated performances initiate an idea in Georg's and the anthropotechnical mind: that Georg resembles this young woman's husband. However, perhaps this *husband* never existed, that it is only a placeholder of an absent *subject* whose spectral voice awaits a corporeal instantiation.

The relationality between Georg and this young woman (who is later identified as Marie) undergoes an ongoing process of transduction. Halfway through the film, Georg looks for a doctor to take care of Heinz's son, Driss. Some émigrés in the café suggest that he visit a man called Richard. When he visits Richard's apartment, he finds this young woman in bed. After seeing Driss, Richard buys Georg dinner, and he confesses to Georg that he is addicted to this woman, who is waiting for her husband, named Weidel, in Marseille. Richard once missed his boat to Mexico because Marie disembarked and stayed in the city for Weidel. During their conversation, Marie enters the café and sits down beside Richard. She refuses to eat and she leaves almost immediately to search for Weidel. Despite the fact that Georg sits opposite her, she looks through Georg as though he did not exist. In her eyes, Georg has yet been transindividuated with her.

In this light, "Georg" is transindividuated with Marie with a double subjectivity—Georg-as-Georg and Georg-as-Weidel. After dinner, Georg visits Richard's apartment again and finds Marie alone, who is packing some of her clothes in order to sell them. After Georg has settled down on a chair, Marie finishes packing her clothes. The film intercuts between a medium close-up of Georg and a medium close-up of Marie, thus isolating them from each other physically and mentally. Marie asks Georg a question that was raised earlier by Weidel in a voiceover: "Who is to forget first? The one who is left behind or the one who leaves?" In other words, how long does it take for someone who has abandoned someone—or who has been abandoned—to surrender the overwhelming burden of the preindividual?

After asking that question, Marie begins a confession of her story with Weidel. Her voice is overlapped with Weidel's, who reiterates her narration by assuming Georg's perspective in the room, though he addresses Georg in the third person. According to this double voice, Marie abandoned Weidel in Paris and fled with Richard to Marseille. She later learned that Weidel was also heading to Marseille. She also learned that someone (Georg) was supposed to deliver both her farewell letter and Weidel's traveling documents to him in Paris. Later, some people told her that they had seen him (Georg-as-Weidel) in Marseille, so she set out to look for him.

At this juncture, the film cuts to a montage of different moments at which she runs up to Georg and taps his shoulder. As these moments unfold, Marie says that it seems like she has always missed him (Weidel), even though the cinematic consciousness knows that she has always managed to catch him (Georg-as-Weidel). She simply does not realize that Georg is Weidel. By the end of the montage, a handheld camera follows Marie down the street. As she turns back and looks directly into the camera, Georg's voice (offscreen) calls her name: "Marie." By the time Marie finishes her confession, Georg sits down beside her in a medium two-shot. He then caresses her and asks her to let him take care of her.

In the beginning of this scene, Georg appears as Georg, and as their isolated medium close-ups indicate, Georg-as-Georg forms no relation whatsoever with Marie. However, once her confession begins, the relationality between them is in-formed through the mediation of Weidel's spectral voice. In other words, the karmic impulses between Marie and Weidel in-form a layout of conditions, which enables Weidel to be corporealized as Georg. This process takes place microperceptually, from one moment of affect to another. This process of becoming also affects the formation of the romantic feeling between Marie and Georg-as-Georg. When we hear Georg's voice calling Marie from the perspective of the camera, it is Georg's consciousness that the camera embodies. In other words, in this process of becoming, Georg, through caring for the *relationality-as-it-is,* is individuated, subjectivized, and autonomized not as a consumer of love but as a caretaker of it.

Still, Georg's individuation, subjectivization, and autonomization have yet to be completed. Georg's promise to take care of Marie is best understood as: "I failed to deliver those letters to Weidel; let me be Weidel and care for you." In this sense, Georg cares for Marie (the other) on behalf of another other (Weidel)—or the Other: the commanding voice/authority that has been dictating Marie and his own thoughts, actions, and speeches. In short, Weidel can be considered the vocalization of karma. In the subsequent sequences, Georg atones for his failure by applying for a transit visa for Marie and arranging for her passage to Mexico.

Even though the film does not clarify whether any of these characters are Jewish, atonement is a specifically Jewish concept. Therefore, we need to analyze his act within the Jewish framework. In the Jewish tradition, the definition of atonement is a subject of rabbinic and scholarly debate. However, a common underlying assumption is that it cannot be achieved under a commandment or for a purpose. In this case, Georg re-performs his (and Weidel's) failure by falling into all the trappings that are scripted by karma. On their taxi ride to the dock to board the ship, Georg feels content that they can finally live their lives as Weidel and Marie. Instead, Marie tells Georg that she is expecting to reunite with Weidel on the boat. Realizing that he has been acting in accordance with karma, he gets out of the taxi and returns to the hotel. He then offers his documents and tickets to Richard. Nevertheless, the next day, he finds out that the boat Marie and Richard took, *The Montreal*, has hit a mine and sunk. However, Georg's self-sacrifice can be regarded as an act of atonement. According to the Wayiqra' (Leviticus), in atonement, the sinner needs to let go of the relationality that constitutes the act of trespassing in the first place, so that one can arrive at—and return to—a state/nonstate of nondifferentiation between the sacred and the profane.[37] As in the concept of emptiness in Buddhism, atonement in the Jewish tradition requires a mindfulness that there has been no trespasser, no trespassed, and no act of trespassing in the first place.

If we see *Transit* as a journey of atonement and realize that different human lives are transindividuated out of a layout of unlivable conditions, two other relationships—one between Georg and Driss and the other between Georg and the German Jewish woman—offer us a further insight into how atonement and reparation operate microperceptually.

Georg and Driss meet for the first time when Georg delivers Heinz's letter and belongings to Heinz's wife. She is not at home, and Driss (who is half-Moroccan) is playing soccer on the sidewalk outside their apartment building. Georg and Driss bond as they play soccer together. When Driss's mother (who is of Moroccan descent) comes home, Heinz realizes that she is mute. He delivers the news of Heinz's death to her through Driss as a sign-language translator.

Okay... A little this way...

. FIGURE 30. Georg and Driss heat up a tiny ball of lead on top of a candle
with mindfulness in *Transit*.

Later in the film, Georg visits Driss again. Driss is sick and home
alone. Georg stays around for him. When Driss feels better, he tells
Georg that the radio has been broken. Georg then takes the radio to the
living room, where he fixes it. As Olivia Landry points out, when the
apartment becomes bathed in the late-afternoon sun, its color temperature is unusually warm for the film.[38] Georg's repair of the radio is conveyed with an alternation between a medium shot of Georg, a medium
shot of Driss, a medium two-shot of them looking at a candle together
(which Georg uses to heat up a small ball of lead; see Figure 30), and a
high-angle medium close-up of his hands handling the mechanical parts
with surgical precision. This image-consciousness is therefore remarkably intimate. Each micromovement of Georg's hand and each glance
between Georg and the son crystallize the affective intensities of the
here and now. As a result, Georg, Driss, and all the technical objects in the
environment are retransindividuated at each microperception as an
instantiation of mindful nondifferentiation and care.

After the radio is fixed, they turn it on and it plays an instrumental
version of a nursery rhyme, along with which Georg sings. Its lyrics are
about different animals going home after a long day of work. Then,
Heinz's wife returns. She asks Georg to sing the song again, despite the
fact that she cannot hear it physically. In a medium two-shot, Heinz's
wife occupies the middle of the frame. She stares, mesmerized, at Georg,
who occupies the right of frame and whose profile is out of focus. In one
single take, Georg sings all the verses of the nursery rhyme. In this shot,

each microperception of the vibration of Georg's voice, listened to or felt by all the sentient bodies that are in-formed by it *here and now* (including the spectators'), constitutes a milieu that is severed from all those desires, avarices, frustrations, and delusions that drive—and are driven by—a failed ecology. *Here and now,* a new seed or potentiality is deposited in the *ālaya*-consciousness that atonement and reparation are possible microperceptually, even in an ecology that seems to be beyond repair.

Yet this kinship between Georg and Driss does not last long. Later in the film, Georg brings the boy to the port to play in an amusement park. He then takes him to an ice cream parlor across the street from the U.S. Consulate and asks Driss to wait there while he goes to pick up his documents. When he returns to the ice cream parlor, he finds Driss sulking and asks him if he is planning to leave. In the soundtrack, Weidel's voiceover indicates in third person that Georg sees Driss crying. The film then cuts to a series of shots/reverse shots, in which Georg, *guided* by Weidel, gives Driss a hug and explains that he needs to flee. In a medium close-up over Driss's shoulders, Driss pushes Georg onto the ground and runs away from him. The camera pans up and follows Driss as he dashes across the street.

Here, the camera employs a telephoto lens that keeps the running boy in focus, whereas the background is out of focus, thus keeping the anthropotechnical consciousness's attention to: (1) the drifting gaze of Georg, who occupies a physical position close to the camera; and (2) the moving body of Driss and his drifting away from both Georg and the camera, forming the frame's middle milieu. In so doing, the anthropotechnical consciousness becomes mindful of their process of detransindividuation—once the acts of atonement, reparation, and care have been fulfilled. A few days later, when Georg visits the apartment again, he finds it being occupied by another group of (presumably) migrants. The film implies that Driss and his mother attempted the dangerous crossing of the Pyrénées in order to escape from occupied France.

The transformation of the apartment into a "camp" sends a sensual shock to the anthropotechnical body. Suddenly, the cinematic consciousness becomes mindful that all living beings are forms, whose appearance and disappearance are always in transit. If all forms are actualized relationalities, which are perceptual-conceptual instantiations of a *roomful of dust* (potentialities; see the introduction, as well as chapters 2 and 3), illuminated transiently by the operation of a layout of overlapping *ālaya*-consciousnesses, these dust particles simply drift from one position to another. As they drift, the forms being instantiated also emerge and perish in accordance with the principles of dependent originations. Not only are these lives drifting, also drifting are the karmic impulses (Weidel's voice) and the drifting actor-patient who seems to assume individuality, subjectivity, and agency during the journey (Georg/Weidel).

This idea is further illustrated toward the end of the film. Georg runs into a German Jewish woman whom he has encountered several times in the Consulate and the café. Before this scene, this woman was always accompanied by two dogs, who had been left behind in Marseille by an American couple who promised her an invitation letter to the United States in exchange for her caretaking. In this scene, however, she is no longer accompanied by the dogs. She treats Georg for lunch and expresses her disgust in the animals. After lunch, they stroll through Marseille's Panier neighborhood. In two long shots, Georg and this woman walk across the backyard of the Musée des Civilisations de l'Europe et de la Méditerranée from frame left to frame right. Weidel's voice now assumes the role of Georg, who describes Georg's impression of that walk and what the woman says.

By the end of their stroll, they stop in front of a high embankment and she asks him for a cigarette. He lights one for her in a medium two-shot. In the voiceover, Weidel describes in third person that Georg feels *aufgehoben,* which Landry translates, in accordance with Georg Wilhelm Friedrich Hegel (1770–1831), as "sublated" or "lifted." *Aufgehoben,* however, can also mean relieved, canceled, or annulled.[39] These meanings correspond to the Buddhist concept of *nirvāṇa:* a release from relationalities. In this state/nonstate, Georg is capable of listening to her and engaging in her suffering with equanimity. In a medium close-up, Georg lights his own cigarette in profile as he turns away from the woman (offscreen), with a faint smile on his face. The film then cuts to a medium shot of him still looking away from where the woman is supposed to be; yet the woman is no longer there. For a brief moment, the relationality between Georg and the woman is dephased, and as the relationality is *lifted,* so is her *form.* Nonetheless, Georg and the anthropotechnical consciousness soon realize that the woman has jumped off the embankment.

In Mahāyāna philosophy, *nirvāṇa* and engagement—like emptiness and form—are neither the same nor different, neither not the same nor not different. By committing suicide, this woman is only extinguishing the operation of the six consciousnesses that constitute her transient sense of individuality, subjectivity, and agency. Death leaves behind an active layout of potentialities that are still engaged in cycles of life and death. To be fully released from relationalities, as I explained earlier in this chapter, is to engage fully in the formational process that instantiates them from one moment to another. By being mindful of the karmic impulses that initiate each thought from one moment to another, the consciousness can gradually take agency over the ontopower to affect—and be affected by—each potentiality.

By the end of *Transit,* Georg hands Weidel's manuscript to the actor Matthias Brandt (the bartender; Weidel's voice), a gesture that indicates his/our surrender of karma to karma. Yet, as an image-consciousness, *life* is constantly in the process of in-forming and changing, and these changes are manifestations and reflections of those karmic traces that produce what we perceive and conceptualize as *movement.* Therefore, the film ends with a medium close-up of Georg in the café, with the offscreen sound of the doorbell ringing, followed by the footsteps of a person wearing high heels (a signature of Marie). Georg looks up toward the camera with a smile, and the film cuts to black, thus enabling the anthropotechnical consciousness to *accept* the karmic cycle of relationality as *the way it is.*

In equanimity, there lies benevolence, compassion, and empathy. It is out of a fully embodied experience of all the *violent* sensations and affections of suffering that an insight can be arrived at and to which it can be returned. It is in this sense that nonviolence is not a disengagement from violence, especially since every moment of our process of becoming involves violence. Rather, it is a mindful engagement of every microperceptual violence *here and now,* so that we can preempt inflicting acts of violence on others and on ourselves, and to enable the cause of and reason for violence to be fully dissolved.

Together, we have failed ourselves. Yet, no failure is beyond repair, even if we find ourselves in the ruins of humanity, where ruination *is* the symptom of humanity. What remains from our utter failure is karma, which operates perpetually, and cannot be conceived otherwise.

How we exercise each karmic impulse—as an ontopower—will determine whether we are going to proliferate our symptoms and attach to
them repeatedly, or instead to rewrite them so that we can engage in
form equanimously. This can be done, one karmic impulse at a time,
from one *kṣaṇa* to another, not by looking at the past or anticipating a
better future, but by fully engaging in this *kṣaṇa*. Only then can we arrive
home—*lakṣaṇa-śūnyatā* (form-emptiness)—and realize that *I exist* neither in the past nor in the future, but *here and now.*

MULTILINGUAL GLOSSARY OF BUDDHIST TERMS, NAMES, AND TITLES

This glossary contains only Buddhist—not all non-European—terms, names (of persons, places, and schools), and literary titles and genres. Please refer to the "Note on Languages" section of the book for a detailed explanation of the transliteration systems employed within and for instructions on Middle Chinese pronunciation.

This glossary is divided into three sections: (1) Terms [T]; (2) Names [N]; and (3) Literary Titles and Genres [L]. In each section:

1. Pāli and/or Sanskrit terms appear in the following order: Pāli/ Sanskrit; full-form Chinese characters (Middle Chinese transliteration, when applicable/Modern Mandarin pinyin); Japanese Kanji (Modern Japanese transliteration); English translation (unless either the original Pāli or Sanskrit term is part of the modern English vocabulary or there is no English translation).
2. Terms, names, and titles originated in Chinese (marked with [C]) appear in the following order: Middle Chinese transliteration (when applicable)/pinyin, Chinese characters; modern Japanese transliteration (when applicable), Kanji; English translation (when applicable).
3. Terms, names, and titles originated in Japanese (marked with [J]) appear in the following order: Japanese transliteration (when applicable), Kanji; English translation (when applicable).

4. The name "Thích Nhất Hạnh" is listed in the following order: Vietnamese; Chinese translation; Japanese translation; English.

5. Chapter titles in Pāli and/or Sanskrit are listed as subentries after the titles of the literary text in which they are found. These chapter titles are also indexed and searchable as main entries.

6. Citations are listed as subentries either after the literary texts from which they are cited, or after the persons to which they are attributed.

7. Cross references are indicated by *See* and *See also* in this glossary, with the following exceptions:

two realities: (2r)
three self-natures: (3)
four insights: (4i)
five aggregates: (5)
five awarenesses: (5aw)
six perfections: (6)
twelve *nidānas:* (12)
H'ua'ngiɐm scholars: (h)
Middle Way scholars: (m)
Pure Land scholars: (pl)
Thenthʌi scholars: (t)
Yogācāra scholars: (y)
Zen scholars and schools: (z)

TERMS [T]

adhipati-pratyaya; 增上緣 (*tsəngdzhiɐ`ng jiuɛn/zengshang yuan*); 增上緣 (*zōjō en*); dominant condition. See also *nidānas* [T]

adhyavasāyas; 用 (*jiòng/yong*); 用 (*yō*); modifications of self-nature or functions. See also *ātmakatva* [T]; *lakṣanas* [T]

ālambana-pratyaya; 境界緣 (所緣緣) [*k'iǎengk'ɛi jiuɛn* (*śiʌ'jiuɛn jiuɛn*)/ *jingjie yuan* (*suoyuan yuan*)]; 境界縁 (所緣緣) [*kyōkai en* (*shoen'en*)]; foundational condition. See also *nidānas* [T]

ālaya; 阿賴耶 (*ʔalàjia/alaiye*); 阿賴耶 (*araya*); storehouse

anantara-pratyaya; 無間緣 (*miok'ɛn jiuɛn/mujian yuan*); 無間縁 (*mugen en*); seed condition. See also *nidānas* [T] *ānāpānasati/ānāpānasmṛti;* 安那般那念 (*ʔannǎpuannǎ nèm/annapanna nian*); 安那般那念 (*annahanna nen*); mindfulness of breathing. See also *satipaṭṭhāna/smṛtyupasthāna* [T]

anattā/anātman; 無我 (*mɪo'ngǎ/wuwo*); 無我 (*muga*); nonself. See also *anicca/anitya* [T]; *ātman* [T]

anicca/anitya; 無常 (*mɪodzhɪɐng/wuchang*); 無常 (*mujō*); impermanence. See also *anattā/anātman* [T]

anupalabdha; 不可得 (*pɪutkhǎtək/bukede*); アヌパラブダ (*anuparabuda*); unattainable. *See also* Tathāgatagarbha [T]

anuttarasamyaksambodhi; 阿耨多羅三藐三菩提 (*ʔanəùtalaasammɪčusambuodei/anouduoluosanmiaosanputi*); 阿耨多羅三藐三菩提 (*anokutara-sanmyakusanbodai*); absolute mindfulness. See also *citta* [T]; *vijñaptis* [T]; *viññāṇa/vijñāna* [T]

arahant/arhat; 阿羅漢 (*ʔalahàn/aluohan*); 阿羅漢 (*arakan*); enlightened being

āśraya; 依 (*ʔɪi/yi*); 依 (*i*); shelter. See also *parāvrtti* [T]

ātmakatva; 體 (*thǎi/ti*); 體 (*tai*); self-nature. See also *adhyavasāyas* [T]; *lakṣanas* [T]

ātman; 我 (*ngǎ/wo*); 我 (*ga*); self. See also *anattā/anātman* [T]

ātmaviparyāsa; 我顛倒 (*ngǎ tentǎu/wo diandao*); 我顛倒 (*ga tentō*); misapprehension of nonself as self. See also *viparyāsas* [T]

avijjā/avidyā (12); 無明 (*mɪom'iæng/wuming*); 無明 (*mumyō*); unenlightenment or ignorance

avyākata/avyākṛta; 無記 (*mɪokì/wuji*); 無記 (*muki*); unmarked

āyatana (12); 六塵 (*lɪukdh'ɪin/liuchen*); 六塵 (*rokujin*); external forms

bhava/bhāva (12); 有 (*hɪǔ/you*); 有 (*u*); existence. See also *suñña/śūnya* (*śūnyatā*) [T]

bhikkhus; 比丘 (*pǐukhɪu/biqiu*); 比丘 (*biku*); monks

bījas; 種子 (*tshɪǒngtsǐ/zhongzi*); 種子 (*shushi*); seeds or potentialities

bodhisattva; 菩薩 (*buosat/pusa*); 菩薩 (*bosatsu*); enlightened sentient being. *See also* Avalokiteśvara [N]; Mahāsthāmaprāpta [N]; Metteyya/Maitreya [N]

Brahman; 梵 (*Bùɐm/Fan*); 梵 (*Bon*); ultimate being

brahmavihārās; 四無量心 (*sɪù mɪolɪɐng sɪim/si wuliang xin*); 四無量心 (*shi muryō shin*); four heightened states of mind. See also *karuṇā* [T]; *mettā/maitrī* [T]; *muditā* [T]

catuṣkoṭi; 四句 (*sɪikɪò/siju*); 四句 (*shiku*); four-cornered negation

cetiya; 舍利子 (*shɪàlɪìtsǐ/shelizi*); 仏舍利 (*Busshari*); relics

citta; 心 (*siim/xin*); 心 (*shin*); consciousness, disembodied mind, or absolute mindfulness (depending on the context). See also *anuttarasamyaksambodhi* [T]; *vijñaptis* [T]; *viññāṇa/vijñāna* [T]

dāna (6); 佈施 (*puòshiɛ/bushi*); 布施 (*huse*); letting go

darśana bhāga; 能緣 (*nəngjiuɛn/nengyuan*); 能緣 (*nōen*); potentiality to perceive and conceptualize. See also *nimitta bhāga* [T]

dhammās/dharmas; 法 (*pɥɐp/fa*); 法 (*hō*); forms and their emptiness

dukkha/duḥkha; 苦 (*khuǒ/ku*); 苦 (*ku*); suffering

dveṣa; 瞋 (*tshim/chen*); 瞋 (*shin*); anger and frustration. See also *kilesas/kleśas* [T]

dvirūpatā; 二相性 (*ñɯsiɛngsièng/erxiangxing*); 二相性 (*nisōshō*); double initiation. *See also* Dinna/Dignāga [N]

dǐi/shi [C], 事; *ji*, 事; consciousness. See also *lǐ/li* [T]

dziěmnguò/jianwu (z) [C], 漸悟; *zengo*, 漸悟; gradual awakening. See also *tuànnguò/dunwu* [T]

dzɯsièng/zixing (z) [C], 自性; *jishō*, 自性; self-nature. See also *citta*

gātha; 偈 (*g'ièi/jie*); 偈 (*ge*); verse

gensō [J], 還相; returning from. See *ōsō;* Tanabe Hajime [N]

hetu-pratyaya; 因緣 (*ʔiɯnjiuɛn/yinyuan*); 因緣 (*innen*); cause-condition. See *nidānas* [T]

hetuvidyā; 因明 (*ʔiɯm'iæng/yinming*); 因明 (*inmyō*); illuminating causes or logic

h'uàidəu/huatou (z) [C], 話頭; *watō*, 話頭; logical puzzle

jarāmaraṇa (12); 老死 (*lǎus'ɯ/laosi*); 老死 (*rōshi*); decay, and death or extinction

jāti (12); 生 (*sh'æng/sheng*); 生 (*shō*); birth

jhana/dhyāna; 禪定 (*dzhiɛndèng/chanding*); 禅定 (*zenjō*); concentration

jñeyāvaraṇa; 所知障 (*śiʌˋth'iɛ tshiɛˋng/suozhi zhang*); 所知障 (*shochi shō*); obstruction of the ultimate emptiness or actual existence by taking forms as knowledge. See also *kilesas/kleśas* [T]

kʌˋm/gan [C], 感; *kan*, 感; be vocated by. See also *kamma/karma* [T]

kamma/karma; 業 (*ngiɐp/ye*); 業 (*gō*); karma. See also *kʌˋm/gan* [T]; *tsiɛu/zhao* [T]

karesansui [J], 枯山水; rock garden

kartṛkaraṇe; 具格 (*giòk'æk/juge*); 具格 (*gukaku*); seeking shelter in agency

karuṇā; 悲 (*p'ɯ/bei*); 悲 (*hi*); compassion. See also *brahmavihārās*

kaya; 身 (*shim/shen*); 身 (*shin*); body

khandhas/skandhas; 五蘊 (*ngŭoʔɨun/wuyun*); 五蘊 (*goun*); formal
 aggregates

khanti/kṣānti (6); 忍辱 (*ɲǐmɲɨok/renru*); 忍耐 (*nintai*); patience and
 receptivity

khɨɨ/qi [C], 氣; *ki,* 気; air or subtle energy

khungthɨung mièuhɨŭ/kongzhong miaoyou [C], 空中妙有; *kūchū myōu,*
 空中妙有; existence is initiated intricately out of the liminality
 between emptiness and existence. *See also* Thenthʌi/Tiantai [N];
 Th'ièngiǐ/Zhiyi [N]

kilesas/kleśas; 煩惱障 (*bʉennău tshiɐ`ng/fannao zhang*); 煩悩障 (*bonnō*
 shō); afflictions. See also *dveṣa* [T]; *jñeyāvaraṇa* [T]; *moha* [T];
 rāga [T]

k'iǎng/jing [C], 境; *kyō,* 境; milieu or image

kṛtyanuṣṭhānajñāna (4i); 成所作智 (*dzhiɛngśiʌˇtsak th'iè/chengsuozuo*
 zhi); 成所作智 (*jōshosa chi*); mindfulness of what must be
 performed

kṣaṇa; 刹那 (*tśh'atnǎ/channa*); 刹那 (*setsuna*); moment or smallest unit
 of time

kungʔàn/gong'an [C], 公案; *kōan,* 公案

kwetdèng sɨm/jueding xin (5aw) [C], 決定心; *kettei shin,* 決定心; determining awareness

lakṣanas; 相 (*sɨɛng/xiang*); 相 (*sō*); forms. See also *suñña/śūnya*
 (*śūnyatā*) [T]

lǐ/li [C], 理; *ri,* 理; technicity. See also *džǐ/shi* [T]

mādhyamaka; 中觀 (*thɨungkuan/zhongguan*); 中観 (*chūkan*); middle way

manas; 末那 (*muatnǎ/mona*); 末那 (*mana*)

manasikara; 作意 (*tsakʔì/zuoyi*); 作意 (*sakui*); impulse

māṇavaka; 摩納縛伽（儒童）[*muanʌpbʉɛkgɨa (niodhung)/monabojia*
 (*rutong*)]; 儒童 [*judō*]; ignorance as self-nature

mantra; 咒 (*tshɨù/zhou*); マントラ (*mantora*)

mettā/maitrī; 慈 (*dzi/ci*); 慈 (*ji*); benevolence. See also *brahmavihārās*

moha; 癡 (*thh'i/chi*); 癡 (*chi*); delusion. See also *kilesas/kleśas* [T]

muditā; 喜 (*hǐ/xi*); 喜 (*ki*); empathy. See also *brahmavihārās*

nāma; 名 (*miɛng/ming*); 名 (*myō*); naming

nāmarūpa (12); 名色 (*miɛngśik/mingse*); 名色 (*myōshiki*); naming and
 in-forming

nibbāna/nirvāṇa; 涅槃 (*netbuan/niepan*); 涅槃 (*nehan*)

nidānas; 緣起 *(jiuɛnkhǐ/yuanqi);* 縁起 *(engi);* dependent originations.
   See also *adhipati-pratyaya* [T]; *ālambana-pratyaya* [T]; *anantara-pratyaya* [T]; *hetu-pratyaya* [T]; *samanatara-pratyaya* [T]

ñiɛ̌mdzièng siɪm/ranjing xin (5aw) [C], 染淨心; *senjō shin,* 染浄心; polluting or purifying awareness

nihsvabhāvatā; 無自性性 *(mɪodzɪ̀ɪsièng sièng/wuzixing xing);* 無自性性 *(mujishō shō);* self-nature-less-ness

nimitta bhāga; 所緣 *(śɪʌˈjiuɛn/suoyuan);* 所縁 *(shoen);* potentiality to generate signs. See also *darśana bhāga* [T]

niṣedha; 存在的否定 *(cunzai de fouding);* 存在の否定 *(sonzai no hitei);* existential negation. See also *paryudāsa* [T]

nityaviparyāsa; 常顛倒 *(zhiɛng tentǎu/chang diandao);* 常顛倒 *(jō tentō);* misapprehension of impermanence as permanence. See also *viparyāsas* [T]

ōsō [J], 往相; going toward. See also *gensō* [T]; Tanabe Hajime [N]

paññā/prajñā; 智慧 *(th'iɛ̀hwèi/zhihui);* 智慧 *(chie);* insight

papañcas; 戲論 *(h'iɛ̀lùən/xilun);* 戲論 *(keron);* perceptual-conceptual proliferations

paramārtha (2r); 勝義諦 *(shɪngngˈiɛ̀ tèi/shengyi di);* 勝義諦 *(shogi tai);* ultimate reality

pāramī/paramita; 波羅蜜多 *(pualamɪɪtta/boluomiduo);* 波羅蜜 *(haramitsu);* perfections

paratantra-svabhāva (3); 依他起性 *(ʔiithakhǐ sièng/yitaqi xing);* 依他起性 *(etaki shō);* nature of being initiated out of dependent originations

parāvrtti; 轉依 *(th'iuɛ̌nʔii/zhuanyi);* 転変 *(tenpen);* reversal. See also *āśraya* [T]

parikalpitah-svabhāva (3); 偏計所執性 *(phiɛnkèiśɪʌˈtsiɪp sièng/pianjisuozhi xing);* 偏計所執性 *(hengeshoshū shō);* nature of being initiated out of the dependent originations between internal and external forms

paryudāsa; 名詞的否定 *(mingci de fouding);* 名詞の否定 *(meishi no hitei);* implicative negation. See also *niṣedha* [T]

passaddhi/prasrabhi; 輕安 *(khiɛngʔan/qin'an);* 軽安 *(keian);* tranquility

phassa/sparśa (12); 觸 *(tshɪok/chu);* 触 *(shoku);* contact

pīti/prīti; 喜 *(hǐ/xi);* 喜 *(ki);* rapture

pratyaveksanāprajñā (4i); 妙觀察智 *(miɛ̀ukuantshhˈɛt th'iɛ̀/miaoguancha zhi);* 妙観察智 *(myōkanzatchi);* reflection insight

puggala/pudgala; 普特伽羅 *(phuɔ̌dhəkgɪala/putejialuo);*
   補特伽羅 *(futogara);* individuality

puruṣa; 神我 *(zhiɯnngǎ/shenwo);* プルシャ *(purusha);* spirit or agency

ʔɯtnèm samtshen/yinian sanqian [C], 一念三千; *ichinen sanzen,* 一念三千; one thought-impulse in-forms an awareness that constitutes three thousand billion universes. *See also* Thenthʌi/Tiantai [N]; Th'ièngiǐ/Zhiyi [N]

rāga; 貪 *(thʌm/tan);* 貪 *(don);* avarice. See also *kilesas/kleśas* [T]

rūpa (5; 12); 色 *(śik/se);* 色 *(shiki);* form

sabhāva; 自性 *(dzɯsièng/zixing);* 自性 *(jishō);* self-nature (different from *citta*)

saḷāyatanas/ṣaḍāyatanas (12); 六入 *(lɯukñɯɯp/liuru);* 六内処 *(rokunaisho);* internal forms

samādhi; 三摩地（三昧）[*sammuadɯ (sammuʌi)/samodi (sanmei)*]; 三昧 [*sanmai*]; concentration

samanatara-pratyaya; 等無間縁 *(tǎng mɯok'ɛn jiuɛn/deng mujian yuan);* 等無間縁 *(tō mugen en);* matching condition. See also *nidānas*

sammuti/saṃvṛti (3r); 世俗諦 *(shièziɯok tèi/shisu di);* 世俗諦 *(sezoku tai);* conventional reality

saṃsāra; 流轉（輪廻）[*lɯuth'iuĕn (liuɯnhùʌi)/liuzhuan (lunhui)*]; 輪廻 [*rinne*]; cycle (transmigration)

saṅgha/sangha; 僧伽 *(sənggɯa/sengjia);* 僧 *(sō);* monastic community

saṅkhāra/saṃskara (5; 12); 行 *(h'æng/xing);* 行 *(gyō);* volition

sañña/saṃjñā (5); 想 *(sɯenˇg/xiang);* 想 *(sō);* perception

śāstra; 論 *(lùən/lun);* 論 *(ron);* treatise

sati/smṛti; 正念 *(tshièngnèm/zhengnian);* 正念 *(shōnen);* awareness or mindfulness

satipaṭṭhāna/smṛtyupasthāna; 四念住 *(sìɯ nèmdh'ɯò/si nianzhu);* 四念処 *(shi nenjo);* establishing mindfulness. See also *ānāpānasati/ ānāpānasmṛti* [T]

sh'iùɯñiĕ sɯɯm/shuai'er xin (5aw) [C], 率爾心; *sotsuji shin,* 率爾心; sudden awareness

sɯɯm/xin/shin [C]. See *citta*

sīla/śīla (6); 持戒 *(dh'ik'èi/chijie);* 戒 *(kai);* discipline

śuciviparyāsa; 淨顛倒 *(dzièng tentǎu/jing diandao);* 浄顛倒 *(jō tentō);* misapprehension of our impure body as pure. See also *viparyāsas*

sukhaviparyāsa; 樂顛倒 *(lak tentǎu/le diandao);* 楽顛倒 *(raku tentō);* misapprehension of those afflictions produced by sensations and affections as happiness. See also *viparyāsas* [T]

suñña/śūnya (śūnyatā); 空 *(khung/kong);* 空 *(kū);* emptiness. See also
 bhava/bhāva [T]

svasaṃvedana/svasaṃvitti; 自證分 *(dzìɪtshiˋngpiun/zizhengfen);* 自証分
 (jishōbun); potentiality to take the act of seeing and the signs being
 seen as self-evident

taṇhā/tṛṣṇā (12); 愛 *(ʔʌì/ai);* 愛 *(ai);* longing or desire

tathatā/tathātā; 如是（真如）[*ñiʌdzhiě (tshiɪmñiʌ)/rushi (zhenru)];* 如是
 （真如）[*nyoze (shinnyo)];* thusness or *the way it is*

tǒngliu siɪm/dengliu xin (5aw) [C], 等流心; *tōru shin,* 等流心; ontological
 awareness

tri-sahasra-mahā-sahasra-lokadhātu; 三千大千世界 *(samtshen dàithsen
 shiɛ̀ik'ɛ̀i/sanqian daqian shijie);* 三千大千世界 *(sanzen daisen sekai);*
 three thousand billion universes

tsiɛu/zhao [C], 招; *shō* 招; vocate. See also *kʌˇm/gan* [T]; *kamma/karma* [T]

tuɜ̀nnguò/dunwu (z) [C], 頓悟; *tongo,* 頓悟; sudden awakening. See also
 dziěmnguò/jianwu

upādāna (12); 取 *(tshiǒ/qu);* 取 *(shu);* attachment

upekkha/upekṣā (4b); 捨 *(shiǎ/she);* 捨 *(sha);* equanimity

vedanās (5; 12); 覺受 *(k'ʌkdzhiǔ/jueshou);* 受 *(ju);* sensations and
 affections

vijñaptis; 識（表）[*shik (piěu)/shi (biao)];* 識（表）[*shiki (hyō)];* consciousness (representation). See also *viññāṇa/vijñāna* [T]

viññāṇa/vijñāna; 識 *(shik/shi);* 識 *(shiki);* consciousness. See also
 vijñaptis [T]

viparyāsas; 顛倒 *(tentǎu/diandao);* 顛倒 *(tentō);* reversal. See also
 ātmaviparyāsa [T]; *nityaviparyāsa* [T]; *śuciviparyāsa* [T];
 sukhaviparyāsa [T]

viriya/vīrya (6p); 精進 *(tsiɛngtzsìɪn/jingjin);* 精進 *(shōjin);* diligence

zangedō [J], 懺悔道. *See also* Tanabe Hajime [N]

ziɪmgiu siɪm/xunqiu xin (5aw) [C], 尋求心; *jingu shin,* 尋求心; seeking
 awareness

NAMES [N]

Amitābha; 阿彌陀佛 *(ʔamiɛɖɑ Biut/Amituo Fo);* 阿弥陀仏 (Amida
 Butsu); *See also* Dharmākara [N]; Sukhāvatī [N]

Ānanda; 阿難 *(ʔa'nan/A'nan);* 阿難 (Anan)

Asaṅga (y); 無著 *(Mioth'iʌ/Wuzhu);* 無着 (Mujyaku). See also
 Abhidharma-samuccaya [L]; Vasubandhu [N]; *Yogācārabhūmi-Śāstra* [L]

Ashoka; 阿育王 (ʔajiuk Huɐng/Ayu Wang); アショーカ (Ashōka)

Aśvaghoṣa (y); 馬鳴 (M'ăm'iæng/Maming); 馬鳴 (Memyō). See also
    Mahāyāna śraddhotpādaśāstra [L]

Avalokiteśvara; 觀自在(觀世音)菩薩 [Kuɑnddzìɪdzʌì (Kuanshièiʔ'iɪm)
    Buosɑt/Guanzizai (Guanshiyin) Pusa]; 観自在(観世音)菩薩
    [Kanjizai (Kanzeon) Bosatsu]. *See also* bodhisattva [T]

Bhāviveka (m); 清辯 (Tshiɛngb'iĕn/Qingbian); 清弁 (Shōben)

Buddhaghosa (y); 覺音 (K'ʌkʔ'iɪm/Jueyin); ブッダゴーサ (Buddagōsa)

Buddhasimha (y); 獅子覺 (Sh'iɪtsĭk'ʌk/Shizijue); 獅子覚 (Shishikaku)

Cārvāka; 順世論 (Zhiùɪnshièilùən/Shunshilun); 順世派 (Junseiha);
    materialism

Ching-kung (pl) [C], 淨空

Chittamatra/Cittamātra; 唯識 (Jiuɪshɨk/Weishi); 唯識 (Yuishiki);
    Consciousness or Manifestation Only. *See also* Yogachara/
    Yogācāra [N]

Dharmākara; 法藏 (Puɐpdzɑng/Fazang); 法蔵 (Hōzō); *See also*
    Amitābha [N]; Sukhāvatī [N]

Dharmakīrti (y); 法稱 (Puɐptshɨng/Facheng); 法称 (Hosshō)

Dharmapāla (y); 護法 (Huòpuɐp/Hufa); 護法 (Gohō)

Dinna/Dignāga (y); 陳那 (Dh'iɪnnă/Chenna); 陳那 (Jinna). See also
    dvirūpatā [T]

Dùngsh'ɛn Liɐngk'èi/Dongshan Liangjie (z) [C], 洞山良介; Tōzan
    Ryōkai, 洞山良介

Duŏzhiùɪn/Dushun (h) [C], 杜順; Tojun, 杜順

Dzaudùng/Caodong (z) [C], 曹洞; Sōtō, 曹洞

Dzhiɛn/Chan [C], 禪; Zen,禅

Dzièngthǔo/Jingtu [C], 淨土; Jōdo 浄土; Pure Land. *See also*
    Jōdo Shinshū [N]

Fang, Thomé, H. [C: Fang Dongmei], 方東美

Feng Zikai [C], 豐子愷

Hoi-yan [C: Hairen], 海仁

H'ua'ngiɐm/Huayan [C], 華嚴; Kegon, 華厳. See also *Avataṃsaka Sūtra* [L]

Hwèihuɐˇn/Huiyuan (pl) [C], 慧遠; Eon, 慧遠

Hwèinəng/Huineng (z) [C], 慧能; Enō, 慧能: *Hagi dzìɪsièng pŭən dzì
    kɨotsɨok?/Heqi zixing ben zi juzu?* [C], 何期自性本自俱足?; *Nanzo-
    kisen, jishō wa hon'yori gusoku serukotoo?,* 何ぞ期せん、自性は本より
    具足せることを。; Who would expect that self-nature [the
    Tathāgatagarbha], in itself, has always been adequately there?

Hwendzàng/Xuanzang (y) [C], 玄奘; Genjyō, 玄奘. See also
　　Vijñapatimātratāsiddhi [L]

Imamichi Tomonobu [J], 今道　友信

Jainism; 耆那教 (Giˀnǎkˀau/Qi'najiao); ジャイナ教 (Jainakyō)

Jinling kejingchu [C], 金陵刻經處; Jinling Sutra Publishing House

Jōdo Shinshū [J], 浄土真宗. *See* Dzièngthŭo/Jingtu [N]

Kaliṅga-rāja; 歌利王 (Kalìɪ Huɐng/Geli Wang); カリンガ王 (Karinga-ō)

Liang Qichao [C], 梁啟超

Liɪmtsèi Ng'ièhwen/Linji Yixuan (z) [C], 臨濟義玄; Rinzai Gigen,
　　臨済義玄

Lokeśvararāja; 世自在王佛 (Shièidzìɪdzʌìhuɐng Bɨut/Shizizaiwang
　　Fo); 世自在王仏 (Sejizaiō Butsu)

Lü Cheng (y) [C], 呂澂

Mahāsāṃghikas; 大眾部 (Dàitshiùng buǒ/Dazhong bu); 大衆部
　　(Daishu bu); Commoners. See also Therāvada [N]

Mahāsthāmaprāpta; 大勢至菩薩 (Dàishièitshìɪ Buosɑt/Dashizhi Pusa);
　　勢至菩薩 (Seishi Bosatsu). *See also* bodhisattva [T]

Mahāyāna; 大乘 (Dàizɨng/Dasheng); 大乘 (Daijō)

Metteyya/Maitreya; 彌勒 (Mɪɛlək/Mile); 弥勒 (Miroku). *See also*
　　bodhisattva [T]

Nāgārjuna; 龍樹 (Lɪongdzhɪò/Longshu); 龍樹 (Ryūju). See also
　　Mūlamadhyamakakārikā [L]; *Mahāprajñāpāramitāśāstra* [L]

Nālandā; 那難陀 (Nǎnɑndɑ/Nanantuo); ナーランダ (Nāranda)

Nanjō Bunyū (pl) [J], 南条　文雄

Nishitani Keiji [J], 西谷　啓治

Ouyang Jian (Ouyang Jingwu) [C], 歐陽漸（歐陽境無）

Sakyamuni/Śākyamuni; 釋迦牟尼 (Shɪɛkgɨamɪun'ɪɪ/Shijiamouni);
　　釈迦牟尼 (Shakamuni)

Sarvāstivāda; 説一切有部 (Shiuɛtˀiɪttshethiǔ buǒ/Shuoyiqieyou bu);
　　説一切有部 (Setsuissaiubu). *See also* Therāvada [N]

Shaku Soyen (Shaku Sōen) [J], 釈　宗演

Sheng-yen [C], 聖嚴

Shinran (pl) [J], 親鸞

Shubūti; 須菩提 (Sɨobuodei/Xuputi); 須菩提 (Shubodai)

Śramaṇa; 沙門 (Sh'amuən/Shamen); 沙門 (Shamon)

Sthaviras; 上座部 (Dzhɪɛˋngdzuàbuǒ/Shangzuobu); 上座部
　　(Dzhɪɛˋ Jōzabu); Elders. *See also* Therāvada

Sthiramati (y); 安慧 (ˀɑnhwèi/Anhui); 安慧 (Anne)

Sukhāvatī; 極樂 (Gɨklɑk/Jile); 極楽 (Gokuraku); Pure Land; *See also* Amitābha [N]; Dharmākara [N]

Su Manshu [C], 蘇曼殊

Suzuki Teitarō Daisetz (Suzuki Daisetzu Teitarō) [J], 鈴木　大拙　貞太郎

Taixu (z) [C], 太虛

Tanabe Hajime [J], 田辺　元. See also *gensō* [T]; *ōsō* [T]; *zangedō* [T]

Tanxu (t) [C], 倓虛

Tathāgata; 如來 (Ñɨʌlʌi/Rulai); 如来 (Nyorai); neither moving nor not moving, or Buddhahood

Tathāgatagarbha; 如來藏 (Ñɨʌlʌidzɑng/Rulaizang); 如来蔵 (Nyoraizō); the womb from which Buddhahood is conceived. See also *anupalabdha* [T]

Thenthʌi/Tiantai [C], 天台; Tendai, 天台. See also *khungthɨung miɛuhɨǔ/kongzhong miaoyou* [T]; Th'iɛ̀ngɨǐ/Zhiyi [N]

Therāvada; 上座部佛教 (Dzhiɛ`ngdzuàbuǒ Bɨutk'au/Shangzuobu Fojiao); 上座部仏教 (Jōzabu Bukkyō). See also Mahāsāṃghikas [N]; Sarvāstivāda [N]; Sthaviras [N]

Thích Nhất Hạnh (z) [Vietnamese]; 釋一行; 釈一行; Thich Nacht Hanh

Th'iɛ̀ngɨǐ/Zhiyi (t) [C], 智顗; Chigi, 智顗. See also *khungthɨung miɛuhɨǔ/kongzhong miaoyou [T]; ʔiitnɛ̀m samtshen/yinian sanqian/ichinen sanzen* [T]; Thenthʌi/Tiantai [N]

Tshɛngngɥɐn H'ængsi/Qingyuan Xingsi (z) [C], 青原行思; Seigen Gyōshi, 青原行思

Tusita/Tuṣita; 兜率天 (Tɘush'iuɪtthen/Doushuaitian); 兜率天 (Tosotsuten)

Upāli; 優婆離 (ʔɨubuɑliɛ/Youpoli); ウパリ (Upari)

Vaiśālī; 毘舍離 (Bɪɪshiàliɛ/Pisheli); ビシャリ (Bishari)

Vajrayāna; 密宗 (M'iɪttsuong/Mizong); 密教 (Mikkyō)

Vasubandhu (y); 世親 (Shiɛ̀itshim/Shiqin); 世親 (Seshin). See also *Abhidharmakośakārikā* [L]; Asaṅga [N]

Vedic; 吠陀 (Bɥɐɩ̀dɑ/Feituo); ベーダ (Bēda)

Wang Guowei [C], 王國維

Xuyun (z) [C], 虛雲

Yang Wenhui (y) [C], 楊文會

Yinguang (pl) [C], 印光

Yin Shun (m) [C], 印順

Yogachara/Yogācāra; 瑜伽行派（唯識）[Jiogiɑh'æŋph'ɛ̀ (Jiuɪshɪk)/ Yujiaxingpai (Weishi)]; 瑜伽行派（唯識）[Yugagyōha (Yuishiki)]. *See also* Chittamatra/Cittamātra [N]

Yuanying (z) [C], 圓瑛

Zhina neixueyuan [C], 支那內學院; China Inner Studies Institute

LITERARY TITLES AND GENRES [L]

Abhidhamma/Abhidharma; 阿毘達磨 (ʔabiɪdatmua/Apidamo); 阿毘達磨 (*Abidatsuma*); meta-discourse. *See also* Asaṅga [N]; *Abhidharmakośakārikā* [L]; *Abhidharma-samuccaya* [L]; Vasubandhu [N]

Abhidharmakośakārikā;《阿毘達磨俱舍論》[ʔabiɪdatmua kioshià lùən/ Apidamo jushe lun]; 『阿毘達磨俱舍論』[*Abidatsuma kusha ron*]; *Verses on the Treasury of Abhidharma. See also* Vasubandhu [N]

Abhidharma-samuccaya;《阿毘達磨集論》[ʔabiɪdatmua dziɪp lùən/ Apidamo ji lun]; 『阿毘達磨集論』[*Abidatsuma shū ron*]; *Compendium of Abhidharma. See also* Asaṅga [N]; *Yogācārabhūmi-Śāstra* [L]

āgamas;《阿含經》[ʔahʌm keng/ahan jing]; 『阿含経』[*agon kyō*]: *Khīṇā jāti, vusitaṃ brahmacariyaṃ, kataṃ karaṇīyam, nāparaṃ itthattāyā'ti pajānāti"ti*; 我生已盡，梵行已立，所作已作，自知不受後有 (*Ngǎsh'æng jǐdzǐn, bùɛmh'æng jǐliɪp, śiʌ'tsak jǐtsak, dzìɪth'iɛ piutdzhiǔ həùhiǔ/Wosheng yijin, fanxing yili, suozuo yizuo, zizhi bushou houyou*); 我生已盡、梵行已立、所作已作、自知不受後有 (*Gashō ijin, bongyō iritsu shosa isaku, jichi fujyu goy ū*); My life has exhausted, my monastic living has come to perfection, what needs to be done has been done, there is no coming back to another state of being.

Avataṃsaka Sūtra;《大方廣佛華嚴經》[*Dàipʉɛngkwǎng Bɪut H'ua'ngiɛm keng/Dafangguang Fo Huayan jing*]; 『大方広仏華厳経』[*Daihōkō Butsu Kegon kyō*]. *See also* H'ua'ngiɛm/Huayan [N]

"Daṇḍavaggo." *See Dhammapada* [L]

Dhammapada;《法句經》[Pʉɛpkiò keng/Faju jing]; 『法句経』[*Hokku gyō*]: "Daṇḍavaggo"; 〈懲罰〉["Dh'iŋbʉɛt"/"Chengfa"]; 「懲罰」["Chōbatsu"]

"Gatāgataparīkṣā." *See Mūlamadhyamakakārikā* [L]; Nāgārjuna [N]

"Kālaparīkṣā." *See Mūlamadhyamakakārikā* [L]; Nāgārjuna [N]

"Karmaphalaparīkṣa." *See Mūlamadhyamakakārikā* [L]; Nāgārjuna [N]

Kathāvatthu;《論事》[Lùəndʑì/Lunshi]; 『論事』[*Ronji*]

Madhupiṇḍika Sutta;《密丸經》[*M'iɪthuan keng/Miwan jing*];『密丸経』
[*Mitsumaru kyō*]

Mahāprajñāpāramitāśāstra;《大智度論》[*Dàith'iɛ̀duò lùən/Dazhidu lun*];
『大智度論』[*Daichido ron*]; *Treatise on the Great Prajñāpāramitā. See
also* Nāgārjuna [N]

Mahā Satipaṭṭhāna Sutta;《大念處經》[*Dài nèmtshhiʌˋ keng/Da nianchu
jing*];『大念処経』[*Dai nenjo kyō*]

Mahāvaṃsa;《大史》[*Dàiśǐ/Dashi*];『マハーワンサ』[*Mahāwansa*]

Mahāyāna śraddhotpādaśāstra;《大乘起信論》[*Dàizing khǐsìn lùən/
Dasheng qixin lun*];『大乘起信論』[*Daijō kishin ron*]; *Awakening of
Faith in the Mahāyāna. See also* Aśvaghoṣa [N]

Mūlamadhyamakakārikā;《中論》[*Thɨung lùən/Zhong lun*];『中論』[*Chū
ron*]; *Fundamental Verses of the Middle Way:* (1) "Gatāgataparīkṣā";
〈觀去來〉["*Kuankhiʌˋlʌi*"/"*Guanqulai*"];「観去来」["*Kankyo-
rai*"]; "On Movement"; (2) "Kālaparīkṣā";〈觀時〉
["*Kuandzhi*"/"*Guanshi*"];「観時」["*Kanji*"]; "On time"; (3)
"Karmaphalaparīkṣa";〈觀業〉["*Kuanngiɛp*"/"*Guanye*"];「観業」
["*Kangō*"]; "On karma." *See also* Nāgārjuna [N]

Prajñāpāramitāhṛdaya;《般若波羅蜜多心經》[*Puonñǐa pualamiɪtta siɪm
keng/Bore boluomiduo xin jing*];『般若波羅蜜多心経』[*Hannya
haramitta shingyō*]; *Heart Sutra: iha śāriputra: rūpaṃ śūnyatā
śūnyataiva rūpaṃ; rūpān na pṛthak śūnyatā śunyatāyā na pṛthag
rūpaṃ; yad rūpaṃ sā śūnyatā; ya śūnyatā tad rūpaṃ. evam eva vedanā
saṃjñā saṃskāra vijñānaṃ;* 舍利子，色不異空，空不異色，色即是
空，空即是色，受想行識，亦復如是 (*Shiàlìɪtsǐ, śik pɪutjì khung, khung
pɪutjì śik, śik tsɪkdzhiě khung, khung tsikdzhiě śik, dzhiǔ sɪeˇng h'æng
shik, jɪɛkbɪuk ñiʌdzhiě/Shelizi, se buyi kong, kong buyise, se jishi kong,
kong jishi se, shou xiang xing shi, yifu rushi*); 舍利子、色不異空、空不
異色、色即是空、空即是色、受想行識、亦復如是 (*Sharishi, shiki fui
kū, kū fui shiki, shiki sokuze kū, kū sokuze shiki, ju sō gyō shiki, yakubu
nyoze*); Here, O Śāriputra, form is emptiness and the very emptiness
is form; emptiness does not differ from form, form does not differ
from emptiness; whatever is form, that is emptiness, whatever is
emptiness, that is form, the same is true of feelings, perceptions,
impulses, and consciousness [Edward Conze, *Buddhist Wisdom Books:
Containing* The Diamond Sutra *and* The Heart Sutra (London: George
Allen and Unwin, 1958; repr. New York: Random House, 2001), 86.]

Samantapāsādikā;《善見呂毘婆沙》[*Dzhiěnkèn lⅰʌˋbⅰⅰbuash'a/Shanjian lüpiposha*];『善見呂毘婆沙』[*Zenken robibasha*]

Saṃdhinirmocana Sūtra;《解深密經》[*Khě shiⅰmm'iⅰt keng/Jie shenmi jing*];『解深密経』[*Gejinmikkyo*]; *Sutra of the Explanation of the Profound Secrets*

Saṃyuktāgama;《雜阿含經》[*Dzʌp ʔahʌm keng/Za ahan jing*];『雜阿含経』[*Zō agon kyō*]; *Connected Discourses*

Sukhāvatīvyūha Sūtra (and the shorter version);《無量壽經》(《佛說阿彌陀經》) [*Mⅰolⅰɐngdzhⅰù keng (Bⅰutshⅰuɛt ʔamⅰɛda keng)/Wuliangshou jing (Foshuo Amituojing)*];『無量寿経』(『阿弥陀経』) [*Muryōju kyō (Amida kyō)*]; *Infinite Life Sutra* and the *Shorter Sukhāvatīvyūha Sutra*

Śūraṅgama Sūtra;《大佛頂首楞嚴經》[*Dài Bⅰuttěng Shⅰǔlʌngngⅰɐm keng/Da Foding Shoulengyan jing*];『大仏頂首楞厳経』[*Dai Butchō Shuryōgonkyō*]

suttas/sūtra; 契經 (*khèikeng/qijing*); 経 (*kyō*)

Tipiṭaka/Tripiṭaka; 三藏 (*Samdzang/Sanzang*); 三蔵 (*Sanzō*)

Upanishads; 奧義書 (*ʔàu'ng'ièshⅰʌ/Aoyishu*); ウパニシャッド (*Upanishaddo*)

Vajracchedikā Prajñāpāramitā Sūtra;《金剛般若波羅蜜經》[*K'iⅰmkang puonñĭa pualamiⅰt keng/Jingang bore boluomi jing*];『金剛般若波羅蜜経』[*Kongō hannya haramitsu kyō*]; *Diamond Sutra*

Vijñapatimātratāsiddhi;《成唯識論》[*Dzhⅰɐng jiⅰushⅰk lùən/Cheng weishi lun*];『成唯識論』[*Jō yuishiki ron*]; *Discourse on the Perfection of Consciousness-Only. See also* Hwendzàng/Xuanzang [N]

vinaya; 毘奈耶（律）[*bⅰmàijia (liuⅰt)/pinaiye (lü)*]; 律 (*ritsu*); monastic regulations

Yogācārabhūmi-Śāstra;《瑜伽師地論》[*Jⅰogⅰash'iⅰ dùlùən/Yujiashi dilun*];『瑜伽師地論』[*Yugashi jiron*]; *Treatise on the Foundation for Yoga Practitioner. See also* Asaṅga [N]; *Abhidharma-samuccaya* [L]

NOTES

INTRODUCTION

1. Gilles Deleuze, *Cinéma 1. L'image-mouvement* (1983; repr., Paris: Éditions de Minuit, 2015); Gilles Deleuze, *Cinéma 2. L'image-temps* (1985; repr., Paris: Éditions de Minuit, 2017); Gilbert Simondon, *Du mode d'existence des objets techniques* (1958; repr., Paris: Éditions Aubier, 2012); Gilbert Simondon, *L'individuation psychique et collective* (1989; repr., Paris: Aubier, 2007). For a discussion of Simondon's work (in relation to Deleuze), see, for example, Arne de Boever, Alex Murray, Jon Foffe, and Ashley Woodward, eds., *Gilbert Simondon: Being and Technology* (2012; repr., Edinburgh: Edinburgh University Press, 2013); Muriel Combes, *Gilbert Simondon and the Philosophy of the Transindividual* [1999], trans. Thomas Lamarre (Cambridge, Mass.: MIT Press, 2013); see also Lamarre, "Afterword: Humans and Machines," in Combes, *Gilbert Simondon and the Philosophy of the Transindividual,* 79–108. In this book, I use as my base texts the French editions of most of the books that were originally published in that language. However, for quotations that are drawn from their standardized translations, I will refer to their English editions, unless otherwise stated.

2. The definition of "affect" in this book is based on Benedict de Spinoza, *Ethics* [1667], trans. G. H. R. Parkinson (Oxford, U.K.: Oxford University Press, 2000), 3P1CP2 (165–66) and 3P8–12 (171–74).

3. See Brian Massumi, *Ontopower: War, Powers, and the State of Perception* (Durham, N.C.: Duke University Press, 2015); Brian Massumi, *Politics of Affect* (Cambridge, U.K.: Polity Press, 2015); Erin Manning, *Relationscapes: Movement, Art, Philosophy* (Cambridge, Mass.: MIT Press, 2009); see also Deborah Levitt, *The Animatic Apparatus: Animation, Vitality, and the Futures of the Image* (Alresford, Hants: Zero Book, 2018).

4. Thomas Lamarre, *The Anime Ecology: A Genealogy of Television, Animation, and Game Media* (Minneapolis: University of Minnesota Press, 2018), 11–12.

5. Simondon, *Du mode d'existence des objets techniques*.

6. André Bazin, "Ontologie de l'image photographique" [1945], in *Qu'est-ce que le cinéma? 1. Ontologie et langage* (Paris: Éditions du Cerf, 1958), 18.

7. See Philip Rosen, *Change Mummified: Cinema, Historicity, Theory* (Minneapolis: University of Minnesota Press, 2001).

8. William Brown, *Supercinema: Film-Philosophy for the Digital Age* (New York: Berghahn, 2013); Shane Denson, *Discorrelated Images* (Durham, N.C.: Duke University Press, 2020), 3–17 and 21–50.

9. Lev Manovich, *The Language of New Media* (Cambridge, Mass.: MIT Press, 2001), 293–303.

10. Thomas Elsaesser, "Afterword—Digital Cinema and the Apparatus: Archaeologies, Epistemologies, Ontologies," in *Cinema and Technology: Cultures, Theories, Practices*, eds. Bruce Bennett, Marc Furstenau, and Adrian Mackenzie (Basingstoke: Palgrave Macmillan, 2008), 227–29.

11. Vivian Sobchack, "The Scene of the Screen: Envisioning Photographic, Cinematic, and Electronic 'Presence,'" in *Carnal Thoughts: Embodiment and Moving Image Culture* (Berkeley: University of California Press, 2004), 138–47; Laura Mulvey, *Death 24x a Second: Stillness and the Moving Image* (London: Reaktion Books, 2006); Mary Ann Doane, *The Emergence of Cinematic Time: Modernity, Contingency, the Archive* (Cambridge, Mass.: Harvard University Press, 2002); Laura Marks, *Touch: Sensuous Theory and Multisensory Media* (Minneapolis: University of Minnesota Press, 2002).

12. Lamarre, *The Anime Ecology*, 16–17; Levitt, *The Animatic Apparatus*.

13. Stanley Cavell, *The World Viewed, Enlarged Edition* (1971; repr., Cambridge, Mass.: Harvard University Press, 1979), 20, 72, 101–8, and 188; Markos Hadjioannou, *From Light to Byte: Toward an Ethics of Digital Cinema* (Minneapolis: University of Minnesota Press, 2012), 178–82. For a discussion of Cavell's theory and its pertinence to contemporary cinema and media, see D. N. Rodowick, *Elegy for Theory* (Cambridge, Mass.: Harvard University Press, 2014), 73–74.

14. Victor Fan, *Cinema Approaching Reality: Locating Chinese Film Theory* (Minneapolis: University of Minnesota Press, 2015), 40–41.

15. See note 8.

16. D. N. Rodowick, *Reading the Figural, or, Philosophy after the New Media* (Durham, N.C.: Duke University Press, 2001), 219–21; Sobchack, "The Scene of the Screen," 138–47.

17. This idea was "presaged" before the digital debate by Jean Baudrillard, *Simulacra and Simulation* [1981], trans. Sheila Faria Glaser (Ann Arbor,: University of Michigan Press, 1994). For a discussion of Baudrillard in relation to contemporary media, see Levitt, *The Animatic Apparatus*, 66–82.

18. Bernard Stiegler, *La technique et le temps,* in three volumes (1994, 1996, and 2001; repr. as a single volume, Paris: Fayard, 2018); Peter Sloterdijk, "Anthropo-Technology," *New Perspective Quarterly* 31, no. 1 (January 2014): 40–47; Peter Sloterdijk, *You Must Change Your Life: On Anthropotechnics,* trans. Wieland Hoban (2009; repr., Cambridge, U.K.: Polity Press, 2015).

19. Bernard Stiegler, *La Faute d'Épiméthée,* in *La technique et le temps,* 21–311; Gilbert Simondon, *Two Lessons on Animal and Man* [2004], trans. Drew S. Burk (Minneapolis: Univocal Publishing, 2011).

20. Gilbert Simondon, *L'individu et sa genèse physico-biologique* (1964; repr., Paris: Éditions Jérôme Millon, 1995), 30.

21. Ted Nannicelli and Malcolm Turvey, "Against Post-Cinema," *Cinéma et Cie: International Film Studies Journal,* nos. 26–27 (2016): 33–44.

22. Denson, *Discorrelated Images,* 54–56.

23. Yuk Hui, *On the Existence of Digital Objects* (Minneapolis: University of Minnesota Press, 2016), 3–21.

24. Deleuze, *Cinéma 1,* 83–84; see also his discussion prior to this point on 9–81. See also Deleuze, *Cinéma 2,* 203–91. The word *agencement* is translated by Brian Massumi as "assemblage" in Deleuze and Félix Guattari, *A Thousand Plateaus: Capitalism and Schizophrenia* [1980], trans. Massumi (Minneapolis: University of Minnesota Press, 1987; repr., London: Continuum International Publishing Group, [2004] 2012). Rodowick prefers to use the word "arrangement," which foregrounds its mobility and transience as a process; see *Reading the Figural,* 219–21.

25. Lamarre, "Afterword," 82–85.

26. Spinoza, *Ethics,* 1S11 (83–84).

27. Combes, *Gilbert Simondon and the Philosophy of the Transindividual,* 30.

28. Combes, *Gilbert Simondon and the Philosophy of the Transindividual,* 25–50.

29. Yen P'ei, "Genben bupai Fojiao yuanqi guan suo zhankai de qiji" [The turning point of the theory of dependent originations proposed by early sectarian Buddhisms], in *Fojiao de yuanqi guan* [On the concept of dependent originations in Buddhism] (1981; repr., Taipei: Tianhua chuban shiye, 1997), 34.

30. Thomas Elsaesser and Malte Hagener, *Film Theory: An Introduction through the Senses* (New York: Routledge, 2010), vii.

31. Hajime Tanabe, *Philosophy as Metanoetics* [1946], trans. Takeuchi Yoshinori, Valdo Viglielmo, and James W. Heisig (1986; repr., Nagoya: Chisokudō, 2016), 73; Thomé H. Fang, *Zhongguo Dasheng Foxue* [Chinese Mahāyāna Buddhism, 1974–75] (2012; repr., Beijing: Zhonghua shuju, 2014), 1:14.

32. For a history of the *Connected Discourses,* see Sujato, *A History of Mindfulness: How Insight Worsted Tranquillity in the Satipaṭṭhāna Sutta* (Taipei: Buddha Education Foundation, 2005; repr. Kerikeri: Santipada, 2012), 31–36. Huang Jiashu, Za ahan jing *xuanji* [*Saṃyuktāgama:* A selection], *suttas* trans. Guṇabhadra (1999; repr., Taipei: Buddhall, 2017), SA-298 (178). For dependent originations, see note 29; for the

Great Schism, see Buddhaghosa, *The Inception of Discipline, and the Vinaya Nidāna: Being a Translation and Edition of the Bāhiranidāna of Bucchaghosa's Samantapāsādikā*, Vinaya commentary by N. A. Jayawickrama (London: Luzac, 1962).

33. Fyodor Stcherbatsky, *Buddhist Logic* [1930–32] (1993; repr., Delhi: Motilal Banarsidass Publishers, 2008), 1:119–45.

34. Lydia Liu, *The Clash of Empires: The Invention of China in Modern World Making* (2004; repr., Cambridge, Mass.: Harvard University Press, 2006), 12–13. For translation studies of Buddhist texts, see Jiang Wu and Lucille Chia, eds., *Spreading Buddha's Word in East Asia: The Formation and Transformation of the Chinese Buddhist Canon* (New York: Columbia University Press, 2016).

35. Gayatri Chakravorty Spivak, "Translator's Preface," in Jacques Derrida, *Of Grammatology* [1967], trans. Spivak (1976; repr., Baltimore: Johns Hopkins University Press, 1997), xiv; see also Derrida, 62.

36. For a detailed discussion, see Fang, *Zhongguo Dasheng Foxue*, 1:24–28.

37. Dushun, *Zhu* Huayan *Fajie guanmen* [Methods of observing the dharma realms according to the *Avataṃsaka Sūtra*, with annotations], annotated by Fei Xiu, in the *Taishō Shinshū Daizōkyō* [*TSD*], ed. Takakusu Junjirō, et al. (Tokyo: *Taisho Tripitaka* Publication Association, 1924–34), 45, no. 1884.

38. William Edward Soothill and Lewis Hodous, *A Dictionary of Chinese Buddhist Terms* (London: Kegan Paul, Trench, Trubner, 1937).

39. Immanuel Kant, *Critique of Pure Reason: Unified Edition* [1781 and 1787], trans. Werner S. Pluhar (Indianapolis: Hackett Publishing, 1996).

40. Stcherbatsky, *Buddhist Logic*, volumes 1 and 2.

41. Shu-mei Shih, "Global Literature and the Technologies of Recognition," *PMLA* 119, no. 1, *Literatures at Large* (January 2004): 25–27.

42. Combes, *Gilbert Simondon and the Philosophy of the Transindividual*, 68.

43. Aijaz Ahmad, "Jameson's Rhetoric of Otherness and the 'National Allegory,'" in *Theory, Classes, Nations, Literatures* (London: Verso, 1992), 95–122; Gayatri Chakravorty Spivak, "Can the Subaltern Speak?," in *Marxism and the Interpretation of Culture*, eds. Cary Nelson and Lawrence Grossberg (Urbana: University of Illinois Press, 1988), 276–86. Ahmad's argument was a retort to Fredric Jameson, "Third-World Literature in the Era of Multinational Capitalism," *Social Text*, no. 15 (1986): 65–88.

44. Fan, *Cinema Approaching Reality*, 1–8 and 17–36.

45. Aaron Gerow, "Introduction: The Theory Complex," in *Decentering Theory: Reconsidering the History of Japanese Film Theory, Review of Japanese Culture and Society*, no. 22 (December 2010): 1–13.

46. Sheldon H. Lu, "Agitation or Deep Focus?: Early Chinese Film History and Theory," *Harvard Journal of Asiatic Studies* 76, nos. 1 and 2 (2016): 205–7.

47. Chen Kuan-hsing, *Asia as Method: Toward Deimperialization* (Durham, N.C.: Duke University Press, 2010), 211–56; Gayatri Chakravorty Spivak, *Other Asias* (Malden, Mass.: Blackwell Publishing, 2008).

48. Yamamoto Naoki, *Dialectics without Synthesis: Japanese Film Theory and Realism in a Global Frame* (Berkeley: University of California Press, 2020), 7–8.

49. Marc Steinberg and Alexander Zahlten, "Introduction," in *Media Theory in Japan*, eds. Steinberg and Zahlten (Durham, N.C.: Duke University Press, 2017), 1–5.

50. See the *Mahā Satipaṭṭhāna Sutta* (DN 22), in dhammatalks.org, https://www.dhammatalks.org/suttas/DN/DN22.html, accessed May 31, 2020.

51. I thank Haun Saussy for his insight in "Exquisite Cadavers Stitched from Fresh Nightmares: Of Memes, Hives, and Selfish Genes," in *Comparative Literature in an Age of Globalization,* ed. Saussy (Baltimore: Johns Hopkins University Press, 2006), 3–42.

52. Stcherbatsky, *Buddhist Logic,* 1:21–22; Asaṅga, *Yujiashi di lun* [*Yogācārabhūmi-śāstra* or *Discourse on the Stages of Yogic Practice*], trans. Xuanzang (Taipei: Buddha Educational Foundation, 2014), §9:16–20 (1:321–29); Huang Jiashu, Za ahan jing *daodu* [*Saṃyuktāgama:* A reading guide], *suttas* trans. Guṇabhadra (1999; repr., Taipei: Buddhall, 2006), SA-1–7 (253–56), 11 (262–63), 58 (264–67), 68 (278–79), 262 (281–85), 274 (292–93), 297 (295–96), 309 (299–300), 319 (302), 322 (304–5), 335 (308–9), 1171 (315–17), and 1173 (319–22); see also Nāgārjuna, *Dazhidulun* [*Mahāprajñāpāramitāśāstra* or *Great Treatise on the Perfection of Wisdom*], trans. Kumārajīva (Taipei: Shihua guoji gufen youxian gongsi, 2007), §5:35–36 (1:233–34).

53. Stcherbatsky, *Buddhist Logic,* 1:16–21.

54. Buddhaghosa, *The Inception of Discipline.*

55. Anālayo, *The Dawn of Abhidharma* (Hamburg: Hamburg University Press, 2014).

56. See note 52.

57. This term, *saṅkhāra/saṃskara,* also refers to transmigration, popularly known as reincarnation.

58. In this book, the singular form "consciousness" refers to our impression of a unified consciousness, whereas the plural forms "consciousnesses" or numbered "consciousnesses" refer to particular domains. This practice is customary in Buddhist studies.

59. Huang, Za ahan jing *daodu*, SA-293 (326–27), 296 (330–32), 300 (337–38), 364 (341–42), 373 (344–46), 388 (348), and 404 (353–54). For a modern discussion, see Stcherbatsky, *Buddhist Logic,* 1:119–45; Tam Shek-wing, *Sichong yuanqi shen borë* [*Four kinds of dependent originations and profound insight*] (2005; repr., Taipei: Buddhall, 2014); see also Yen P'ei, *Fojiao de yuanqi guan,* 1–32; Yin Shun, *Fofa gailun* [A basic discussion of Buddhist theories, 1949] (2010; repr., Beijing: Zhonghua shuju, 2016), 98–104.

60. Yin Shun, *Shuo Yiqieyou bu weizhu de lunshu yu lunshi zhi yanjiu* [*A study of the śāstras and philosophers of and related to the Sarvāstivāda*] (Taipei: Zhengwen chubanshe, 1968), 91–120.

61. *Kathāvatthu* [Points of controversy, dated circa 240 B.C.E.], ed., Arnold C. Taylor (London: Pali Text Society by H. Frowde, 1894–97), XII:264–71; this phrase can be found in many *suttas* in the *Connected Discourses*—see, for example, Huang, Za ahan jing *daodu,* SA-1 (253), my translation. In this book, all subsequent uncredited translations are mine, unless otherwise stated.

62. *Kathāvatthu* [Points of controversy].

63. Richard F. Gombrich, "How the Mahāyāna Began," in *The Buddhist Forum,* ed. Tadeusz Skorupski (London: School of Oriental and African Studies, 1990), 1:21–30; Donald S. Lopez Jr., "Authority and Orality in the Mahāyāna," *Numen* 42, no. 1 (1995): 21–47; David McMahan, "Orality, Writing and Authority in South Asian Buddhism: Visionary Literature and the Struggle for Legitimacy in the Mahayana," *History of Religions* 37, no. 3 (February 1998): 249–74; A. K. Warder, *Indian Buddhism* (1970; repr., Delhi: Motilal Banarsidass Publishers, 2004), 4–5.

64. Edward Conze, *Buddhist Wisdom Books: Containing* The Diamond Sutra *and* The Heart Sutra (London: George Allen and Unwin, 1958; repr., New York: Random House, 2001), 86; Conze's translation.

65. Nan Huai-chin, The Diamond Sutra *Explained* [lectures given in 1980; transcriptions first published in 2001], trans. Hue En (Pia Giammasi) (Florham Park, N.J.: Primordia Media, 2003), §2, 43; my emphasis.

66. Nan, The Diamond Sutra *Explained;* Za ahan jing [*Saṃyuktāgama*], in *TSD* 2, no. 99, SA-26 (142), 297 (177), 300–301 (179), 912 (483), 961 (515), and 1164 (656).

67. Yin Shun, Zhongguan lunsong *jiangji* [Lectures on the *Mūlamadhyamakakārikā*] (1952; repr., Taipei: Zhengwen chubanshe, 2014), §7 (142–72).

68. Nāgārjuna, *Dazhidulun.*

69. Yin Shun, Zhongguan lunsong *jiangji,* §17 (280–83).

70. Hong Xue, *Weishixue gailun* [Consciousness-only studies: A general introduction] (Chengdu: Bashu chubanshe, 2016), 8–23; Stcherbatsky, *Buddhist Logic,* 1:31–47.

71. Thich Nhat Hanh, "Fifty Verses on the Nature of Consciousness," in *Understanding Our Mind* (1989; repr., Berkeley, Calif.: Parallax Press, 2001), §16–21.

72. One of the best summaries of this theory can be found in Lo Shi-hin, *Weishi fangyu* [*Introduction to Yogācāra Buddhism*] (Hong Kong: Dharmalakṣaṇa Buddhist Institute, 2008).

73. Han Qingjing, *Dasheng* Apidamo jilun *bieshi* [An annotated anthology of discourses on the *Abhidharma-samuccaya* (Compendium of Abhidharma) of the Mahayana faith] (Hong Kong: Zhongguo Fojiao wenhua yanjiusuo, 1998), §1 (28); Yen P'ei, Jushe lunsong *jiangji* [Lectures on the *Abhidharmakośakārikā*] (Taichung: Zhonghua dadian bianyinhui, 1971), §4 (2:514–25).

74. The analogy of a roomful of dust comes from *Śūraṅgama Sūtra (Leng Yeng Ching)*, trans. Charles Luk (New Delhi: Munshiram Manoharlal Publishers, 2000), 22.

75. See Yin Shun, *Rulaizang zhi yanjiu* [A study of the Tathāgatagarbha] (Taipei: Zhengwen chubanshe, 1983).

76. Bodhi, "Mahā Kaccāna: Master of Doctrinal Exposition," Wheel Publication no. 405/406 (Kandy: Buddhist Publication Society, 1995), 1204 note 229; also see Kañukurunde Ñāṇananda, *Concept and Reality in Early Buddhist Thought: An Essay on* Papañca *and* Papañca-Saññā-Saṅkhā [1971] (Sri Lanka: Dharma Grantha Mudrana Bhāraya, 2012).

77. See note 31.

78. Ñāṇananda, *Concept and Reality in Early Buddhist Thought*, 5–6.

79. Bazin, "Ontologie de l'image photographique," 18.

80. See Deleuze, *Cinéma 1*, 173; Deleuze, *Expressionism in Philosophy: Spinoza* [1968], trans. Martin Joughin (New York: Zone Books, 1989), 89; see also Spinoza, *Ethics*, 1S11 (83–84).

81. Deleuze, *Cinéma 2*, 7–164; Henri Bergson, *L'Évolution créatrice* [1907] (Geneva: Éditions Albert Skira, 1940); Henri Bergson, *Matière et mémoire. Essai sur la relation du corps à l'esprit* (1939; repr., Paris: Presses Universitaires de France, 2019).

82. Deleuze, *Cinéma 1*, 87.

83. Deleuze, *Cinéma 2*, 109.

84. Fok To-fui, *Liuzu tanjing* [*Platform Sutra of the Sixth Patriarch*] (Hong Kong: The Dharmasthiti Group, 2015), §1 (111).

85. Nāgārjuna, *Dazhidulun*, §20 (2:863–906).

86. Among the works being discussed are Vivian Sobchack, *The Address of the Eye: A Phenomenology of Film Experience* (Princeton, N.J.: Princeton University Press, 1992); Gilbert Simondon, "Psychologie du cinéma (niédit)" (1960), in *Sur la technique (1953–1983)* (Paris: Presses Universitaires de France, 2014), 355–62; Stiegler, *La technique et le temps;* Massumi, *Ontopower;* and Massumi, *Politics of Affect.*

87. Tomonobu Imamichi, *Higashi nishi no tetsugaku* [Philosophies of East and West] (Tokyo: TBS-Britannica, 1981); Martin Heidegger, *Being and Time*, trans. John Macquarrie and Edward Robinson (San Francisco: HarperSanFrancisco, 1962), §64–65 (367–80); Fok, *Liiuzu tanjing*, §1 (111); Massumi, *Politics of Affect*, 160.

88. Richard Gombrich, "Buddhist Aesthetics?," *Journal of the Oxford Centre for Buddhist Studies* 5 (November 2013): 136.

89. Charles Sanders Peirce, *The Essential Peirce: Selected Philosophical Writings* (Bloomington: University of Indiana Press, 1998), 2:155, 191–95, 204–11, 226–42; Charles Sanders Peirce, *Pragmatism as a Principle and Method of Right Thinking: The 1903 Lectures on Pragmatism* (Albany: State University of New York Press, 1997), 199–201. See also, Massumi, *Ontopower*, 257 note 16.

90. See, for example, Shaku Soyen, "Arbitration Instead of War," in *The World's Parliament of Religions: An Illustrated and Popular Story of the World's First Parliament of Religions, Held in Chicago in Connection with the Columbian Exposition of 1893*, ed. John Henry Barrows (Chicago: Parliament Publishing Company, 1893), 2:1285; Shaku Soyen, "The Law of Cause and Effect as Taught by Buddha," in Barrows, ed., *The World's Parliament of Religions*, 2:829–31; see also Frederick Franck, ed., *The Buddha Eye: An Anthology of the Kyoto School and Its Contemporaries* (1982; repr., Bloomington, Ind.: World Wisdom, 2004).

91. See Yang Wenhui, *Deng budeng guan zalu* [On non-differentiation and differentiation] (Taipei: Xinwenfeng chuban gongsi, 1973); see also Ouyang Jian, *Faxiang zhulun xuhekan: Fodi jinglun xu* [An integrated study of the various *śāstras* of the Dharmakasana school: Introduction to the *Buddhabhūmi-sūtra-śāstra*] (Nanking: Zhina neixueyuan, 1920).

92. See Wang Guowei, *Wang Guowei meilun wenxuan* [Selected essays on aesthetics by Wang Guowei], ed. Liu Gangqiang (Changsha: Hunan renmin chubanshe, 1987); Chu Kuang-ch'ien, *Tan mei: Gei qingnian de di shisan feng xin* [On beauty: The thirteenth letter to youth] (1932; repr., Shanghai: Kaiming shudian, 1949); Chu, *Wenyi xinlixue* [Psychology of art and literature] (Shanghai: Kaiming shudian, 1936); Zong Baihua, *Meixue yu yijing* [Aesthetics and *yijing*] (Beijing: Renmin chubanshe, 1987); Lam Nin-tung, *Jing you* [Mirroring-journeying] (Hong Kong: Su Yeh Publications, 1985); see also Lam Nin-tung, "Zhongguo dianying de kongjian yishi" [The spatializing consciousness of Chinese cinema], *Zhongguo dianying yanjiu* [*An Interdisciplinary Journal of Chinese Film Studies*], no. 1 (1983): 58–85.

93. Giorgio Agamben, *State of Exception* [2003], trans. Kevin Attell (Chicago: University of Chicago Press, 2005).

94. *The Mahāvaṃsa*, trans. Wilhelm Geiger (London: H. Frowde, 1908), §25; Nāgārjuna, *Dazhidulun*, §12:1–49 (1:505–53).

1. MEONTOLOGY

1. André Bazin, "Ontologie de l'image photographique" and "Le mythe du cinéma total," in *Qu'est-ce que le cinéma? 1. Ontologie et langage* (Paris: Éditions du Cerf, 1958), 11–19 and 21–26.

2. I have already discussed the various ontological arguments proposed in relation to the digital debate in this book's introduction.

3. Bazin, "Ontologie de l'image photographique," 14–15 and 18.

4. Jean-Paul Sartre, *L'imaginaire: Psychologie phénoménologique de l'imagination* (Paris: Éditions Gallimard, 1940), 55–63; Dudley Andrew, *André Bazin* (New York: Oxford University Press, 1978), 70–73.

5. André Malraux, *Esquisse d'une psychologie du cinéma* (Paris: Gallimard, 1946; repr., Paris: Nouveau Monde, 2003); Andrew, *André Bazin*, 70–73. According to Andrew, the English translation was published as an essay.

6. Michel Foucault, *Power/Knowledge: Selected Interviews and Other Writings, 1927–1977,* ed. C. Gordon (New York: Pantheon Books, 1980), 194–96; qtd. Giorgio Agamben, "What Is an Apparatus" [2006], in *"What Is an Apparatus?" and Other Essays* [2008], trans. David Kishik and Stefan Pedatella (Stanford, Calif.: Stanford University Press, 2009), 2.

7. Shu-mei Shih, "Global Literature and the Technologies of Recognition," *PMLA* 119, no. 1, *Literatures at Large* (January 2004): 25–27.

8. Aijaz Ahmad, "Jameson's Rhetoric of Otherness and the 'National Allegory,'" in *Theory, Classes, Nations, Literatures* (London: Verso, 1992), 95–122; Gayatri Chakravorty Spivak, "Can the Subaltern Speak?," in *Marxism and the Interpretation of Culture,* eds. Cary Nelson and Lawrence Grossberg (Urbana,: University of Illinois Press, 1988), 276–86. Ahmad's argument was a retort to Fredric Jameson, "Third-World Literature in the Era of Multinational Capitalism," *Social Text,* no. 15 (1986): 65–88.

9. Kañukurunde Ñaṇananda, *Concept and Reality in Early Buddhist Thought: An Essay on* Papañca *and* Papañca-Saññā-Saṅkhā [1971] (Sri Lanka: Dharma Grantha Mudrana Bhāraya, 2012); Bodhi, "Mahā Kaccāna: Master of Doctrinal Exposition," Wheel Publication no. 405/406 (Kandy: Buddhist Publication Society, 1995), 1204 note 229.

10. Ñaṇananda, *Concept and Reality in Early Buddhist Thought,* 5–6.

11. Hajime Tanabe, *Philosophy as Metanoetics* [1946], trans. Takeuchi Yoshinori, Valdo Viglielmo, and James W. Heisig (1986; repr., Nagoya: Chisokudō, 2016), 73; Thomé H. Fang, *Zhongguo Dasheng Foxue* [Chinese Mahāyāna Buddhism, 1974–75] (2012; repr., Beijing: Zhonghua shuju, 2014), 1:14.

12. See notes 9 and 10.

13. See the discussion in the introduction.

14. For the history of the *Connected Discourses,* see Sujato, *A History of Mindfulness: How Insight Worsted Tranquillity in the Satipaṭṭhāna Sutta* (Taipei: Buddha Education Foundation, 2005; repr., Kerikeri: Santipada, 2012), 31–36. Huang Jiashu, *Za ahan jing xuanji* [*Saṃyuktāgama:* A selection], *suttas* trans. Guṇabhadra (1999; repr., Taipei: Buddhall, 2017), SA-298 (178). My translation refers to the definition offered by Yen P'ei, "Genben bupai Fojiao yuanqi guan suo zhankai de qiji" [The turning point of the theory of dependent originations proposed by early sectarian Buddhisms], in *Fojiao de yuanqi guan* [On the concept of dependent originations in Buddhism] (1981; repr., Taipei: Tianhua chuban shiye, 1997), 34. For the Great Schism, see Buddhaghosa, *The Inception of Discipline, and the Vinaya Nidāna: Being a Translation and Edition of the Bāhiranidāna of Bucchaghosa's Samantapāsādikā,* Vinaya commentary by N. A. Jayawickrama (London: Luzac, 1962).

15. Wei Yin, "Fojiao de yinguo lun" [Buddhist theory of dependent originations], in *Fojiao zhexue sixiang lunji* [Anthology of critical essays on Buddhist

philosophy], ed. Chang Man-t'ao (Taipei: Dasheng wenhua chubanshe, 1978), 1:218.

16. For the definition of an unmoved mover, see Aristotle, *Aristotle's Metaphysics*, trans. Joe Sachs (1999; repr., Santa Fe, N.M.: Green Lion Press, 2002), XII, 1072a.

17. V. V. Kobychev and S. B. Popov, "Constraints on the Photon Charge from Observations and Extragalactic Sources," *Astronomy Letters* 31, no. 3 (2005): 147–51; Matthew D. Schwartz, *Quantum Field Theory and the Standard Model* (Cambridge, U.K.: Cambridge University Press, 2014), 66.

18. Chi Fa, "Yinyuan lun" [On dependent originations], in *Fojiao genben wenti yanjiu* [Studies of the fundamental questions in Buddhism], ed. Chang Man-tao (Taipei: Dasheng wenhua chubanshe, 1978), 1:87 and 95–96; Yen P'ei, "Genben bupai Fojiao yuanqi guan suo zhankai de qiji," 45.

19. This piece of information is known to most cinematographers.

20. W. S. Boyle and G. E. Smith, "Charge Coupled Semiconductor Devices," *Bell System Technical Journal* 49, no. 4 (April 1970): 587–93.

21. P. A. Cheremkhin, V. V. Lesnichii, and N. V. Petrov, "Use of Spectral Characteristics of DSLR Cameras with Bayer Filter Sensors," *Journal of Physics: Conference Series*, no. 536 (2014): 2.

22. Gilbertt F. Amelio, "Charge-Coupled Devices," *Scientific American* 230, no. 2 (February 1974): 22–31.

23. See Neil R. Carlson, *Physiology of Behaviour, Eleventh Edition* (Upper Saddle River, N.J.: Pearson Education, 2013), 187–89; David Hubel, *Eye, Brain, and Vision* (New York: Scientific American Library, 1988); Semir Zeki, *A Vision of the Brain* (Oxford: Blackwell Scientific Publications, 1993).

24. See Lamberto Maffei and Adriana Fiorentini, "The Visual Cortex as a Spatial Frequency Analyser," *Vision Research* 13, no. 7 (July 1973): 1255–67; Kalanit Grill-Spector and Rafael Malach, "The Human Visual Cortex," *Annual Review of Neuroscience* 27 (2004): 649–77.

25. See note 24; see also J. Moran and R. Desimone, "Selective Attention Gates Visual Processing in the Extrastriate Cortex," *Science* 299, no. 4175 (August 23, 1985): 782–84; Charles D. Gilbert and Torsten N. Wiesel, "Receptive Field Dynamics in Adult Primary Visual Cortex," *Nature*, no. 356 (March 12, 1992): 150–52.

26. Chi Fa, "Yinyuan lun," 88.

27. Huang, Za ahan jing *xuanji*, SA-189, 196–97, 200, 212, 215, 231–33, 236, 249–50, 252, 254, 265, 273, 277, 304, 311, 334–35, 1172, 1774 (105–47); Asaṅga, *Yujiashi di lun* [*Yogācārabhūmi-śāstra* or *Discourse on the Stages of Yogic Practice*], trans. Xuanzang (Taipei: Buddha Educational Foundation, 2014), §9:16–20 (1:321–29); Nāgārjuna, *Dazhidulun* [*Mahāprajñāpāramitāśāstra* or *Great Treatise on the Perfection of Wisdom*], trans. Kumārajīva (Taipei: Shihua guoji gufen youxian gongsi, 2007), §5:35–36 (1:233–34). For a modern discussion, see Fyodor

Stcherbatsky, *Buddhist Logic* (1930–32) (1993; repr., Delhi: Motilal Banarsidass Publishers, 2008), 1:119–45; Tam Shek-wing, *Sichong yuanqi shen borë [Four kinds of dependent originations and profound insight]* (2005; repr., Taipei: Buddhall, 2014); Yen P'ei, *Fojiao de yuanqi guan,* 1–32; see also Yin Shun, *Fofa gailun* [A basic discussion of Buddhist theories, 1949] (2010; repr., Beijing: Zhonghua shuju, 2016), 98–104.

28. Ñaṇananda, *Concept and Reality in Early Buddhist Thought,* 5–6; Yin Shun, *Zhongguan lunsong jiangji* [Lectures on the *Mūlamadhyamakakārikā*] (1952; repr., Taipei: Zhengwen chubanshe, 2014), §17 (277).

29. See note 27.

30. Christian Metz, "The Imaginary Signifier," trans. Ben Brewster, *Screen* 16, no. 2 (Summer 1975): 48–50.

31. Vivian Sobchack, "What My Fingers Knew: The Cinesthetic Subject, or the Vision in the Flesh," in *Carnal Thoughts: Embodiment and Moving Image Culture* (Berkeley: University of California Press, 2004), 53–84.

32. See note 27.

33. Gilbert Simondon, "La mentalité technique" (1961), in *Sur la technique (1953-1983)* (Paris: Presses Universitaires de France, 2014), 299.

34. See note 6.

35. Gilles Deleuze, *Cinema 2: The Time-Image* [1985], trans. Hugh Tomlinson and Robert Galeta (1989; repr., Minneapolis: University of Minnesota Press, 2001), 27–28. As stated in note 1 of the introduction, the English edition is used here because the quotation is taken from it.

36. See *Kathāvatthu* [Points of controversy, dated circa 240 B.C.E.], ed. Arnold C. Taylor (London: Pali Text Society by H. Frowde, 1894–97), XII (264–71).

37. See the *Shelifu Apitan lun [Śāriputrābhidharma-śāstra]*, in *TSD* 25, no. 1548, §15 (144) and §25 (217).

38. Yin Shun, *Zhongguan lunsong jiangji,* §17 (280–83).

39. *Za ahan jing* [Saṃyuktāgama], in *TSD* 2, no. 99, SA-102 (59–61).

40. Ferdinand de Saussure, *Écrits de linguistique générale* (Paris: Éditions Gallimard, 2002), 25–45 and 82–83.

41. Dignāga, *Wuxiang si chen lun* [On the formlessness of sense data], in *Chen Na si lun* [The four *śāstras* by Dignāga], trans. Xuanzang (Nanking: Zhina neixueyuan, 1932), §1 (*Wu:* 1–4).

42. Dharmapāla, *The Netti-pakaraṇa: With Extracts from Dhammapāla's Commentary,* ed. E. Hardy (London: Oxford University Press, 1902).

43. Xuanzang, *Cheng weishi lun* [*Vijñapatimātratāsiddhi* or *Discourse on the Perfection of Consciousness-Only*], in *TSD* 31, no. 1585, §1 (1–2).

44. *Jie shenmi jing* [Saṃdhinirmocana *Sūtra* or *Sūtra of the Explanation of the Profound Secrets*], trans. Xuanzang (Putian: Guanghua si, 2010), §4 (138).

45. Stcherbatsky, *Buddhist Logic,* 1:115–18, 436–39, and 482–86; Henri Bergson, *L'Évolution créatrice* [1907] (Geneva: Éditions Albert Skira, 1940), 19–24.

46. Stcherbatsky, *Buddhist Logic,* 1:183.

47. Kuiji, *Bian* Zhongbian lun *shuji* [On the *Madhyāntavibhāgakārikā* or On the *Verses Distinguishing the Middle and the Extremes*] (Taipei: Xin wenfeng chuban gonsi, 1975).

48. William Brown, *Supercinema: Film-Philosophy for the Digital Age* (New York: Berghahn, 2013), 37–39; Lev Manovich, *The Language of New Media* (Cambridge, Mass.: MIT Press, 2001), 302 and 287–333, Manovich's emphasis.

49. See Shane Denson, *Discorrelated Images* (Durham, N.C.: Duke University Press, 2020); Markos Hadjioannou, *From Light to Byte: Toward an Ethics of Digital Cinema* (Minneapolis: University of Minnesota Press, 2012).

50. Brown, *Supercinema;* D. N. Rodowick, *Reading the Figural, or, Philosophy after the New Media* (Durham, N.C.: Duke University Press, 2001), 210–17; Vivian Sobchack, "The Scene of the Screen: Envisioning Photographic, Cinematic, and Electronic 'Presence,'" in *Carnal Thoughts,* 140–41.

51. Bazin, "Ontologie de l'image photographique," 15. In this book, I use my own translation of Bazin's original French text unless otherwise stated. This is because the Hugh Grey translation misses some nuances in the French text.

52. Aristotle, *Physics,* in *The Complete Works of Aristotle,* ed. Jonathan Barnes (Princeton, N.J.: Princeton University Press, 1984), 2§1 (329); qtd. Bernard Stiegler, Calif., *La technique et le temps,* in three volumes (1994, 1996, and 2001; repr. as a single volume, Paris: Fayard, 2018), 21.

53. Plato, *Ion,* trans. Paul Woodruff, in *Plato: Complete Works,* ed. John M. Cooper (Indianapolis: Hackett Publishing Company, 1997), 533d and 533e (941).

54. Giorgio Agamben, *The Man Without Content* [1994], trans. Georgia Albert (Stanford, Calif.: Stanford University Press, 1999), 72–73.

55. Sartre, *L'imaginaire,* 40.

56. Bazin, "Ontologie de l'image photographique," 11.

57. Bazin, "Ontologie de l'image photographique," 16.

58. Bazin, "Ontologie de l'image photographique," 11.

59. Roland Barthes, *Camera Lucida: Reflections on Photography* [1980], trans. Richard Howard (New York: Hill and Wang, 1981), 95.

60. Charles Sanders Peirce, "On a New List of Categories" [1867], in *Peirce on Signs: Writings on Semiotic by Charles Sanders Peirce,* ed. James Hoopes (Chapel Hill: University of North Carolina Press, 1991), 23.

61. Manovich, *The Language of New Media,* 302; Manovich's emphasis.

62. See Thomas Lamarre, *The Anime Machine: A Media Theory of Animation* (Minneapolis: University of Minnesota Press, 2009), 3–206; Thomas Lamarre, *The Anime Ecology: A Genealogy of Television, Animation, and Game Media* (Minneapolis: University of Minnesota Press, 2018); Thomas Lamarre, "From Animation to *Anime:* Drawing Movements and Moving Drawings," *Japan Forum* 14, no. 2 (2002): 329–67.

63. See Lamarre's discussions in *The Anime Machine* and in *The Anime Ecology.*

64. Metz, "The Imaginary Signifier," 51.

65. Sartre, *L'imaginaire*, 55–63.

66. Renyou, *Chenna xianliang lilun ji qi Hanchuan quanshi* [*Dignāga's Theory of Perception and Its Chinese Interpretations*] (Taipei: Dharma Drum Culture, 2015), 186–87.

67. Nan Huai-chin, The Diamond Sutra *Explained* [lectures given in 1980; transcriptions first published in 2001], trans. Hue En (Pia Giammasi) (Florham Park, N.J.: Primordia Media, 2003), §32 (303).

68. Pier Paolo Pasolini, "Cinema of Poetry," trans. Bill Nichols from the French version, trans. Marianne de Vettimo and Jacques Bontemps, in *Movies and Methods*, ed. Nichols (Berkeley: University of California Press, 1976), 1:544–45. Pasolini presented this paper with Christian Metz and Umberto Eco in the Mostra Internazionale del Nuovo Cinema. See Christian Metz, *Film Language: A Semiotics of the Cinema* [1968], trans. Michael Taylor (1974; repr., Chicago: University of Chicago Press, 1991), 62–72 and 114–16; see also Umberto Eco, "On the Contribution of Film to Semiotics," *Quarterly Review of Film Studies* 2, no. 1 (February 1977): 1–14.

69. Pasolini, "Cinema of Poetry," 1:555; Gilles Deleuze, *Cinéma 2. L'image-temps* (1985; repr., Paris: Éditions de Minuit, 2017), 42. Deleuze uses the term *cinemes* in place of stylemes.

70. Olga Solovieva, *Christ's Subversive Body: Practices of Religions Rhetoric in Culture and Politics* (Chicago: Northwestern University Press, 2017), 170–73.

71. Thomas Elsaesser, *Film History as Media Archaeology: Tracking Digital Cinema* (Amsterdam: Amsterdam University Press, 2016), 191–208.

72. Thomas Elsaesser, "The Mind-Game Film," in *Puzzle Film: Complex Storytelling in Contemporary Cinema*, ed. Warren Buckland (Malden, Mass.: Blackwell, 2009), 14–16. For a more elaborate discussion, see Elsaesser's posthumous monograph, *The Mind-Game Film: Distributed Agency, Time Travel, and Productive Pathology*, eds. Warren Buckland, Dana Polan, and Seung-hoon Jeong (New York: Routledge, 2021).

73. Elsaesser, "The Mind-Game Film," 22–25 and 32–33; Walter Benjamin, "The Work of Art in the Age of Its Technological Reproducibility: Second Version" (1936), in *Walter Benjamin: Selected Writings, Volume 3, 1935-1938*, trans. Edmund Jephcott, Howard Eiland, and others, eds. Eiland and Michael Jennings (Cambridge, Mass.: Belknap Press of Harvard University Press, 2002), 3:107–8. Elsaesser's concept is critiqued by David Bordwell in *The Way Hollywood Tells It: Story and Style in Modern Movies* (Berkeley: University of California Press, 2006), 7–9.

74. I wish to thank the London representatives of Heavenly Pictures for Bi Gan's biography and the production information.

75. This account is a summary of my observation in the IFFR in 2020. Regarding Bi Gan, see "Director's Q&A," Kino Lorber, 2018 Cannes Film Festival,

Cannes, 2018; see also Jiwei Xiao, "Creating a Cinema of Dream and Memory: An Interview with Bi Gan," *Cineaste* (Summer 2019): 17–21.

76. Luke Robinson, *Independent Chinese Documentary: From the Studio to the Street* (Basingstoke, U.K.: Palgrave Macmillan, 2013), 29. Robinson cites the following sources: Qiu Zhijie, "Xuyan: Zhongyaode shi xianchang" [Preface: The scene is what's important], in *Zhongyaode shi xianchang* [The scene is what's important] (Beijing: Renmin daxue chubanshe, 2003), 2; Wu Wenguang, *Jingtou xiang ziji de yanjing yiyang* [The camera is like my eye] (Shanghai: Shanghai wenyi chubanshe, 2001), 215; Wu Wenguang, "*Xianchang*: He jilu fangshi youguan de shu" [*Xianchang*: A book about documentary], in *Xianchang* [Document 1], ed. Wu Wenguang (Tianjin: Tianjin shehui kexueyuan chubanshe, 2000), 274; Zhang Zhen, "Introduction. Bearing Witness: Chinese Urban Cinema in the Era of 'Transformation,'" in *The Urban Generation: Chinese Cinema and Society at the Turn of the Twenty-First Century*, ed. Zhang (Durham, N.C.: Duke University Press, 2007), 20.

77. "Bi Gan: Wo ba dianying jiiao mianbi siguo" [Bi Gan: I call cinema a form of repentance], Wangyi, https://web.archive.org/web/20180317232140/; http://news.163.com/16/0714/02/BRTDCP0O00014Q4P.html (July 14, 2016), accessed February 25, 2020.

78. Denson, *Discorrelated Images*, 21–110; Yuk Hui, *On the Existence of Digital Objects* (Minneapolis: University of Minnesota Press, 2016), 75–105.

79. Lamarre, *The Anime Ecology*, 10–29.

2. THE KARMA-IMAGE

1. Sheng-yen is also the founder of the Zen monasteries and various institutions Dharma Drum in Jinshan, New Taipei City.

2. Sheng-yen, *Shengyan Fashi jiao mozhao chan* [*Master Sheng Yen Teaches* utkuṭuka-stha] (Taipei: Dharma Drum, 2004).

3. *Lengqie'abaduoluo baojing* [*Laṅkāvatāra Sūtra*], in *TSD* 16, no. 670, §4 (36–45).

4. See Fyodor Stcherbatsky, *Buddhist Logic* [1930–32] (1993; repr., Delhi: Motilal Banarsidass Publishers, 2008), 1:106–8.

5. Immanuel Kant, *Critique of Pure Reason: Unified Edition* [1781 and 1787], trans. Werner S. Pluhar (Indianapolis: Hackett Publishing, 1996), §4–8 (85–104); Henri Bergson, *L'Évolution créatrice* [1907] (Geneva: Éditions Albert Skira, 1940), 21–23.

6. Gilles Deleuze, *Cinéma 1. L'image-mouvement* (1983; repr., Paris: Éditions de Minuit, 2015), 20–22.

7. Gilles Deleuze, *Cinéma 2. L'image-temps* (1985; repr., Paris: Éditions de Minuit, 2017), 266–90.

8. Deleuze, *Cinéma 2*, 48–50.

9. Gilles Deleuze, *Cinema 1: The Movement-Image* [1983], trans. Hugh Tomlinson and Barbara Babberjam (1986; repr., Minneapolis: University of Minnesota Press, 2001), 11. As indicated in chapter 1, note 1, I refer to the English edition here because the quotation in the main text is taken from it. In the rest of this book, the French edition is indicated by the French word "*Cinéma*," whereas the English edition is indicated by the English word "*Cinema*."

10. Benedict de Spinoza, *Ethics* [1667], trans. G. H. R. Parkinson (Oxford, U.K.: Oxford University Press, 2000), 1S11 (83–84).

11. The term *prajñā* is usually translated as wisdom (that is, the ability to apprehend/be apprehended by *the way it is*), insight (that is, a glimpse of *the way it is*), or enlightenment (that is, the complete disconcealment of *the way it is* after ignorance has been removed). The term "insight" best fits the purpose here.

12. Huang Jiashu, Za ahan jing *xuanji* [*Saṃyuktāgama*: A selection], *suttas* trans. Guṇabhadra (1999; repr., Taipei: Buddhall, 2017), SA-1, 8, 9, 11, 13, 18, 22, 25, 29–30, 37, 42, 46, 53, 57, 60–61, 64, 72, 80, 103, 109, 260, 262, 265, 267, and 270 (39–102).

13. The term "classical Hollywood style" was first proposed by David Bordwell, Janet Staiger, and Kristin Thompson in *The Classical Hollywood Cinema: Film Style and Mode of Production to 1960* (New York: Columbia University Press, 1985). In this book, the "classical period" indicates Hollywood cinema from 1926 to 1960. This term was first contested by Miriam Hansen, in "The Mass Production of the Senses: Classical Cinema as Vernacular Modernism," *Modernism/Modernity* 6, no. 2 (1999): 59–77. Though Deleuze himself does not use the term "classical cinema," the kinds of films that Deleuze discusses in *Cinema 1* roughly correspond to Bordwell, Staiger, and Thompson's definition of "classical cinema." See Deleuze, *Cinéma 2,* 266–90.

14. D. N. Rodowick, *Gilles Deleuze's Time Machine* (Durham, N.C.: Duke University Press, 1997), 194–98.

15. Kant, *Critique of Pure Reason,* §4–6 (86–88).

16. Deleuze, *Cinéma 1,* 9–12.

17. Ervin S. Ferry, "Persistence of Vision," *American Journal of Science* 44, no. 261 (September 1892): 192.

18. Joseph Anderson and Barbara Anderson, "The Myth of Persistence of Vision Revisited," *Journal of Film and Video* 45, no. 1 (Spring 1993): 6–7; Max Wertheimer, "Experimental Studies on the Seeing of Motion," in *Classics in Psychology,* ed. Thorne Shipley (New York: Philosophical Library, 1961), 1076–77; Hugo Münsterberg, *The Photoplay: A Psychological Study* [1916]; repr., *The Film: A Psychological Study* (New York: Dover Publications, 1970), 2–26 and 29.

19. Anderson and Anderson, "The Myth of Persistence of Vision Revisited," 4–5; Peter Mark Roget, "Explanation of an Optical Deception in the Appearance

of the Spokes of a Wheel When Seen through Vertical Apertures," *Philosophical Transactions,* part 1 (1825): 131–40; Terry Ramsaye, *A Million and One Nights* (New York: Simon and Schuster, 1926); Arthur Knight, *The Liveliest Art* (New York: New American Library, 1957).

20. Kalanit Grill-Spector and Rafael Malach, "The Human Visual Cortex," *Annual Review of Neuroscience* 27 (2004): 649–77; Charles D. Gilbert and Torsten N. Wiesel, "Receptive Field Dynamics in Adult Primary Visual Cortex," *Nature,* no. 356 (March 12, 1992): 150–52; Lamberto Maffei and Adriana Fiorentini, "The Visual Cortex as a Spatial Frequency Analyser," *Vision Research* 13, no. 7 (July 1973): 1255–67; J. Moran and R. Desimone, "Selective Attention Gates Visual Processing in the Extrastriate Cortex," *Science* 299, no. 4175 (August 23, 1985): 782–84.

21. Anderson and Anderson, "The Myth of Persistence of Vision Revisited," 8–11; Paul Kolers, *Aspects of Motion Perception,* International Series of Monographs in Experimental Psychology, vol. 16 (New York: Pergamon Press, 1972), 39.

22. Deleuze, *Cinema 1,* 9.

23. *Za ahan jing* [Saṃyuktāgama], in *TSD* 2, no. 99, SA-79 (41).

24. Daoping, "Shijian zai Fofa shang xitong de yanjiu" [A systematic study of the Buddhist concepts of time], in *Fojiao zhexue sixiang lunji* [Anthology of critical essays on Buddhist philosophy], ed. Chang Man-t'ao (Taipei: Dasheng wenhua chubanshe, 1978), 2:244–50.

25. Yin Shun, *Zhongguan lunsong jiangji* [Lectures on the *Mūlamadhyamakakārikā*] (1952; repr., Taipei: Zhengwen chubanshe, 2014), §17 (280–83).

26. Yin Shun, *Zhongguan lunsong jiangji,* §19 (342–52).

27. Yin Shun, *Zhongguan lunsong jiangji,* §19 (350–52).

28. Deleuze, *Cinéma 1,* 23–45.

29. See note 13.

30. Christian Metz, *Film Language: A Semiotics of the Cinema* [1968], trans. Michael Taylor (1974; repr., Chicago: University of Chicago Press, 1991), 108–46.

31. Bordwell, Staiger, and Thompson, *The Classical Hollywood Cinema,* 1–84; David Bordwell, *Narration in the Fiction Film* (Madison: University of Wisconsin Press, 1985), 156–204.

32. See Rodowick, *Gilles Deleuze's Time Machine,* 121–210.

33. Gilles Deleuze, *Expressionism in Philosophy: Spinoza* [1968], trans. Martin Joughin (New York: Zone Books, 1989), 89; Spinoza, *Ethics,* 1S11 (83–84).

34. Deleuze, *Expressionism in Philosophy,* 93.

35. Deleuze, *Cinema 1,* 58–59, emphases in the original translation; Bergson, *L'Évolution créatrice,* 300–303; repr., Henri Bergson, *Matière et mémoire. Essai sur la relation du corps à l'esprit* (1939; repr., Paris: Presses Universitaires de France, 2019), 36.

36. Henri Bergson, *Matter and Memory,* trans. Nancy Margaret Paul and W. Scott Palmer (New York: Zone Books, 1988), 30.

37. Deleuze, *Cinema 1*, 60 and 64–65.

38. Deleuze, *Cinéma 1*, 145–72. Deleuze's theorization of the close-up is taken from Béla Balázs, *L'Esprit du cinéma* (1930; repr., Paris: Payot, 2011), 131 and 205. Meanwhile, his theorization of the long shot is based on Balázs, *Le cinéma. Nature et évolution d'un art nouveau* (1948; repr., Paris: Payot, 2011), 167. Rodowick, *Gilles Deleuze's Time Machine*, 65–66.

39. Deleuze, *Cinéma 1*, 173; *Cinema 1*, 123.

40. Deleuze, *Cinéma 1*, 196–265.

41. Deleuze, *Cinema 1*, 110–17; Robert Bresson, *Notes sur le cinématographe* (1975; repr., Paris: Gallimard, 1995), 95–96.

42. Rodowick, *Gilles Deleuze's Time Machine*, 64; Deleuze, *Cinema 1*, 102–3.

43. Kañukurunde Ñaṇananda, *Concept and Reality in Early Buddhist Thought: An Essay on* Papañca *and* Papañca-Saññā-Saṅkhā [1971] (Sri Lanka: Dharma Grantha Mudrana Bhāraya, 2012), 5–6.

44. Immanuel Kant, *Critique of the Power of Judgement* [1790], trans. Paul Guyer and Eric Matthews, ed. Guyer (Cambridge, U.K.: Cambridge University Press, 2000), §1–29 (1–159); Arthur Schopenhauer, *The World as Will and Presentation* [1818–19], trans. Richard E. Aquila (New York: Pearson Longman, 2008), Book 1, §1 (1:31).

45. Deleuze, *Cinéma 2*, 13.

46. Deleuze, *Cinema 1*, 218.

47. Bergson, *L'Évolution créatrice*, 101–10. For a discussion of Bergson's mysticism, see Sarah Cooper, *Soul of Film Theory* (New York: Palgrave Macmillan, 2013).

48. Yen P'ei, "Genben bupai Fojiao yuanqi guan suo zhankai de qiji" [The turning point of the theory of dependent originations proposed by early sectarian Buddhisms], in *Fojiao de yuanqi guan* [On the concept of dependent originations in Buddhism] (1981; repr., Taipei: Tianhua chuban shiye, 1997), 12–13.

49. Plotinus, *Enneads*, ed. Lloyd P. Gerson, trans. George Boys-Stones, John M. Dillon, Lloyd P. Gerson, R. A. H. King, Andrew Smith, and James Wilberding (Cambridge, U.K.: Cambridge University Press, 2018), 2:iv; qtd. Deleuze, *Expressionism in Philosophy*, 172.

50. *Śūraṅgama Sūtra (Leng Yeng Ching)*, trans. Charles Luk (New Delhi: Munshiram Manoharlal Publishers, 2000), 22. Here, I am using this *Sūtra* as a philosophical text. Its authenticity as a religious text, however, has been controversial. See Chang Man-tao, ed., *Dasheng qixin lun yu Lengyan jing kao bian* [On the historical authenticity of the *Awakening of Faith of the Mahāyāna* and the *Śūraṅgama Sūtra*] (Taipei: Dasheng wenhua chubanshe, 1978).

51. Stcherbatsky, *Buddhist Logic*, 1:530–31.

52. Stcherbatsky, *Buddhist Logic*, 1:533–34.

53. Up until this point, I have been using the term "impetus" to indicate this enduring force. In this particular section, however, I use the term "force"

(on the formal level) to differentiate it from the notion of "impetus" (on the technical level).

54. Han Qingjing, *Dasheng* Apidamo jilun *bieshi* [An annotated anthology of discourses on the *Abhidharma-samuccaya* (Compendium of Abhidharma) of the Mahayana faith] (Hong Kong: Zhongguo Fojiao wenhua yanjiusuo, 1998), §1 (28).

55. Yen P'ei, Jushe lunsong *jiangji* [Lectures on the *Abhidharmakośakārikā*] (Taichung: Zhonghua dadian bianyinhui, 1971), §4 (514–25).

56. Dharmapāla, *Dasheng guang* Bailun *shilun* [On the interpretations of the *Śataśāstra*], *TSD* 30, no. 1571, §6 (67–76).

57. Bhāviveka, *Dasheng changzhen lun* [On proving the emptiness of Madhyamaka], vol. 1, in *TSD* 30, no. 1578, §2 (12). For a summary of this debate, see Wan Chün, "Guanyu kong you de wenti" [On emptiness and existence], in Chang, ed., *Fojiao zhexue sixiang lunji,* 1:252–53.

58. Shantarakshita, *The Adornment of the Middle Way: Shantarakshita's Madhyamakalankara with Commentary by Jamgön Mipham,* trans. Padmakara Translation Group (Boston: Shambhala Publications, 2005), 386.

59. Plotinus, *Enneads,* 2:iv; qtd. Deleuze, *Expressionism in Philosophy,* 172.

60. *Jie shenmi jing* [*Saṃdhinirmocana Sūtra* or *Sūtra of the Explanation of the Profound Secrets*], trans. Xuanzang (Putian: Guanghua si, 2010), §4 (138).

61. See note 12. The term *ālaya*-consciousness is not used in the *Connected Discourses.*

62. Han, *Dasheng* Apidamo jilun *bieshi,* §1 (28).

63. Deleuze, *Cinema 1,* 218.

64. Han, *Dasheng* Apidamo jilun *bieshi,* §4 (158–59).

65. Han, *Dasheng* Apidamo jilun *bieshi,* §4 (159–63).

66. Han, *Dasheng* Apidamo jilun *bieshi,* §4 (161–63).

67. Metz, *Film Language,* 108–10.

68. See Susan Courtney, *Hollywood Fantasies of Miscegenation: Spectacular Narratives of Gender and Race, 1903-1967* (Princeton, N.J.: Princeton University Press, 2005).

69. Thierry Kuntzel, *Title TK. Notes, 1974-1992,* ed. Anne-Marie Duguet (Paris: Anarchive, 2006); Raymond Bellour, *Analyse du filim* (Paris: Albatros, 1979).

70. Viktor Shklovsky, *Theory of the Prose,* trans. Benjamin Sher (Normal, Ill.: Dalkey Archive Press, 1993).

71. See Sigmund Freud, *The Uncanny* [1919], in *The Uncanny,* trans. David McLintock (New York: Penguin, 2003), 121–62.

72. Richard Dyer, *White* (London: Routledge, 1997), 2–3.

73. Jacques Lacan, "Le stade du miroir comme formateur de la function du Je," in *Écrits I* (1966; repr., Paris: Éditions du Seuil, 1999), 92–99.

3. THE INSIGHT-IMAGE

1. D. N. Rodowick, *Gilles Deleuze's Time Machine* (Durham, N.C.: Duke University Press, 1997), 186–93 and 194–98.

2. Gilles Deleuze, *Cinema 2: The Time-Image* [1985], trans. Hugh Tomlinson and Robert Galeta (1989; repr., Minneapolis: University of Minnesota Press, 2001), 5–6. As stated in chapter 1, note 1, I use the French editions of Deleuze's books as my base texts, and I refer to the English editions whenever I quote directly from them. The French editions are indicated with the word "Cinéma," whereas the English editions are indicated with the word "Cinema."

3. Charles Sanders Peirce, "On a New List of Categories" [1867], in *Peirce on Signs: Writings on Semiotic by Charles Sanders Peirce*, ed. James Hoopes (Chapel Hill: University of North Carolina Press, 1991), 23.

4. Deleuze, *Cinema 2*, 17.

5. Henri Bergson, *Matière et mémoire. Essai sur la relation du corps à l'esprit* (1939; repr., Paris: Presses Universitaires de France, 2019), 114–16; qtd. Gilles Deleuze, *Cinéma 2. L'image-temps* (1985; repr., Paris: Éditions de Minuit, 2017), 62.

6. Deleuze, *Cinema 2*, 44; Deleuze's emphasis.

7. See note 5.

8. Bergson, *Matière et mémoire*, 116; Deleuze, *Cinema 2*, 56.

9. See Deleuze, *Cinéma 2*, 122 note 33; see also Clément Rosset, "Archives," *La Nouvelle Revue française*, no. 373 (February 1984): 80–84.

10. Deleuze, *Cinéma 2*, 67–68. I thank Maureen Turim for her comment on my reading of this film.

11. Deleuze, *Cinéma 2*, 67–68.

12. Ben McCann, Le Jour se lève: *French Film Guide* (London: I. B. Tauris, 2014), 108–109; see also Richard Dyer, "No Place for Homosexuality: Marcel Carné's *L'Air de Paris* (1954)," 2d ed., in *French Film: Texts and Contexts,* eds. Susan Hayward and Ginette Vincendeau (London: Routledge, 2000), 63–77.

13. Deleuze, *Cinema 2*, 68.

14. Han Qingjing, *Dasheng* Apidamo jilun *bieshi* [An annotated anthology of discourses on the *Abhidharma-samuccaya* (Compendium of Abhidharma) of the Mahayana faith] (Hong Kong: Zhongguo Fojiao wenhua yanjiusuo, 1998), §4 (158–59).

15. Deleuze, *Cinema 2*, 81.

16. Deleuze, *Cinema 2*, 294 note 22.

17. See Hoy-yan, Da Foding Shoulengyan jing *jiangji* [*Lectures on the Śūraṅgama Sūtra*] (Tainan: Heyu chubanshe, 2011), 253; Yuanynig, Da Foding Shoulengyan jing *jiangyi* [*Lecture notes on the Śūraṅgama Sūtra*] (Tainan: Heyu chubanshe, 2009), 154–59.

18. See note 16.

19. Melvin McLeod, "Love and Liberation," in *Courage and Compassion: A Thich Nhat Hanh Reader* (Plum Village, France: Lion's Roar, 2019), 5.

20. Deleuze, *Cinéma 2*, 246 and 274; here, Deleuze refers to the third chapter of Bergson, *Matière et memoir*, 147–98.

21. Deleuze, *Cinema 2*, 81.

22. Giorgio Agamben, *The Time that Remains: A Commentary on the Letter to the Romans* [2000], trans. Patricia Dailey (Stanford, Calif.: Stanford University Press, 2005), 59–87.

23. Fok To-fui, *Liuzu tanjing* [*Platform Sutra of the Sixth Patriarch*] (Hong Kong: The Dharmasthiti Group, 2015), §1 (111).

24. Deleuze, *Cinema 2*, 99–100.

25. Thomé H. Fang, "A Critical Exposition of the Bergsonian Philosophy of Life" (master's thesis, University of Wisconsin, Madison, 1922), 30–33; Bergson, *Matière et mémoire*, 81–146.

26. Thomé H. Fang, "Jiu yuanqi lun tan Zhongguo Dasheng Foxue sixiang yanbian guocheng zhong yanzhong de yinan" [On the most serious conundrum in the evolution of Chinese Mahāyāna philosophy based on the theory of dependent originations], in *Fojiao zhexue sixiang lunji* [Anthology of critical essays on Buddhist philosophy], ed. Chang Man-t'ao (Taipei: Dasheng wenhua chubanshe, 1978), 1:319–96.

27. Tiago de Luca and Nuno Barradas Jorge, "Introduction: From Slow Cinema to Slow Cinemas," in *Slow Cinema*, eds. De Luca and Jorge (Edinburgh: Edinburgh University Press, 2016), 2.

28. Mary Ann Doane, *The Emergence of Cinematic Time: Modernity, Contingency, the Archive* (Cambridge, Mass.: Harvard University Press, 2002), 160 and 163; qtd. De Luca and Jorge, "Introduction," 5.

29. *Mahā Satipaṭṭhāna Sutta* (DN 22), §1, in dhammatalks.org, https://www.dhammatalks.org/suttas/DN/DN22.html, accessed May 31, 2020.

30. Deleuze, *Cinema 2*, 100; Louis Hjelmslev, *Prolégomènes à une théorie du langage* (Paris: Éditions de Minuit, 1968), 85. Here, Deleuze refers to *Matière et mémoire*, 181–89.

31. William James, *The Principles of Psychology* (New York: H. Holt, 1890), 2:611 and 629–30; here, he refers to E. R. Clay, *The Alternative: A Study in Psychology* (London: Macmillan and Co., 1882), 151. For a discussion of this concept, see David Lapoujade, *William James: Empiricism and Pragmatism* [1997], trans. Thomas Lamarre (Durham, N.C.: Duke University Press, 2020), 17 and 38.

32. Fang, "Jiu yuanqi lun," 1:319–96.

33. Alain Robbe-Grillet, *L'Année dernière à Marienbad* (Paris: Minuit, 1961).

34. Deleuze, *Cinema 2*, 123.

35. Brian Massumi, *Politics of Affect* (Cambridge, U.K.: Polity Press, 2015), 53; Brian Massumi, *Ontopower: War, Powers, and the State of Perception* (Durham, N.C.: Duke University Press, 2015), 66.

36. Foon Tsai, *Liuzu tanjing jiangyi* [Lectures on the *Liuzu tanjing*], Hong Kong Buddhist Youth Association, Hong Kong, September–October 2018, 16–23.

37. Sheng-yen, *Wufa zhi fa* [*The Method of No-Method*, 2008], trans. Shan Dexing (Beijing: Zhongguo youyi chubanshe, 2016), 60; Thich Nhat Hanh, *Zhengnian de qiji* [*The Miracle of Mindfulness: An Introduction to the Practice of Meditation*, 1975], trans. He Ting-chao (Taipei: Oak Tree Publishing, 2003), 150.

38. Charles Sanders Peirce, *The Essential Peirce: Selected Philosophical Writings* (Bloomington: University of Indiana Press, 1998), 2:155, 191–95, 204–11, 226–42; Charles Sanders Peirce, *Pragmatism as a Principle and Method of Right Thinking: The 1903 Lectures on Pragmatism* (Albany: State University of New York Press, 1997), 199–201; Massumi, *Ontopower*, 257 note 16. Massumi also refers to Alfred North Whitehead, *Process and Reality: Corrected Edition* (New York: The Free Press, 1978).

39. Xuanzang, *Cheng weishi lun* [*Vijñapatimātratāsiddhi or Discourse on the Perfection of Consciousness-Only*], in *TSD* 31, no. 1585, §8 (56–63).

40. Xuanzang, *Cheng weishi lun,* §8 (56–63).

41. Nāgārjuna, *Dazhidulun* [*Mahāprajñāpāramitāśāstra or Great Treatise on the Perfection of Wisdom*], trans. Kumārajīva (Taipei: Shihua guoji gufen youxian gongsi, 2007), §26 (2:1136–37).

42. Robert Barnett, "Documentaries by Tibetans in Tibet: The Digital Era," in *Latse Journal,* no. 7 (2011–12): 48; Tenzing Sonam, "Quiet Storm: Pema Tseden and the Emergence of Tibetan Cinema," in *Latse Journal,* no. 7 (2011–12): 36; Tsering Shakya, "*Old Dog (Khyi rgan)* Directed by Pema Tseden and *The Sun-Beaten Path (Dbus Lam Gyi Nyi Ma)* Directed by Sonthar Gyal," http://lhakardi aries.com/2011/11/30/old-dog-khyi-rgan-directed-by-pema-tsetan-the -sun-beaten-path-dbus-lam-gyi-nyi-ma-directed-by-sonthar-gyal/, accessed March 20, 2015; Dan Smyer Yu, "Pema Tseden's Transnational Cinema: Screening a Buddhist Landscape of Tibet," *Contemporary Buddhism: An Interdisciplinary Journal* 15, no. 1 (2014): 126.

43. Tenzing, "Quiet Storm," 37–38 and 41–44.

44. Tsering, "*Old Dog (Khyi rgan).*"

45. Smyer Yu, "Pema Tseden's Transnational Cinema," 126; Wai-Ping Yau, "Reading Pema Tseden's Films as Palimpsests," *Journal of Chinese Cinemas* 10, no. 2 (2016): 120–34; Ahup Grewal, "Contested Tibetan Landscapes in the Films of Pema Tseden," *Journal of Chinese Cinemas* 10, no. 2 (2016): 135–49; Kwai-Cheung Lo, "Buddha Found and Lost in the Chinese Nation of 'Diversity in Unity': Pema Tseden's Films as a Buddhist Mode of Reflexivity," *Journal of Chinese Cinemas* 10, no. 2 (2016): 150–65.

46. Smyer Yu, "Pema Tseden's Transnational Cinema," 139.

47. Yau, "Reading Pema Tseden's Films as Palimpsests," 120. Here, Yau uses the term "dichotomies" instead of "differences." Nonetheless, if we follow the way in which the idea of the palimpsest was discussed by Derrida, "differences" would be a more proper term. See Jacques Derrida, *Of Grammatology* [1967], trans.

Gayatri Chakravorty Spivak (1976; repr., Baltimore: Johns Hopkins University Press, 1997).

48. Grewal, "Contested Tibetan Landscapes in the Films of Pema Tseden," 139.

49. For desubjectivization, see *Vacarme*, " 'I Am Sure That You Are More Pessimistic than I Am . . .': An Interview with Giorgio Agamben," trans. Jason Smith, *Rethinking Marxism* 16, no. 2 (April, 2004): 115–24.

50. Teresa de Lauretis, *Technologies of Gender* (Bloomington: Indiana University Press, 1987), 1–30; Shu-mei Shih, "Global Literature and the Technologies of Recognition," *PMLA* 119, no. 1: *Literatures at Large* (January 2004): 17.

51. Lam Nin-tung, "Zhongguo dianying de kongjian yishi" [The spatializing consciousness of Chinese cinema], *Zhongguo dianying yanjiu* [*An Interdisciplinary Journal of Chinese Film Studies*], no. 1 (1983): 19–23; see also Victor Fan, "Mirroring-Drifting—Lam Nin-tung and Film Aesthetics," *Asian Cinema* 27, no. 1 (2016): 39.

52. Fan, conversation with Pema Tseden, Hong Kong Baptist University, Hong Kong, 2018. I thank Jessica Yeung for her invitation.

53. Chris Berry, "Pema Tseden and the Tibetan Road Movie: Space and Identity beyond the 'Minority Nationality Film,' " *Journal of Chinese Cinemas* 10, no. 2 (2016): 94.

54. Mao Zedong, "Wei renmin fuwu" [Serve the people], in *Mao Zhuxi yu lu* [*Quotations of Mao Zedong*], ed. People's Liberation Army General Political Department (1965; repr., Guangzhou: Guangdong Xinhua yinshuachang, 1966), 149; Mao Tse-tung, "Serve the People" (September 8, 1944) in *Quotations of Mao Zedong* (1967), September 2, 2016, https://www.marxists.org/reference/archive/mao/selected-works/volume-3/mswv3_19.htm#bm2, accessed April 4, 2020. This speech was originally given on September 8, 1944, in the memorial for Zhang Side given by the Central Military Commission; see "Wei renmin fuwu" [Serve the people], in *Mao Zedong xuanji* [Selected essays by Mao Zedong] (1960; repr., Beijing: Remin chubanshe, 1991), 1004.

55. Fan, conversation with Pema Tseden.

56. Yau, "Reading Pema Tseden's Films as Palimpsests," 132.

57. Berry, "Pema Tseden and the Tibetan Road Movie," 94; Yau, "Reading Pema Tseden's Films as Palimpsests," 133.

58. Tenzing, "Quiet Storm," 37–38 and 41–44.

59. Victor Fan, *Extraterritoriality: Locating Hong Kong Cinema and Media* (Edinburgh: Edinburgh University Press, 2019).

60. *Vacarme*, " 'I Am Sure That You Are More Pessimistic than I Am . . . ,' " 115–24.

61. Mao Zedong, "Wei renmin fuwu," 149; Mao Tse-tung, "Serve the People."

4. CINEMA ECOLOGY

1. Melvin McLeod, "Love and Liberation," *Courage and Compassion: A Thich Nhat Hanh Reader* (Plum Village, France: Lion's Roar, 2019), 5.

2. These seven attachments are enumerated in Xuanzang's translation of the *Diamond Sutra*. See Lo Shi-hin, Nengduan jingang borë boluo miduo jing zuanshi • Borë boluomiduo xin jing *jianglu* [*Vajracchedikā Prajñāpāramitā Sūtra: A revised edition with interpretation • Prajñāpāramitā Hṛdaya sūtra: Lectures*] (Hong Kong: Dharmalakshana Buddhist Institute, 2007), 44.

3. Ching-kung, Liuzu tanjing *jiangji* [Lectures on the *Platform Sutra*, 1981], ed. Ch'iu Shu-chen (Taipei: Huazang Jingzong xuehui, 2019), 165.

4. Vivian Sobchack, "The Scene of the Screen: Envisioning Photographic, Cinematic, and Electronic 'Presence,'" in *Carnal Thoughts: Embodiment and Moving Image Culture* (Berkeley: University of California Press, 2004), 138–47; William Brown, *Supercinema: Film-Philosophy for the Digital Age* (New York: Berghahn, 2013); Shane Denson, *Discorrelated Images* (Durham, N.C.: Duke University Press, 2020).

5. Brian Massumi, *Politics of Affect* (Cambridge, U.K.: Polity Press, 2015), 53; Brian Massumi, *Ontopower: War, Powers, and the State of Perception* (Durham, N.C.: Duke University Press, 2015).

6. Nāgārjuna, *Dazhidulun* [*Mahāprajñāpāramitāśāstra* or *Great Treatise on the Perfection of Wisdom*], trans. Kumārajīva (Taipei: Shihua guoji gufen youxian gongsi, 2007), §20 (2:863–906).

7. Jean-Pierre Meunier, "Part I, *The Structures of the Film Experience: Filmic Identification*" [1969], trans. Daniel Fairfax, in *The Structures of the Film Experience by Jean-Pierre Meunier: Historical Assessments and Phenomenological Expansions*, eds. Julian Hanich and Fairfax (Amsterdam: Amsterdam University Press, 2019), 46–48; Maurice Merleau-Ponty, *Phenomenology of Perception*, trans. Donald A. Landes (London: Routledge, 2012), xx; Angelo Hesnard, *Psychanalyse du lien interhumain* (Paris: Presses Universitaires Françaises, 1957), 26–27.

8. Jean-Paul Sartre, *L'imaginaire. Psychologie phénoménologique de l'imagination* (Paris: Éditions Gallimard, 1940), 44–45; this argument is adopted by André Bazin, "Théâtre et cinéma" [June–July 1951], in *Qu'est-ce que le cinéma? II. Le cinéma et les autres arts* (1959; repr., Paris: Éditions du cerf, 1969), 93–96.

9. Meunier calls this our three attitudes of identification; see *The Structures of the Film Experience*, 38–68.

10. Henri Bergson, *Matière et mémoire. Essai sur la relation du corps à l'esprit* (1939; repr., Paris: Presses Universitaires de France, 2019), 19–21.

11. Meunier, *The Structures of the Film Experience*, 123; qtd. Vivian Sobchack, "'Me, Myself, and I': On the Uncanny in Home Movies," in Hanich and Fairfax, eds., *The Structures of the Film Experience by Jean-Pierre Meunier*, 206.

12. Vivian Sobchack, *The Address of the Eye: A Phenomenology of Film Experience* (Princeton, N.J.: Princeton University Press, 1992), 4.

13. Maurice Merleau-Ponty, *The Visible and the Invisible*, ed. Claude Lefort, trans. Alphonso Lingus (Evanston, Ill.: Northwestern University Press, 1968), 155; qtd. Sobchack, *The Address of the Eye*, 4.

14. Sobchack, *The Address of the Eye*, 3 and 11.

15. Gilles Deleuze, *Cinema 1: The Movement-Image*, trans. Hugh Tomlinson and Barbara Babberjam (1986; repr., Minneapolis: University of Minnesota Press, 2001), 57.

16. Vivian Sobchack, "From Screen-Scape to Screen-Sphere: A Meditation in Medias Res," in *Screens: From Materiality to Spectatorship*, eds. Dominique Chateau and José Moure (Amsterdam: Amsterdam University Press, 2016), 157–75.

17. Shane Denson, *Discorrelated Images* (Durham, N.C.: Duke University Press, 2020), 21–72.

18. Gilbert Simondon, "Psychasociologie du cinéma (niédit)" (1960), in *Sur la technique (1953–1983)* (Paris: Presses Universitaires de France, 2014), 356.

19. Gilbert Simondon, "Anthropo-technologie (inédit)" (1961), in *Sur la technique*, 368.

20. Gilbert Simondon, "Objet technique et conscience modern (inédit)" (1961), in *Sur la technique*, 364; Simondon's emphasis.

21. Kañukurunde Ñaṇananda, *Concept and Reality in Early Buddhist Thought: An Essay on* Papañca *and* Papañca-Saññā-Saṅkhā [1971] (Sri Lanka: Dharma Grantha Mudrana Bhāraya, 2012), 5–6.

22. Bernard Stiegler, *La technique et le temps*, in three volumes (1994, 1996, and 2001; repr. as a single volume, Paris: Fayard, 2018), 782–83.

23. Walter Benjamin, "The Work of Art in the Age of Its Technological Reproducibility: Second Version" [1936], in *Walter Benjamin: Selected Writings, Volume 3, 1935–1938*, trans. Edmund Jephcott, Howard Eiland, and others, eds. Eiland and Michael Jennings (Cambridge, Mass.: Belknap Press of Harvard University Press, 2002), 3:107–8.

24. Bernard Stiegler, *Technics and Time, 3: Cinematic Time and the Question of Malaise* [2001], ed. Stephen Barker (Stanford, Calif.: Stanford University Press, 2011), 59.

25. Theodor Adorno and Max Horkheimer, *La dialectique de la raison* [1947] (Paris: Gallimard, 1974).

26. Stiegler, *La technique et le temps*, 682–738.

27. Stiegler, *La technique et le temps*, 801–42.

28. Peter Sloterdijk, *Critique of Cynical Reason* [1983], trans. Michael Eldred (Minneapolis: University of Minnesota Press, 1987); Peter Sloterdijk, *You Must Change Your Life: On Anthropotechnics*, trans. Wieland Hoban (2009; repr., Cambridge, U.K.: Polity Press, 2015), 281–84.

29. Peter Sloterdijk, "Anthropo-Technology," *New Perspective Quarterly* 31, no. 1 (January 2014): 41.

30. Benedict de Spinoza, *Ethics* [1667], trans. G. H. R. Parkinson (Oxford, U.K.: Oxford University Press, 2000), 3P1C (165–66).

31. Spinoza, *Ethics*, 3P2 (166).

32. Spinoza, *Ethics*, 3P8–12 (171–74).

33. Brian Massumi, *Politics of Affect* (Cambridge, U.K.: Polity Press, 2015), 48–51.

34. *Mahā Satipaṭṭhāna Sutta* (DN 22), §A4, in dhammatalks.org, https://www.dhammatalks.org/suttas/DN/DN22.html, accessed May 31, 2020.

35. *Mahā Satipaṭṭhāna Sutta*, §B.

36. See Thich Nhat Hanh, *Zhengnian de qiji* [*The Miracle of Mindfulness: An Introduction to the Practice of Meditation*, 1975], trans. He Ting-chao (Taipei: Oak Tree Publishing, 2003), 149–50; Miaojing, *Sinianchu jiangji* [*Lectures on the Satipaṭṭhāna*] (Hong Kong: Buddhist Youth Association, 2017), 33–43.

37. *Mahā Satipaṭṭhāna Sutta*, §D2 and D5b; Miaojing, *Sinianchu jiangji*, 44–58.

38. This final part is not from the Theravādin tradition, but is taken from the *Jie shenmi jing* [*Saṃdhinirmocana Sūtra*, or *Sūtra of the Explanation of the Profound Secrets*], trans. Xuanzang (Putian: Guanghua si, 2010), §4 (138); this is also the teaching explicated by Thich Nhat Hanh, *Xin ru yimu tian* [*Understanding Our Mind: 50 Verses on Buddhist Psychology*], trans. Guanxingzhe (Taipei: Oak Tree Publishing, 2017).

39. Massumi, *Politics of Affect*, 206–8.

40. Massumi, *Politics of Affect*, 53; Massumi, *Ontopower*, 66.

41. Foon Tsai, Liuzu tanjing jiangyi [*Lectures on the Liuzu tanjing*], Hong Kong Buddhist Youth Association, Hong Kong, September–October 2018, 16–23; Sheng-yen, *Wufa zhi fa* [*The Method of No-Method*, 2008], trans. Shan Dexing (Beijing: Zhongguo youyi chubanshe, 2016), 60; Thich Nhat Hanh, *Zhengnian de qiji*, 150; Charles Sanders Peirce, *The Essential Peirce: Selected Philosophical Writings* (Bloomington: University of Indiana Press, 1998), 2:155, 191–95, 204–11, 226–42; Charles Sanders Peirce, *The Essential Peirce: Selected Philosophical Writings* (Bloomington: University of Indiana Press, 1998), 199–201; Massumi, *Ontopower*, 257 note 16.

42. Erin Manning, *Relationscapes: Movement, Art, Philosophy* (Cambridge, Mass.: MIT Press, 2009), 23–24.

43. Martin Heidegger, *Being and Time*, trans. John Macquarrie and Edward Robinson (San Francisco: HarperSanFrancisco, 1962), §64 (367).

44. Heidegger, *Being and Time*, §64 (368).

45. Heidegger, *Being and Time*, §65 (370).

46. Heidegger, *Being and Time*, §65 (371–80).

47. Imamichi Tomonobu, *Higashi nishi no tetsugaku* [Philosophies of East and West] (Tokyo: TBS-Britannica, 1981), 67.

48. Fok To-fui, *Liuzu tanjing* [*Platform Sutra of the Sixth Patriarch*] (Hong Kong: The Dharmasthiti Group, 2015), §1 (111).

49. Nan Huai-chin, The Diamond Sutra *Explained* [lectures given in 1980; transcriptions first published in 2001], trans. Hue En (Pia Giammasi) (Florham Park, N.J.: Primordia Media, 2003), §18 (203).

50. *The Śūraṅgama Sūtra: A New Translation*, trans. Buddhist Text Translation Society (Ukiah, Calif.: Buddhist Text Translation Society, 2009), 74. Although the Charles Luk translation I have used in the previous chapters is considered the authoritative English edition, the new Californian translation is clearer in this specific passage.

51. Massumi, *Politics of Affect*, 160; Muriel Combes, *Gilbert Simondon and the Philosophy of the Transindividual* [1999], trans. Thomas Lamarre (Cambridge, Mass.: MIT Press, 2013), 32–38 and 112.

52. Thich Nhat Hanh, *Zhengnian de qiji*, 160–64.

53. Massumi, *Ontopower*; Massumi, *Politics of Affect*, 64.

54. Karl Marx and Friedrich Engels, *The German Ideology: Parts 1 and 3* (1832) (1939; repr., New York: International Publishers, Inc., 2011), 27–43.

55. See Victor Fan, *Cinema Approaching Reality: Locating Chinese Film Theory* (Minneapolis: University of Minnesota Press, 2015), 43–74; Thomas Lamarre, *The Anime Ecology: A Genealogy of Television, Animation, and Game Media* (Minneapolis: University of Minnesota Press, 2018), 12–21; Stiegler, *La technique et le temps*, 636.

56. Massumi, *Politics of Affect*, 116–17.

57. Judith Butler, *Gender Trouble: Feminism and the Subversion of Identity* (New York: Routledge, 1999), 163–80.

58. See note 51.

59. Massumi, *Politics of Affect*, 58.

60. Lamarre, *The Anime Ecology*, 10–21.

61. Mouloud Boukala, *Le dispositif cinématographique, un processus pour [re] penser l'anthropologie* (Paris: Téraèdre, 2009), 50–52. See Jean-Louis Baudry, "Le Dispositif," *Communications*, no. 23 (1975), *Psychanalyse et cinema*: 56–72; Christian Metz, "The Imaginary Signifier," trans. Ben Brewster, *Screen* 16, no. 2 (Summer 1975): 14–76; Jacques Aumont, *L'image* (Paris: Nathan 2000), 101.

62. Stiegler, *La technique et le temps*, 631–79.

63. Francesco Casetti, *The Lumière Galaxy: 7 Key Words for the Cinema to Come* (New York: Columbia University Press, 2015), 3–4.

64. Casetti, *The Lumière Galaxy*, 81–85; Stanley Cavell, *The World Viewed, Enlarged Edition* (1971; repr., Cambridge, Mass.: Harvard University Press, 1979), 20, 72, 101–8, and 188.

65. Yuk Hui, *Recursivity and Contingency* (London: Rowman and Littlefield, 2019), 9–10.

66. Manning, *Relationscapes*, 24; Markos Hadjioannou, *From Light to Byte: Toward an Ethics of Digital Cinema* (Minneapolis: University of Minnesota Press, 2012), 177–209.

67. Massumi, *Politics of Affect*, 58.

68. Massumi, *Politics of Affect*, 112–16.

69. Nāgārjuna, *Dazhidulun* [*Mahāprajñāpāramitāśāstra* or *Great Treatise on the Perfection of Wisdom*], trans. Kumārajīva (Taipei: Shihua guoji gufen youxian gongsi, 2007), §31 (2:1331–93); Yen P'ei, *Jushe lunsong jiangji* [Lectures on the *Abhidharmakośakārikā*] (Taichung: Zhonghua dadian bianyinhui, 1971), §5 (2:736–38); *Apidamo Dapiposha lun* [*Abhidharma Mahāvibhāṣa Śāstra*], trans. Xuanzang, in *TSD* 27, no. 1545, §104 (721–27); Dharmatrāta, *Za Apitan xin lun* [*Sajyuktābhidharma-hrdaya śāstra*], trans. Samghavarman, in *TSD* 28, no. 1552, §8; Xuanzang, *Cheng weishi lun* [*Vijñapatimātratāsiddhi* or *Discourse on the Perfection of Consciousness-Only*], in *TSD* 31, no. 1585, §1 (2); Fabao, *Jushe lun shu* [Commentaries on the *Abhidharmakośakārikā*], in *TSD* 41, no. 1822, §19 (358–413); Zhiyan, ed., *Huayan jing neizhang mendeng Kongmu zhang*, in *TSD* 45, no. 1870, §3 (35–56); Yang Jie, *Zong jing lu* [*On the citta as mirror*], in *TSD* 48, no. 2016, §39 (344–51).

70. Teresa de Lauretis, "Film and the Visible," in *How Do I Look?: Queer Film and Video*, ed. Bad Object-Choices (Seattle: Bay Press, 1991), 223.

71. Earl Jackson Jr., *Strategies of Deviance: Studies in Gay Male Representation* (Durham, N.C.: Duke University Press, 1995), 1–3.

72. Richard Fung, "Looking for My Penis: The Eroticized Asian in Gay Video Porn," in Bad Object-Choices, ed., *How Do I Look?*, 145–68; Kobena Mercer, "Skin Head Sex Thing: Racial Difference and the Homoerotic Imaginary," in Bad Object-Choices, ed., *How Do I Look?*, 169–222.

73. Petrus Liu, *Queer Marxism in Two Chinas* (Durham, N.C.: Duke University Press, 2015), 34–84.

74. Tze-lan Deborah Sang, "Translating Homosexuality: The Discourse of Tongxing'ai in Republican China (1912–1949)," in *Tokens of Exchange: The Problem of Translation in Global Circulations*, ed. Lydia Liu (Durham, N.C.: Duke University Press, 1999), 292–98; Giovanni Vitiello, *The Libertine's Friend: Homosexuality and Masculinity in Late Imperial China* (Chicago: University of Chicago Press, 2011), 1–14.

75. For a discussion of LGBTQI+ rights in Hong Kong, see Amy Barrow and Joy L. Chia, "Pride or Prejudice? Sexual Orientation, Gender Identity and Religion in Post-colonial Hong Kong," *Hong Kong Law Journal* 46, no. 1 (2016): 89–104.

76. Jason McGrath, *Postsocialist Modernity: Chinese Cinema, Literature, and Criticism in the Market Age* (Stanford, Calif.: Stanford University Press, 2008), 28–55.

77. Liu, *Queer Marxism in Two Chinas*, 34–84.

78. Victor Fan, *Extraterritoriality: Locating Hong Kong Cinema and Media* (Edinburgh: Edinburgh University Press, 2019), 249–50; Lü Yidu, "Goujian hexie shehui yu Zhongguo dianying fazhan chuyi" [On constructing a harmonious society and the development of Chinese cinema], in *Zhongguo dianying xin bainian: Hezuo yu fazhan* [A new century of Chinese cinema: Coproduction and development], ed. China Film Producers' Association (Beijing: Zhongguo dianying chubanshe, 2006), 27–31. For more on the concept of socialist harmonious society, see "Minzhu fazhi, gongping zhengyi, chengxin youai, chongman huoli, anding youxu, ren yu ziran hexie xiangchu" [Democratic rule of law, fairness and justice, honesty and fraternity, energy and liveliness, stability and order, and the harmonious coexistence between human and nature], *People.com.cn*, *People's Daily*, October 12, 2006, http://www.people.com.cn/GB/32306/54155/57487/4913154.html, accessed August 25, 2015; see also, "Shiliujie Zhongquanhui kaimu; Zhuozhong yanjiu goujian hexie shehui wenti" [The Sixteenth Central Committee of the CCP opened: On the construction of a harmonious society], *People.com.cn*, *People's Daily*, October 8, 2006, http://theory.people.com.cn/GB/40557/44459/44461/4890703.html, accessed August 25, 2015.

79. Kwai Cheung Lo and Laikwan Pang, "Hong Kong: Ten Years after Colonialism," *Postcolonial Studies* 10, no. 4 (2007): 350.

80. For a discussion of the term *tongzhi*, see Song Hwee Lim, *Celluloid Comrades: Representations of Male Homosexuality in Contemporary Chinese Cinemas* (Honolulu: University of Hawai'i Press, 2006), 7–13. Regarding *tongxing'ai*, see Sang, "Translating homosexuality," 292–98.

81. Karl Schoonover and Rosalind Galt, *Queer Cinema in the World* (Durham, N.C.: Duke University Press, 2016), 7.

82. See Ferdinand de Saussure, *Écrits de linguistique générale* (Paris: Éditions Gallimard, 2002), 28–30.

83. See Jacques Derrida, *Of Grammatology* [1967], trans. Gayatri Chakravorty Spivak (1967; repr., Baltimore: Johns Hopkins University Press, 1997), 62.

84. Chen Mo and Zhiwei Xiao, "Chinese Underground Films: Critical Views from China," in *From Underground to Independent: Alternative Film Culture in Contemporary China,* eds. Paul Pickowicz and Yingjin Zhang (Lanham, Md.: Rowman and Littlefield, 2006), 146; Qu Chunjing, "Dianying wenxian jiazhi yu yishu pinwei: Tan xinshengdai dianying de chengbai" [Film's documentary and artistic values: Newborn generation film's success and failure], in Chen Xihe and Shi Chuan, *Duoyuan yujing zhong de xinshengdai dianying* [Newborn generation films in multiple contexts: Essays on Chinese newborn generation film] (Shanghai: Xuelin chubanshe, 2003), 192.

85. See "First Festival Program," in Beijing Queer Film Festival, http://www.bjqff.com/?cat=21, accessed December 15, 2015.

86. Bao Hongwei, "Queer as Catachresis: The Beijing Queer Film Festival in Cultural Translation," in *Chinese Film Festivals: Sites of Translation*, eds. Chris

Berry and Luke Robinson (London: Palgrave Macmillan, 2016), 79–100; see also, Bao Hongwei, *Queer Comrades: Gay Identity and Tongzhi Activism in Postsocialist China* (Copenhagen: Nordic Institute of Asian Studies, 2018), 119–48.

87. Bao, *Queer Comrades*, 119–48; see also "Political Ceremonies: Caravans and USBs," in Beijing Queer Film Festival, http://www.bjqff.com/?cat=192, accessed December 15, 2015.

88. "Zhonghua Renmin Gongheguo dianying chanye cujin fa" (Law to expatriate the [development of] the film industry of the People's Republic of China), The National People's Congress of the People's Republic of China, November 7, 2016, http://www.npc.gov.cn/npc/xinwen/2016-11/07/content _2001625.htm, accessed March 17, 2019.

89. Bao, "Queer as Catachresis," 79–100. I also thank David Chalmers for his conversation about the ShanghaiPride Film Festival.

90. Victor Fan, "Ontopower and Queer Radical Changes," in "Queer" Asia, September 3, 2020, https://queerasia.com/victorfan/, accessed September 2020. See Judith Butler, *Notes toward a Performative Theory of Assembly* (Cambridge, Mass.: Harvard University Press, 2015); David Harvey, *A Brief History of Neoliberalism* (Oxford: Oxford University Press, 2005), 7 and 41; see also Massumi, *Politics of Affect*. For the analogy of the box, see Franz Kafka, "Before the Law" [written 1914; published 1916], trans. Willa and Edwin Muir, in *Franz Kafka: The Complete Stories*, ed. Nahum N. Glatzer (New York: Schocken Books, 1983), 3–4.

91. Fan, "Ontopower and Queer Radical Changes."

92. Cui Zi'en and Wang Qi, "The Ruin Is Already a New Outcome: An Interview with Cui Zi'en," *positions: east asia cultures critique* 12, no. 1 (2004): 191; qtd. Bao, *Queer Comrades*, 125.

93. Liu, *Queer Marxism in Two Chinas*, 51.

94. Denson, *Discorrelated Images*, 51–72.

95. For a summary of the situation, see Fang Wan, "How China Changed after 2008 Beijing Olympics," Deutsche Welle, August 8, 2018, https://www.dw .com/en/how-china-changed-after-2008-beijing-olympics/a-44986744, accessed July 13, 2020. I was in Beijing that summer and was in conversation with some of BQFF's organizers.

96. These claims are based on my work as Film Consultant for the Chinese Visual Festival since 2013.

97. James Mudge, "*Martian Syndrome*," in Chinese Visual Festival, http://chinesevisualfestival.org/portfolios/martian-syndrome/, accessed December 15, 2015.

98. Kiki Yu, "Xingdong zhong de 'wo': Diyirencheng jilu" [The self in action], *Zhongguo duli yingxiang* [*Chinese Independent Cinema*], no. 11 (November 2012), no page.

99. Pier Paolo Pasolini, "Cinema of Poetry," trans. Bill Nichols from the French version, trans. Marianne de Vettimo and Jacques Bontemps, in *Movies*

and Methods, ed. Nichols (Berkeley: University of California Press, 1976), 1:544.

100. Gilles Deleuze, *Cinema 2: The Time-Image,* trans. Hugh Tomlinson and Robert Galeta (1989; repr., Minneapolis: University of Minnesota Press, 2001), 81; Fan, *Cinema Approaching Reality,* 80.

5. IN-AESTHETICS

1. See, for example, Donald Richie, *Ozu* (Berkeley: University of California Press, 1974); David Bordwell, *Ozu and the Poetics of Cinema* (Princeton, N.J.: Princeton University Press, 1988); Dudley Andrew and Paul Andrew, *Kenji Mizoguchi: A Guide to References and Resources* (Boston: G. K. Hall, 1981); Dudley Andrew and Carole Cavanaugh, *Sanshō dayū* (London: BFI Publishing, 2000); Gabrielle Finnane, "Wayfaring in the Megacity: Tsai Ming-liang's *Walker* and Lav Diaz's *Melancholia,*" in *Walking and the Aesthetics of Modernity,* eds. Klaus Benesch and François Specq (New York: Palgrave Macmillan, 2016), 115–27; Corrado Neri, "Tsai Ming-liang and the Lost Emotions of the Flesh," *positions: east asia cultures critique* 16, no. 2 (Fall 2008): 389–407; Fran Martin, "The European Undead: Tsai Ming-liang's Temporal Dysphoria," *Senses of Cinema,* no. 27 (July–August 2003), https://minerva-access.unimelb.edu.au/handle/11343/34209, accessed April 21, 2020; Teng-Kuan Ng, "Pedestrian Dharma: Slowness and Seeing in Tsai Ming-liang's Walker," *Religions* 9, no. 7 (2018), https://doi.org/10.3390/rel 9070200, accessed April 21, 2020; Arnika Fuhrmann, *Ghostly Desires: Queer Sexuality and Vernacular Buddhism in Contemporary Thai Cinema* (Durham, N.C.: Duke University Press, 2016), 122–59; Ji-Hoon Kim, "Learning about Time: An Interview with Apichatpong Weerasethakul," *Film Quarterly* 64, no. 4 (Summer 2011): 48–52; Angela O'Hara, "Mysterious Object of Desire: The Haunted Cinema of Apichatpong Weerasethakul," in *Transnational Asian Identities in Pan-Pacific Cinemas: The Reel Asian Exchange,* eds. Philippa Gates and Lisa Funnell (New York: Routledge, 2012); David Teh, "Itinerant Cinema: The Social Surrealism of Apichatpong Weerasethakul," *Third Text* 25, no. 5 (2011): 595–609.

2. Paul Schrader, *Transcendental Style in Film: Ozu, Bresson, Dreyer* (Berkeley: University of California Press, 1972).

3. Richard Gombrich, "Buddhist Aesthetics?," *Journal of the Oxford Centre for Buddhist Studies* 5 (November 2013): 136.

4. Huang Jiashu, Za ahan jing *xuanji* [*Saṃyuktāgama*: A selection], *suttas* trans. Guṇabhadra (1999; repr., Taipei: Buddhall, 2017), SA-815 (335).

5. See the *Sarvāstivāda-vinaya, TSD* 23, no. 1435, 352a, and 355a; discussed in Ju-Hyung Rhi, "From Bodhisattva to Buddha: The Beginning of Iconic Representation in Buddhist Art," *Artibus Asiæ* 54, nos. 3–4 (1994): 220–21.

6. Alfred Foucher, *L'art gréco-bouddhique du Gandhāra. Étude sur les origines de l'influence Classique dans l'art bouddhique d l'Inde et de l'Extrême-Orient* (Paris: Imprimerie Nationale, 1922).

7. Ananda K. Coomaraswamy, *Elements of Buddhist Iconography* (Cambridge, Mass.: Harvard University Press, 1935).

8. Susan L. Huntington, "Early Buddhist Art and the Theory of Aniconism," *Art Journal* 49, no. 4 (Winter 1990): 401–8.

9. Thomé H. Fang, *Zhongguo Dasheng Foxue* [Chinese Mahāyāna Buddhism, 1974–75] (2012; repr., Beijing: Zhonghua shuju, 2014), 13–18 and 97–136; Erik Zürcher, "Buddhist Influence on Early Taoism," *T'oung Pao* 66, no. 1 (January 1980): 84–147.

10. For art criticism, see Yu Anlan, ed., *Hualun congkan* [Theories of painting series] (Beijing: Renmin meishu chubanshe, 1989), in two volumes; for poetic criticism, see He Wenhuan, ed., *Lidai shihua* [Poetic criticism of previous dynasties, eighteenth century] (Shanghai: Yixue shuju, 1927); see also Yan Yu, *Canglang shihua* [Poetic criticism by Yan Canlang, circa 1191–1241] (Beijing: Renmin wenxue chubanshe, 1962); Wu Qiao, *Weilu shihua* [Poetry talks around a stove, circa 1686] (Taipei: Guangwen shuju, 1969).

11. See, for example, Lokesh Chandra, *Tibetan Art* (New Delhi: Niyogi Books, 2008); Jane Casey Singer and Philip Denwood, eds., *Tibetan Art: Towards a Definition of Style* (London: Laurence King, 1997); see also Amy Heller, *Tibetan Art: Tracing the Development of Spiritual Ideals and Art in Tibet, 600–2000 A.D.* (Milan: Editoriale Jaca Book, 1999).

12. For general historical accounts, see, for example, M. Anesaki, *Buddhist Art in Its Relation to Buddhist Ideals: With Special Reference to Buddhism in Japan* (Boston: Houghton Mifflin Company, 1915); Patricia J. Graham, *Faith and Power in Japanese Buddhist Art, 1600–2005* (Honolulu: University of Hawai'i Press, 2007); see also Hiromitsu Washizuka, ed., *Transmitting the Forms of Divinity: Early Buddhist Art from Korea and Japan* (New York: Japan Society, 2003).

13. See, for example, Nanxiu Qian, Richard J. Smith, and Bowei Zhang, *Reexamining the Sinosphere: Cultural Transmissions and Transformations in East Asia* (Amherst, N.Y.: Cambria Press, 2020).

14. See *Dafangguang Fo Huayan jing ru fajie pin* [*Avataṃsaka Sūtra: The Gaṇḍavyūha Sutra*], trans. Divākara, in *TSD* 20, no. 295.

15. Alain Badiou, *Handbook of Inaesthetics* [1998], trans. Alberto Toscano (Stanford, Calif.: Stanford University Press, 2005), xii and 9–10.

16. Nico Baumbach, *Cinema/Politics/Philosophy* (New York: Columbia University Press, 2019), 92–127.

17. Inken Prohl, "California 'Zen': Spirituality Made in America," *Amerikastudien/American Studies* 59, no. 2, Religion and the Marketplace (2014): 193–206.

18. Schrader, *Transcendental Style in Film*, 3; Donald Richie, "A Bibliographical Filmography," *Film Comment* 7, no. 1 (Spring 1971): 4–17; Donald Richie, *Japanese Movies* (Tokyo: Japan Travel Bureau, 1961); Donald Richie, "The Later Films of Yasujiro Ozu," *Film Quarterly* 13, no. 1 (Fall 1959); "A Short Guide to the Aesthetics of Japanese Film," *UniJapan Bulletin,* nos. 11–12 (December 1965): 18–25; Donald

Richie, "Yasujiiro Ozu: The Syntax of His Films," *Film Quarterly* 17, no. 2 (Winter 1963–64): 11–16; Suzuki Daisetz, *Essays in Zen Buddhism,* in three volumes (London: Luzac, 1927, 1933, and 1934); *Zen Buddhism and Its Influence on Japanese Culture* (Kyoto: Eastern Buddhist Society, 1938); Alan Watts, *The Spirit of Zen* (London: Murray, 1936); Alan Watts, *The Way of Zen* (New York: Pantheon, 1957).

19. The term *Western* is highlighted here to emphasize that it should not be taken as an unquestionable nomination. In the case discussed here, the imaginary divide between the *East* and *West* was drawn precisely by showcasing Buddhism and Japan as *technē*.

20. R. John Williams, *The Buddha in the Machine: Art, Technology, and the Meeting of East and West* (New Haven, Conn.: Yale University Press, 2014), 6–20.

21. Shaku Soyen, "The Law of Cause and Effect," in *The World's Parliament of Religions: An Illustrated and Popular Story of the World's First Parliament of Religions, Held in Chicago in Connection with the Columbian Exposition of 1893,* ed. John Henry Barrows (Chicago: Parliament Publishing Company, 1893), 2:829–31.

22. Shaku Soyen, "Arbitration Instead of War," in *The World's Parliament of Religions,* 2:1285; see also Richard Hughes Seager, *The World Parliament of Religions: The East/West Encounter, Chicago, 1893* (Bloomington: Indiana University Press, 2009).

23. John M. Thompson, "Particular and Universal: Problems Posed by Shaku Soen's 'Zen,'" self-published PDF file (2005): 2. For the names of the delegates, see Barrows, ed., *The World's Parliament of Religions.*

24. Thompson, "Particular and Universal," 3–5; see also Margaret H. Dornish, "Aspects of D. T. Suzuki's Early Interpretations of Buddhism and Zen," *The Eastern Buddhist,* New Series 3, no. 1 (June 1970): 47–66.

25. Shōjun Bandō, "D. T. Suzuki's Life in LaSalle," *The Eastern Buddhist,* New Series 2, no. 1 (August 1967): 137–46.

26. Suzuki Teitarō Daisetz, "Self the Unattainable," in *The Buddha Eye: An Anthology of the Kyoto School and Its Contemporaries,* ed. Frederick Franck (1982; repr., Bloomington, Ind.: World Wisdom, 2004), 6–7.

27. Suzuki Teitarō Daisetz, "The Buddhist Conception of Reality," in Franck, ed., *The Buddha Eye,* 93.

28. *Jingtu wujing duben* [The five sutras of Pure Land Buddhism] (Hong Kong: Hong Kong Buddhist Education Foundation, 2000).

29. *Dafangguang Fo Huayan jing;* see also, *Weimojie suoshuo jing* [*Vimalakīrti Nirdeśa*], trans. Kumārajīva, in *TSD* 14, no. 375, §4 (8).

30. Huiyuan, *Dasheng dayi zhang* [The great principles of Mahāyāna Buddhism], in *TSD* 44, no. 1851.

31. Zhiyi, *Mohe zhiguan* [Great *śamatha-vipaśyanā*], *TSD* 46, no. 1911, §5 (71).

32. See, for example, Fujisawa Keiju, *Jōdo monrui jushō daikoroku* [Anthology of essays on Shin Buddhism] (Kyoto: Nagata Bunshōdō, 1998).

33. Hajime Tanabe, *Philosophy as Metanoetics* [1946], trans. Takeuchi Yoshinori, Valdo Viglielmo, and James W. Heisig (1986; repr., Nagoya: Chisokudō, 2016), 113.

34. Tanabe, *Philosophy as Metanoetics*, 168.

35. Tanabe, *Philosophy as Metanoetics*, 71–73.

36. Nishitani Kenji, "Science and Zen," in Franck, ed., *The Buddha Eye,* 125; Nishitani's emphasis.

37. Suzuki Teitarō Daisetz, "Apropos of Shin," in Franck, ed., *The Buddha Eye,* 222.

38. See, for example, Shigemori Mirei, *Karesansui* (Kyoto: Kawahara Shoten, 1965); see also Karl Hennig, *Karesansui. Garten als Ausdruck der Kultur der Muromachi-Zeit* (Hamburg: Gesellschaft für Nature, 1982).

39. Richie, *Ozu;* Noël Burch, *To the Distant Observer: Form and Meaning in the Japanese Cinema* (Berkeley: University of California Press, 1979); Andrew and Andrew, *Kenji Mizoguchi;* Andrew and Cavanaugh, *Sanshō dayū.*

40. Fang, *Zhongguo Dasheng Foxue.*

41. Wu Kang, *Song Ming lixue* [Neo-Confucianism from the Song to Ming dynasties] (1955; repr., Taipei: Huaguo chubanshe, 1962).

42. Lan Chi-fu, "Yang Renshan yu xiandai Zhongguo Fojiao" [Yang Wenhui and modern Chinese Buddhism], *Hua-Kang Buddhist Journal,* no. 2 (1972): 100–103.

43. Lan, "Yang Renshan yu xiandai Zhongguo Fojiao," 102–103. It is unclear to historians whether Su Manshu had ever been ordained.

44. Tanxu, *Yingchen huiyilu* [Memoir of an image in-formed by dust] (Hong Kong: Hong Kong Buddhist Book Distributor, 2002).

45. See Taixu, *Taixu dashi quanshu* [A complete collection of the writings of Taixu] (Taipei: *Taixu dashi quanshu* bianhui weiyuanhui, 1970); Tanxu, *Yingchen huiyilu;* Xuyun, *Xuyun Heshang nianpu* [Annals of Master Xuyun] (Taipei: Wenhai chubnahse, 1972).

46. Yang Wenhui, *Deng budeng guan zalu,* §4, 10–11; Yang, *Chanjiao pian* [Interpretations of Buddhism], in *Yang Renshan quanji* [Complete Collection of works by Yang Wenhui] (Hefei: Huangshan shushe, 2000), 523–29; Lan, "Yang Renshan yu xiandai Zhongguo Fojiao," 106; Zhang Hua, "Yu Riben Jingtu Zhenzong bianlun fayi: 1898–1900" [The debate with Japanese Jōdo Shin Buddhism], in *Yang Wenhui yu Zhongguo jindai Fojiao sixiang zhuanxing* [Yang Wenhui and the transformation of Chinese Buddhist thoughts in recent history], ed. Zhang Hua (Beijing: Zongjiao wenhua chubanshe, 2004), 198–232.

47. Yin Shun, *Dasheng qixinlun jiangji* [Lectures on the *Mahāyāna śraddhotpādaśāstra,* 1950], *śāstra* Aśvaghoṣa (?), trans. Paramārtha (?) (2010; repr., Beijing: Zhonghua shuju, 2014), 54–57; see also Yusuki Ryōei, *Dasheng qixinlun xinshi* [New commentaries of the *Awakening of Faith in the Mahāyāna*], trans. Feng Zikai (Hangzhou: Zhejiang renmin chubanshe, 2015), 66.

48. Yin Shun, Dasheng qixinlun *jiangji,* 54–57.

49. Cheng Gonrang, "Ouyang Jingwu xiansheng de shengping, shiye ji qi Fojiao sixiang de tezhi" [The life, career, and characteristics of his Buddhist thoughts], *Yuanguang Foxue xuebao* [The Yuanguang journal of Buddhist studies], no. 4 (December 1992): 158; Lü Cheng, "Qinjiaoshi Ouyang xiansheng shilüe" [A concise biography of my dearest teacher Master Ouyang], in *Ouyang Jingwu dashi jiniankan* [In memory of Ouyang Jingwu], ed. China Inner Studies Institute, repr. in *Zhonghua Fojiao renwu zhuanji wenxian quanshu* [Complete collection of biographies of figures in Chinese Buddhism], ed. Guojia tushuguan fenguan (Beijing: Xianzhuang shuju, 2005), 48:24241–44; Xu Qingxiang and Wang Guoyan, *Ouyang Jinigwu pingzhuan* [A commentated biography of Ouyang Jingwu] (Nanchang: Baihuazhou wenyi chubanshe, 1995), 48.

50. Cheng, "Ouyang Jingwu xiansheng de shengping," 161–62.

51. Yang, *Deng budeng guan zalu.*

52. Cheng, "Ouyang Jingwu xiansheng de shengping," 167.

53. "Mei Guangyi zhi Yang Wenhui" [Letter from Mei Guangyi to Yang Wenhui], *Deng budeng guan zalu,* §6; discussed in Cheng, "Ouyang Jingwu xiansheng de shengping," 163 note 45.

54. Ouyang, *Faxiang zhulun xuhekan:* Fodi jinglun *xu* [An integrated study of the various *śāstras* of the Dharmakasana school: Introduction to the *Buddhabhūmi-sūtra-śāstra*] (Nanking: Zhina neixueyuan, 1920).

55. Liang Qichao, *Liang Qichao tan Fo* [On Buddhism by Liang Qichao], ed. Zhang Yang (Beijing: Dongfang chubanshe, 2005).

56. "Lü Cheng, Xiong Shili wangfu xiangao" [Letters between Lü Cheng and Xiong Shili], http://www.wuys.com/news/Article_Show.asp?ArticleID=14374, accessed April 26, 2020.

57. Nirmala Sharma, *Kumārajīva: The Transcreator of Buddhist Chinese Diction* (New Delhi: Niyogi Books, 2011).

58. Fang, *Zhongguo Dasheng Foxue,* 24–28.

59. Fang, *Zhongguo Dasheng Foxue,* 17–18. See Friedrich Nietzsche, *Thus Spoke Zarathustra: A Book for All and None* [1883–85], trans. Adrian del Caro (Cambridge, U.K.: Cambridge University Press, 2006); see also Gilles Deleuze's discussion of this concept in relation to the cinema in his *Cinéma 2. L'image-temps* (1985; repr., Paris: Éditions de Minuit, 2017), 129–64.

60. Thomé H. Fang, "Jiu yuanqi lun tan Zhongguo Dasheng Foxue sixiang yanbian guocheng zhong yanzhong de yinan" [On the most serious conundrum in the evolution of Chinese Mahāyāna philosophy based on the theory of dependent originations], in *Fojiao zhexue sixiang lunji* [Anthology of critical essays on Buddhist philosophy], ed. Chang Man-t'ao (Taipei: Dasheng wenhua chubanshe, 1978), 1:368–69.

61. Wang Deyi, *Wang Guowei nianpu* [Wang Guowei: A chronicle] (Taipei: Zhongguo xueshu zhuzuo jiangzhu weiyuanhui, 1967).

62. Yang Bojun, Lunyu *yizhu* [The *Analects* with modern translations and annotations] (1958; repr., Beijing: Zhonghua shuju, 2010), §17.9; qtd. Wang Guowei, "Kongzi zhi meiyu zhuyi" [The aesthetic education of Confucius, 1904], in Wang Guowei, *Wang Guowei meilun wenxuan* [Selected essays on aesthetics by Wang Guowei], ed. Liu Gangqiang (Changsha: Hunan renmin chubanshe, 1987), 6.

63. Wang, "Kongzi zhi meiyu zhuyi," 4.

64. Arthur Schopenhauer, *The World as Will and Presentation* [1818–19], trans. Richard E. Aquila (New York: Pearson Longman, 2008), §19 (1:164); qtd. Ñāṇājīvako, *Schopenhauer and Buddhism* (1970; repr., Kandy, Sri Lanka: Buddhist Publication Society, 1988), 30. For a discussion of Schopenhauer's understanding of Buddhism, see, for example, Peter Abelson, "Schopenhauer and Buddhism," *Philosophy East and West* 43, no. 2 (April 1993): 255–78.

65. Su Shi, "Baohuitang ji" [Hall of painterly treasures], in *Tang Song badajia wenchao* [Anthology of essays by the great eight writers from the Tang and Song dynasties], ed. Sun Boxing (Beijing: Shangwu yinshuguan, 1936), §138–40; qtd. Wang, "Kongzi zhi meiyu zhuyi," 5.

66. Shao Yong, "Guan neiwu pian" [On internal objects], in *Huang ji jingshi shu* [On imperial administration] (Hong Kong: iTVentures, 2006), §7; qtd. Wang, "Kongzi zhi meiyu zhuyi," 7.

67. Yan Yu, *Canglang shihua*; Wang, *Renjian cihua* [On human lyrics] (1910; repr., Beijing: Pushe, 1926), §1–9.

68. Wang, *Renjian cihua*, §26.

69. See Victor Fan, *Cinema Approaching Reality: Locating Chinese Film Theory* (Minneapolis: University of Minnesota Press, 2015), 103–4.

70. Zen *gāthās* are transmitted orally.

71. *Zhu Guangqian ziliao ji* [Anthology of research materials on Chu Kuang-ch'ien] (Hong Kong: Taozhai shuwu, 1974).

72. Chu Kuang-ch'ien, *Tan mei: Gei qingnian de di shisan feng xin* [On beauty: The thirteenth letter to youth] (1932; repr., Shanghai: Kaiming shudian, 1949); Chu, *Wenyi xinlixue* [Psychology of art and literature] (Shanghai: Kaiming shudian, 1936).

73. Mario Sabattini, *Zhu Guangqian and Benedetto Croce on Aesthetic Thought* (Leiden: Brill, 2019), 5–17.

74. Immanuel Kant, *Critique of the Power of Judgement* (1790), trans. Paul Guyer and Eric Matthews, ed. Guyer (Cambridge, U.K.: Cambridge University Press, 2000), 5:272 note (154).

75. Chu, *Tan mei*, 5–10.

76. Chu, *Tan mei*, 24–25.

77. Chu, *Wenyi xinlixue*.

78. Sigmund Freud, "Group Psychology and the Analysis of the Ego," in *The Standard Edition of the Complete Psychological Works of Sigmund Freud*, vol. XVIII (1920–1922), ed. James Strachey (London: Hogarth Press, 1955), 106–7.

79. Pan Guangdan, *Feng Xiaoqing: Yijian yinglian de yanjiu* [Feng Xiaoqing: A study of narcissism, 1927], in *Pan Guangdan wenji* [Collection of writings by Pan Guangdan] (Beijing: Peking University Press, 2000), 1:1–61.

80. Chu, *Wenyi xinlixue.*

81. As Bao Weihong argues, the idea of resonance, informed by both European philosophy and Buddhist worldviews, is a more popular term among Republican filmmakers and critics than identification. See *Fiery Cinema: The Emergence of an Affective Medium in China, 1915–1945* (Minneapolis: University of Minnesota Press, 2015), 91–149.

82. Wu, *Song Ming lixue,* 41.

83. Zhou Ji, *Song sijia ci xuan* [Selections of lyrics by the four great lyricists from the Song dynasty] (Peking: Guangxu wushen xu, 1908), *xu* [introduction]; qtd. Zong Baihua, "Lun wenyi de kongling yu chongshi" [On emptiness-spirituality and fulfillment-concreteness in art and literature], in *Meixue yu yijing* [Aesthetics and *yijing*], 226.

84. Zong, "Lun wenyi de kongling yu chongshi," 228, Zong's emphasis.

85. Zong, "Lun wenyi de kongling yu chongshi," 229.

86. Sikong Tu (attributed), *Ershisi shipin* [Twenty-four poetic criticisms] (Beijing: Beijing Erudition Digital Research Center, 2009), §13; qtd. Zong, "Lun wenyi de kongling yu chongshi," 231.

87. Zhou, *Song sijia ci xuan, xu;* qtd. Zong, "Lun wenyi de kongling yu chongshi," 231.

88. Zou Yigui, *Xiaoshan huapu* [Annotated catalogue of Xiaoshan Studio] (Taipei: Guangwen shuju, 1963); Zong, "Zhongguo shihua zhong suo biaoxian de kongjian yishi" [The spatial consciousness manifested in Chinese poetry and painting, 1949], in *Meixue yu yijing,* 246.

89. Shen Kuo, *Mengxi bitan* [The written talks of Shen Mengxi] (Beijing: Zhonghua shuju, 2015), §17; qtd. Zong, "Zhongguo shihua zhong suo biaoxian de kongjian yishi," 247.

90. Zong, "Zhongguo shihua zhong suo biaoxian de kongjian yishi," 247.

91. Ji Kang, "Siyan zeng xiong xiucai ru jun shi shiba shou" [Eighteen four-syllable poems offered to my scholarly brother on the occasion of his being enlisted], no. 14, *Ji Kang shi quanji* [Complete collection of poems by Ji Kang] (Beijing: Yishu zhongguowang, no year), 6; qtd. Zong, "Zhongguo shihua zhong suo biaoxian de kongjian yishi," 248.

92. Chen Guying and Zhao Jianwei, *Zhou Yi zhuyi yu yanjiu* [*I-ching*: Annotations and studies] (Taipei: Taiwan Shangwu yinshuguan, 1999), §11; qtd. Zong, "Zhongguo shihua zhong suo biaoxian de kongjian yishi," 248.

93. Yan Yu, *Cang Lang shihua,* §5; qtd. Zong, "Zhongguo shihua zhong suo biaoxian de kongjian yishi," 250.

94. Zong, "Zhongguo shihua zhong suo biaoxian de kongjian yishi," 256; Zong's emphasis.

95. Zong, "Zhongguo shihua zhong suo biaoxian de kongjian yishi," 258.

96. Lam Nin-tung, "Zhongguo dianying lilun yanjiu zhong youguan gudian meixue wenti de tantao" [On the investigation into classical aesthetics in the study of Chinese film theory, written 1981], in *Jing you* [Mirroring-journeying] (Hong Kong: Su Yeh Publications, 1985), 32.

97. Han Shangyi, "Dianying meishu yu dianying texing" [Cinematic art and the *cinématique*], in *Lun dianying yu xiju de meishu sheji* [On production designs in the cinema and theater] (Beijing: Zhongguo dianying chubanshe, 1962), 37; qtd. Lam, "Zhongguo dianying lilun yanjiu zhong youguan gudian meixue wenti de tantao," 33.

98. Lam, "Zhongguo dianying lilun yanjiu zhong youguan gudian meixue wenti de tantao," 34–50. Lam refers to Nie Jing, "*Xiaobing Zhang Ga* de sheying gousi ji qita" [The photographic conceptualization of *Little Soldier Zhang Ga* and others], *Dianying yishu* [*Film Art*], no. 1 (1964): 48; also to Zhao Dan, *Yingmu yingxiang chuangzao* [The creation of a screen image] (Beijing: Zhongguo dianying chubanshe, 1980), 88. See also Lo Wai-luk, "Traditional Chinese Aesthetics and Contemporary Chinese Films: Applying the Idea of Qi-yun to Understand the Temporal Structure of Selected Films of Hou Hsiao-hsien," in *East Asian Cinema and Cultural Heritage: From China, Hong Kong, Taiwan to Japan and South Korea,* eds. Shuk-ting Kinnia Yau (New York: Palgrave Macmillan, 2011), 81–100.

99. Lam, "Zhongguo dianying de tedian" [The characteristics of Chinese cinema], in *Jing you,* 58–64.

100. Lam, "Zhongguo dianying de kongjian yishi" [The spatial consciousness of Chinese cinema], *Zhongguo dianying yanjiu* [*An Interdisciplinary Journal of Chinese Film Studies*], no. 1 (1983): 58–85.

101. Scholars and critics including Chris Berry, Law Kar, Tony Rayns, and Shu Kei have raised such a concern in our private conversations.

102. Lam, "Zhongguo dianying de kongjian yishi," 58

103. Lam, "Zhongguo dianying de kongjian yishi," 60; Jean-Louis Baudry, "Le Dispositif," *Communications,* no. 23 (1975), *Psychanalyse et cinema:* 56–72.

104. Nian Xiyao, *Shixue* [The study of vision, 1729] (Beijing: Beijing Erudition Digital Research Center, 2009); qtd. Lam, "Zhongguo dianying de kongjian yishi," 81.

105. The title "Yan lianzhu" is the name of a poetic genre, which is structured by a chain of interrelated political allegories. Lu Ji, "Yan Lianzhu" [Performing a sequence of pearls], in *Lu Ji ji* [Collection of essays by Lu Ji] (Beijing: Zhonghua shuju, 1992); qtd. Lam, "Zhongguo dianying de kongjian yishi," 62.

106. Guo Xi, "Linquan gaozhi: Shanshui xun" [On the way woods and streams are best placed within a landscape of mountains and water], in Yu, ed., *Hualun congkan,* 1:19–23; qtd. Lam, "Zhongguo dianying de kongjian yishi," 62–63.

107. Lam, "Zhongguo dianying de kongjian yishi," 62–63.

108. Cheng Bugao, *Yingtan yijiu* [Memories of the film altar] (Beijing: Zhongguo dianying chubanshe, 1983), 113; qtd. Lam, "Zhongguo dianying de kongjian yishi," 64.

109. Zong Bing, "Hua shanshui xu" [On painting mountains and rivers], in Yu, ed., *Hualun congkan,* 1:1; qtd. Lam, "Zhongguo dianying de kongjian yishi," 64.

110. Lam, "Zhongguo dianying de kongjian yishi," 64.

111. Lam, "Zhongguo dianying de kongjian yishi," 68 and 72–76.

112. *Za ahan jing* [Saṃyuktāgama], in *TSD* 2, no. 99, SA-733 and 737 (413–15).

113. Schrader, *Transcendental Style in Film,* 3.

114. Schrader, *Transcendental Style in Film,* 6–7.

115. See note 18.

116. Richie, "Donald Richie: Japan the Incongruous and Myself," Luce Hall, Yale University, New Haven, October 18, 2006.

117. Richie, *Ozu.*

118. Burch, *To a Distant Observer.*

119. Hasumi Shigehiko, *Yasujirō Ozu,* trans. René de Ceccatty, Hasumi, and Nakamura Ryōji (Paris: Cahiers du cinéma, 1998), 22–25 and 217.

120. Hasumi, *Yasujirō Ozu,* 45–46.

121. Satō Tadao, *Riben dianying de juzhangmen* [The great Japanese film masters], trans. Liao Hsiang-hsiung (Taipei: Zhiwen chubanshe, 1987), 77.

122. Victor Shklovsky, *Résurrection du mot; Littérature et cinématographe,* trans. Andrée Robel (Paris: Lebovici, 1985), 93–101; Yuri Tyniyanov, *The Problem of Verse Language,* trans. and eds. Michael Sosa and Brent Harvey (Ann Arbor, Mich.: Ardis, 1981), 31–47; qtd. Bordwell, *Ozu,* 31.

123. Bordwell, *Ozu,* 31–108.

124. Ozu Yasujirō, *Carnets: 1933-1963,* trans. Pinon-Kawataké (Paris: Éditions Alive, 1996).

125. Jinhee Choi, "Introduction," in *Reorienting Ozu: A Master and His Influence* (New York: Oxford University Press, 2018), 1–15; Jinhee Choi, "Ozuesque as a Sensibility: Or, On the Notion of Influence," in *Reorienting Ozu,* 77–94.

126. Yoshida Kiju, *Ozu's Anti-Cinema,* trans. Miyao Daisuke and Hirano Kyoko (Ann Arbor: Center for Japanese Studies, University of Michigan, 2003).

127. Burch, *To a Distant Observer,* 160–62.

128. Deleuze, *Cinema 2,* 17.

129. Bordwell, *Ozu,* 31–108; Satō, *Riben dianying de juzhangmen,* 77; Yoshida, *Ozu's Anti-Cinema.*

CONCLUSION

1. Laura Mulvey, "Visual Pleasure and Narrative Cinema," *Screen* 16, no. 3 (Autumn 1975): 6–18.

2. Giorgio Agamben, *Homo Sacer: Sovereign Power and Bare Life* [1995], trans. Daniel Heller-Roazen (Stanford, Calif.: Stanford University Press, 1998).

3. Norbert Elias, *The Civilizing Process* (Oxford: Blackwell, 2000); Pierre Bourdieu, *Language and Symbolic Power* (Cambridge, U.K.: Polity Press, 1991); discussed in Thomas Elsaesser, *Film History as Media Archaeology: Tracking Digital Cinema* (Amsterdam: Amsterdam University Press, 2016), 201.

4. *Spectator,* nos. 1–635 (March 1, 1711–December 20, 1714).

5. Giorgio Agamben, *State of Exception* [2003], trans. Kevin Attell (Chicago: University of Chicago Press, 2005).

6. Elsaesser, *Film History as Media Archaeology,* 199–200.

7. Tom Gunning, "The Cinema of Attraction: Early Film, Its Spectator and the Avant-Garde," *Wide Angle* 8, nos. 3–4 (1986): 63–70; André Gaudreault, "Narration and Monstration in the Cinema," *Journal of Film and Video* 39, no. 2 (Spring 1987): 29–36.

8. Charles Musser, *Emergence of Cinema: The American Screen to 1907* (Berkeley: University of California Press, 1994), 159–92, 327–79, and 393–94.

9. Elsaesser, *Film History as Media Archaeology,* 202–5.

10. Muriel Combes, *Gilbert Simondon and the Philosophy of the Transindividual* [1999], trans. Thomas Lamarre (Cambridge, Mass.: The MIT Press, 2013), 32–38 and 112.

11. Brian Massumi, *Politics of Affect* (Cambridge, U.K.: Polity Press, 2015), 112–16.

12. Judith Butler, "The Force of Nonviolence," online lecture for Whitechapel Gallery, July 23, 2020, https://www.whitechapelgallery.org/events/judith-butler/, accessed July 23, 2020; Judith Butler, *The Force of Nonviolence* (New York: Verso, 2020).

13. Gavin Yamey and Clare Wenham, "The U.S. and U.K. Were the Two Best Prepared Nations to Tackle a Pandemic—What Went Wrong?," *Time,* July 1 2020, https://time.com/5861697/us-uk-failed-coronavirus-response/, accessed July 26, 2020.

14. See, for example, Hillary Leung, "Why Wearing a Face Mask Is Encouraged in Asia, but Shunned in the U.S.," *Time,* March 12, 2020, https://time.com/5799964/coronavirus-face-mask-asia-us/, accessed July 27, 2020; see also Shaun O'Dwyer, "You Don't Have to Be Asian to Wear a Face Mask in an Epidemic," in *Japan Times,* March 17, 2020, https://www.japantimes.co.jp/opinion/2020/03/17/commentary/japan-commentary/dont-asian-wear-face-mask-epidemic/, accessed July 27, 2020.

15. See PricewaterhouseCoopers, "Macroeconomic Impact of the COVID-19 in China and Policy Suggestions," in PwC China, July 2020, https://www.pwccn.com/en/covid-19/macroeconomic-impact-covid19-policy-suggestions.pdf, accessed July 27, 2020; Sandhya Keelery, "Impact of the Coronavirus (COVID-19) on the Indian Economy: Statistics and Facts, in Statista, June 24, 2020, https://

www.statista.com/topics/6304/covid-19-economic-impact-on-india/, accessed July 27, 2020; McKinsey and Company, "COVID-19: Briefing Materials: Global Health and Crisis Response," updated July 6, 2020, https://www.mckin sey.com/~/media/McKinsey/Business%20Functions/Risk/Our%20Insights /COVID%2019%20Implications%20for%20business/COVID%2019%20July %2023/COVID-19-Facts-and-Insights-July-23.pdf, accessed July 27, 2020; Andrea Conte, Patrizio Lecca, Stylianos Sakkas, and Simone Salotti, "The Territorial Economic Impact of COVID-19 in the E.U.: A Rhomolo Analysis," in the European Commission, July 2020, https://ec.europa.eu/jrc/en/publication /eur-scientific-and-technical-research-reports/territorial-economic-impact -covid-19-eu-rhomolo-analysis, accessed July 27, 2020.

16. Maike Halterbeck, Gavan Conlon, Rhys Williams, and Joscelyn Miller, "Impact of the COVID-19 Pandemic on University Finances: Report for the University and College Union," *London Economics*, April 2020, https://www.ucu .org.uk/media/10871/LE_report_on_covid19_and_university_finances/pdf /LEreportoncovid19anduniversityfinances, accessed July 27, 2020.

17. Michelle Goldberg, "Trump's Occupation of American Cities Has Begun," *New York Times*, July 20, 2020, https://www.nytimes.com/2020/07/20 /opinion/portland-protests-trump.html, accessed July 27, 2020.

18. Reports on the Hong Kong protests since 2019 can be found in the portal "Hong Kong Protests," *South China Morning Post*, updated daily since June 2019, https://www.scmp.com/topics/hong-kong-protests, accessed July 27, 2020; "Hong Kong Extradition Law Protests," *Hong Kong Free Press*, updated since June 2019, https://hongkongfp.com/hong-kong-extradition-law/, accessed July 27, 2020; Emma Graham-Harrison, "UK Government 'Has' Underestimated Takeup for Hong Kong Resettlement Scheme," *Guardian*, December 12, 2020, https://www.theguardian.com/world/2020/dec/12/uk-government -underestimates-takeup-hong-kong-resettlement, accessed November 4, 2021.

19. See, for example, Lindsay Maizland, "China's Repression of Uighurs in Xinjiang," in Council on Foreign Relations, June 30, 2020, https://www.cfr.org /backgrounder/chinas-repression-uighurs-xinjiang, accessed July 27, 2020; see also, the Uyghur Human Rights Project, updated daily, https://uhrp.org /press-release/%E2%80%9Cideological-transformation%E2%80%9D-records -mass-detention-qaraqash-hotan.html, accessed July 27, 2020.

20. "'Shoot the Traitors': Discrimination Against Muslims under India's New Citizenship Policy," Human Rights Watch, April 9, 2020, https://www.hrw .org/report/2020/04/09/shoot-traitors/discrimination-against-muslims -under-indias-new-citizenship-policy, accessed July 27, 2020.

21. David Fleming and Simon Harrison, *Chinese Urban Shi-nema: Cinematicity, Society and Millennial China* (London: Palgrave Macmillan, 2020). The term *shi* here means a potential force, which is often performative. For background,

see Jean Baudrillard, *Simulacra and Simulation* [1981], trans. Sheila Faria Glaser (Ann Arbor: University of Michigan Press, 1994), and Paul Virilio, *"Ready-made" urbains: Paris* (Paris: Picard, 2000).

22. See, for example, David Meyer, *Control Shift: How Technology Affects You and Your Rights* (No place: David Meyer, 2017); see also Richard Rogers, *Information Politics on the Web* (Cambridge, Mass.: MIT Press, 2004).

23. Butler, *The Force of Nonviolence*, 27.

24. *The Dhammapada*, trans. Nārada Thera (London: J. Murray, 1954), §10.129–34.

25. Michael Jerryson, "Militarizing Buddhism: Violence in Southern Thailand," in *Buddhist Warfare*, eds. Jerryson and Mark Juergensmeyer (Oxford: Oxford University Press, 2010), 179–210.

26. See Jerryson and Juergensmeyer, eds., *Buddhist Warfare*; see also Mahinda Degalle, ed., *Buddhism, Conflict and Violence in Modern Sri Lanka* (London: Routledge, 2006).

27. *The Mahāvaṃsa*, trans. Wilhelm Geiger (London: H. Frowde, 1908), §25.

28. Nāgārjuna, *Dazhidulun* [*Mahāprajñāpāramitāśāstra* or *Great Treatise on the Perfection of Wisdom*], trans. Kumārajīva (Taipei: Shihua guoji gufen youxian gongsi, 2007), §12 (1:505–53).

29. Nan Huai-chin, The Diamond Sutra *Explained* [lectures given in 1980; transcriptions first published in 2001], trans. Hue En (Pia Giammasi) (Florham Park, N.J.: Primordia Media, 2003), §14 (179).

30. Yinguang, "Yu Wei Jinzhou shu" [Letter to Wei Jinzhou], in *Yinguang Fashi wenchao* [Printed essays by Yinguang] (Shanghai: Shangwu yinshuguan, 1921), 2b, §7.

31. Mobbi Ho, "Zheben shu benshen jiushi qiji" [This book itself is a miracle], in Thich Nhat Hanh, *Zhengnian de qiji,* 9–11; Thich Nhat Hanh, *Anger: Wisdom for Cooling the Flames* (New York: Riverhead Books, 2001).

32. Bernard Stiegler, *La technique et le temps,* in three volumes (1994, 1996, and 2001; repr. as a single volume, Paris: Fayard, 2018), 681–738; Combes, *Gilbert Simondon and the Philosophy of the Transindividual,* 32–38 and 112.

33. Sheng-yen, *Shengyan Fashi jiao mozhao chan* [*Master Sheng Yen Teaches* utkuṭuka-stha] (Taipei: Dharma Drum, 2004).

34. Anna Seghers, *Transit,* trans. James A. Glaston (Boston: Little Brown, 1944).

35. Thomas Elsaesser, *Hollywood heute. Geschichte, Gender und Nation im postklassischen Kino* (Berlin: Bertz + Fischer, 2009), 191–92.

36. Olivia Landry, "The Beauty and Violence of *Horror Vacui:* Waiting in Christian Petzold's *Transit* (2018)," *German Quarterly* 93, no. 1 (February 13, 2020), https://onlinelibrary.wiley.com/doi/full/10.1111/gequ.12126, accessed April 1, 2020; Siegfried Kracauer, "Die Wartenden," in *Das Ornament der Masse* (Berlin: Suhrkamp, 1977), 116–17; Martin Heidegger, *Gelassenheit* (Pfullingen: Neske, 1959), 44.

37. See Mary Douglas, "Atonement in Leviticus," *Jewish Studies Quarterly* 1, no. 2 (1993–94): 109–30.

38. Landry, "The Beauty and Violence of *Horror Vacui.*"

39. Landry, "The Beauty and Violence of *Horror Vacui.*" See Georg Wilhelm Friedrich Hegel, *Phenomenology of Spirit* [1807], trans. A. V. Miller (1952; repr., New York: Oxford University Press, 1977), §11–59 (6–38) and §90–131 (58–79).

FILMOGRAPHY

Bi, Gan. *Diqiu zuihou de yewan* [*Long Day's Journey into Night*]. Prod. Shan Zuolong. Zhejiang Huace Film & TV, Dangmai Films, and Huace Pictures. China and France, 2018. 113 mins. DCP. Color and 3D.

Bi, Gan. *Jingang jing* [*The Poet and Singer*]. Prod. Bi Gan. China, 2012. 22 mins. HD. B&W.

Bi, Gan. *Lubian yecan* [*Kaili Blues*]. Prod. Li Zhaoyu, Shan Zuolong, and Wang Zijian. Prod. Heaven Pictures. China, 2015. 113 mins. DCP. Color.

Carné, Marcel. *Le jour se lève* [*Daybreak*]. Prod. Robert and Raymond Hakim. Productions Sigma; AFE. France, 1939. 93 mins. 35 mm. B&W.

Cui, Zi'en. *Xing xing xiang xi xi* [*Star Appeal*]. Prod. Cui Zi'en. Cuizi DV Studio. China, 2004. 86 mins. DV. Color.

Diao, Yinan. *Nanfang chezhan de juhui* [*The Wild Goose Lake*]. Prod. Li Li and Yang Shen. Green Ray Films and Maisong Entertainment Investment. China and France, 2019. 113 mins. DCP. Color.

Djen, Jon Lee (Zheng Junli). *Kumu fengchun* [*Spring Comes to the Withered Tree*]. Prod. Xu Sangchu. Shanghai Film Studio. China, 1961. 96 mins. 35 mm. B&W.

Ford, John. *The Searchers*. Prod. C. V. Whitney Pictures. Warner Brothers. United States, 1956. 119 mins. 35 mm. Color.

Gao, Ming. *Huinan tian* [*Damp Season*]. Prod. Huang Xufeng and Wang Lei. Factory Gate Films and Pokwai Pictures. China, 2020. 109 mins. DCP. Color.

Gu, Xiaogang. *Chunjiang shuinuan* [*Dwelling in the Fuchun Mountain*]. Prod. Suey Chen and Megan Sung. Beijing Qu Jing Pictures. China, 2019. DCP. Color.

Kokoka (Xue Jianjiang). *Canfei kehuan* [*Deformity Sci-fi*]. Prod. Kokoka. Wudianmeixue and Busituzi Studio. China, 2008. 122 mins. DV. Color.

Kokoka (Xue Jianjiang). *Huoxing zonghezheng* [*Martian Syndrome*]. Prod. Kokoka. Wudianmeixue and Busituzi Studio. China, 2010. 83 mins. DV. B&W and Color.

Kwan, Stanley. *Lan Yu*. Prod. Zhang Yongning. Kwan's Creation Workshop and Yongning Creation Workshop. China, 2001. 86 mins. 35 mm. Color.

Li, Jun. *Nongnu* [*Serf*]. Prod. August First Film Studio. China, 1951. 88 mins. 35 mm. B&W.

Liu, Bingjian. *Nannan nünü* [*Men and Women*]. Prod. Li Jinliang. China, 1998. 89 mins. 35 mm. Color.

Ozu, Yasujirō. *Banshun* [*Late Spring*]. Shochiku. Japan, 1949. 108 mins. B&W.

Ozu, Yasujirō. *Otona no miru ehon—Umarete wa mita keredo* [*An Adult's Picture Book View—I Was Born, But...*]. Shochiku. Japan, 1932. 90 mins. B&W.

Ozu, Yasujirō. *Tōkyō monogatari* [*Tokyo Story*]. Prod. Takeshi Yamamoto. Shochiku. Japan, 1953. 136 mins. B&W.

Pema Tseden. *Dbugs lgang* [*Balloon*]. Prod. Huang Xufeng. Beijing Jiu Zhou Tong Ying Digital Cinemas, Factory Gate Films, Mani Stone Pictures, Tang Dynasty Culture Communication, and iQiyi Picture. China, 2019. 102 mins. DCP. Color.

Pema Tseden. *Jinpa*. Prod. Wong Kar-wai and Jacky Pang. Jet Tone Films. China and Hong Kong, 2019. 86 mins. DCP. Color.

Pema Tseden. *Khyi rgan* [*Old Dog*]. Prod. Zhang Xianmin. Himalaya Audio and Visual Culture Communication. China, 2011. 93 mins. HD. Color.

Pema Tseden. *Lhing vjags kyi ma ni rdo vbum* [*The Silent Holy Stones*]. Prod. Pan Peicong and Li An. Youth Film Studio of the Beijing Film Academy. China, 2005. 102 mins. 35 mm. Color.

Pema Tseden. *Tharlo*. Prod. Wu Leilei, Wang Xuebo, and Zhang Xianmin. Heaven Pictures, Beijing YiHe Star Film Production, Beijing Ocean & Time Culture Communication. China, 2015. 123 mins. DCP. B&W.

Pema Tseden. *'Tsol ba* [*The Search*]. Prod. Tian Zhuangzhuang. Himalaya Audio and Visual Culture Communication. China, 2019. 112 mins. DV. Color.

Pema Tseden. *Yangdar* [*The Sacred Arrow*]. Prod. Guo Yonghao. Himalaya Audio and Visual Culture Communication. China, 2014. 96 mins. DCP. Color.

Petzold, Christian. *Transit*. Prod. Antonin Dedet and Florian Koerner von Gustorf. Schramm Film. Germany, 2018. DCP. Color.

Resnais, Alain. *L'Année dernière à Marienbad* [*Last Year in Marienbad*]. Prod. Pierre Courau, Raymond Froment, Robert Dorfmann, Anatole Dauman. Cocinor. France and Italy, 1961. 94 mins. B&W.

Tarkovsky, Andrei. *Stalker*. Prod. Aleksandra Demidova. Mosfilm. Soviet Union, 1979. 161 mins. 35 mm. B&W and Color.

Weerasethakul, Apichatpong. *Sleepcinemahotel*. Prod. International Film Festival Rotterdam. Netherlands, 2018. 21,600 mins. Installation with HD projection. B&W and Color.

Zhang, Shichuan. *Nanfu nanqi* [*The Newly Weds*]. Prod. Zhang Shichuan. Asia Film Company. China, 1913. 30 mins. 35 mm. B&W.

Zhang, Yuan. *Donggong xigong* [*East Palace, West Palace*]. Prod. Willy Tsao. Qulqu'un d'Autre Productions. China, 1998. 90 mins. 35 mm. Color.

Zheng Lu, Xinyuan. *Ta fangjian li de yun* [*The Cloud in Her Room*]. Prod. Wang Zijian. Blackfin Production and Nina Xiao. Hong Kong and China, 2020. 98 mins. DCP. B&W.

INDEX

Abhidhamma/Abhidharma (meta-discourse), 14, 21

affect, affection, and affective, 1, 4, 6, 8–9, 17, 20, 24–25, 27, 33, 47, 59, 73, 83, 85–87, 90, 94–96, 100, 140–41, 157–72, 177–78, 180, 183, 185, 188, 195–97, 208–9, 214, 216, 218, 221–27, 234, 241, 243, 247, 249–50, 256, 261; affinities, 62, 90; engagements, 55, 176–78, 182–84; impulses, 1, 7, 27, 247; insight, 169; intensities, 55, 87, 168, 232, 241–43, 248, 258; milieu and ecology, 68–69; power, 177; qualities, 50; union, 68; transductions and transindividuations, 25, 39. *See also* Chu, Kuang-ch'ien (Zhu Guangqian): affective transference; Deleuze, Gilles: affect and affection; Deleuze, Gilles: affection-image; impulse and impetus: *manasikara*; insight (*paññā/ prajñā*); Kant, Immanuel: affect, affection, and sensation; queer and trans cinema: same-sex affections; Simondon, Gilbert; sensations and affections

(*vedanās*); Spinoza, Baruch (Benedict de): affect and affection

afflictions (*kilesas/kleśas*), 17, 25, 100–110, 120, 125, 141–42, 150–51, 154, 157, 170–72, 177, 180, 189, 197, 206, 216, 212, 229, 242, 247–48; affliction-image, 100, 105–7; anger and frustration (*dveṣa*), 52, 100, 103, 106, 117–18, 125, 142, 153, 172, 216–17, 221, 238, 248, 251, 259; avarice (*rāga*), 52, 100, 103, 172, 259; delusion (*moha*), 52, 100, 103, 142, 153, 172, 238, 251, 259. *See also* obstruction and obstructing

āgamas, 14, 17. See also *Connected Discourses* [*Saṃyuktāgama*]

Agamben, Giorgio: biopolitics, 155, 241; exception, 242; *kairos*, 131; *technē* and *poiesis*, 49. *See also* Aristotle: mimesis and *poiesis;* Deleuze, Gilles: control-society; Deleuze, Gilles: Cronos; Foucault, Michel: biopolitics; Plato: mimesis and *technē*

ālaya and *ālaya*-consciousness (storehouse consciousness),

321

Huayan (H'ua'ngiɐm), 11, 45. *See also*
Dushun (Dŭozhiùɪn)
Hui, Yuk, 5, 69, 174. *See also* digital:
existence
Huineng (Hwèinəng), 170. *See also*
Zen (Dzhiɛn/Chan)
Huiyuan (Hwèihɐeˇn), 206. *See also*
Pure Land

ideology, 172–77, 193, 197, 225
ignorance/unenlightenment (*avijjā/
avidyā*), 1, 8, 13, 15, 18, 39–40, 76,
83, 100, 110, 116, 122, 124–25,
155, 157, 207, 212, 215, 232, 235.
See also enlightenment
Imamichi, Tomonobu, 27, 170.
See also Heidegger, Martin
impermanence (*anicca/anitya*) and
permanence, 10, 14–16, 19, 38,
41, 56, 72, 75–79, 81, 94, 96, 139,
142, 145–49, 159–60, 177, 180–84,
211, 215, 219, 234, 246. See also
kṣaṇa
impulse and impetus (also force),
1–2, 6–10, 15–28, 33–34, 36,
40–41, 46–47, 61, 68, 72–73, 76,
79, 86–90, 92–93, 95–102, 106,
108–11, 114–18, 120, 122, 125–26,
132, 134, 137, 140–42, 146, 150–51,
157, 160, 166–67, 172, 175, 177,
185, 187, 196–97, 206, 208–9, 212,
235, 237–38, 243–44, 246–48, 251,
256–62; *manasikara*, 100–101.
See also Deleuze, Gilles: impulse-
image; Deleuze, Gilles: *puissance
(conatus)*; karma; Spinoza, Baruch
(Benedict de): *conatus*
in-aesthetics, 28, 199, 201–2, 209,
231, 238–39. *See also* Badiou,
Alain: inaesthetics
insight (*paññā/prajñā*), 2, 16, 27,
73–74, 101, 108, 114–15, 117, 126,

128, 131–32, 141–42, 157, 166–67,
169, 177, 180, 182, 204, 206–7,
210, 212–13, 216–17, 219–20, 234,
239, 243, 246–48, 257, 261; image,
25–26, 73–74, 113, 115, 118–26,
130, 134, 142, 154–55, 157, 217,
219, 227–28, 234–35, 239;
mindfulness of what must be
performed (*kṛtyanuṣṭhānajñāna*),
142, 144; reflection
(*pratyaveksanāprajñā*), 169–70,
172. *See also* affect, affection, and
affective; consciousness;
mindfulness (*sati/smṛti*)

Jackson, Earl, Jr., 178. *See also* queer
and trans cinema
Jainism, 14
James, William: specious present, 138.
See also Fang, Thomé H.: present
jing (*jingjie* or milieu or image; also
k'iĕng or *kyō*), 43, 59, 214–20, 223.
See also consciousness; Lam,
Nin-tung; mindfulness (*sati/
smṛti*); Wang, Guowei; Zong,
Baihua
Jinling Sutra Publishing House
(Jinling kejingchu), 209–12.
See also China Inner Studies
Institute; Liang, Qichao; Su,
Manshu; Yang, Wenhui
Jorge, Nuno Barradas, 133. *See also*
slow cinema

Kaliṅga-rāja, 257. See also *Diamond
Sutra* [*Vajracchedikā
Prajñāpāramitā Sūtra*]
Kant, Immanuel: affect, affection,
and sensation, 74, 90, 217–18,
239; aesthetics, 214–15; Buddhism, 11; consciousness, 163,
169; ontology, 5, 207; time, 71,

Victor Fan is reader in film and media philosophy in the Department of Film Studies, King's College London. He is author of *Cinema Approaching Reality: Locating Chinese Film Theory* (Minnesota, 2015) and *Extraterritoriality: Locating Hong Kong Cinema and Media.*